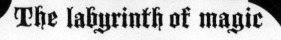

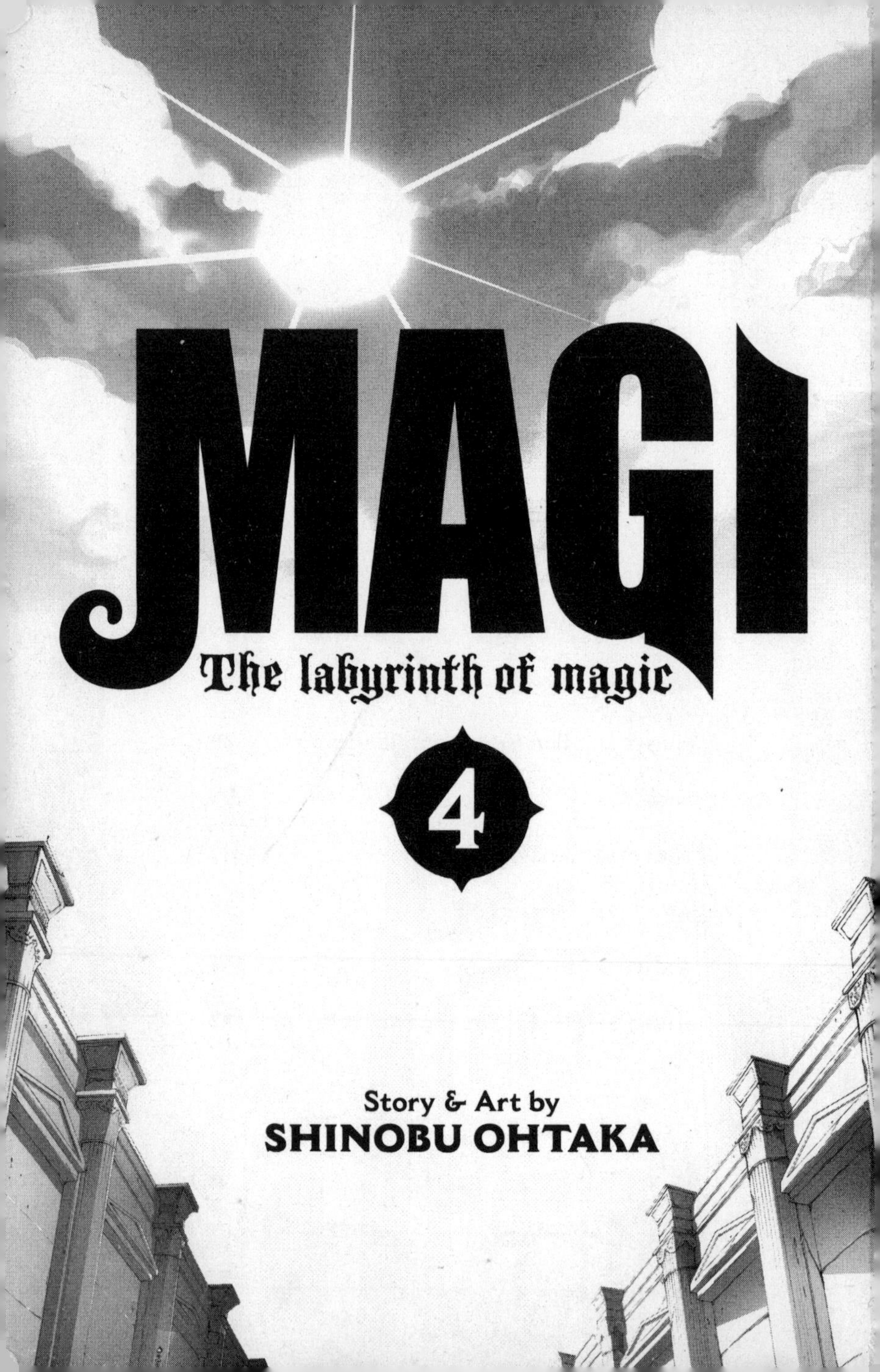

MAGI
The labyrinth of magic

Story & Art by
SHINOBU OHTAKA

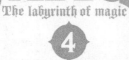

CONTENTS

NIGHT 28	Fanaris Warrior Clan	3
NIGHT 29	Slave	21
NIGHT 30	Miracle	39
NIGHT 31	Feast	57
NIGHT 32	The Road to Balbadd	79
NIGHT 33	His Name Is Sinbad	99
NIGHT 34	Answers	117
NIGHT 35	Dispersion	135
NIGHT 36	Fog Troop	157
NIGHT 37	Gazing at the Moon	177

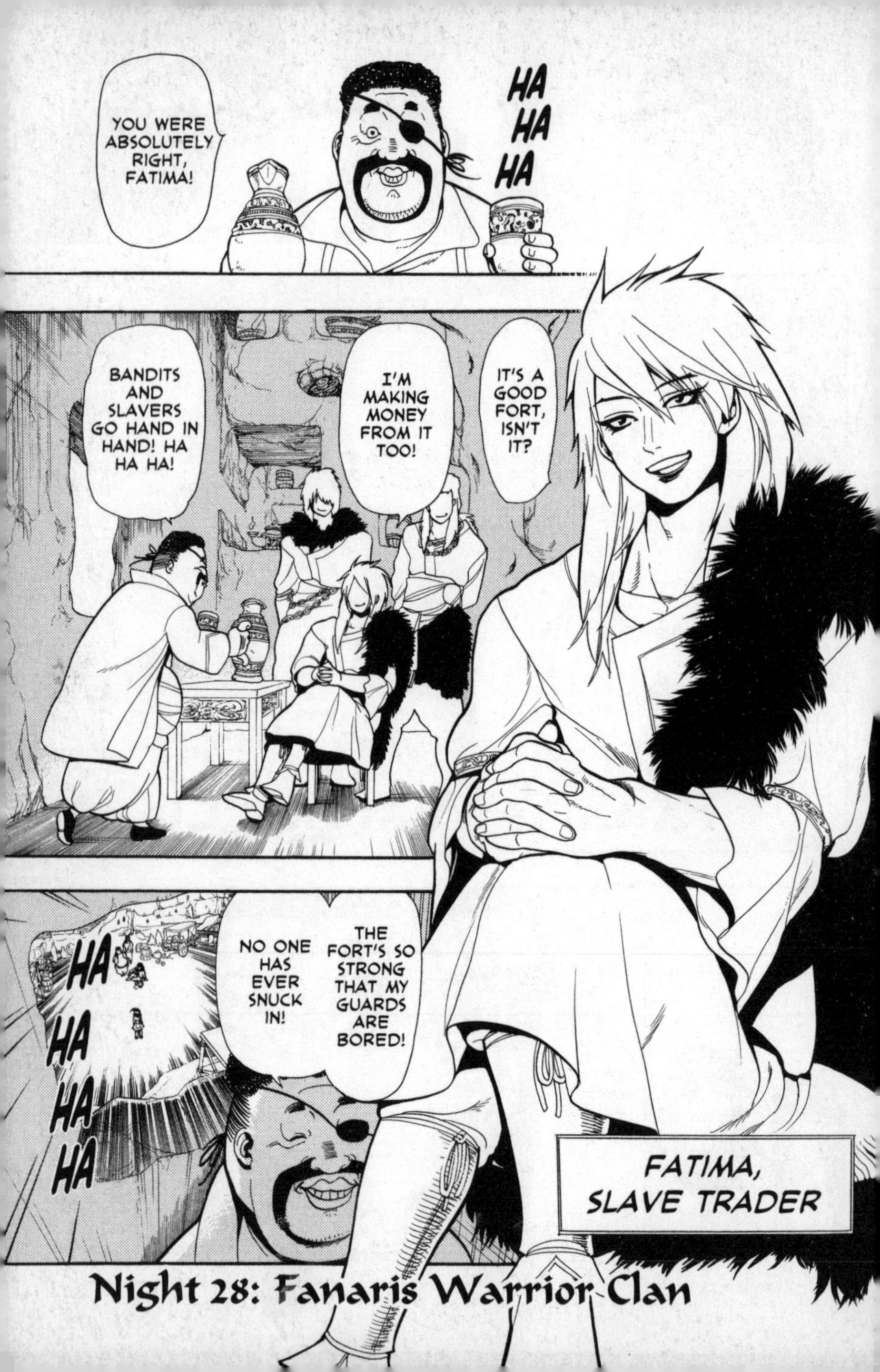
HA HA HA
YOU WERE ABSOLUTELY RIGHT, FATIMA!
FATIMA, SLAVE TRADER
IT'S A GOOD FORT, ISN'T IT?
I'M MAKING MONEY FROM IT TOO!
BANDITS AND SLAVERS GO HAND IN HAND! HA HA HA!
THE FORT'S SO STRONG THAT MY GUARDS ARE BORED!
NO ONE HAS EVER SNUCK IN!
HA HA HA HA HA
Night 28: Fanaris Warrior Clan

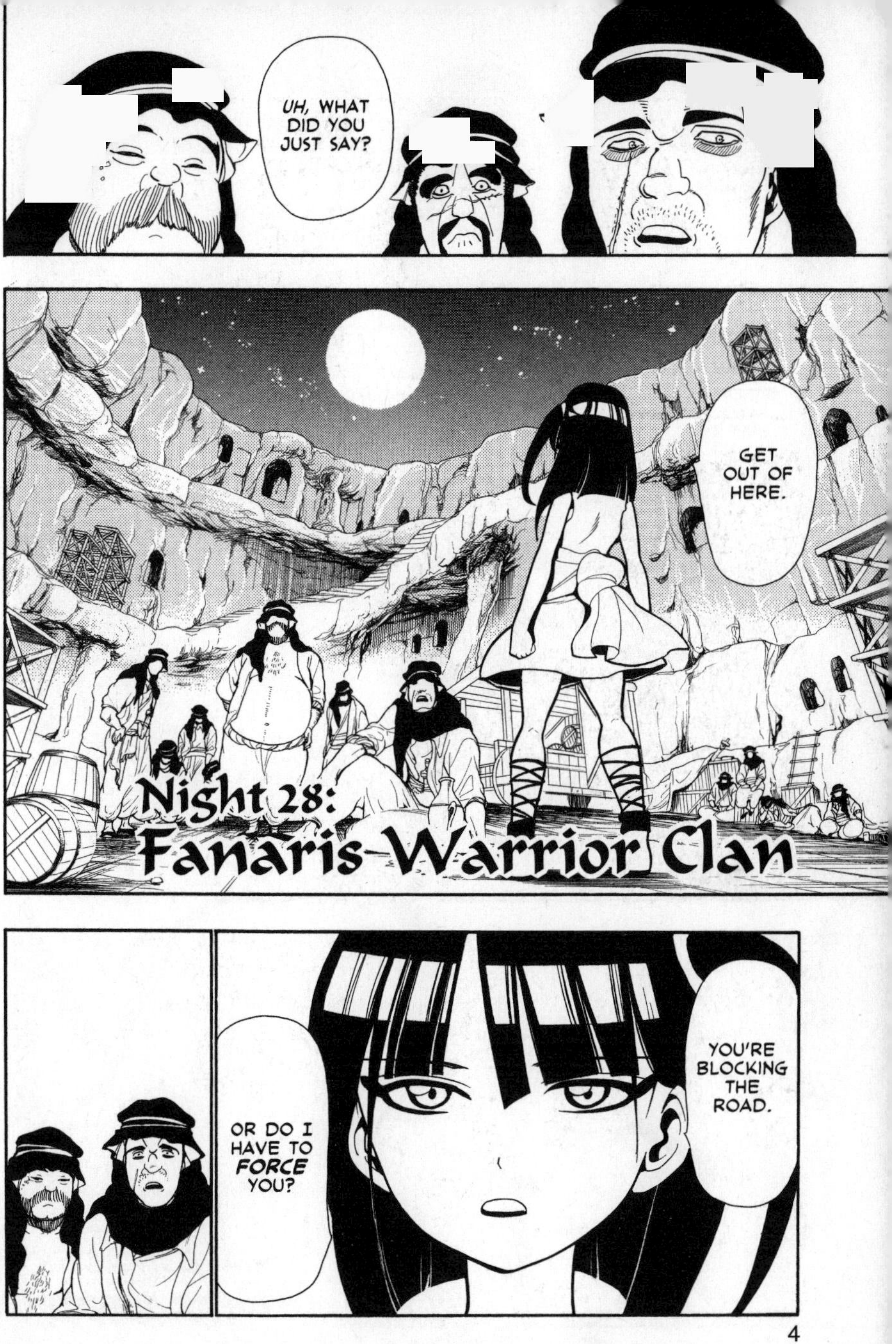

UH, WHAT DID YOU JUST SAY?
GET OUT OF HERE.
Night 28: Fanaris Warrior Clan
YOU'RE BLOCKING THE ROAD.
OR DO I HAVE TO *FORCE* YOU?

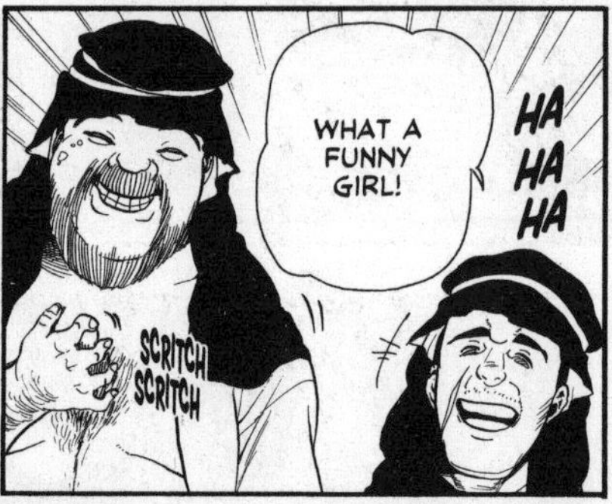
HA HA HA
WHAT A FUNNY GIRL!
SCRITCH SCRITCH
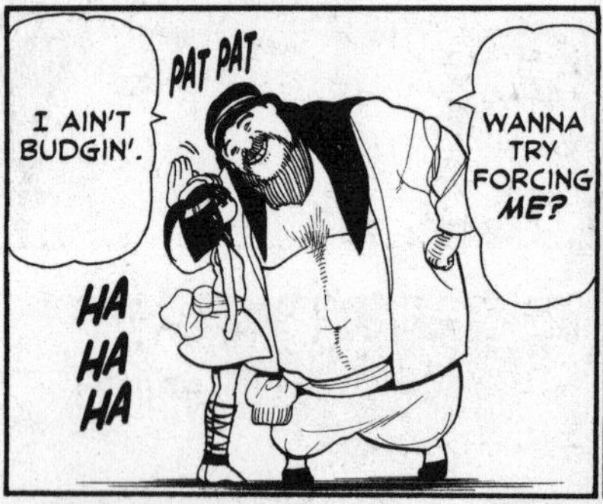
WANNA TRY FORCING *ME?*
PAT PAT
I AIN'T BUDGIN'.
HA HA HA
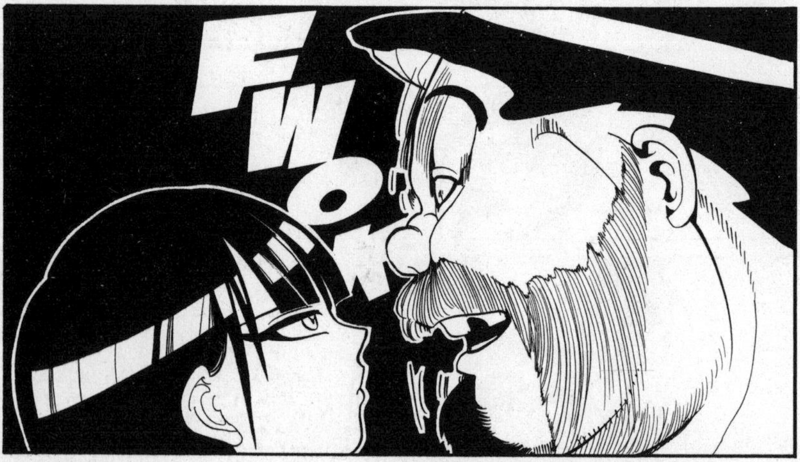
FWOM
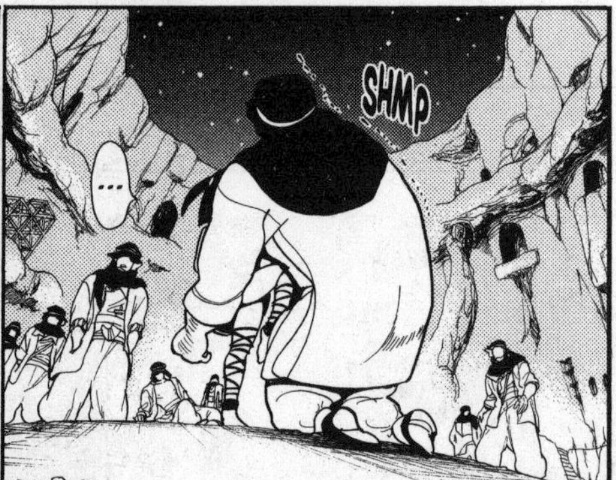
SHMP
...
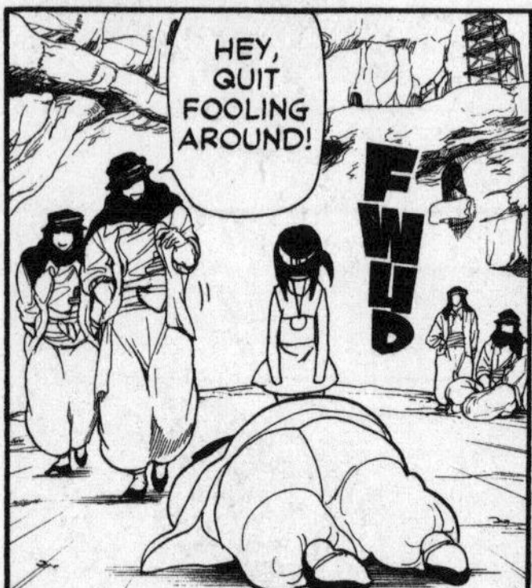
FWUD
HEY, QUIT FOOLING AROUND!

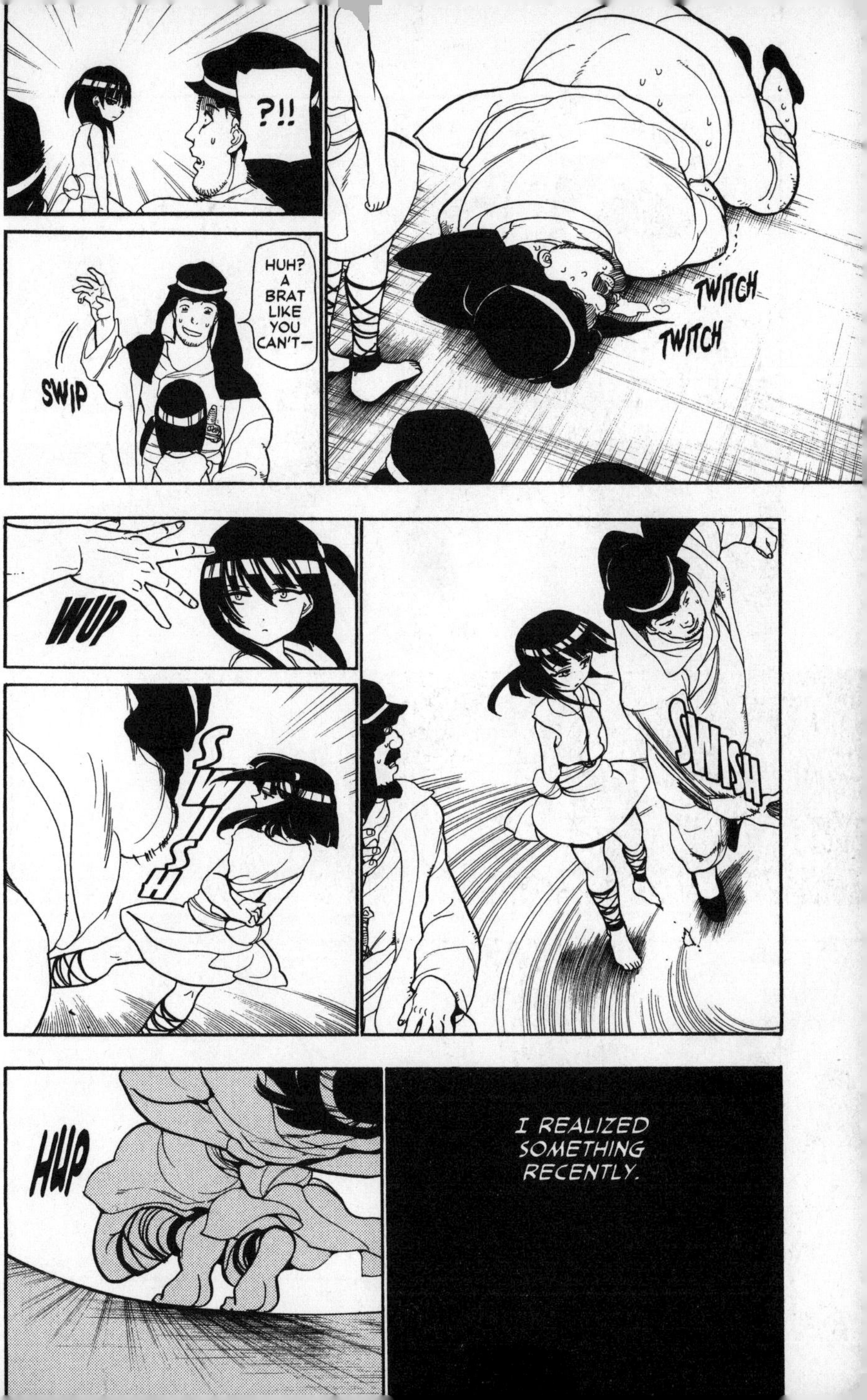
TWITCH
TWITCH
?!!
HUH? A BRAT LIKE YOU CAN'T—
SWIP
SWISH
WUP
SWISH
I REALIZED SOMETHING RECENTLY.
HUP

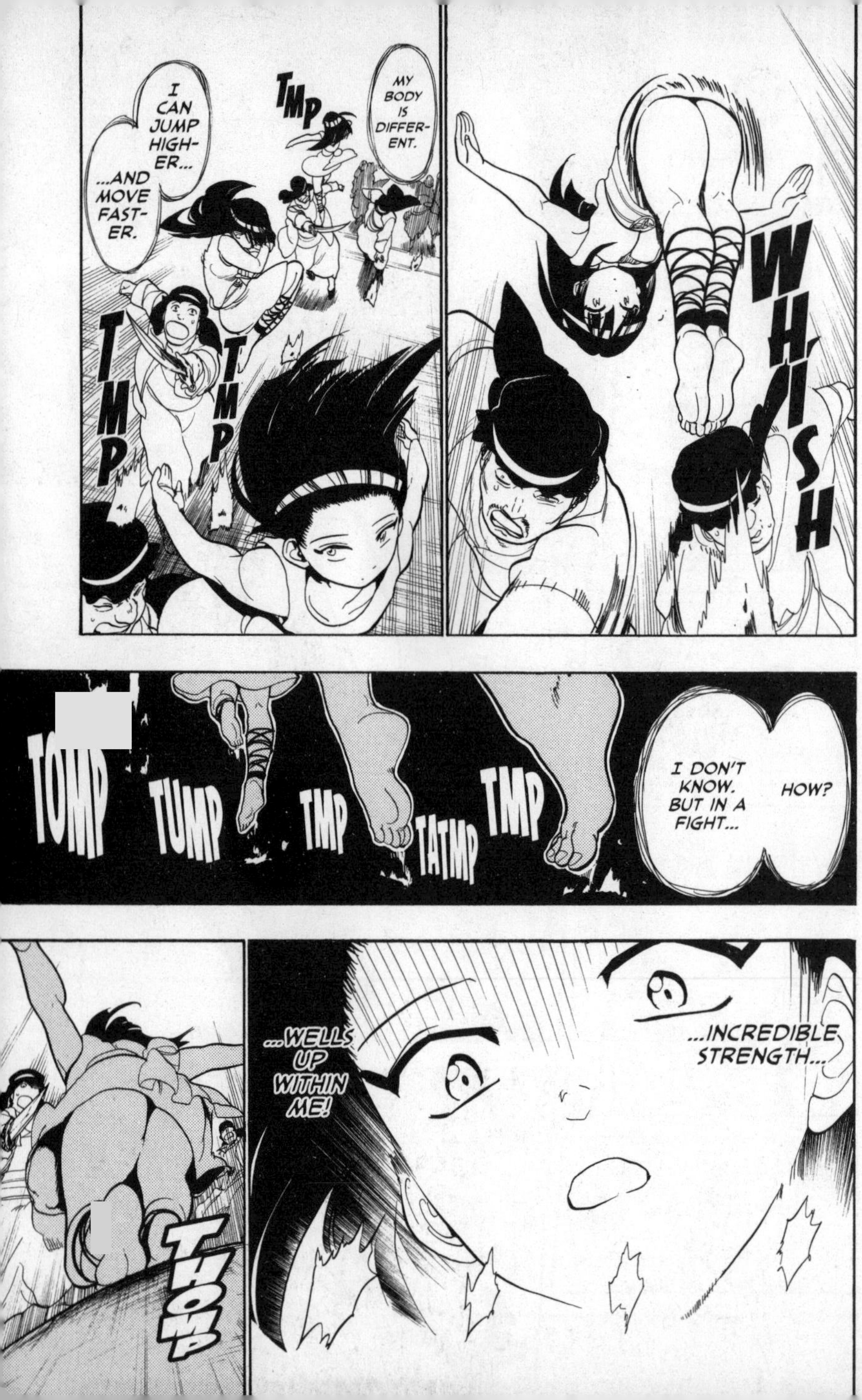
WHISH
MY BODY IS DIFFERENT.
TMP
I CAN JUMP HIGHER...
...AND MOVE FASTER.
TMP
TMP
HOW?
I DON'T KNOW. BUT IN A FIGHT...
TMP
TATMP
TMP
TUMP
TOMP
...INCREDIBLE STRENGTH...
...WELLS UP WITHIN ME!
THOMP

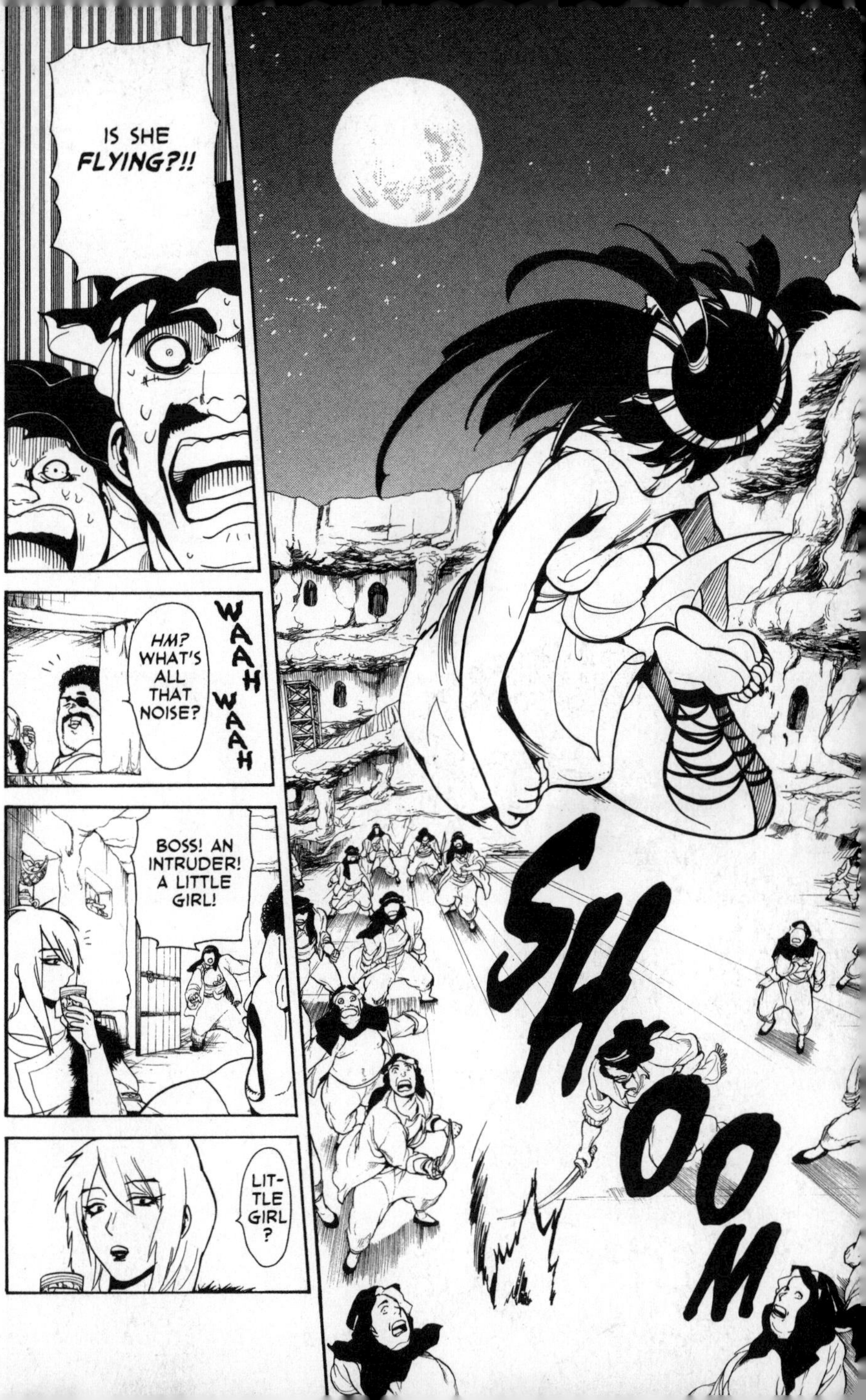
SHOOOM
IS SHE FLYING?!!
WAAH WAAH
HM? WHAT'S ALL THAT NOISE?
BOSS! AN INTRUDER! A LITTLE GIRL!
LIT-TLE GIRL?

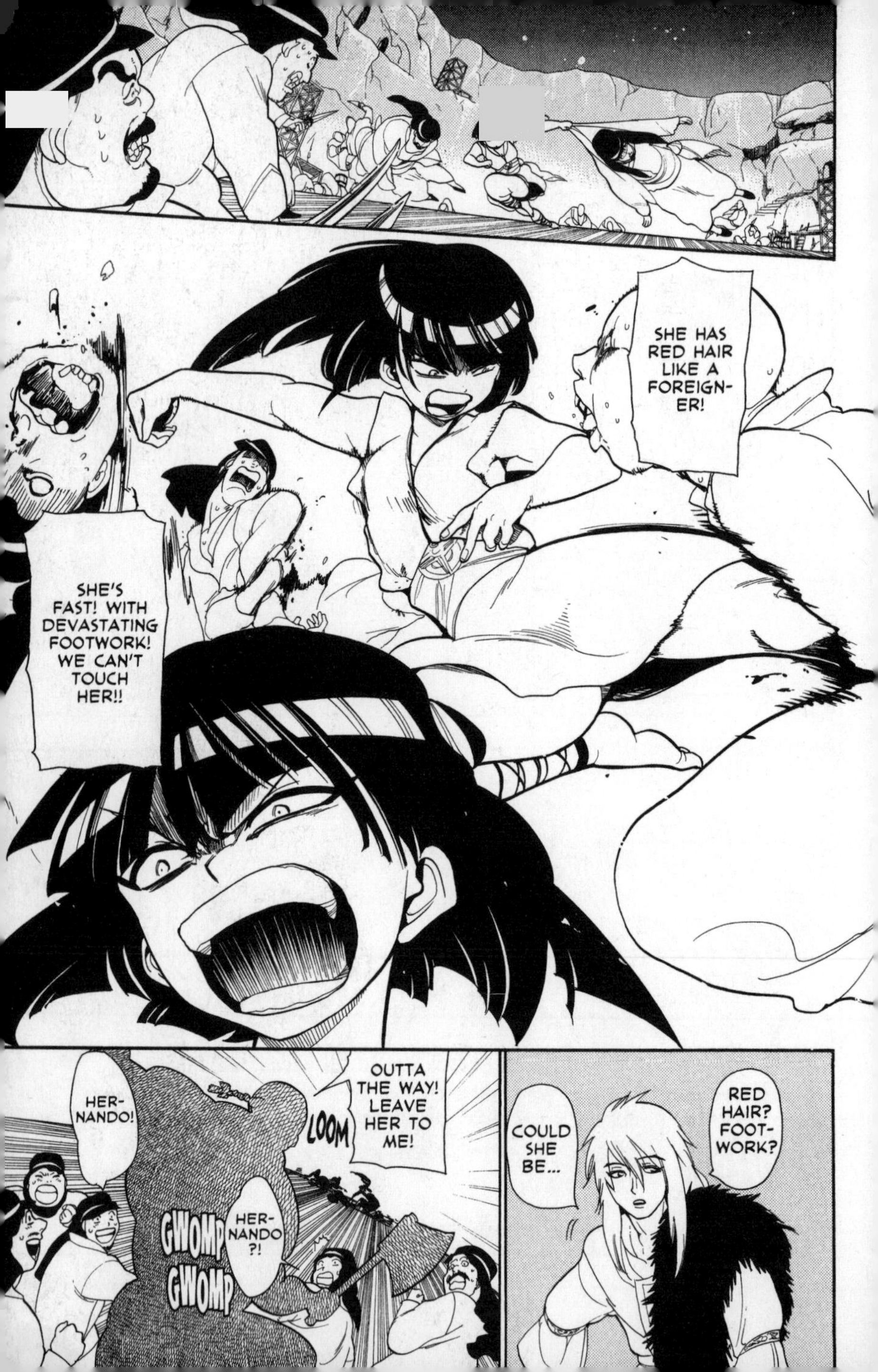
SHE HAS RED HAIR LIKE A FOREIGNER!
SHE'S FAST! WITH DEVASTATING FOOTWORK! WE CAN'T TOUCH HER!!
RED HAIR? FOOTWORK?
COULD SHE BE...
OUTTA THE WAY! LEAVE HER TO ME!
LOOM
HERNANDO!
HERNANDO?!
GWOMP GWOMP

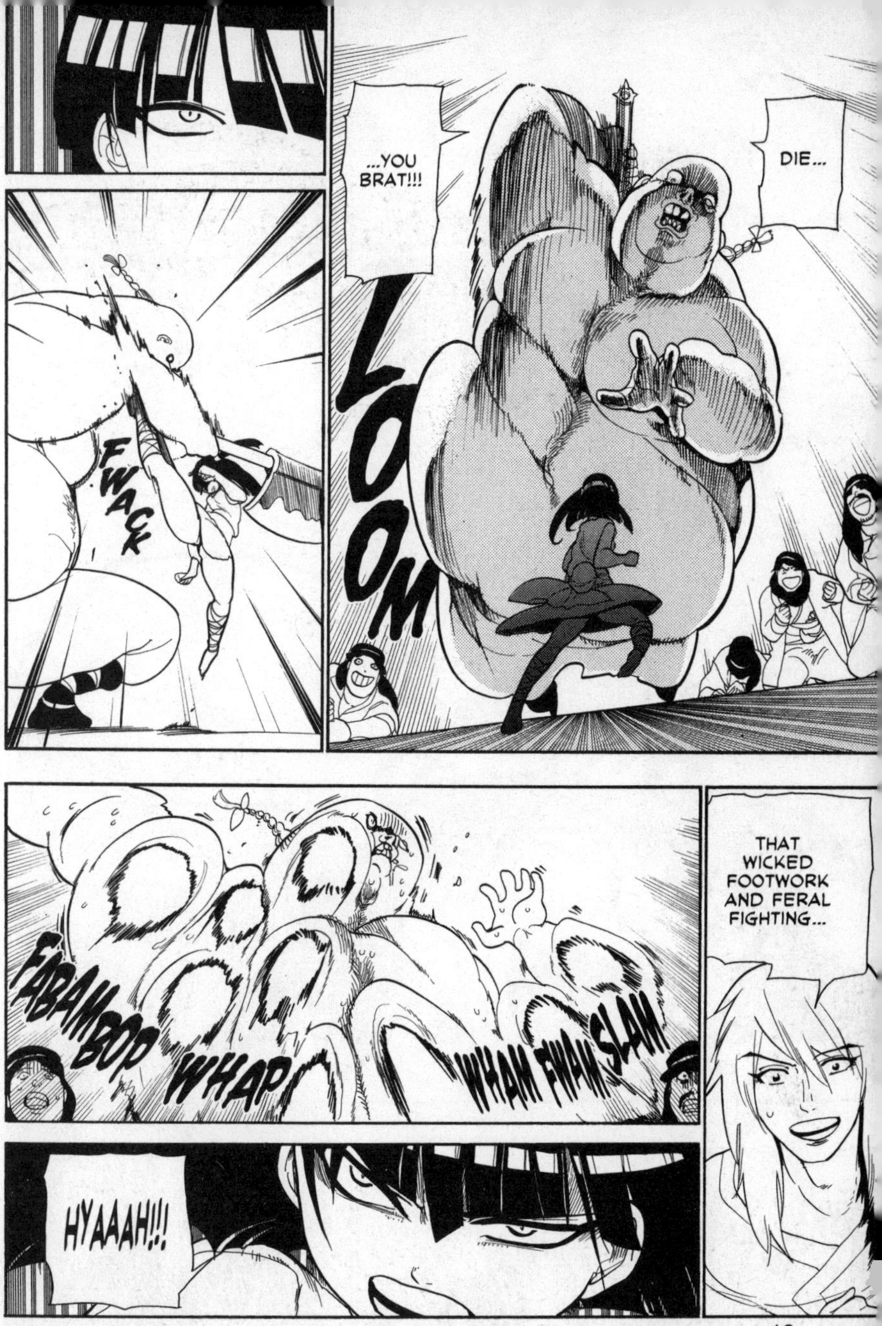
DIE...
...YOU BRAT!!!
LOOM
FWACK
THAT WICKED FOOTWORK AND FERAL FIGHTING...
SLAM
FWAM
WHAM
WHAP
FABAMBOP
HYAAAH!!!

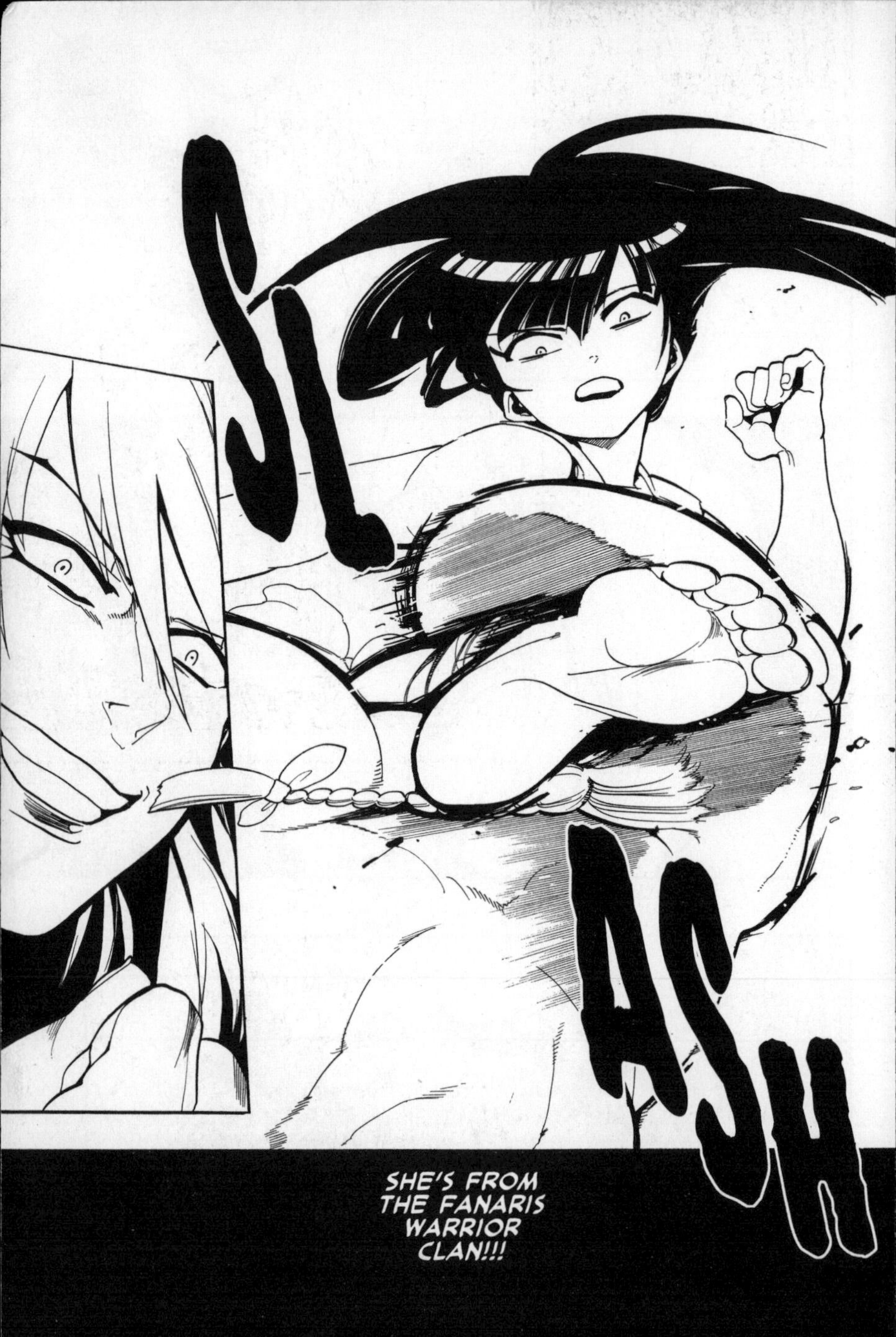
SLASH
SHE'S FROM THE FANARIS WARRIOR CLAN!!!

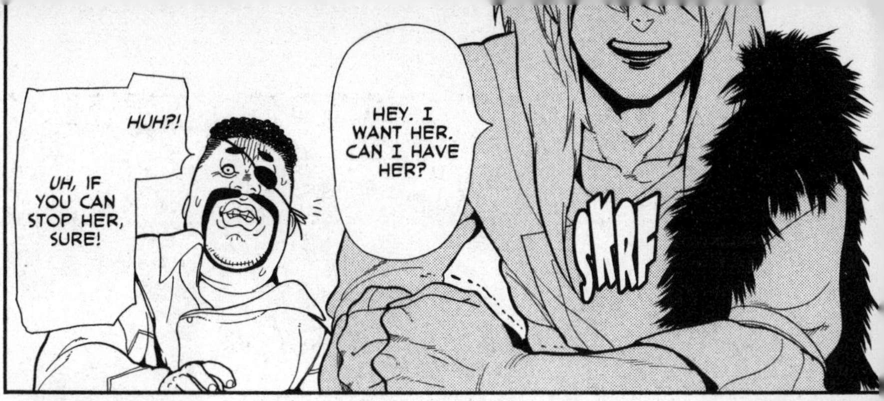
HEY. I WANT HER. CAN I HAVE HER?
SKRF
HUH?!
UH, IF YOU CAN STOP HER, SURE!

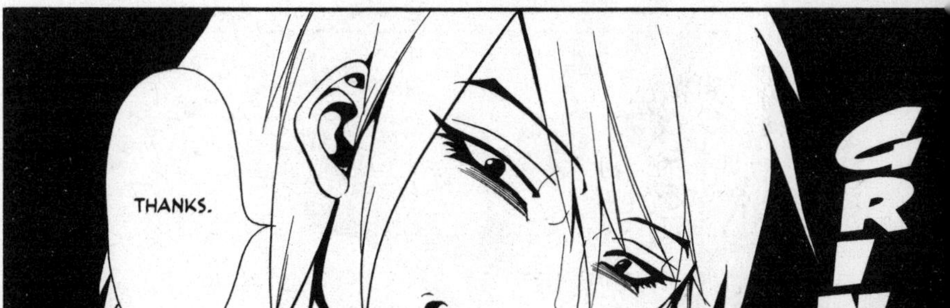
GRIN
THANKS.

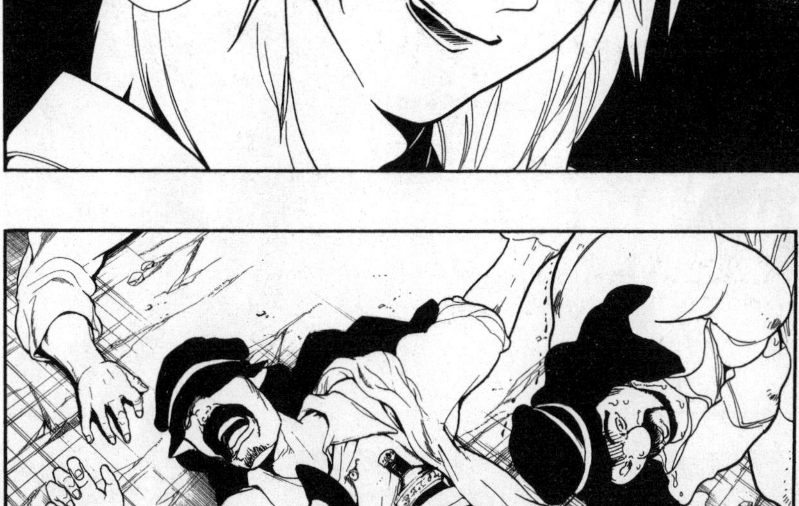

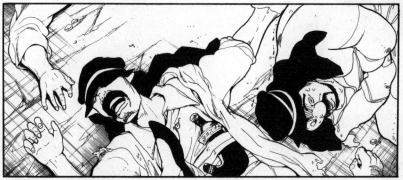

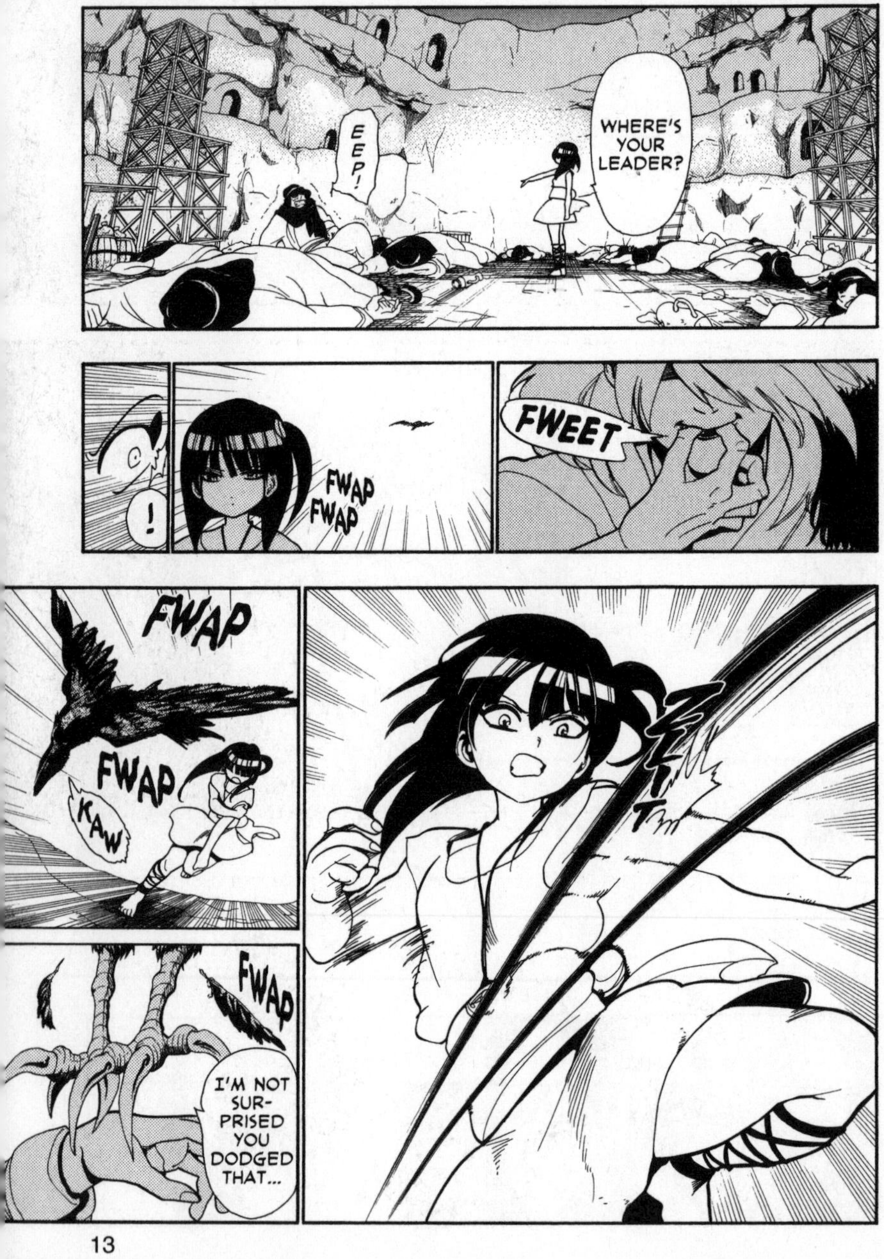
WHERE'S YOUR LEADER?
EEP!
FWEET
FWAP FWAP
!
FWAP
FWAP
KAW
FWAP
I'M NOT SUR-PRISED YOU DODGED THAT...

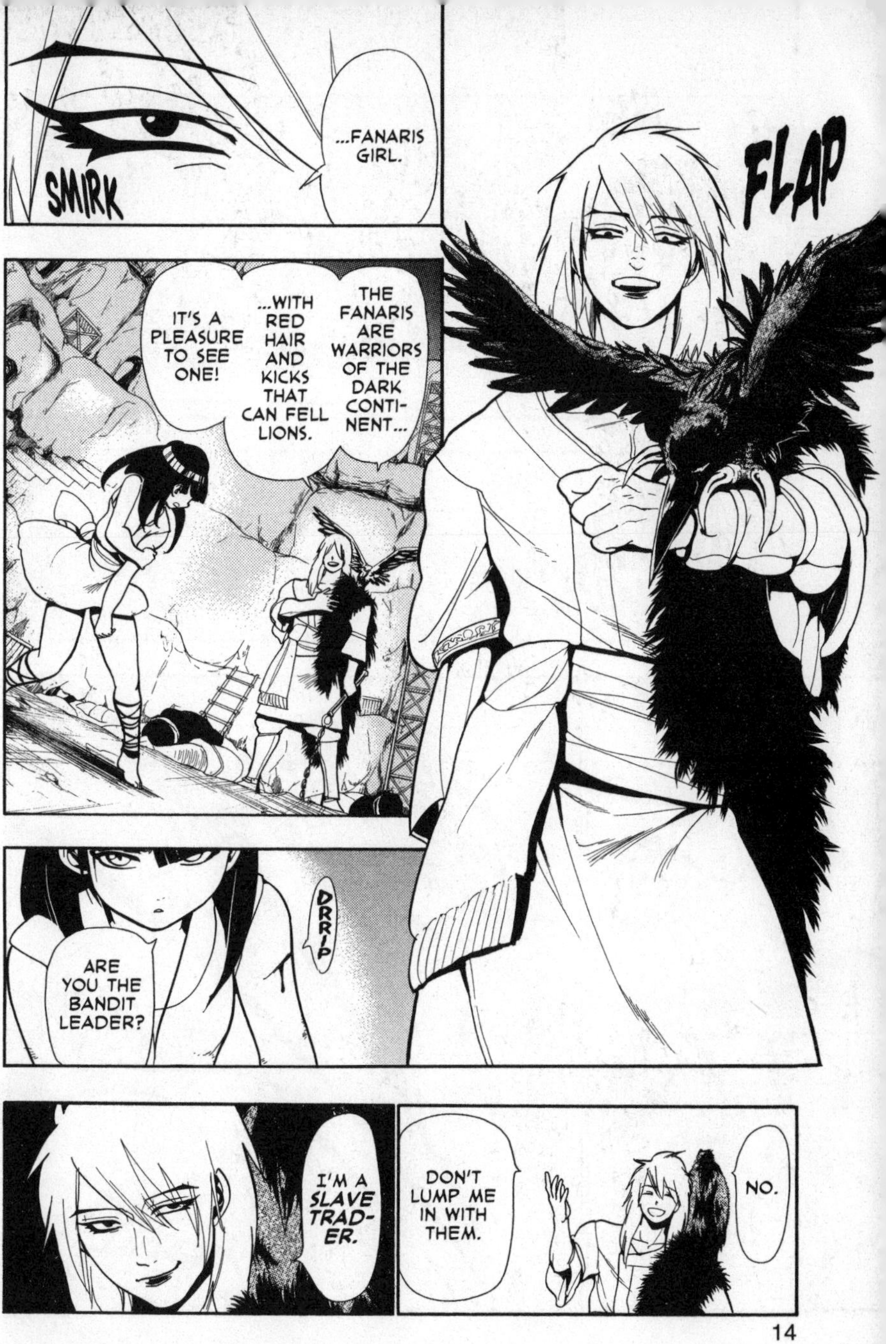
FLAP
SMIRK
...FANARIS GIRL.
THE FANARIS ARE WARRIORS OF THE DARK CONTI-NENT...
...WITH RED HAIR AND KICKS THAT CAN FELL LIONS.
IT'S A PLEASURE TO SEE ONE!
DRRIP
ARE YOU THE BANDIT LEADER?
NO.
DON'T LUMP ME IN WITH THEM.
I'M A *SLAVE TRAD-ER.*

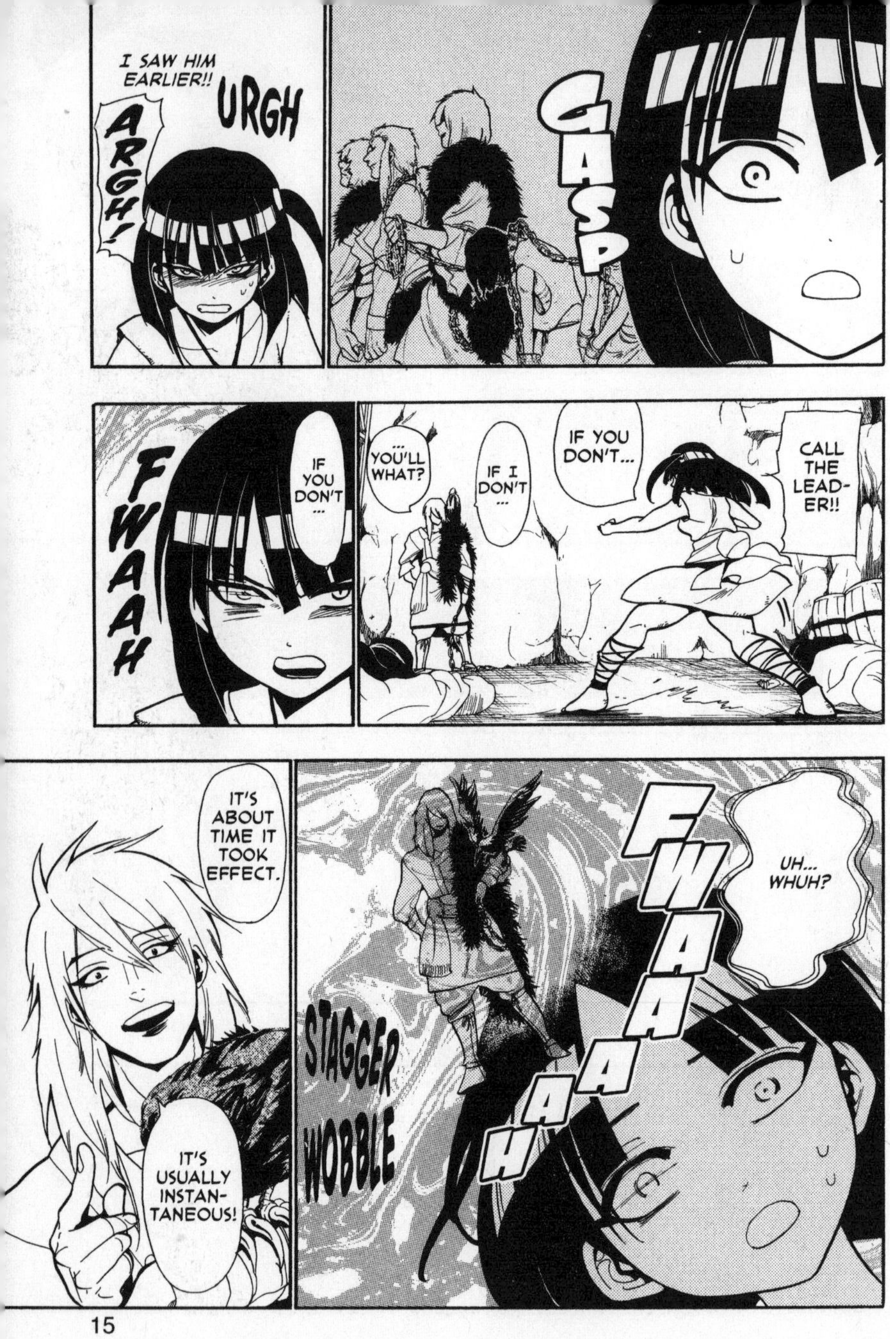
GASP
URGH
I SAW HIM EARLIER!!
ARGH!
CALL THE LEADER!!
IF YOU DON'T...
IF I DON'T ...
...YOU'LL WHAT?
IF YOU DON'T ...
FWAAAH
UH... WHUH?
FWAAAAH
STAGGER WOBBLE
IT'S ABOUT TIME IT TOOK EFFECT.
IT'S USUALLY INSTANTANEOUS!

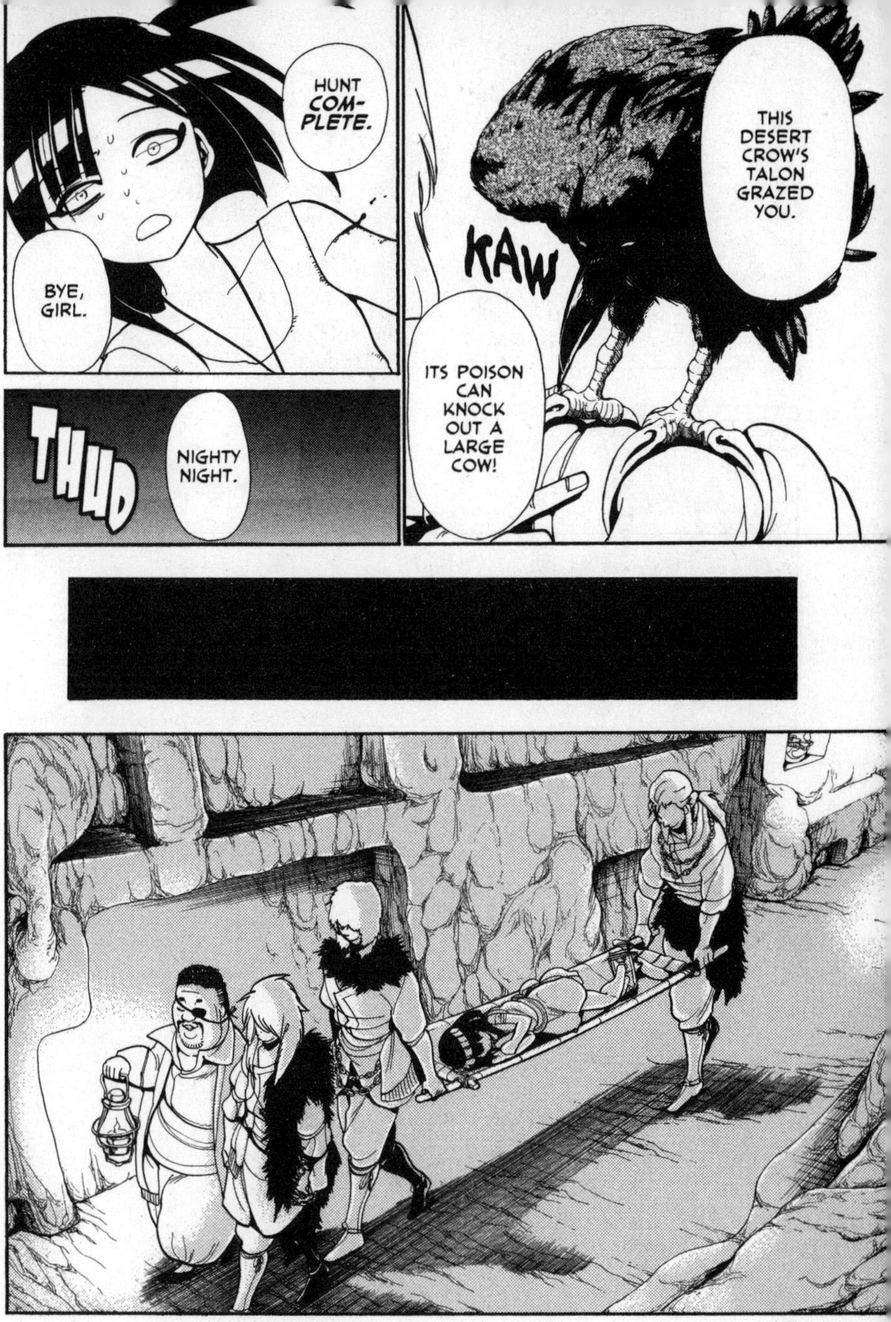
THIS DESERT CROW'S TALON GRAZED YOU.
KAW
ITS POISON CAN KNOCK OUT A LARGE COW!
HUNT COMPLETE.
BYE, GIRL.
NIGHTY NIGHT.
THUD

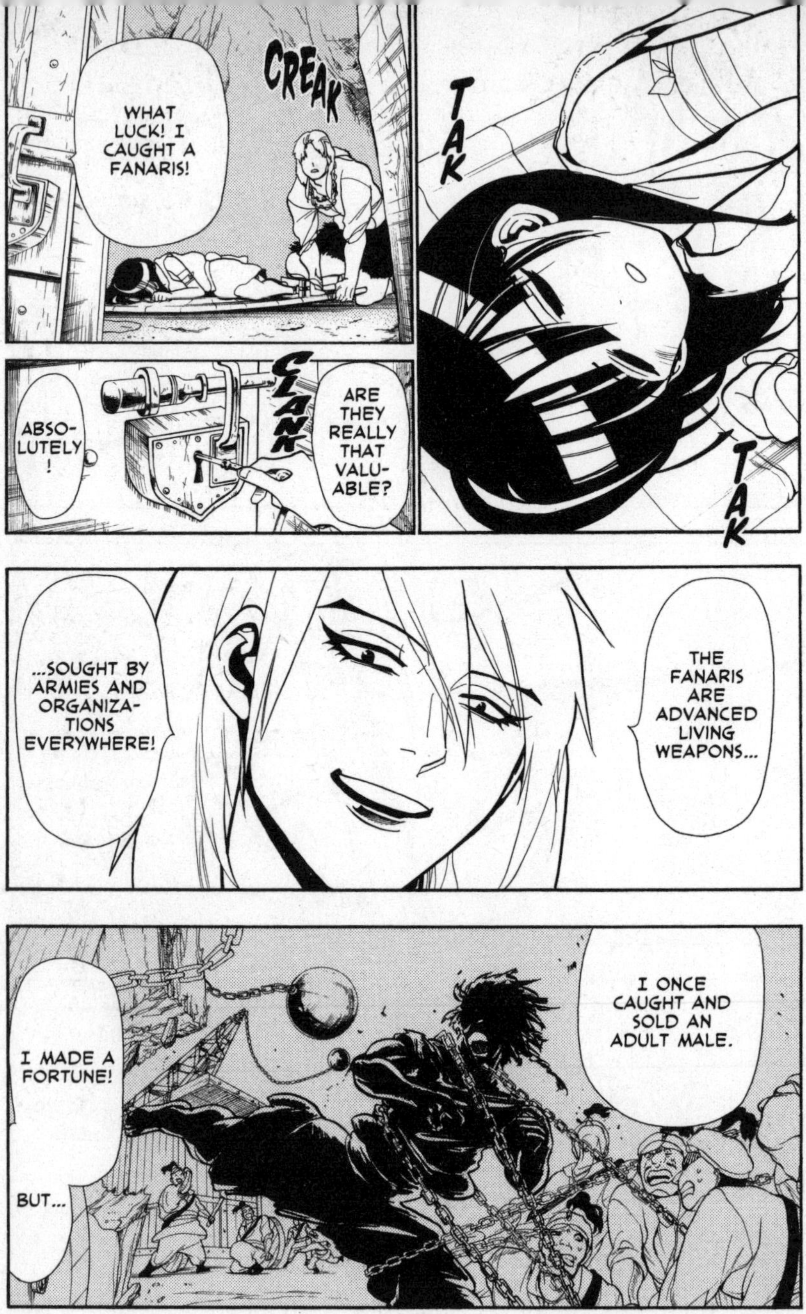
TAK
TAK
CREAK
WHAT LUCK! I CAUGHT A FANARIS!
CLANK
ARE THEY REALLY THAT VALU-ABLE?
ABSO-LUTELY!
THE FANARIS ARE ADVANCED LIVING WEAPONS...
...SOUGHT BY ARMIES AND ORGANIZA-TIONS EVERYWHERE!
I ONCE CAUGHT AND SOLD AN ADULT MALE.
I MADE A FORTUNE!
BUT...

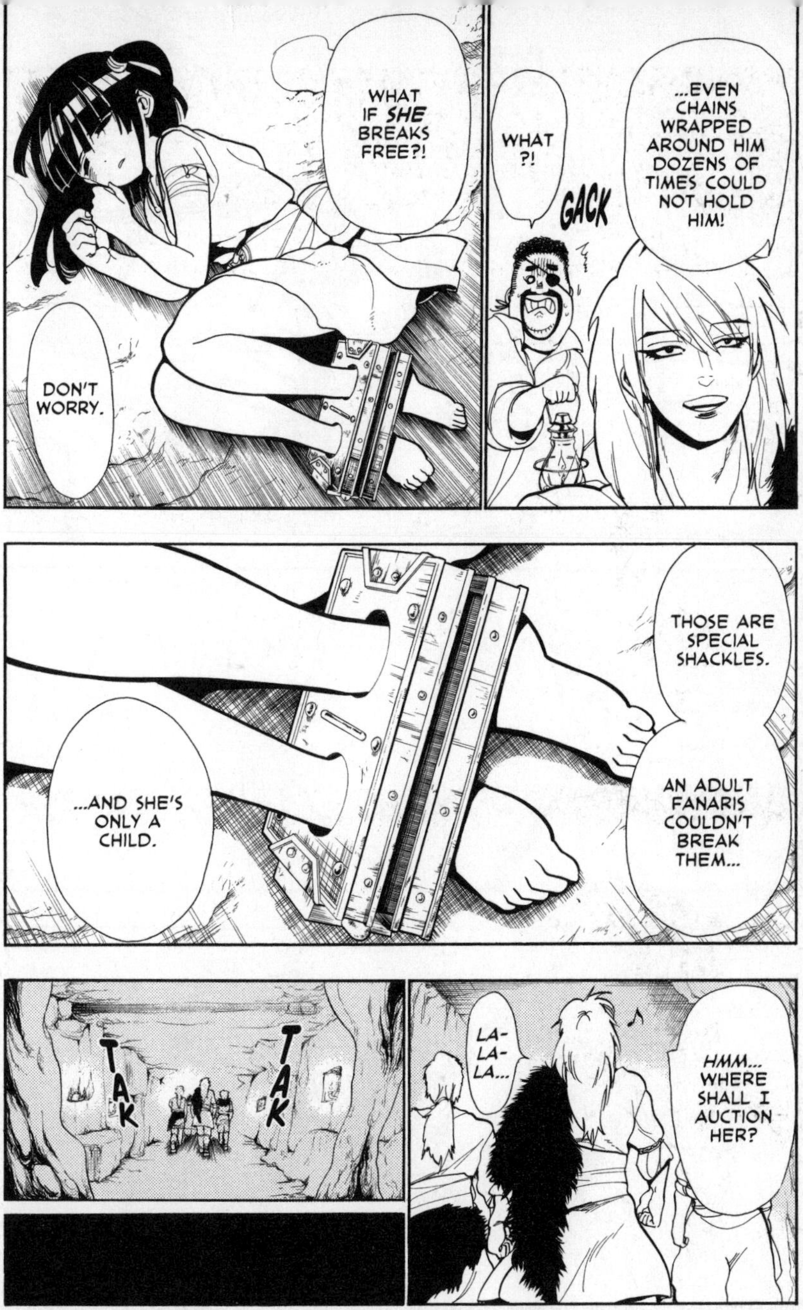
...EVEN CHAINS WRAPPED AROUND HIM DOZENS OF TIMES COULD NOT HOLD HIM!
GACK
WHAT ?!
WHAT IF SHE BREAKS FREE?!
DON'T WORRY.
THOSE ARE SPECIAL SHACKLES.
AN ADULT FANARIS COULDN'T BREAK THEM...
...AND SHE'S ONLY A CHILD.
HMM... WHERE SHALL I AUCTION HER?
LA-LA-LA...
TAK
TAK

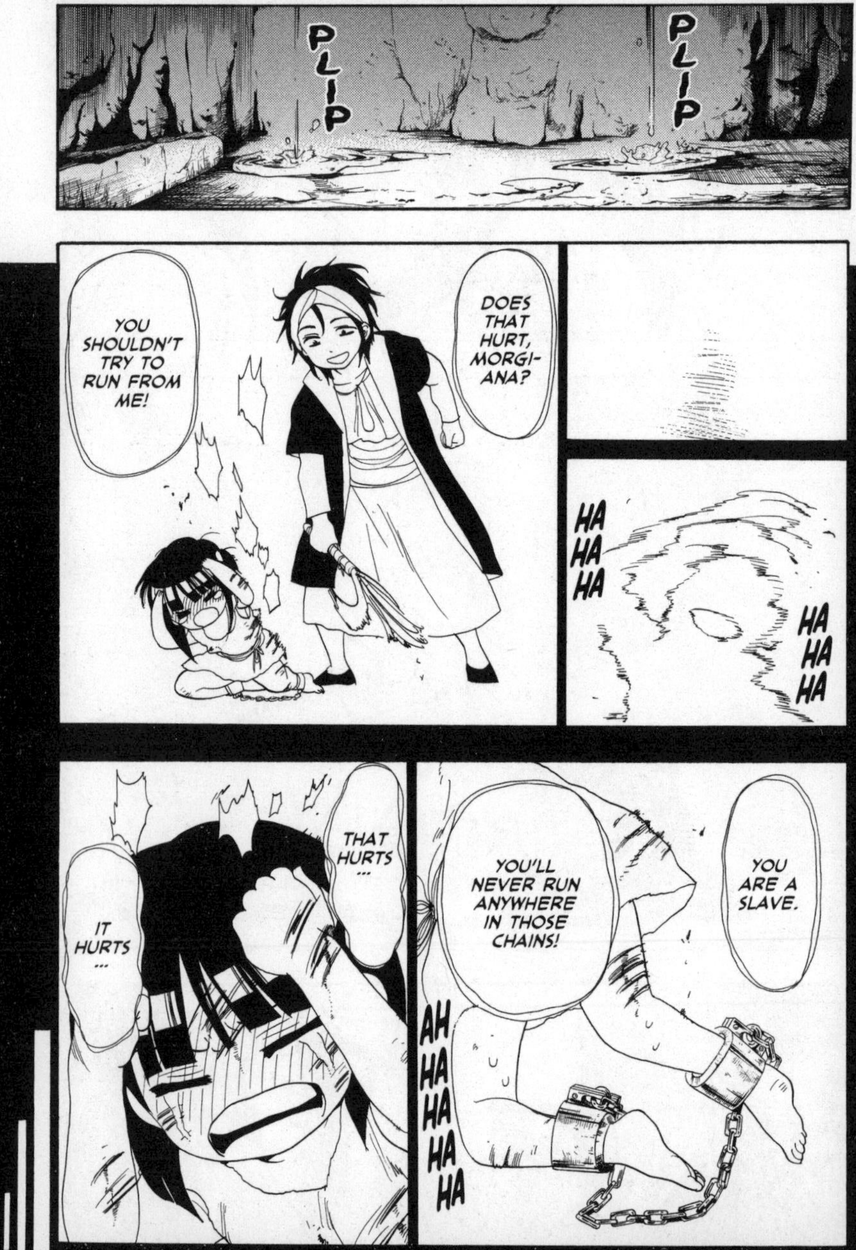
PLIP
PLIP
HA HA HA
HA HA HA
DOES THAT HURT, MORGI-ANA?
YOU SHOULDN'T TRY TO RUN FROM ME!
YOU ARE A SLAVE.
YOU'LL NEVER RUN ANYWHERE IN THOSE CHAINS!
AH HA HA HA HA HA
THAT HURTS ...
IT HURTS ...

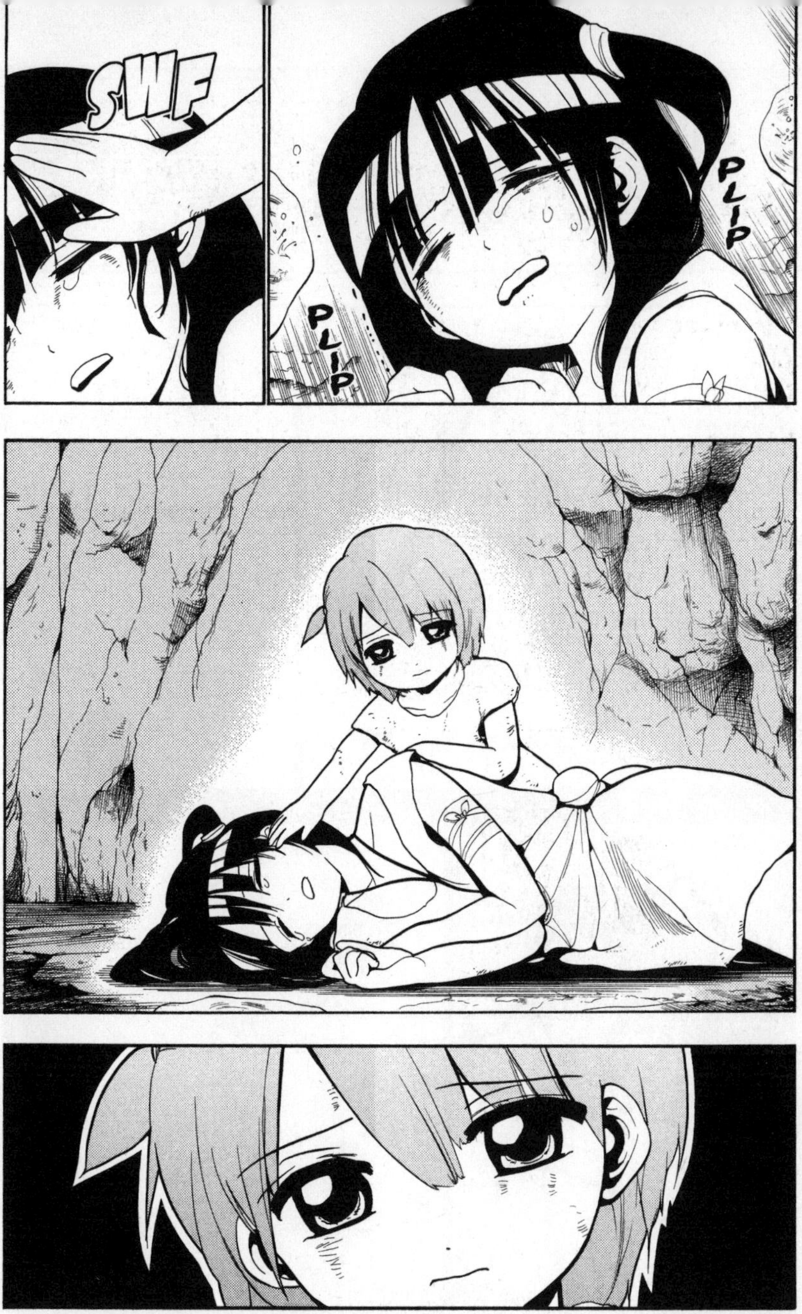
PLIP
PLIP
PLIP
PLIP
SWF

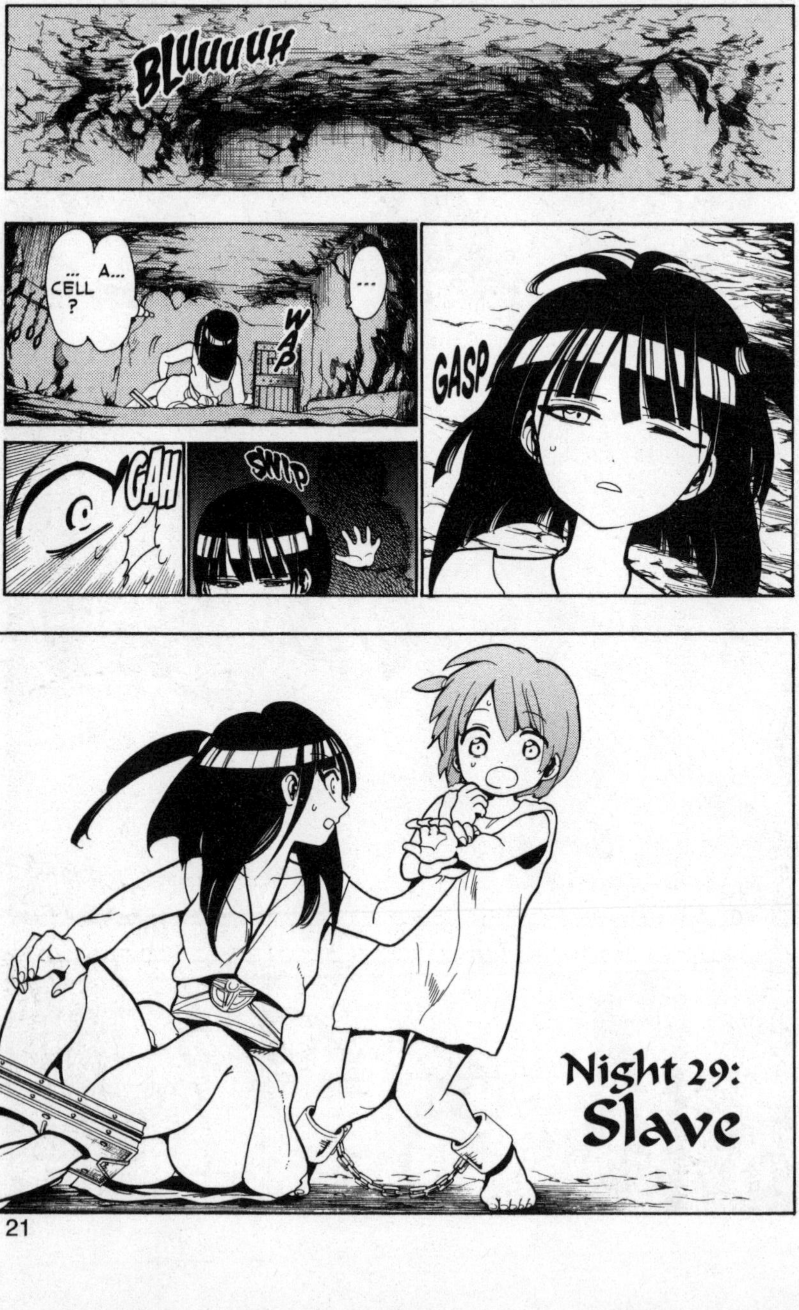
BLUUUUH
GASP
...
WAP
A... ...CELL?
SWIP
GAH
Night 29: Slave

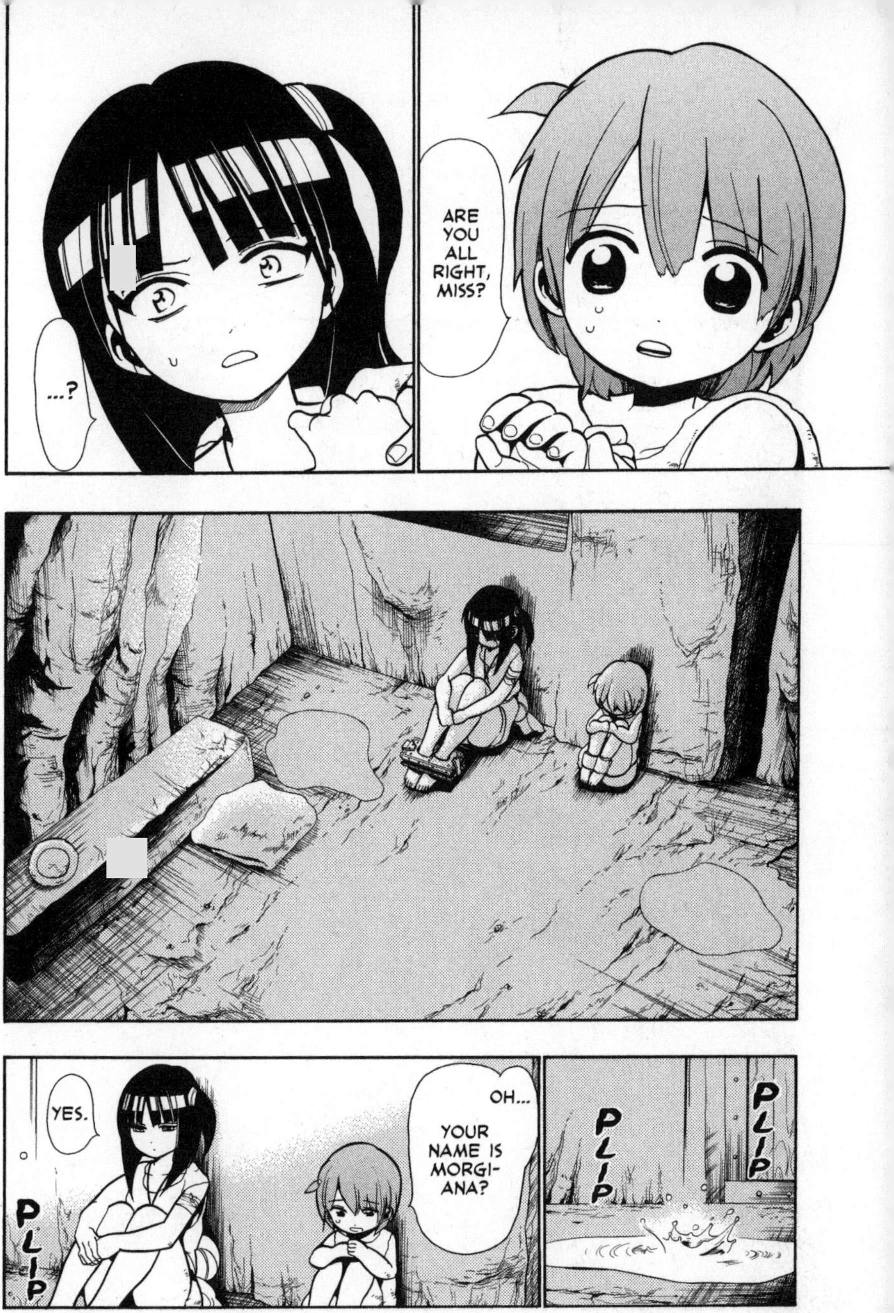
ARE YOU ALL RIGHT, MISS?
...?
PLIP
PLIP
OH...
YOUR NAME IS MORGI-ANA?
YES.
PLIP

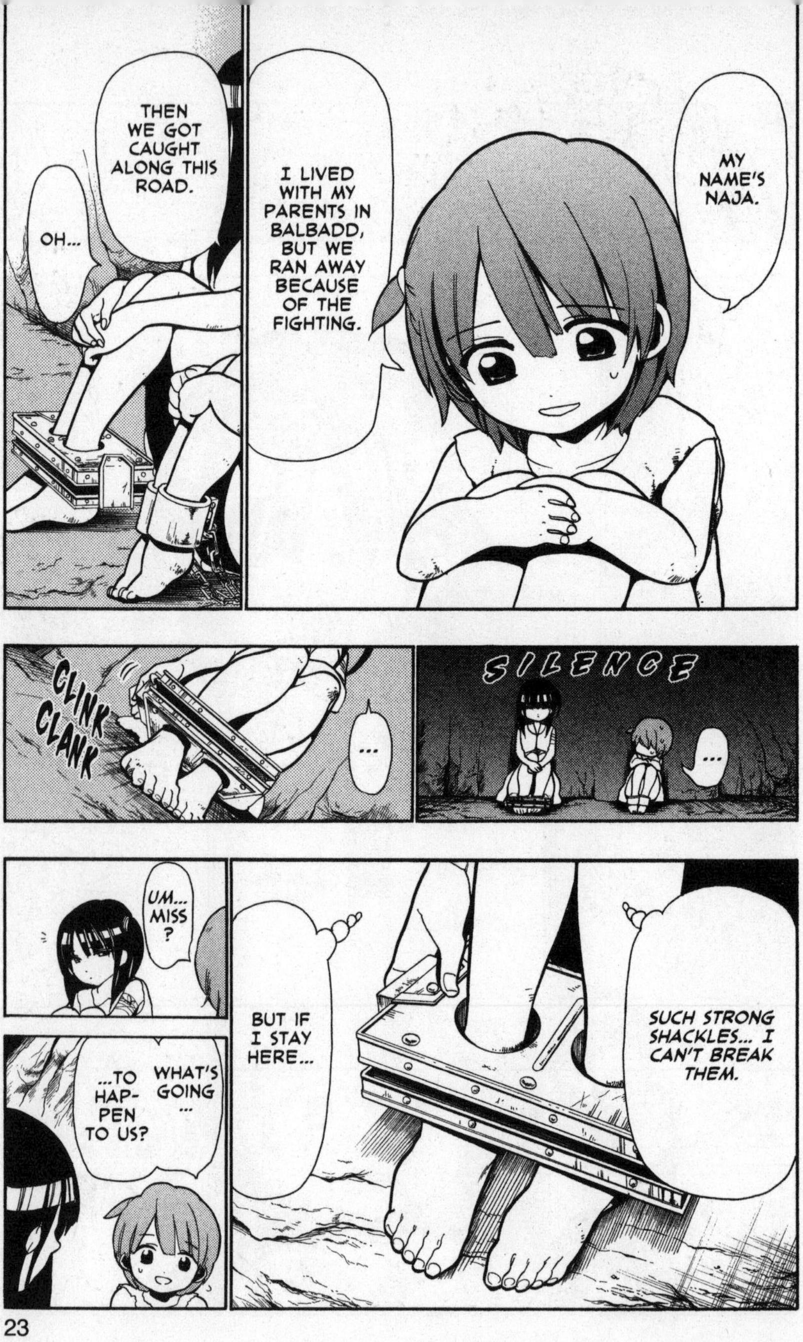
MY NAME'S NAJA.
I LIVED WITH MY PARENTS IN BALBADD, BUT WE RAN AWAY BECAUSE OF THE FIGHTING.
THEN WE GOT CAUGHT ALONG THIS ROAD.
OH...
SILENCE
...
...
CLINK CLANK
SUCH STRONG SHACKLES... I CAN'T BREAK THEM.
BUT IF I STAY HERE...
UM... MISS?
WHAT'S GOING...
...TO HAPPEN TO US?

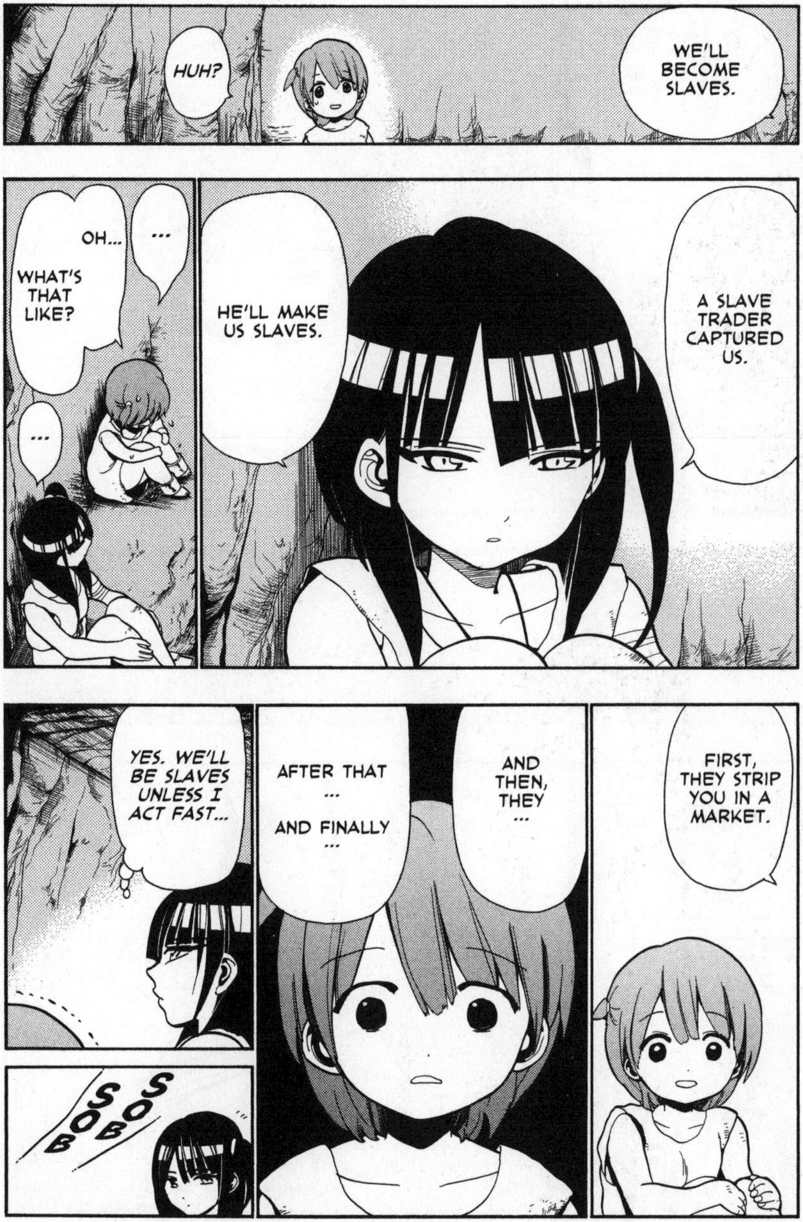
WE'LL BECOME SLAVES.
HUH?
A SLAVE TRADER CAPTURED US.
HE'LL MAKE US SLAVES.
...
OH... WHAT'S THAT LIKE?
...
FIRST, THEY STRIP YOU IN A MARKET.
AND THEN, THEY ...
AFTER THAT ...
AND FINALLY ...
YES. WE'LL BE SLAVES UNLESS I ACT FAST...
SOB SOB

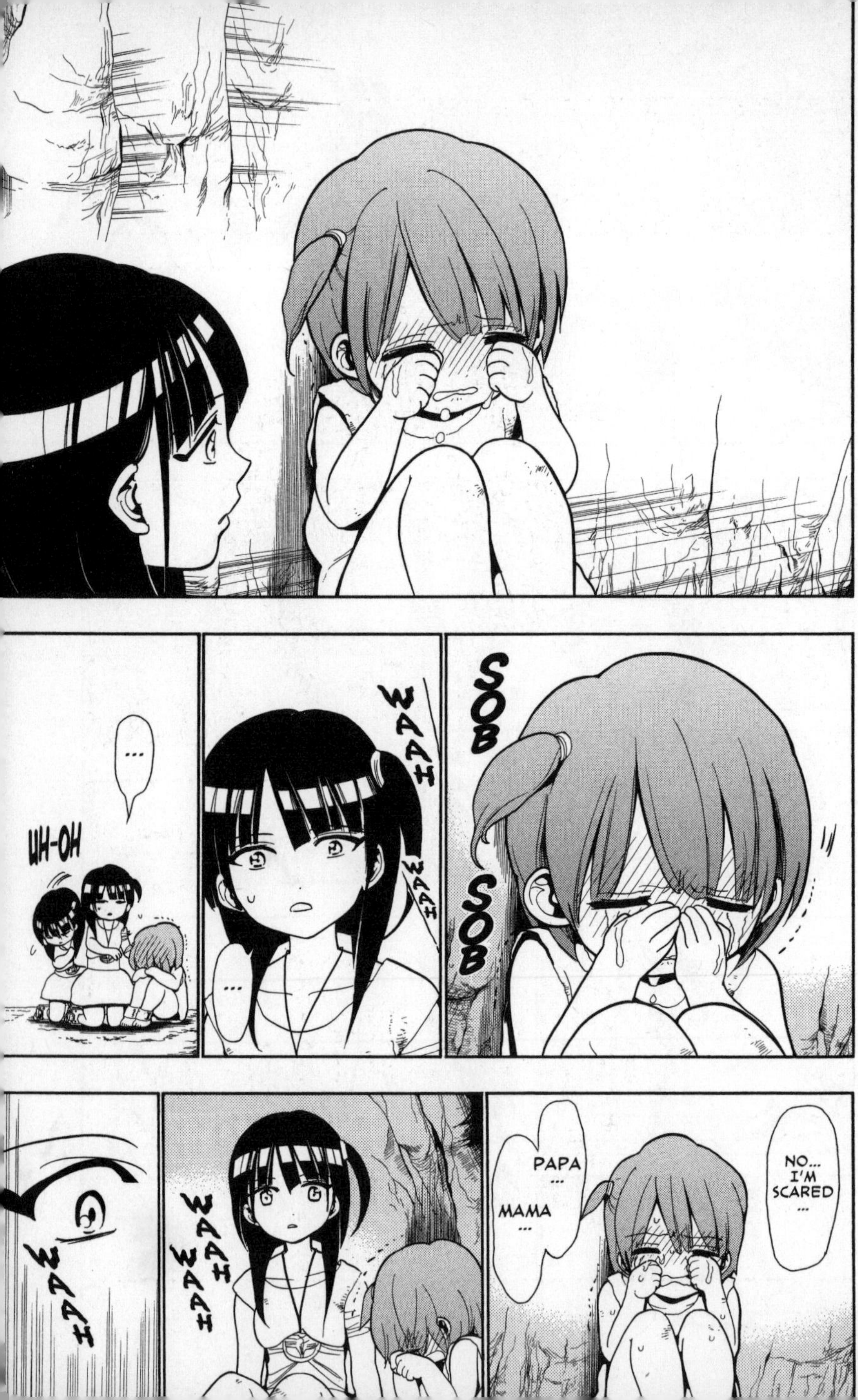
SOB
SOB
WAAH
WAAH
...
...
UH-OH
NO... I'M SCARED ...
PAPA ...
MAMA ...
WAAH
WAAH
WAAH

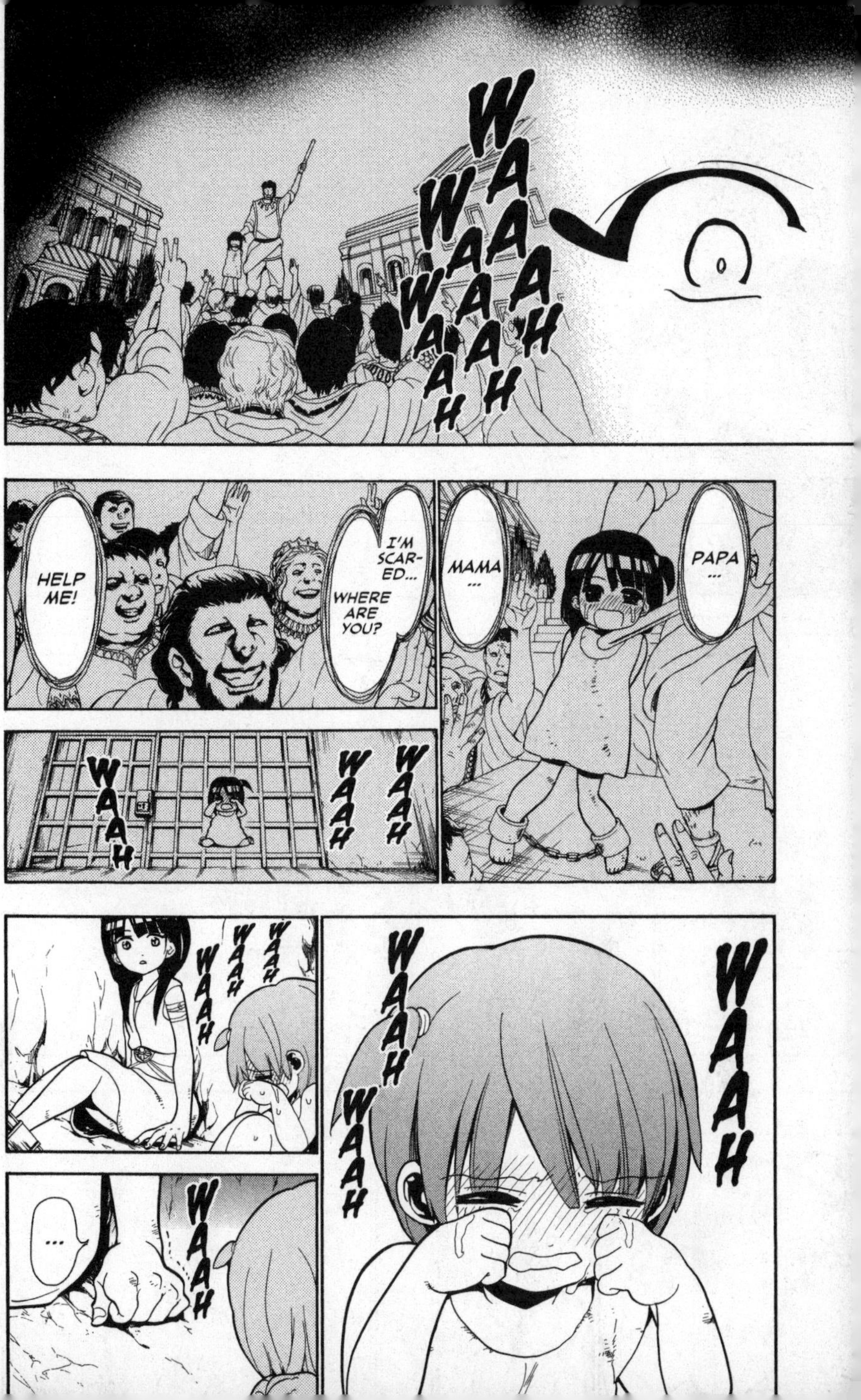
WAAAAAH
WAAAAAH
PAPA...
MAMA...
I'M SCARED-ED...
WHERE ARE YOU?
HELP ME!
WAAH
WAAH
WAAH
WAAAH
WAAH
WAAH
WAAH
WAAH
WAAH
WAAAH
...

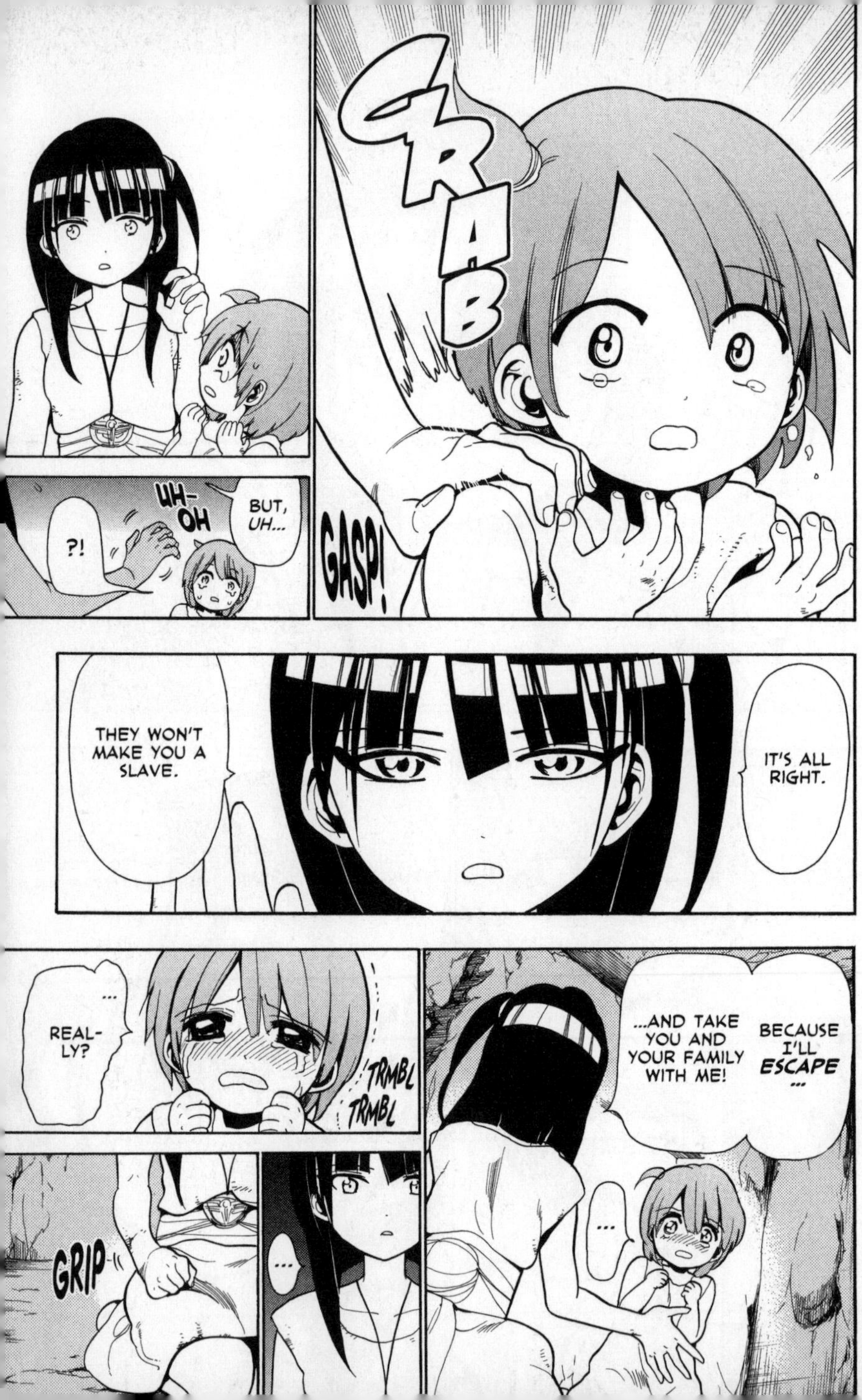
GRAB
GASP!
BUT, UH...
UH-OH
?!
IT'S ALL RIGHT.
THEY WON'T MAKE YOU A SLAVE.
BECAUSE I'LL *ESCAPE* ...
...AND TAKE YOU AND YOUR FAMILY WITH ME!
...
TRMBL TRMBL
... REAL-LY?
...
GRIP

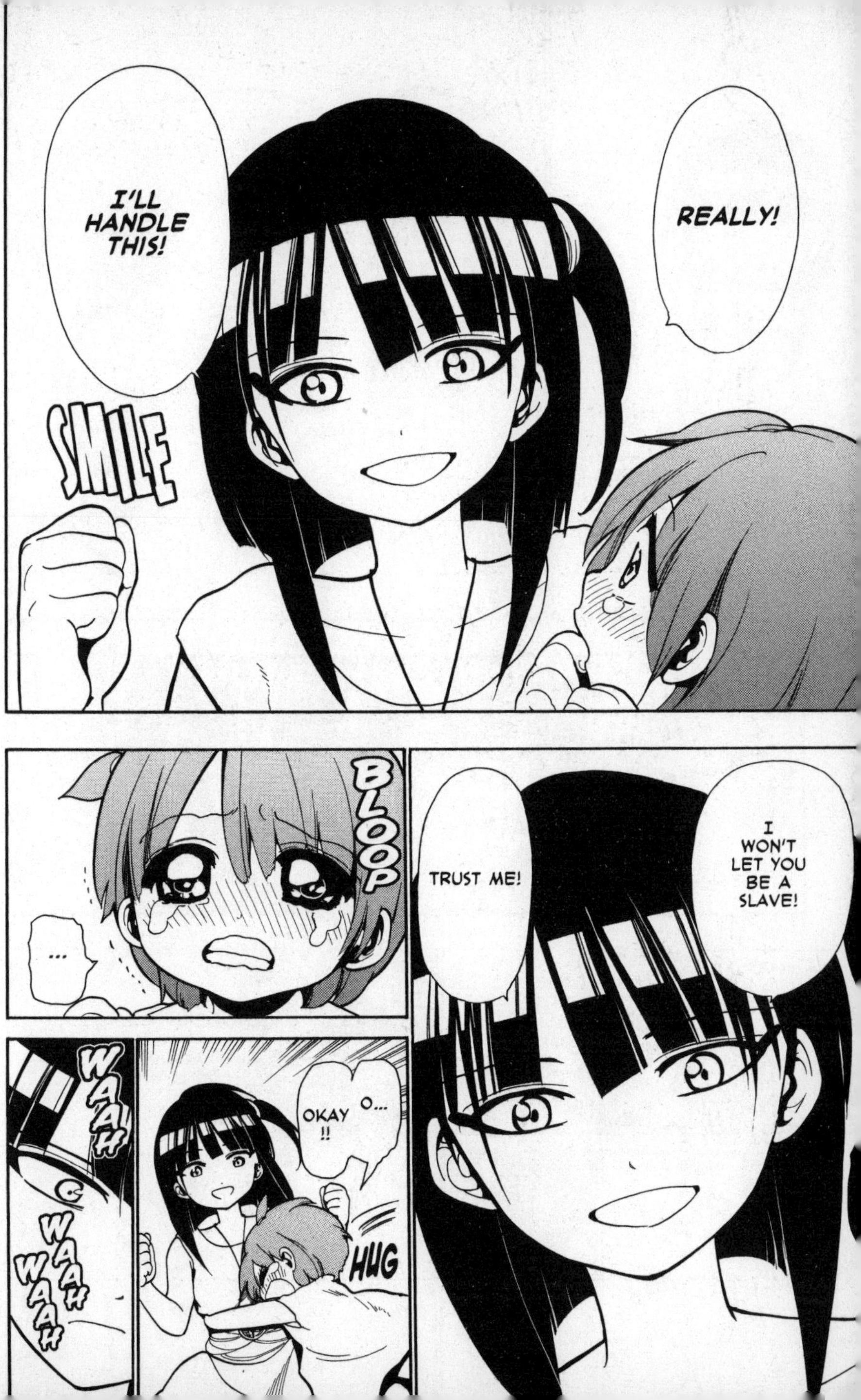
REALLY!
I'LL HANDLE THIS!
SMILE
I WON'T LET YOU BE A SLAVE!
TRUST ME!
BLOOP
...
O... OKAY!!
HUG
WAAH
WAAH
WAAH

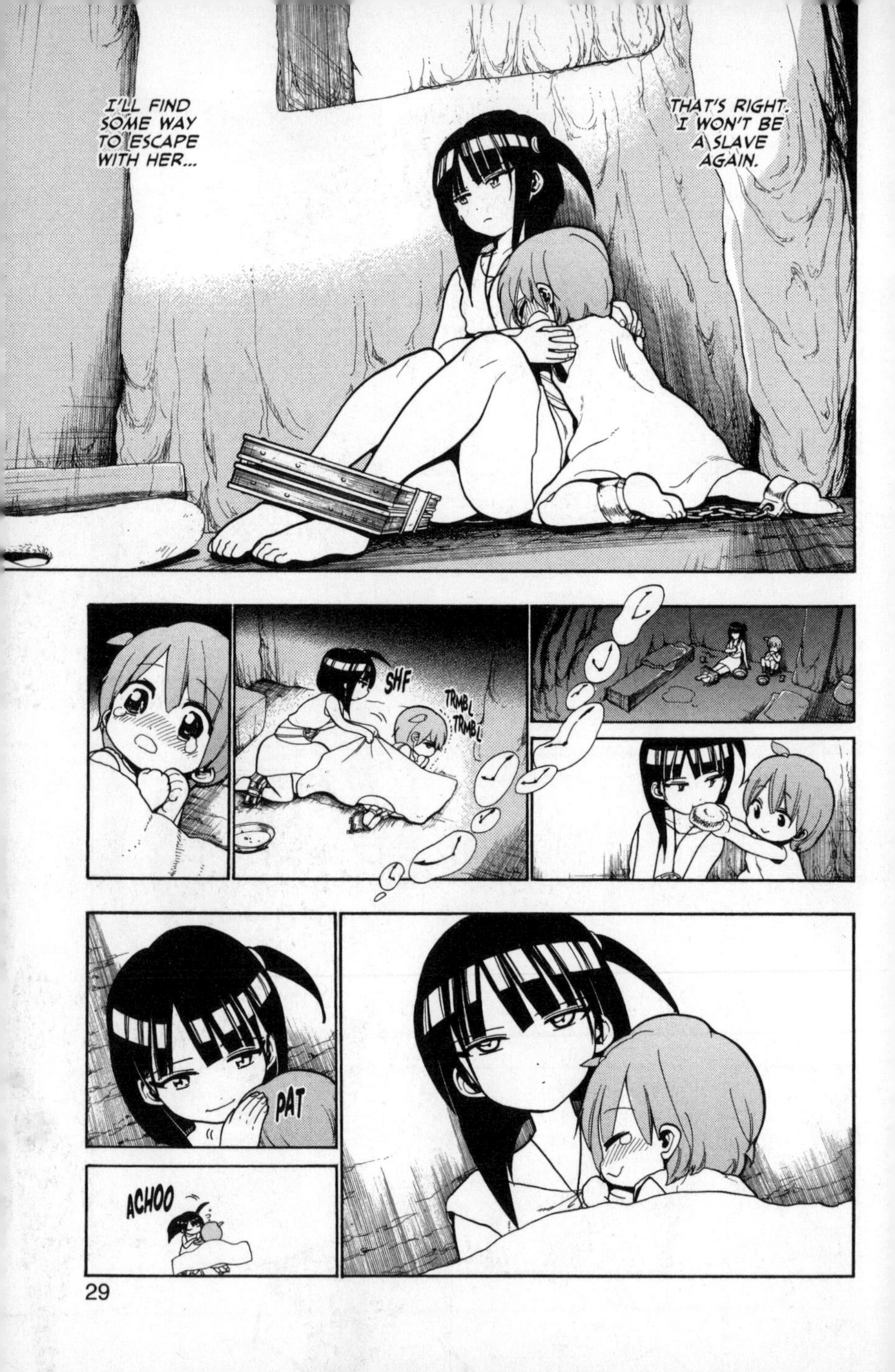
THAT'S RIGHT. I WON'T BE A SLAVE AGAIN.
I'LL FIND SOME WAY TO ESCAPE WITH HER...
SHF
TRMBL TRMBL
PAT
ACHOO

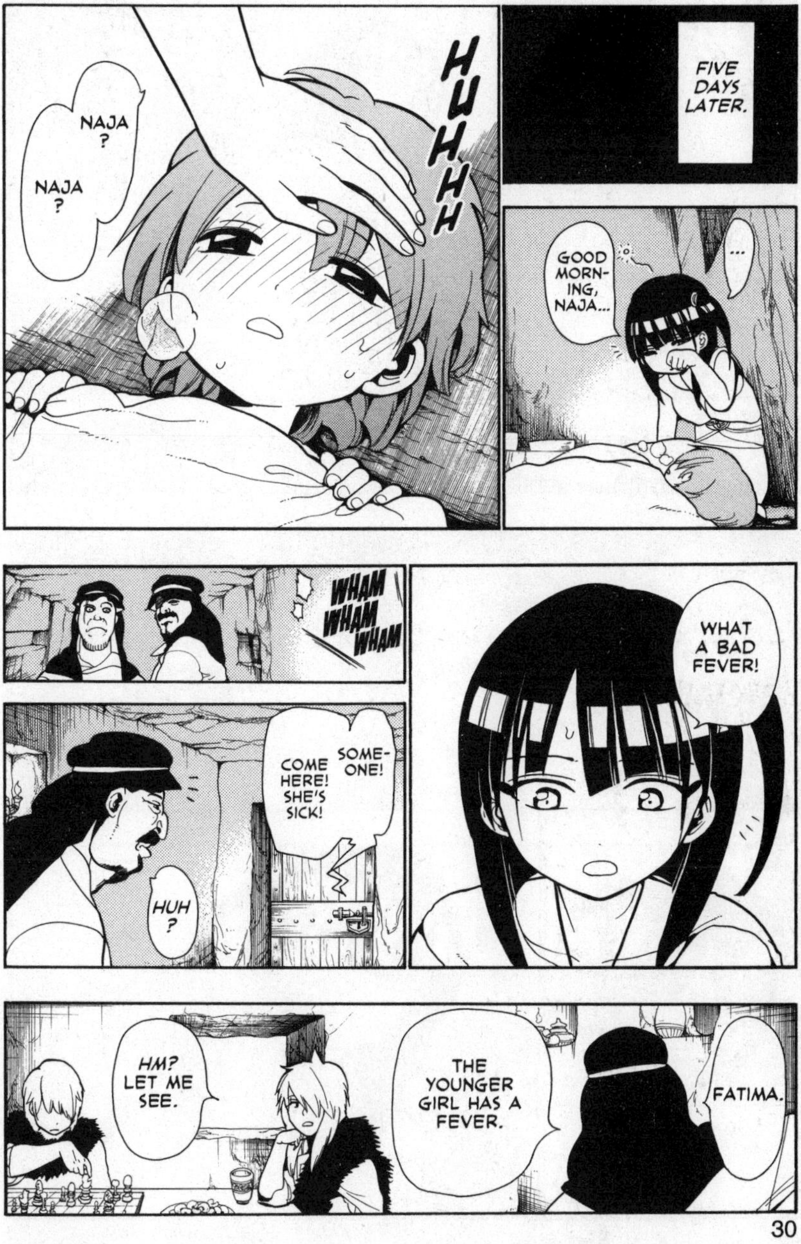
FIVE DAYS LATER.
...
GOOD MORNING, NAJA...
HUHHHH
NAJA?
NAJA?
WHAT A BAD FEVER!
WHAM WHAM WHAM
SOME-ONE!
COME HERE! SHE'S SICK!
HUH?
FATIMA.
THE YOUNGER GIRL HAS A FEVER.
HM? LET ME SEE.

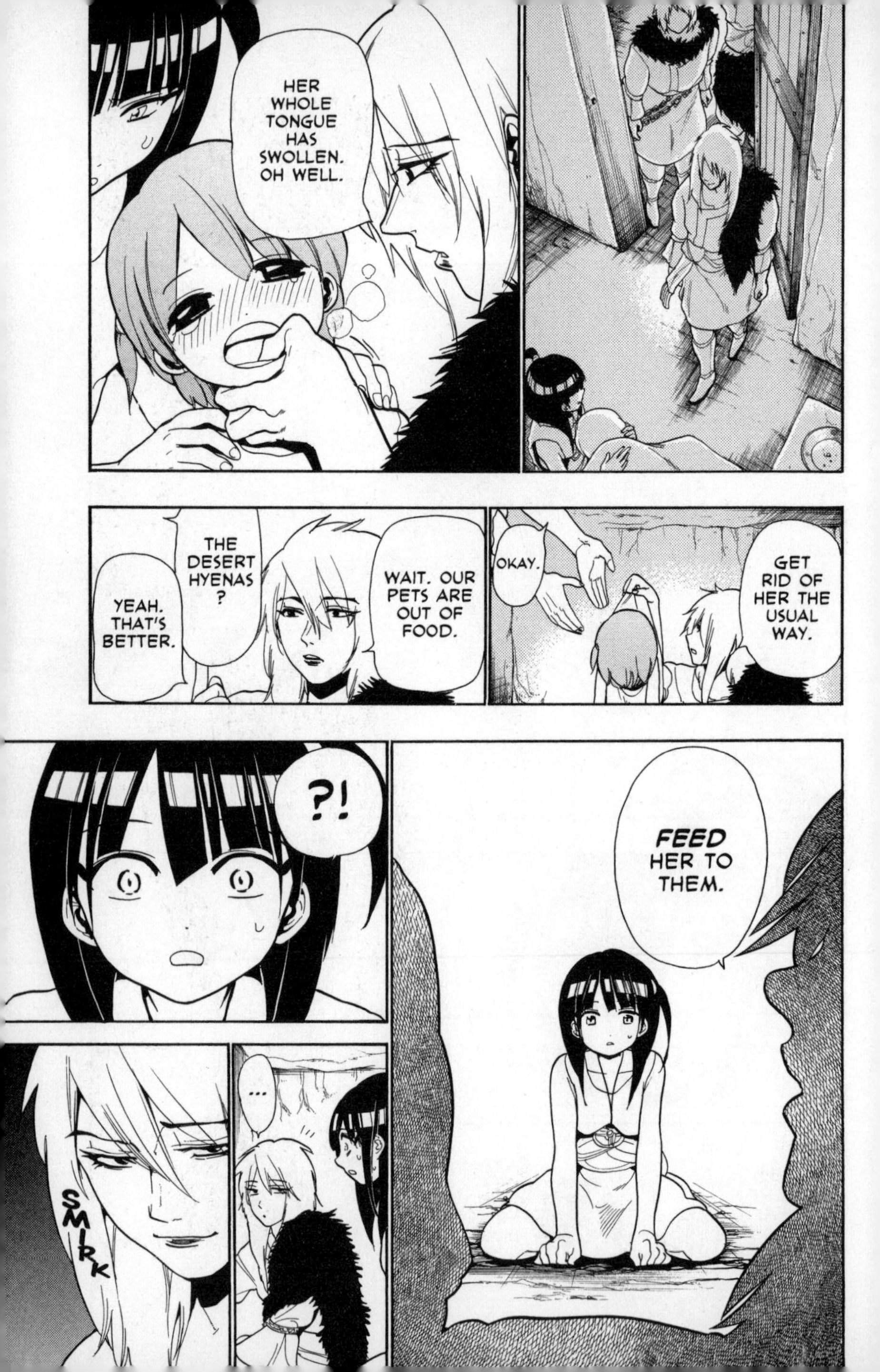
HER WHOLE TONGUE HAS SWOLLEN. OH WELL.
GET RID OF HER THE USUAL WAY.
OKAY.
WAIT. OUR PETS ARE OUT OF FOOD.
THE DESERT HYENAS?
YEAH. THAT'S BETTER.
FEED HER TO THEM.
?!
...
SMIRK

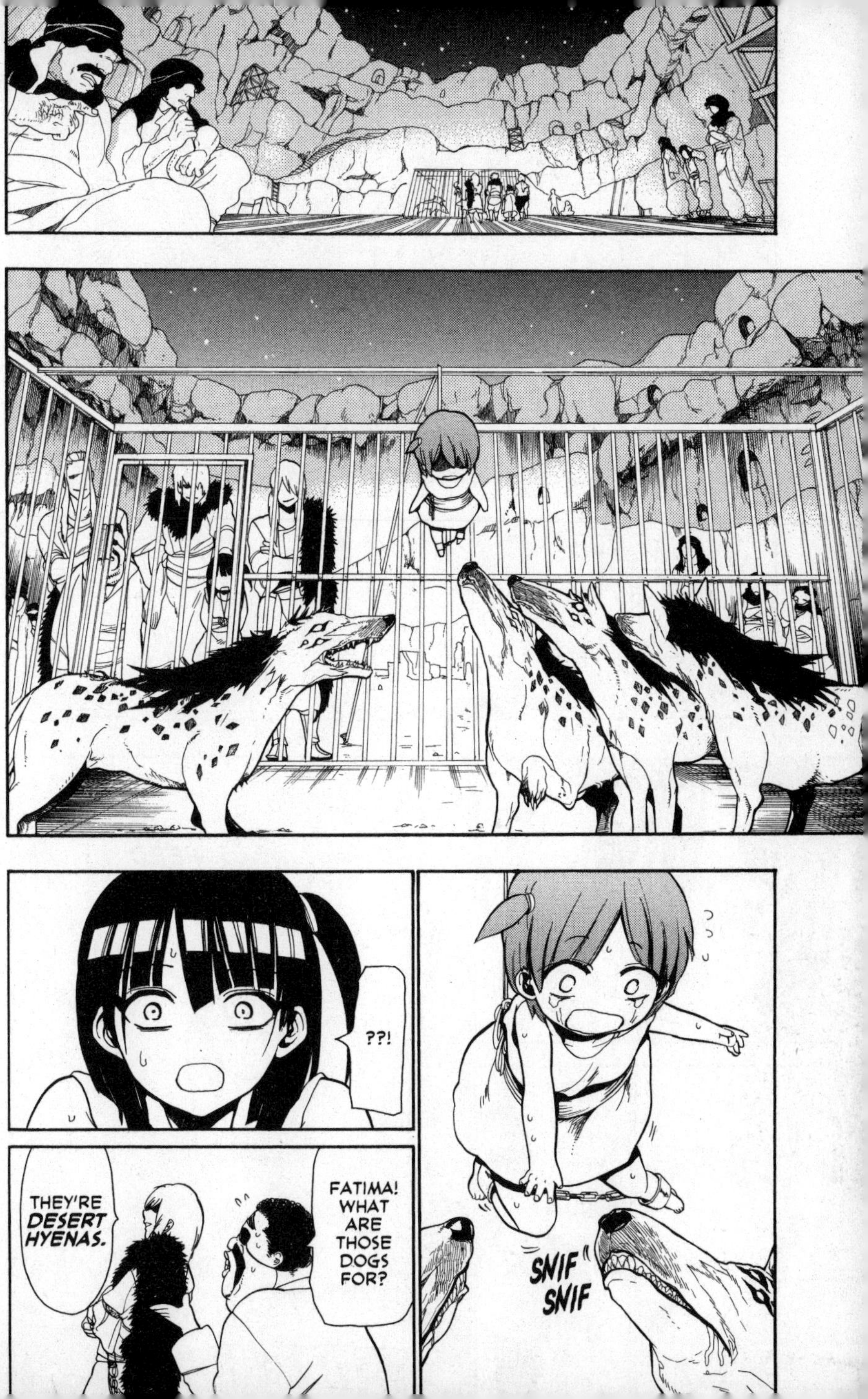
SNIF SNIF
??!
FATIMA! WHAT ARE THOSE DOGS FOR?
THEY'RE DESERT HYENAS.

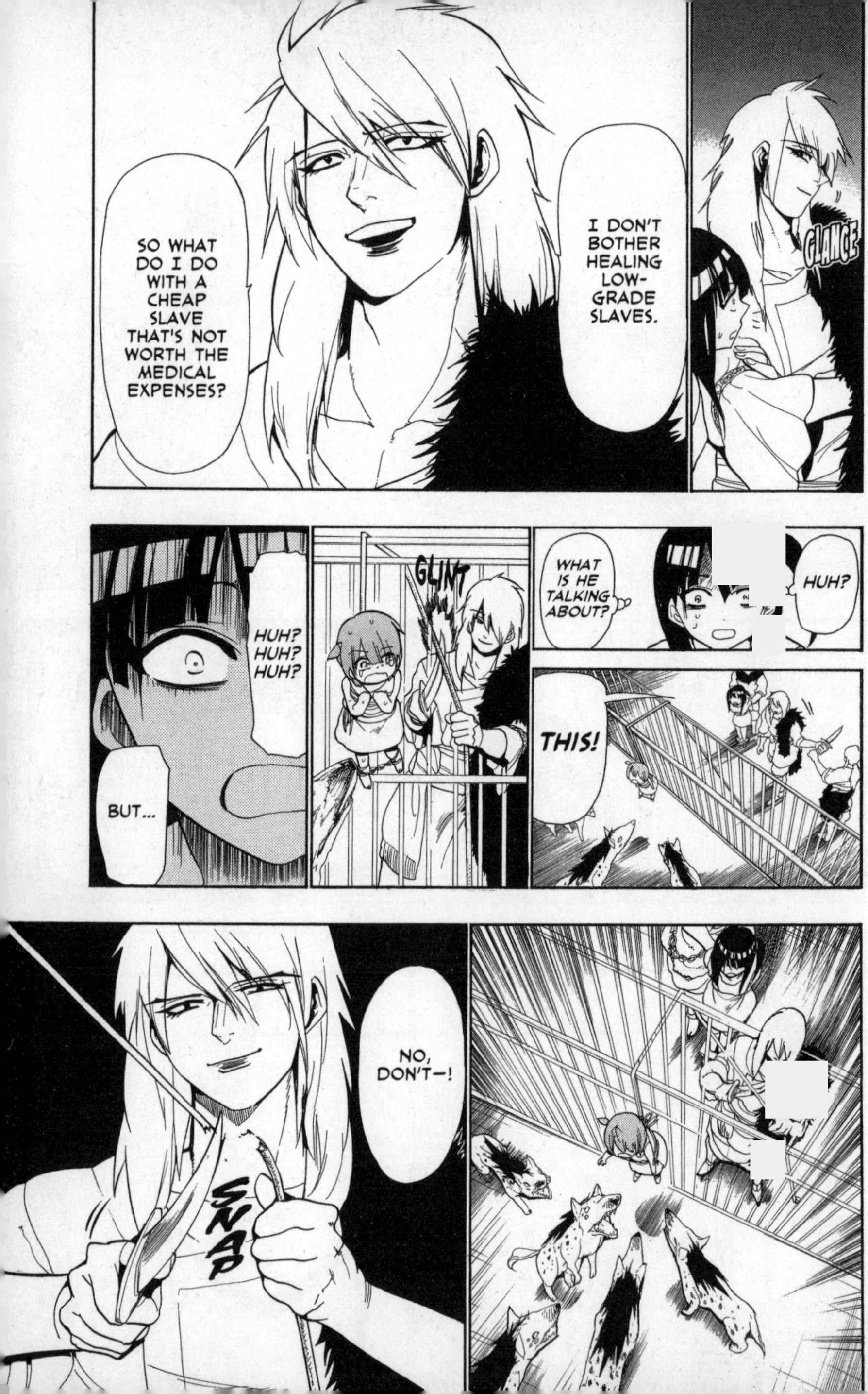
GLANCE
I DON'T BOTHER HEALING LOW-GRADE SLAVES.
SO WHAT DO I DO WITH A CHEAP SLAVE THAT'S NOT WORTH THE MEDICAL EXPENSES?
HUH?
WHAT IS HE TALKING ABOUT?
THIS!
GLINT
HUH? HUH? HUH?
BUT...
NO, DON'T—!
SNAP

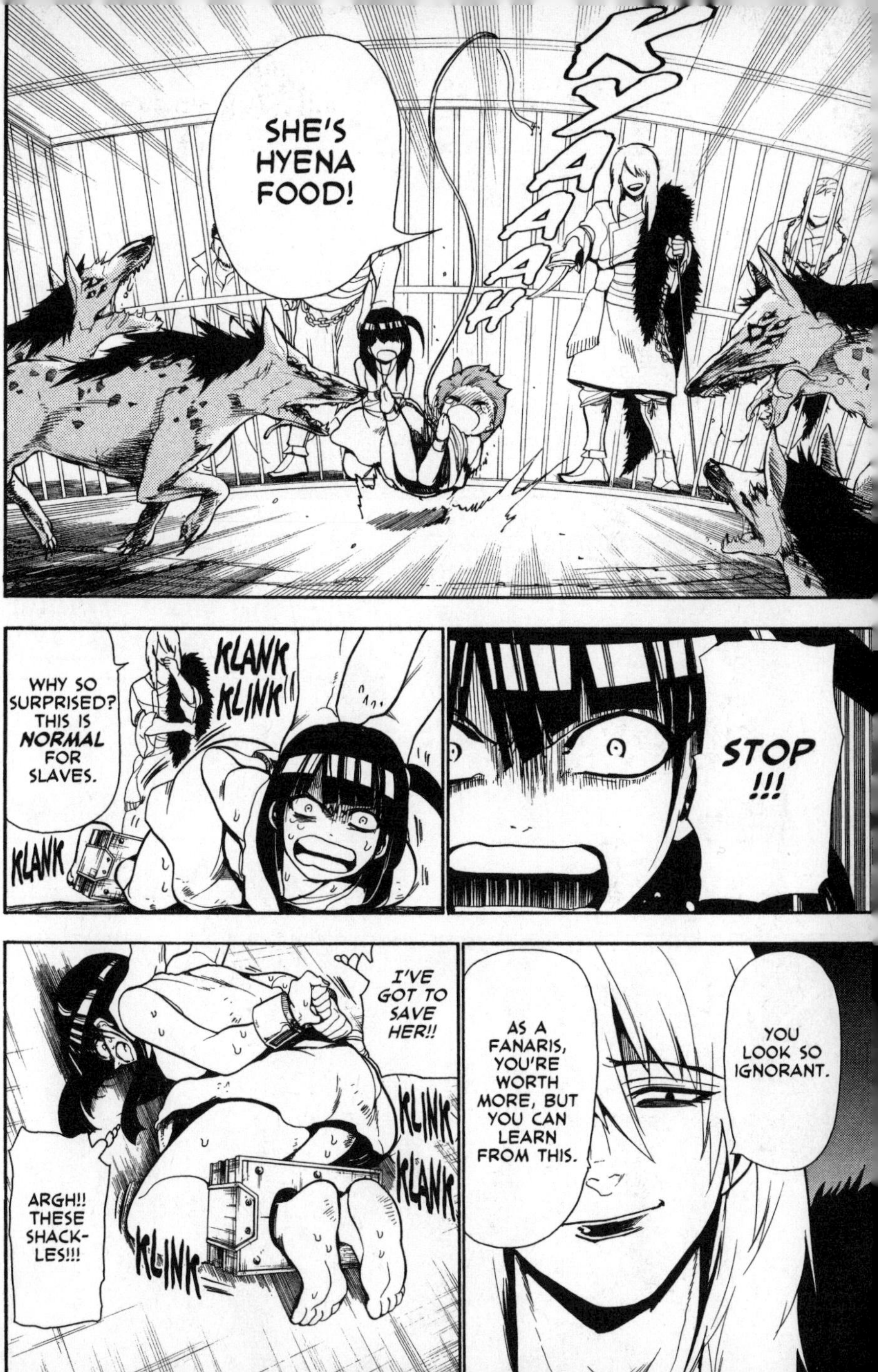
KYAAAAH
SHE'S HYENA FOOD!
STOP!!!
KLANK KLINK
WHY SO SURPRISED? THIS IS *NORMAL* FOR SLAVES.
KLANK
YOU LOOK SO IGNORANT.
AS A FANARIS, YOU'RE WORTH MORE, BUT YOU CAN LEARN FROM THIS.
I'VE GOT TO SAVE HER!!
KLINK
KLANK
ARGH!! THESE SHACK-LES!!!
KLINK

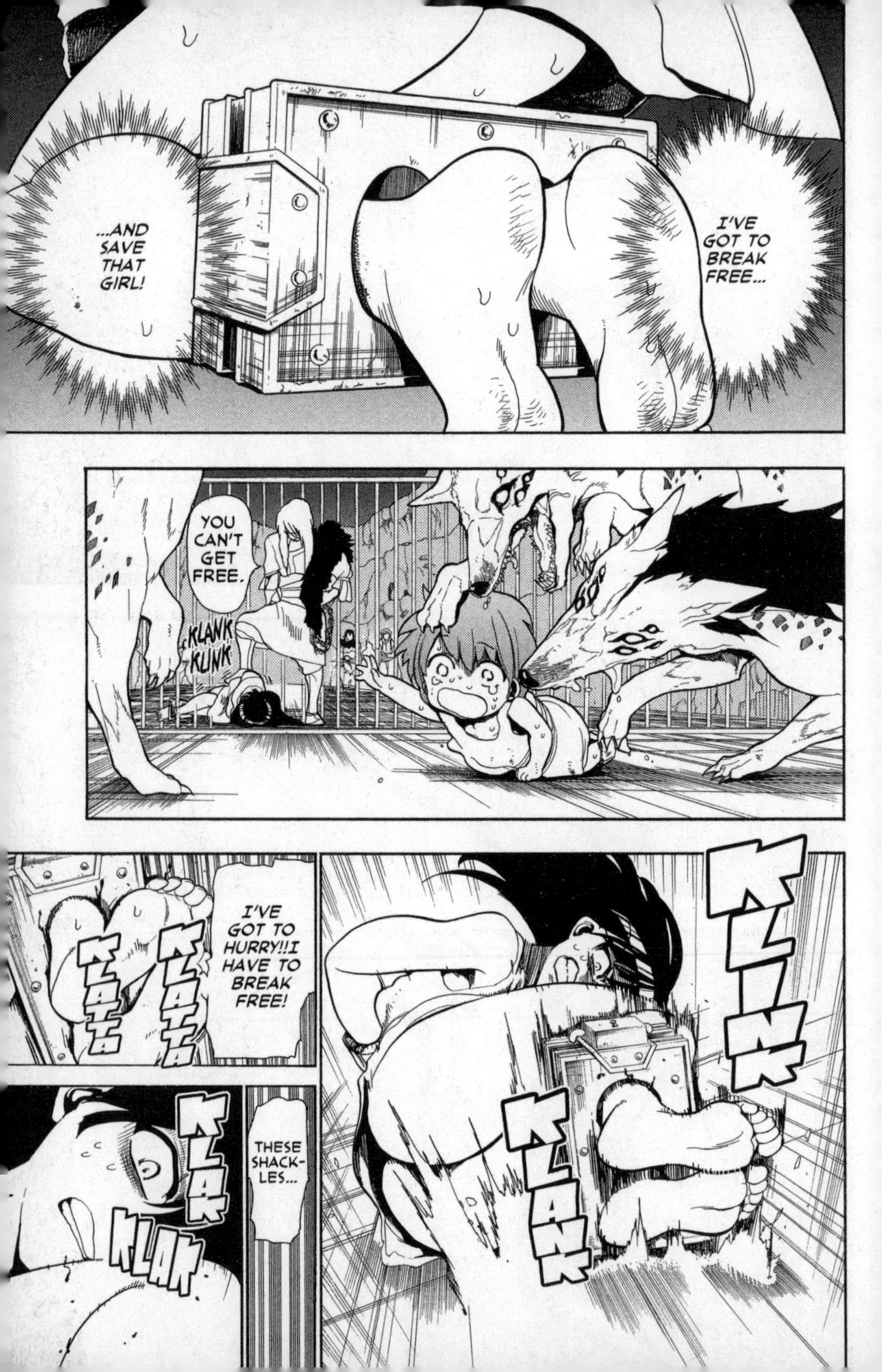
I'VE GOT TO BREAK FREE...
...AND SAVE THAT GIRL!
YOU CAN'T GET FREE.
KLANK KLINK
KLINK
KLANK
I'VE GOT TO HURRY!!I HAVE TO BREAK FREE!
KLATTA
KLATTA
THESE SHACK-LES...
KLAK
KLAK

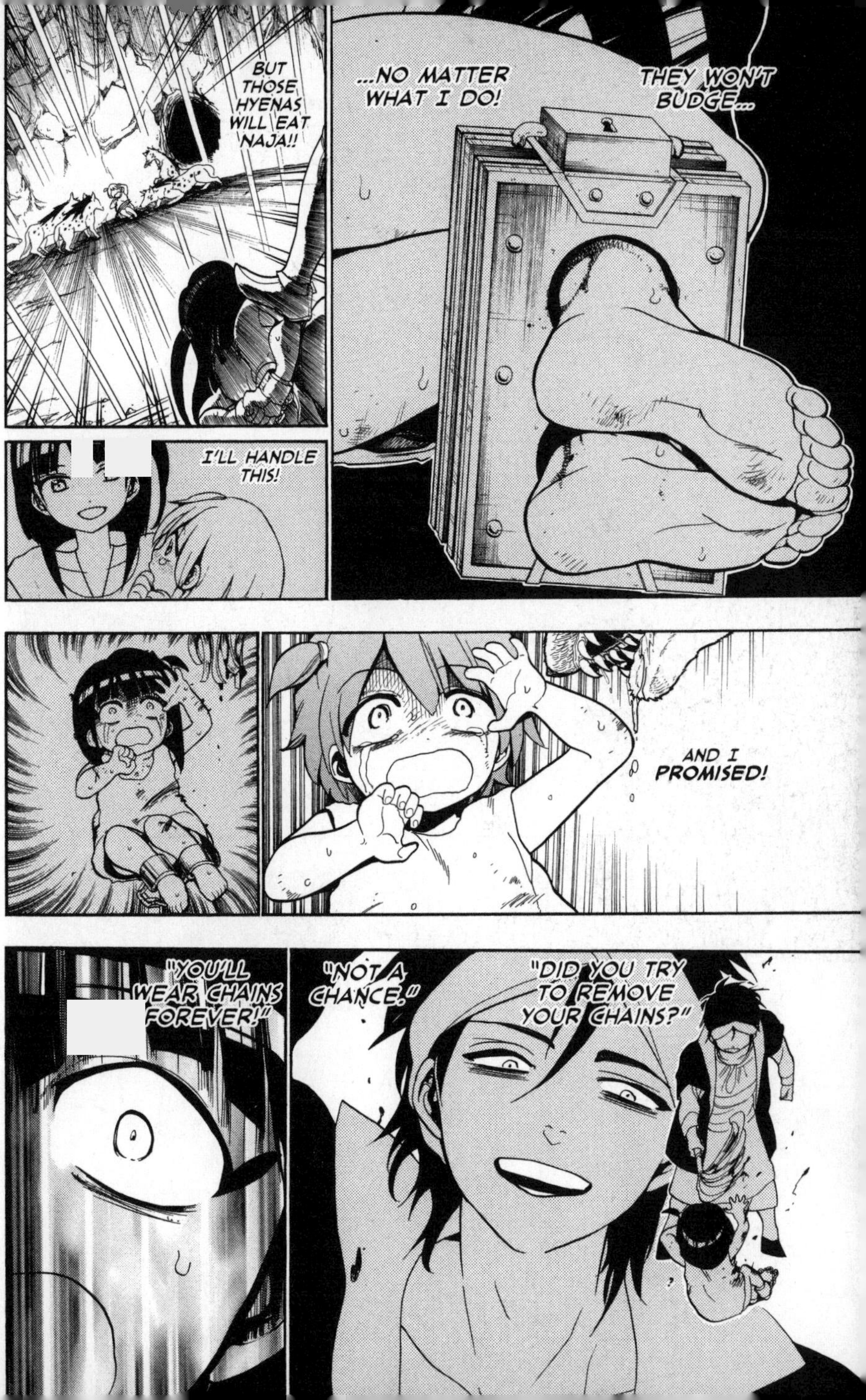
THEY WON'T BUDGE...
...NO MATTER WHAT I DO!
BUT THOSE HYENAS WILL EAT NAJA!!
I'LL HANDLE THIS!
AND I PROMISED!
"DID YOU TRY TO REMOVE YOUR CHAINS?"
"NOT A CHANCE."
"YOU'LL WEAR CHAINS FOREVER!"

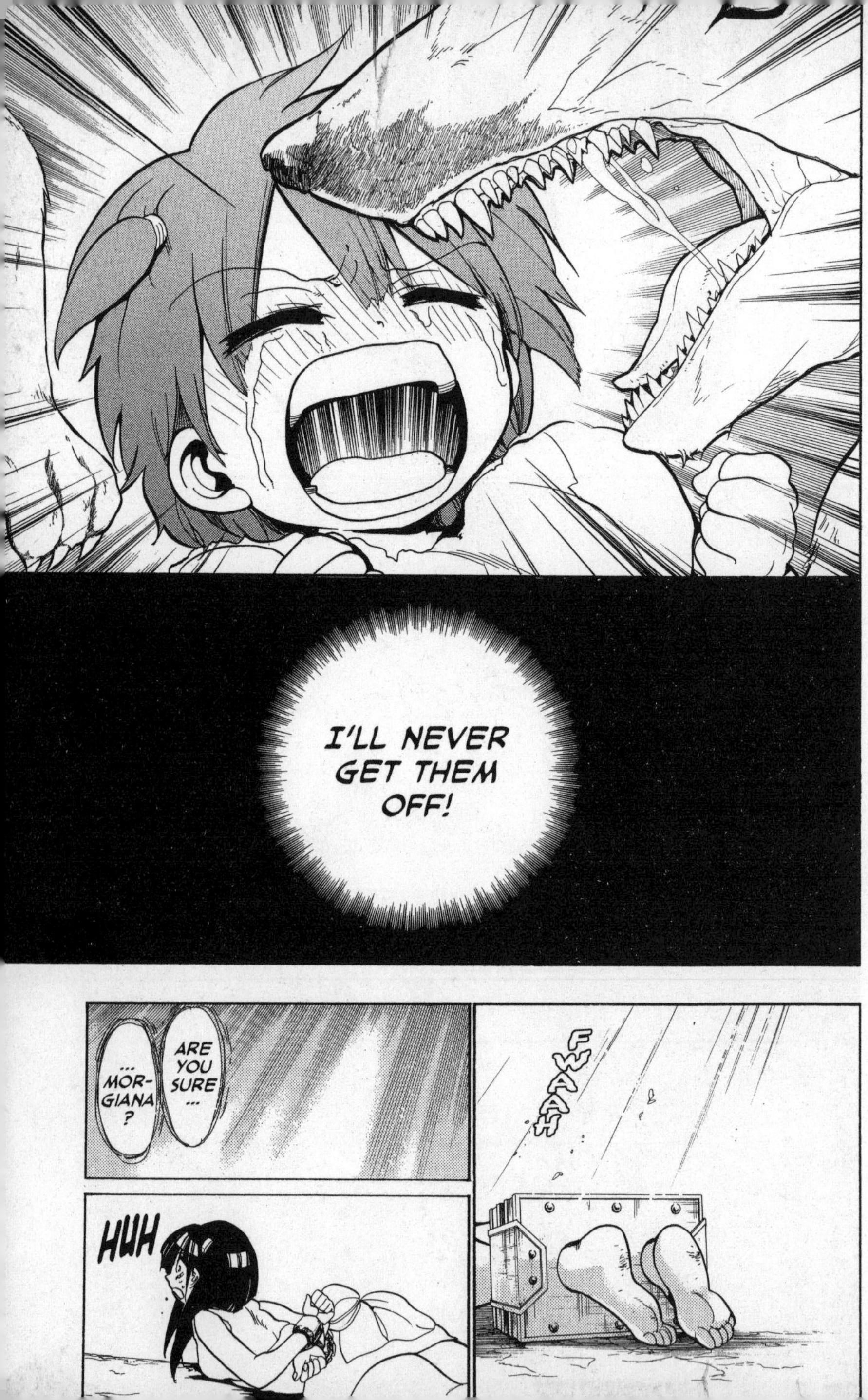
I'LL NEVER GET THEM OFF!
FWAAH
ARE YOU SURE ...
... MOR-GIANA ?
HUH

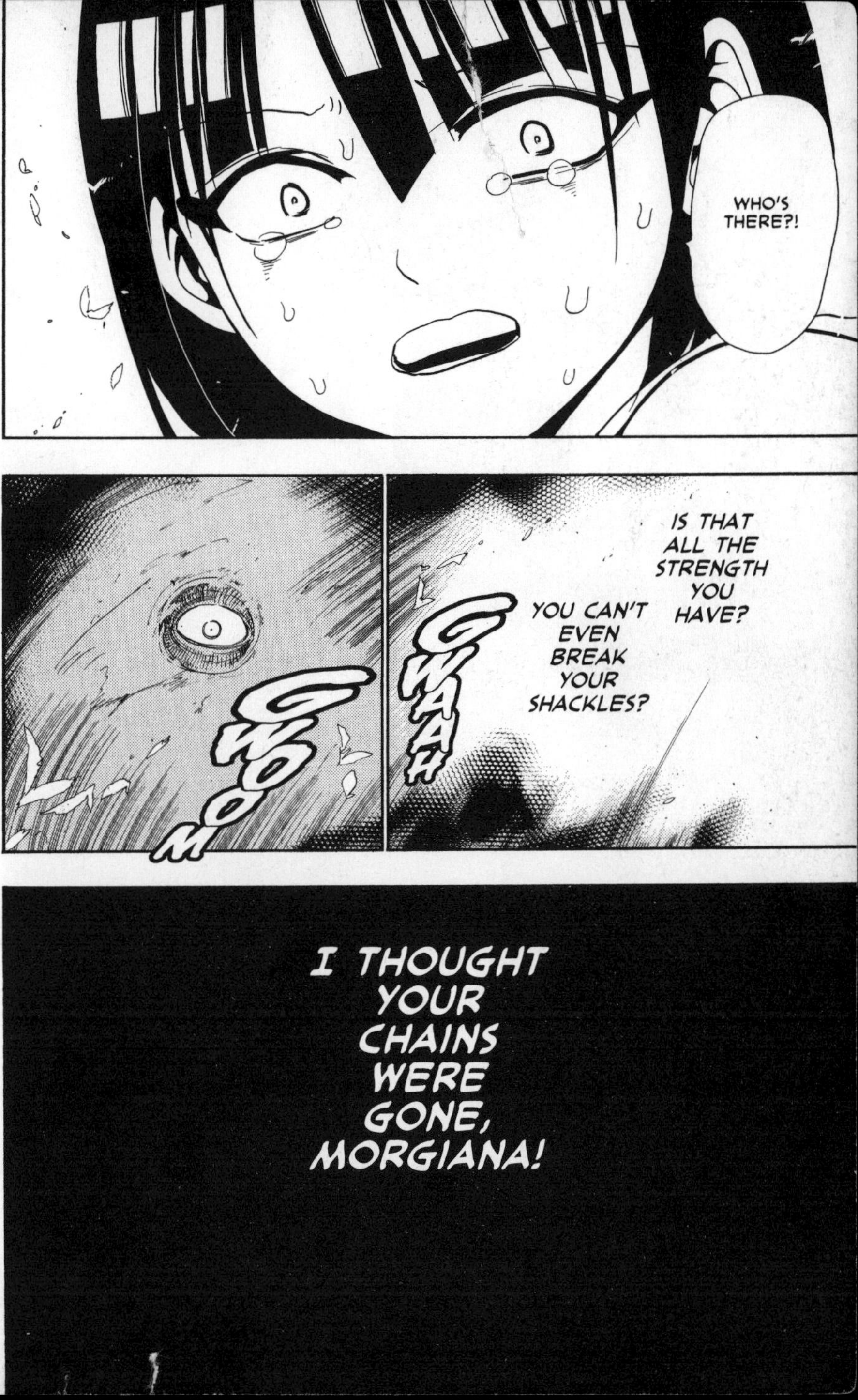
WHO'S THERE?!
IS THAT ALL THE STRENGTH YOU HAVE?
YOU CAN'T EVEN BREAK YOUR SHACKLES?
GWAAH
GWOOOM
I THOUGHT YOUR CHAINS WERE GONE, MORGIANA!

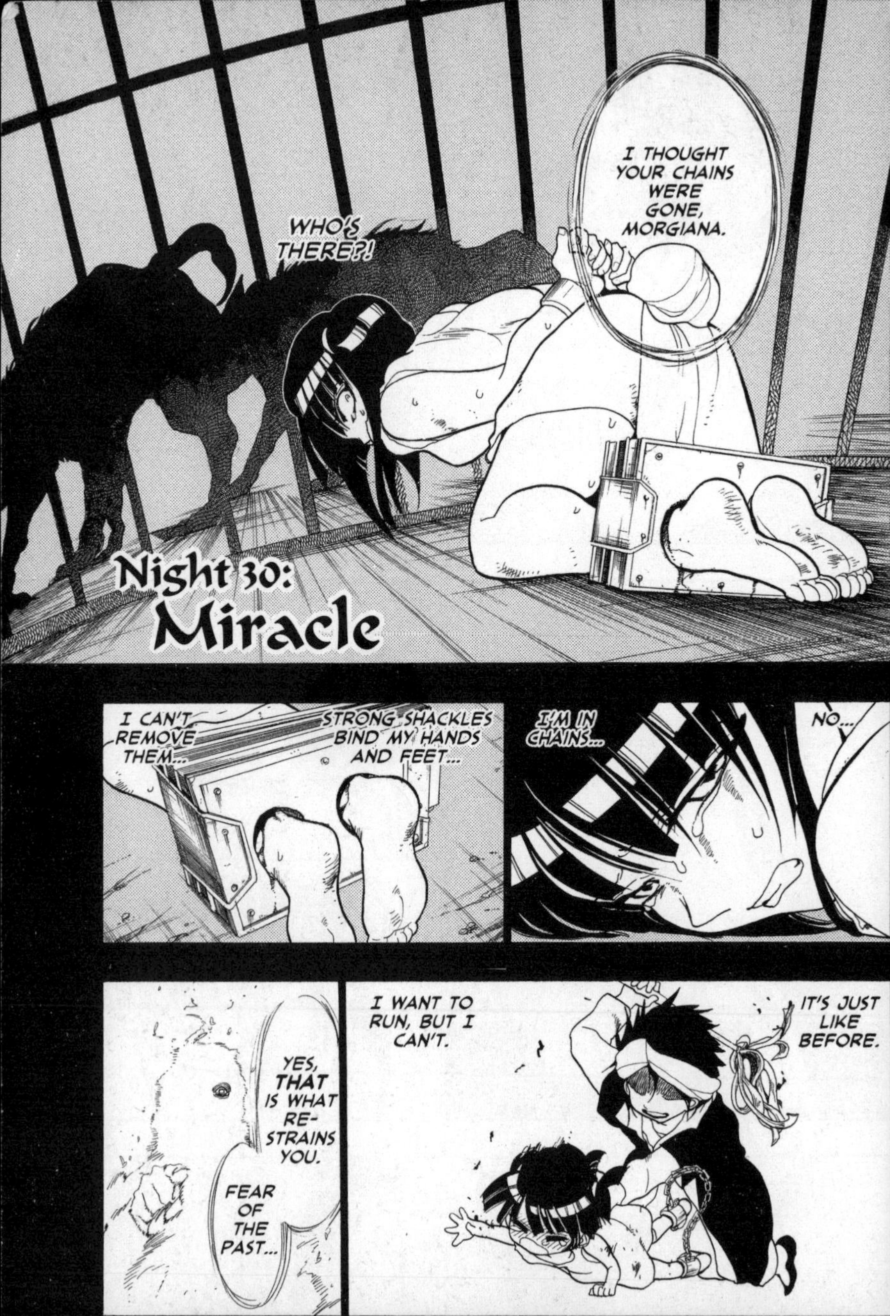
I THOUGHT YOUR CHAINS WERE GONE, MORGIANA.
WHO'S THERE?!
Night 30: Miracle
NO...
I'M IN CHAINS...
STRONG SHACKLES BIND MY HANDS AND FEET...
I CAN'T REMOVE THEM...
IT'S JUST LIKE BEFORE.
I WANT TO RUN, BUT I CAN'T.
YES, THAT IS WHAT RE-STRAINS YOU.
FEAR OF THE PAST...

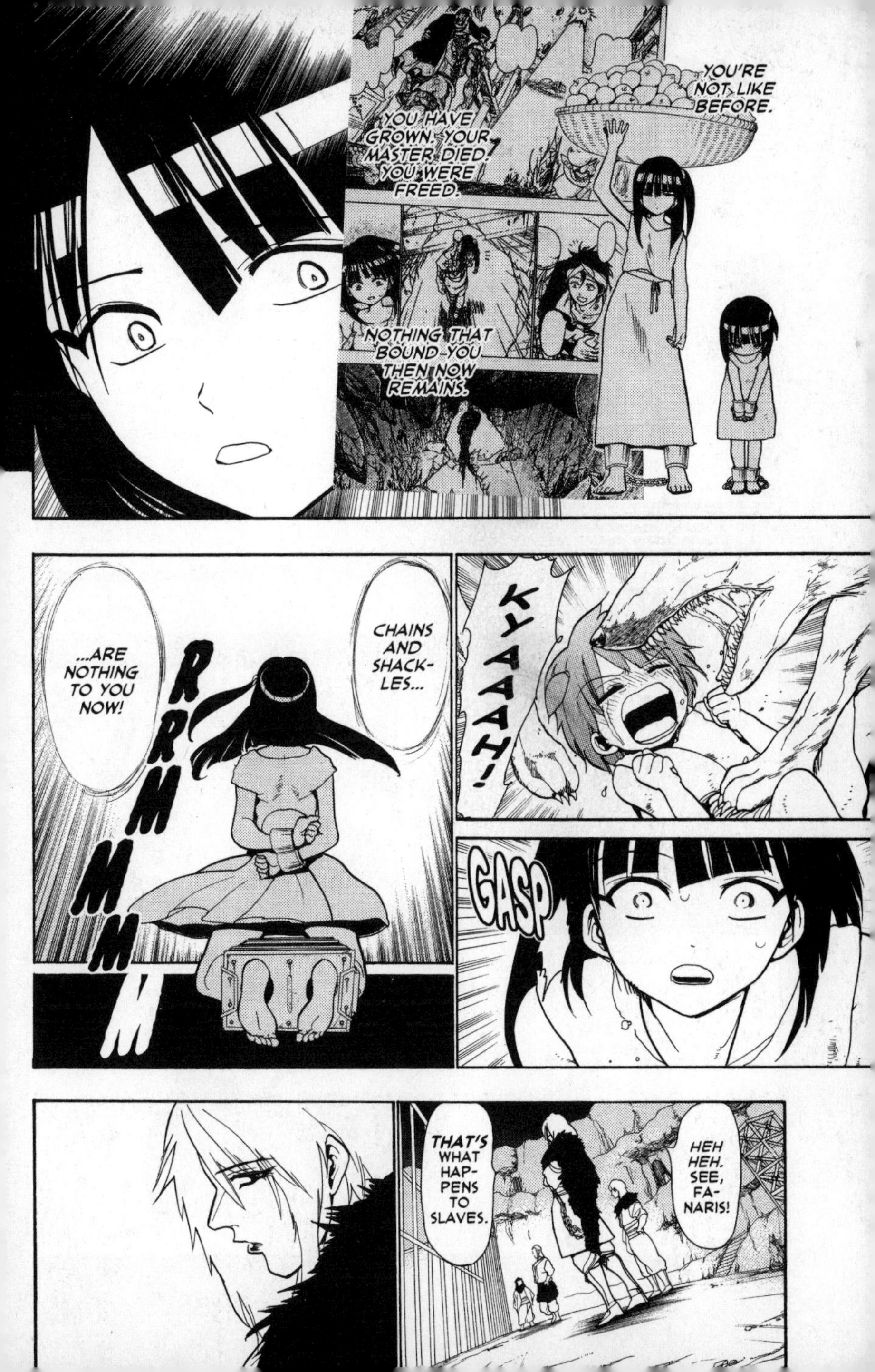
YOU'RE NOT LIKE BEFORE.
YOU HAVE GROWN. YOUR MASTER DIED. YOU WERE FREED.
NOTHING THAT BOUND YOU THEN NOW REMAINS.
KYAAAAH!
GASP
CHAINS AND SHACK-LES...
RRMMMMMMH
...ARE NOTHING TO YOU NOW!
HEH HEH. SEE, FA-NARIS!
THAT'S WHAT HAP-PENS TO SLAVES.

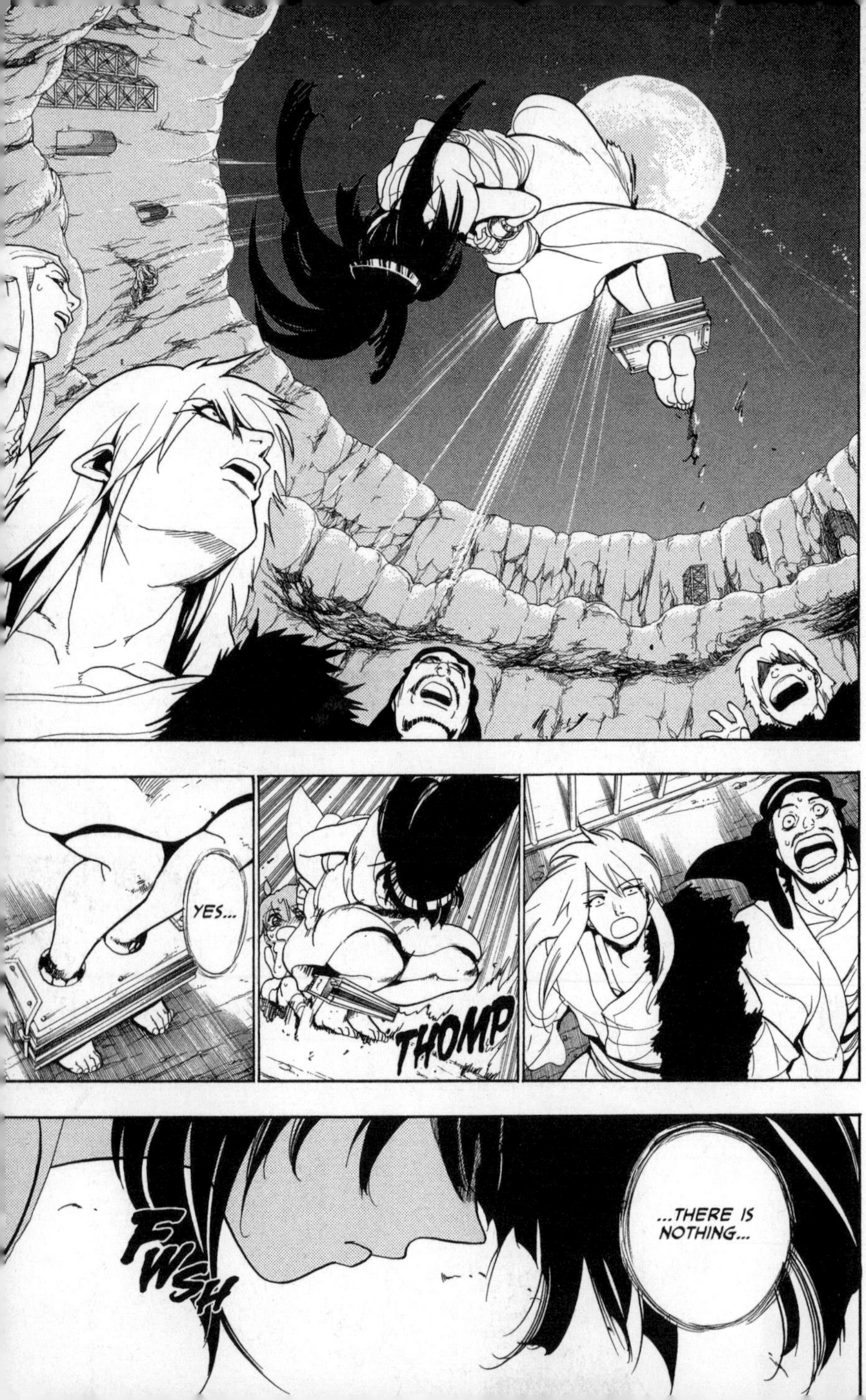
THOMP
YES...
...THERE IS NOTHING...
FWSH

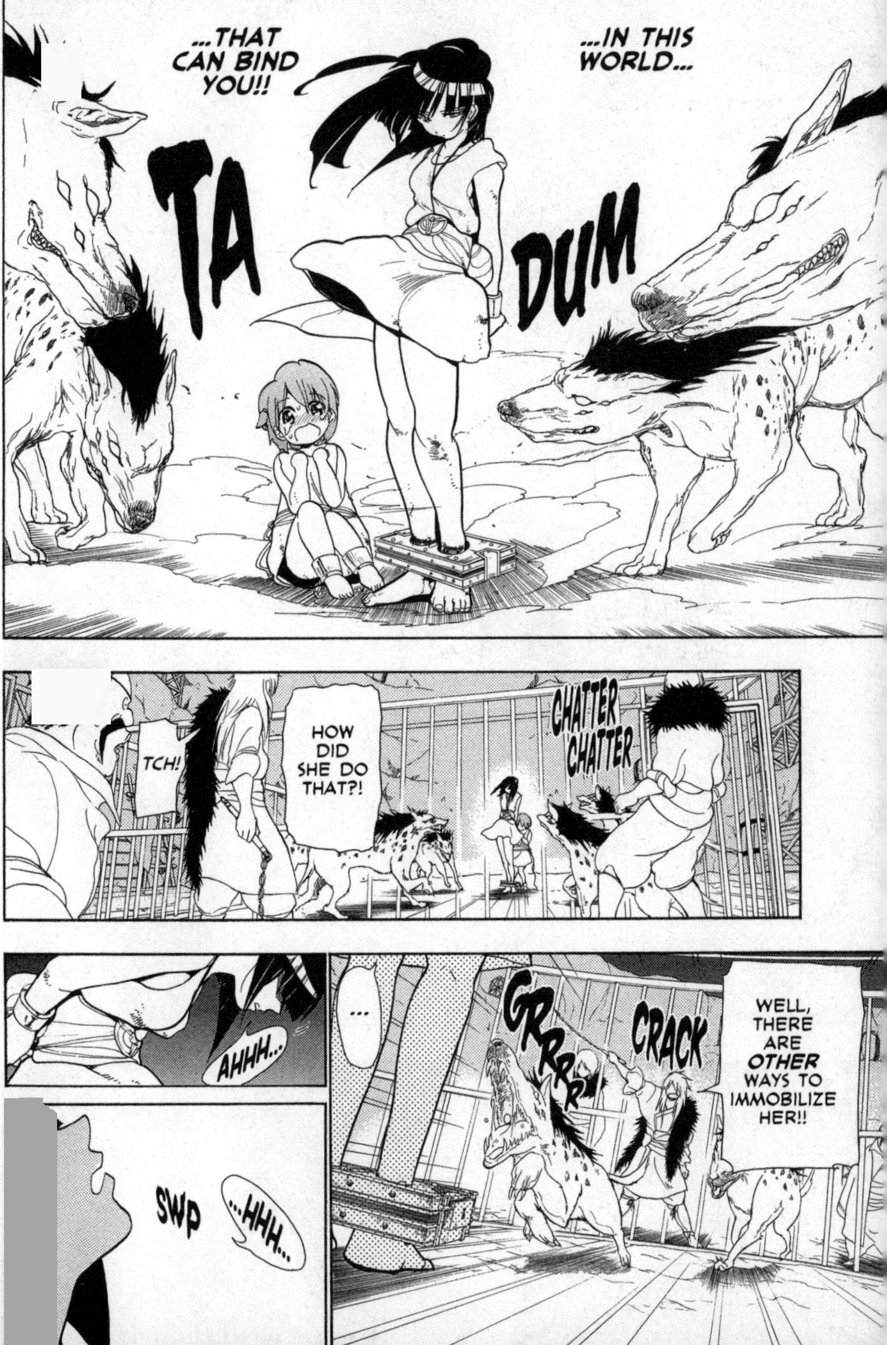
...IN THIS WORLD...
...THAT CAN BIND YOU!!
TA DUM
CHATTER CHATTER
HOW DID SHE DO THAT?!
TCH!
WELL, THERE ARE OTHER WAYS TO IMMOBILIZE HER!!
CRACK
GRRRR
...
AHHH...
...HHH...
SWP

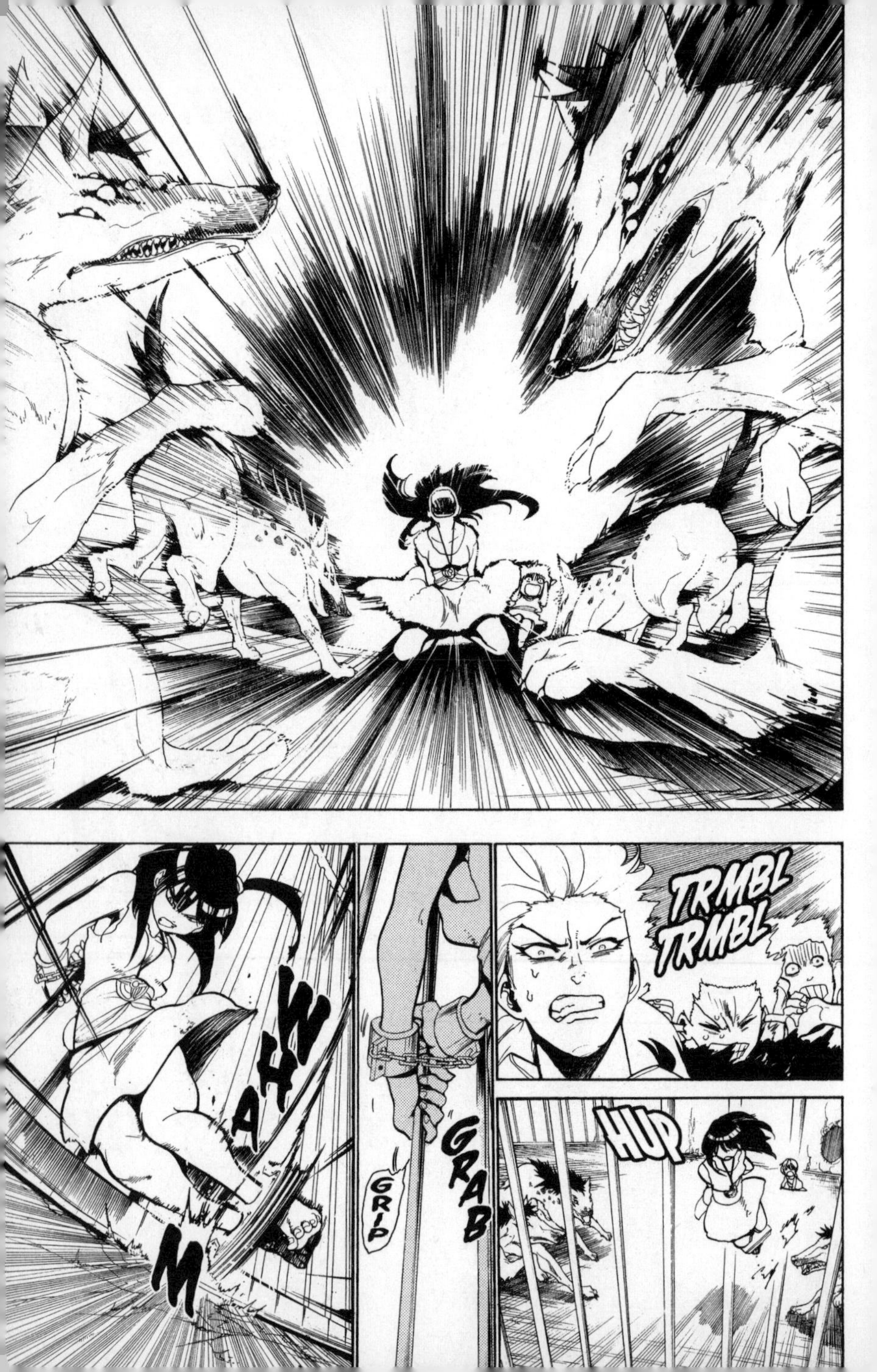
TRMBL TRMBL
HUP
GRAB
GRIP
WHAM

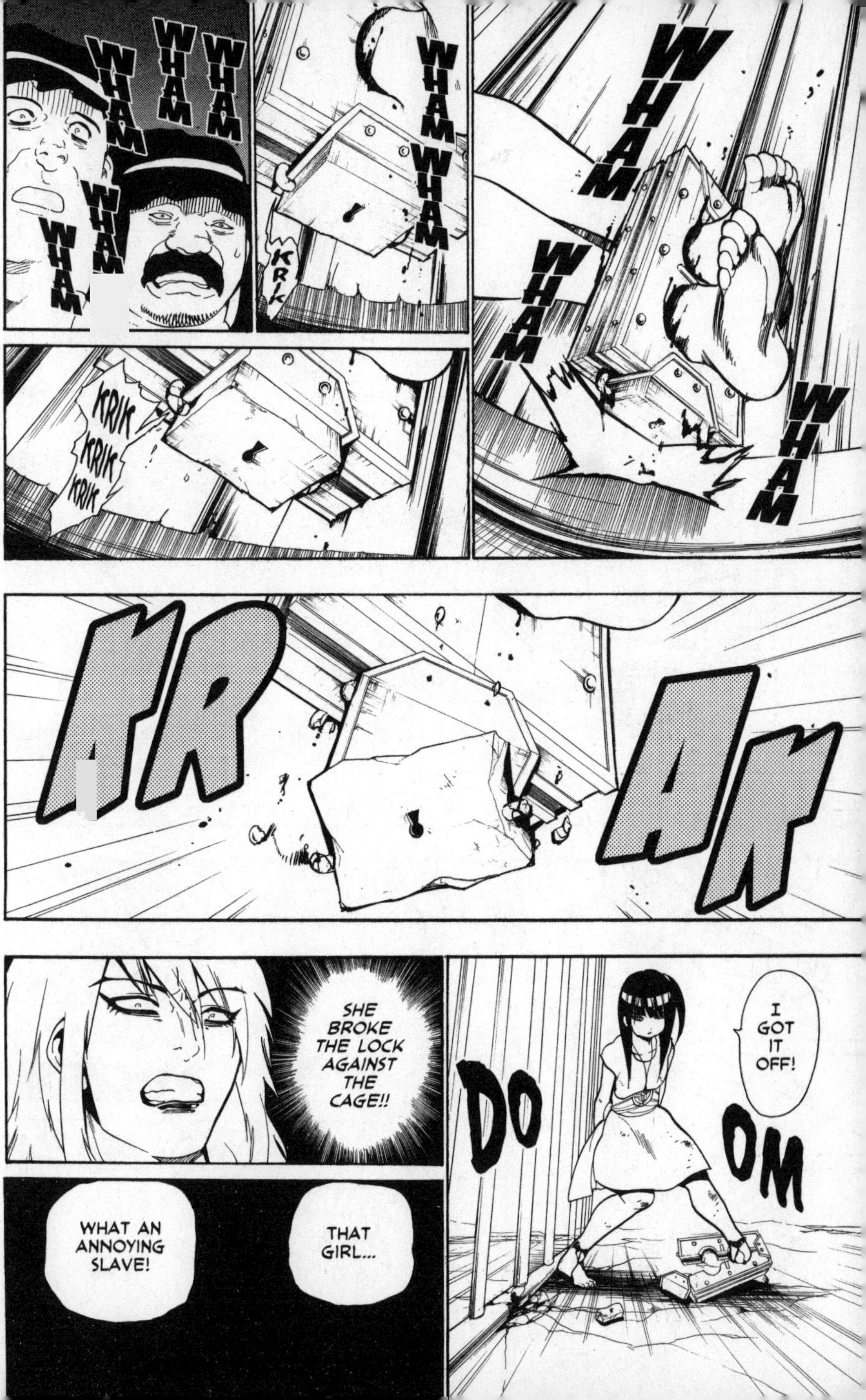
WHAM
WHAM
WHAM
WHAM
WHAM
KRIK
WHAM
WHAM
WHAM
WHAM
WHAM
KRIK
KRIK
KRIK
KRAK
I GOT IT OFF!
DOOM
SHE BROKE THE LOCK AGAINST THE CAGE!!
THAT GIRL...
WHAT AN ANNOYING SLAVE!

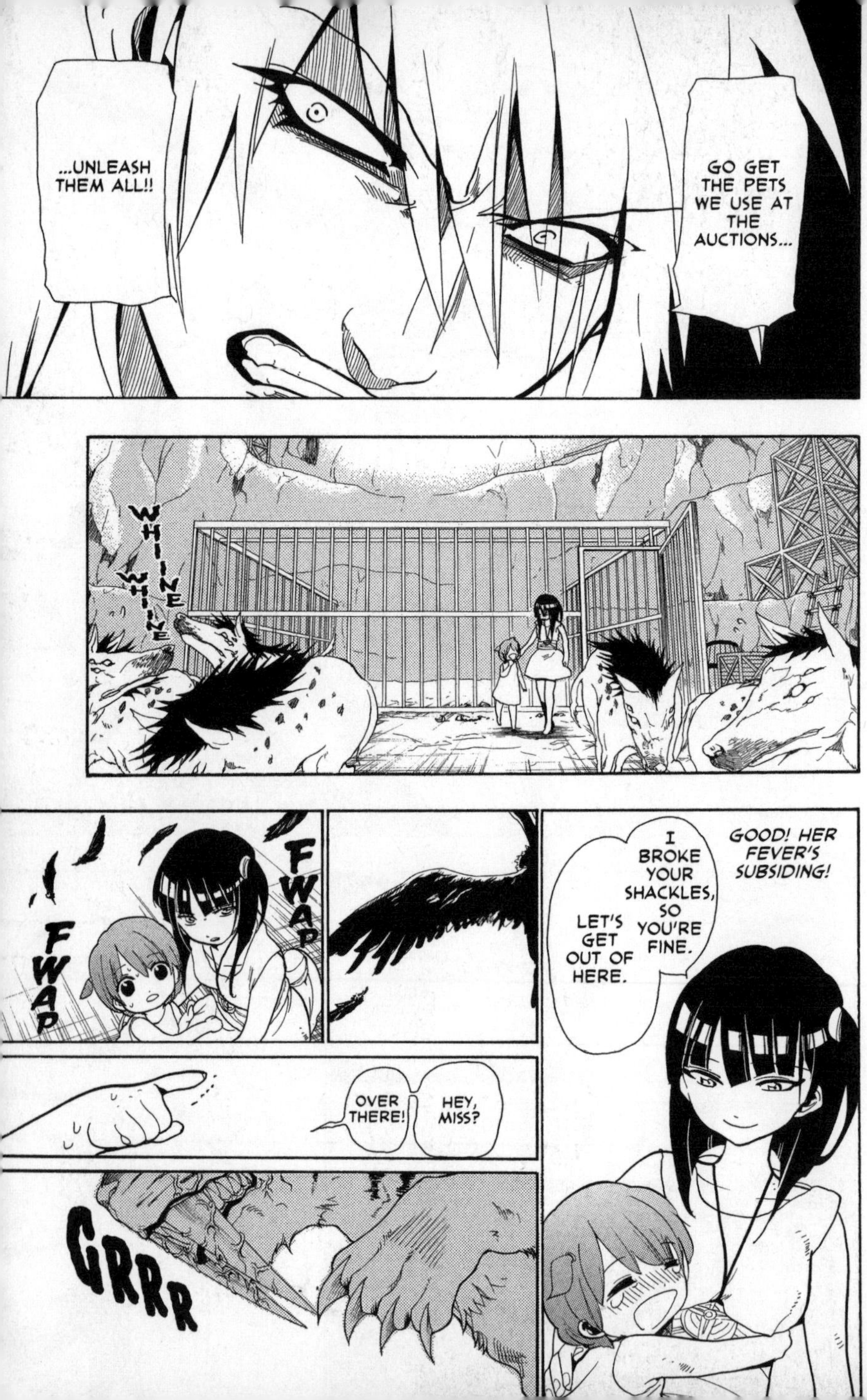
GO GET THE PETS WE USE AT THE AUCTIONS...
...UNLEASH THEM ALL!!
WHIINE
WHIINE
GOOD! HER FEVER'S SUBSIDING!
I BROKE YOUR SHACKLES, SO YOU'RE FINE.
LET'S GET OUT OF HERE.
FWAP
FWAP
HEY, MISS?
OVER THERE!
GRRR

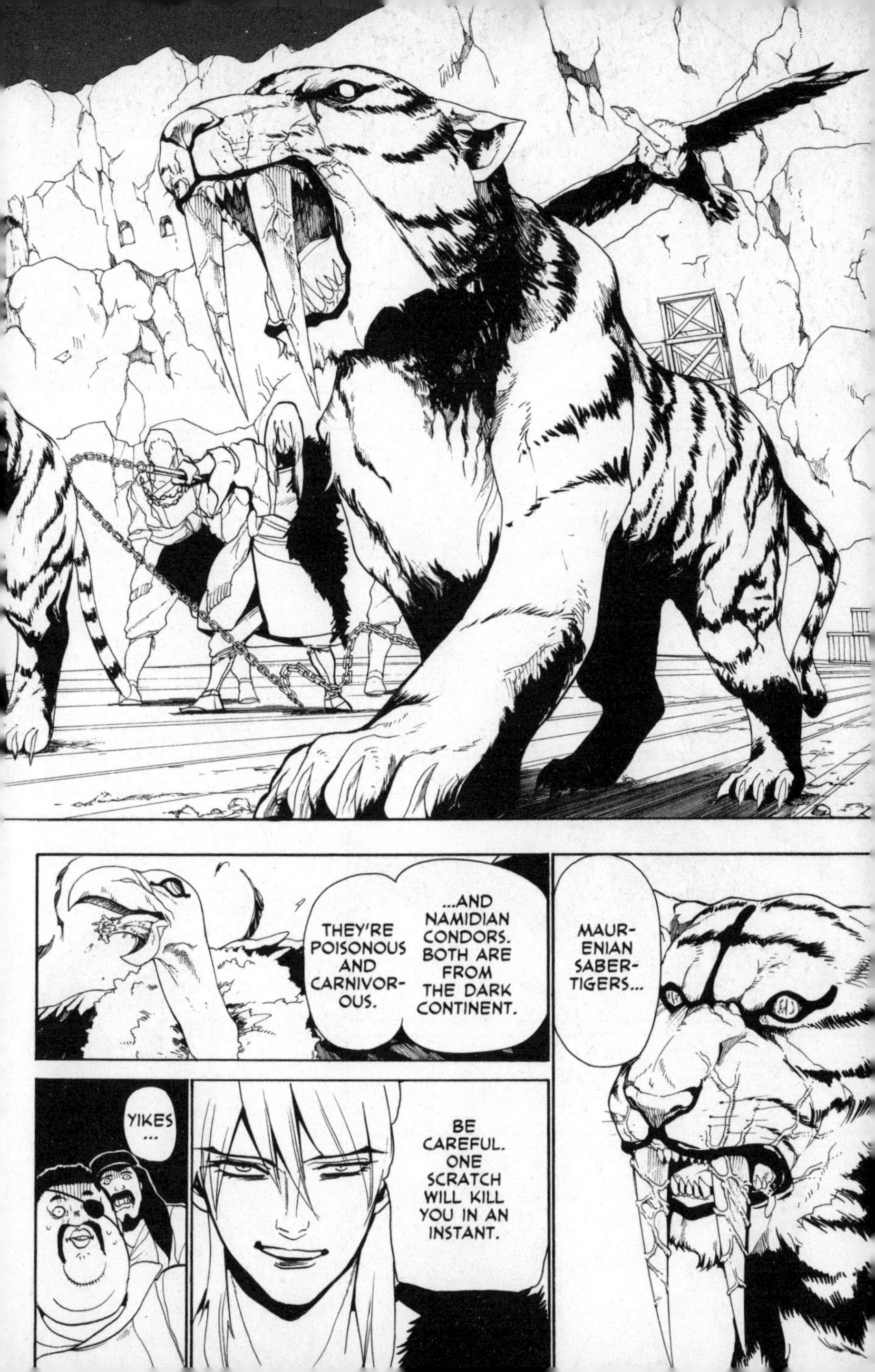
MAUR-
ENIAN
SABER-
TIGERS...
...AND
NAMIDIAN
CONDORS.
BOTH ARE
FROM
THE DARK
CONTINENT.
THEY'RE
POISONOUS
AND
CARNIVOR-
OUS.
BE
CAREFUL.
ONE
SCRATCH
WILL KILL
YOU IN AN
INSTANT.
YIKES
...

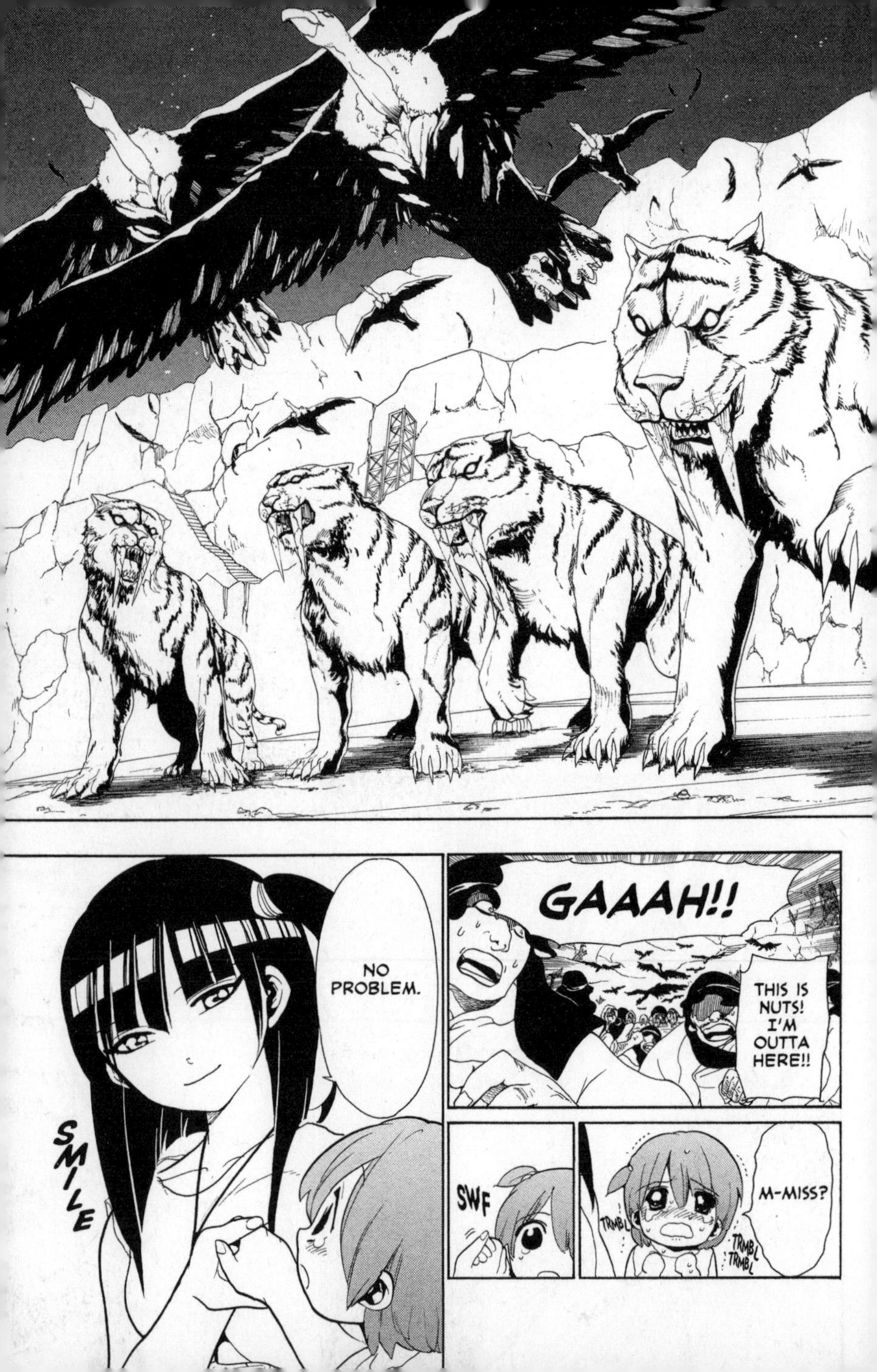
GAAAH!!
THIS IS NUTS! I'M OUTTA HERE!!
TRMBL
TRMBL TRMBL
M-MISS?
SWF
NO PROBLEM.
SMILE

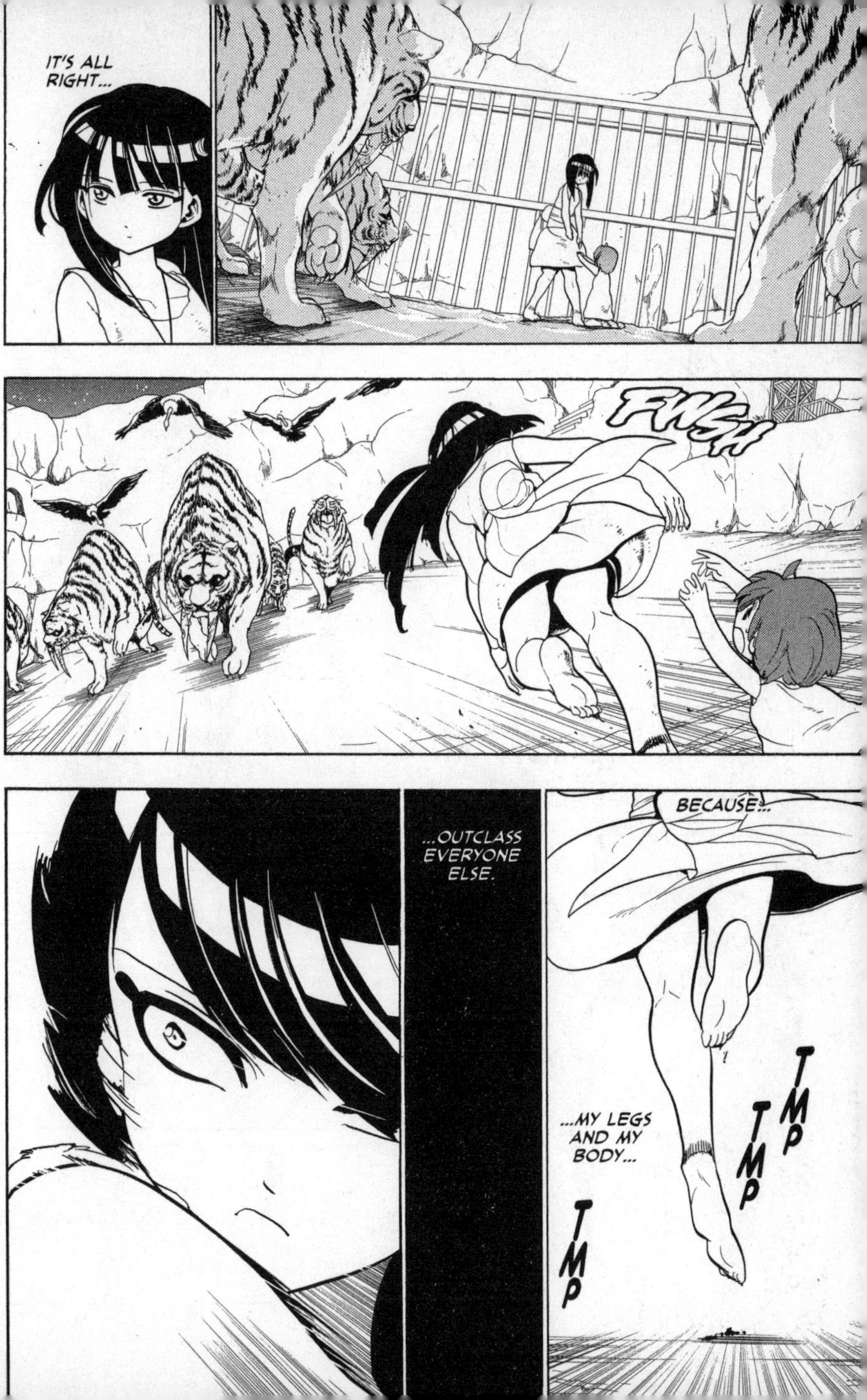
IT'S ALL RIGHT...
FWSH
BECAUSE...
...MY LEGS AND MY BODY...
TMP
TMP
TMP
...OUTCLASS EVERYONE ELSE.

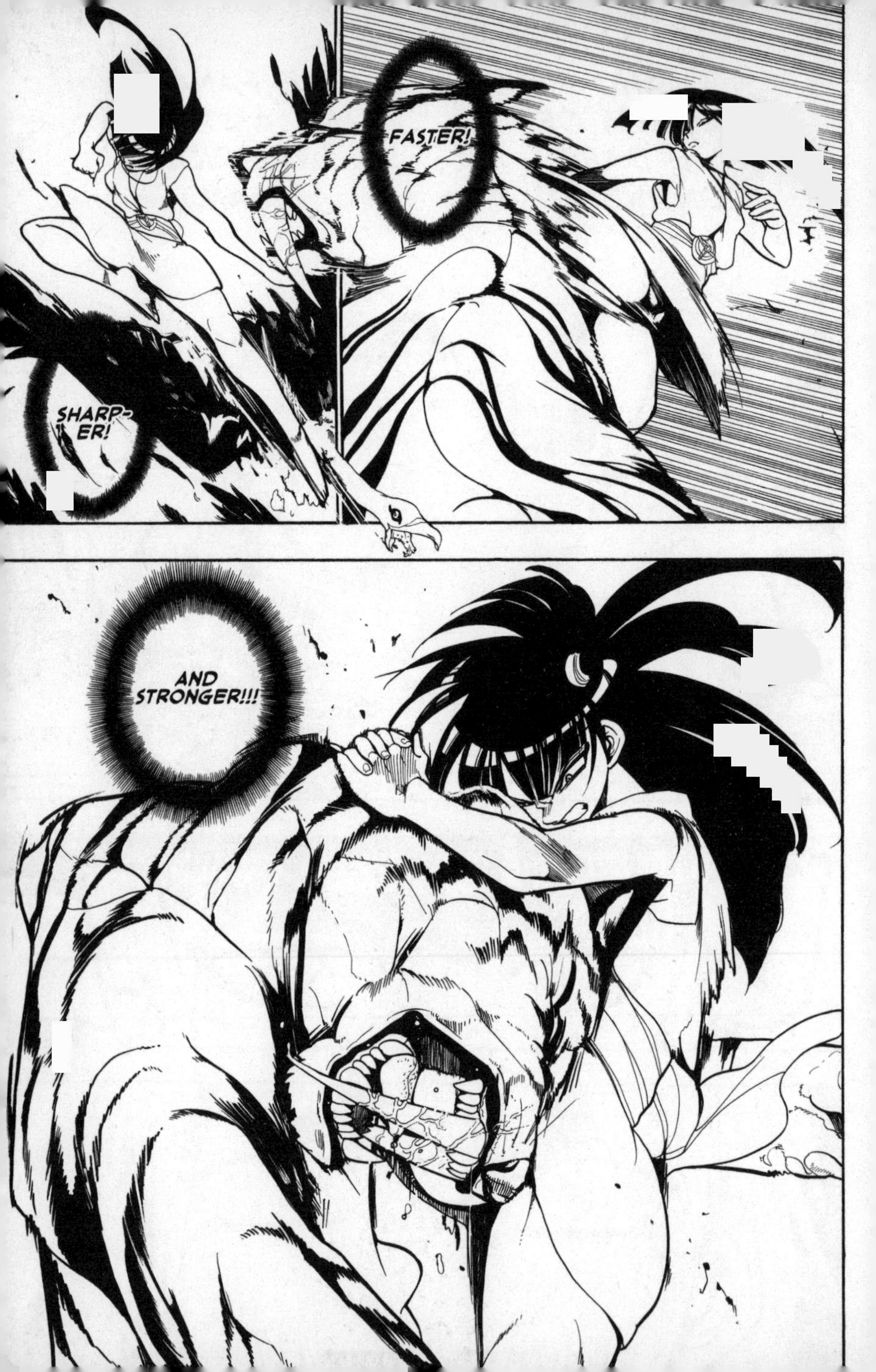
FASTER!
SHARP-ER!
AND STRONGER!!!

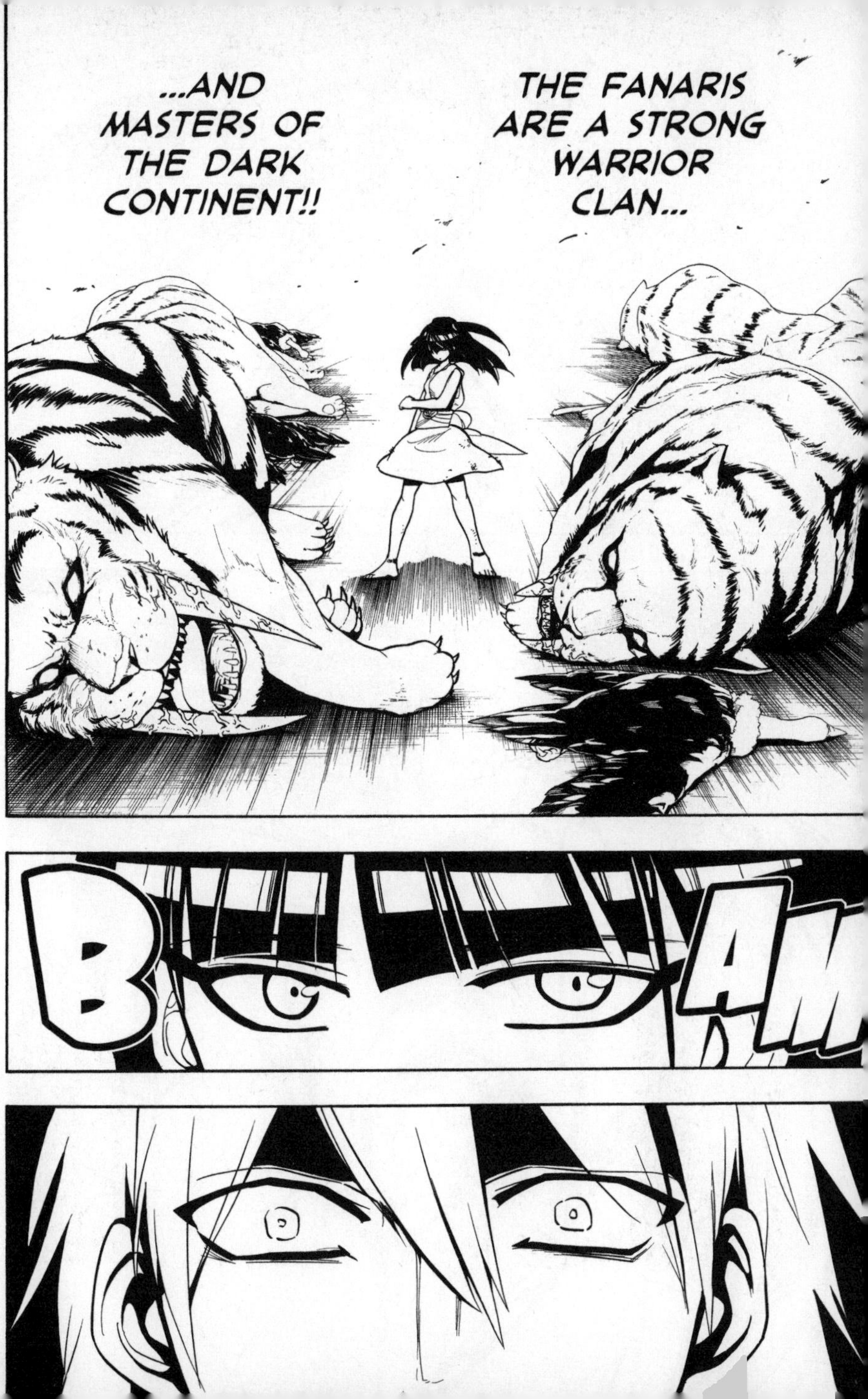
THE FANARIS ARE A STRONG WARRIOR CLAN...
...AND MASTERS OF THE DARK CONTINENT!!
BAM

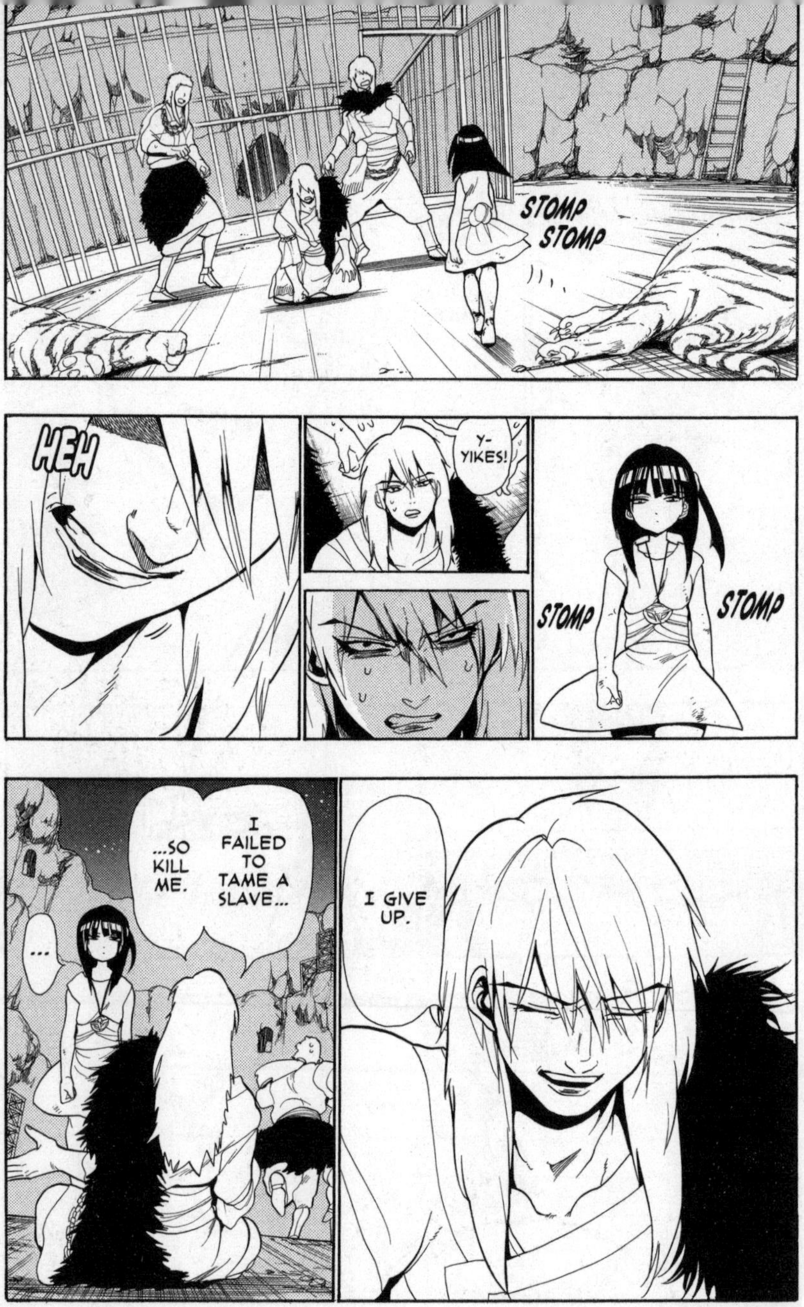
STOMP STOMP
STOMP
STOMP
Y-YIKES!
HEH
I GIVE UP.
I FAILED TO TAME A SLAVE...
...SO KILL ME.
...

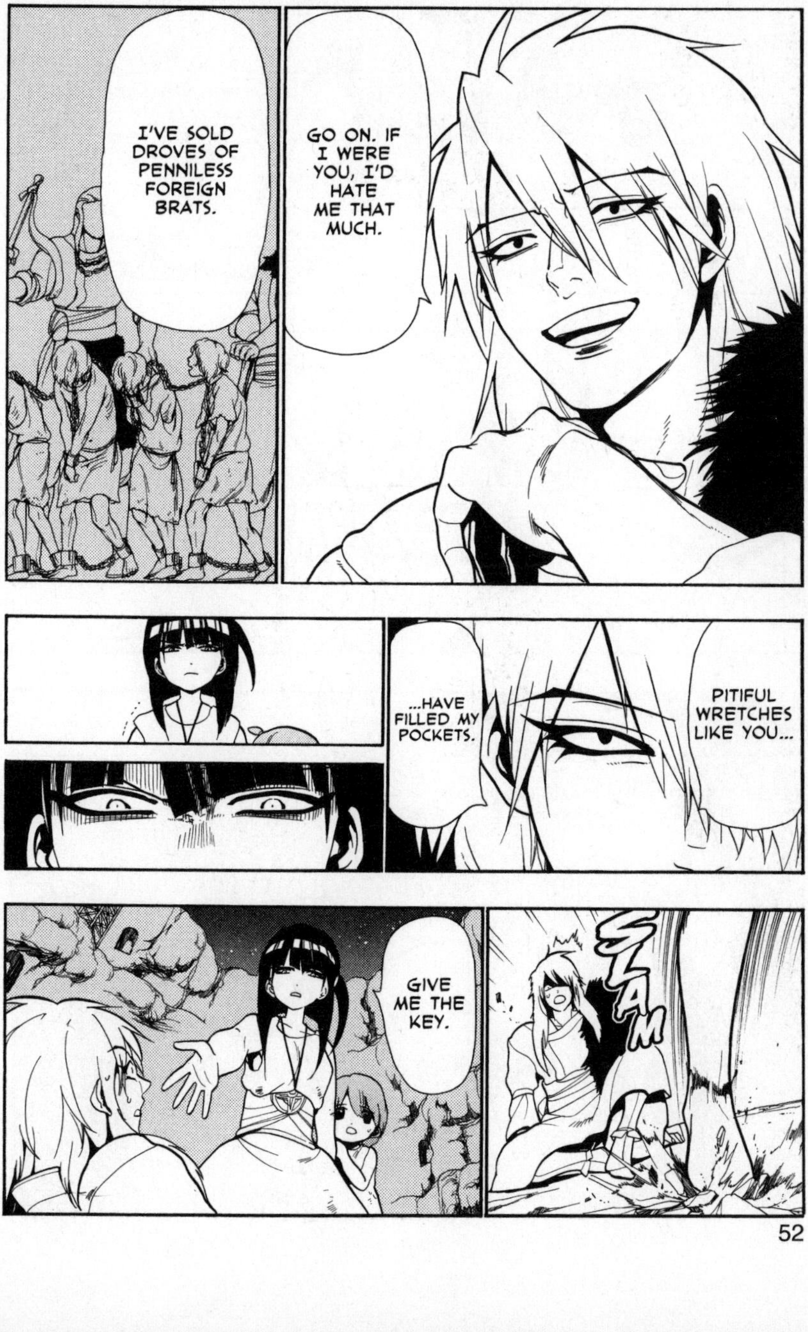
GO ON. IF I WERE YOU, I'D HATE ME THAT MUCH.
I'VE SOLD DROVES OF PENNILESS FOREIGN BRATS.
PITIFUL WRETCHES LIKE YOU...
...HAVE FILLED MY POCKETS.
SLAM
GIVE ME THE KEY.

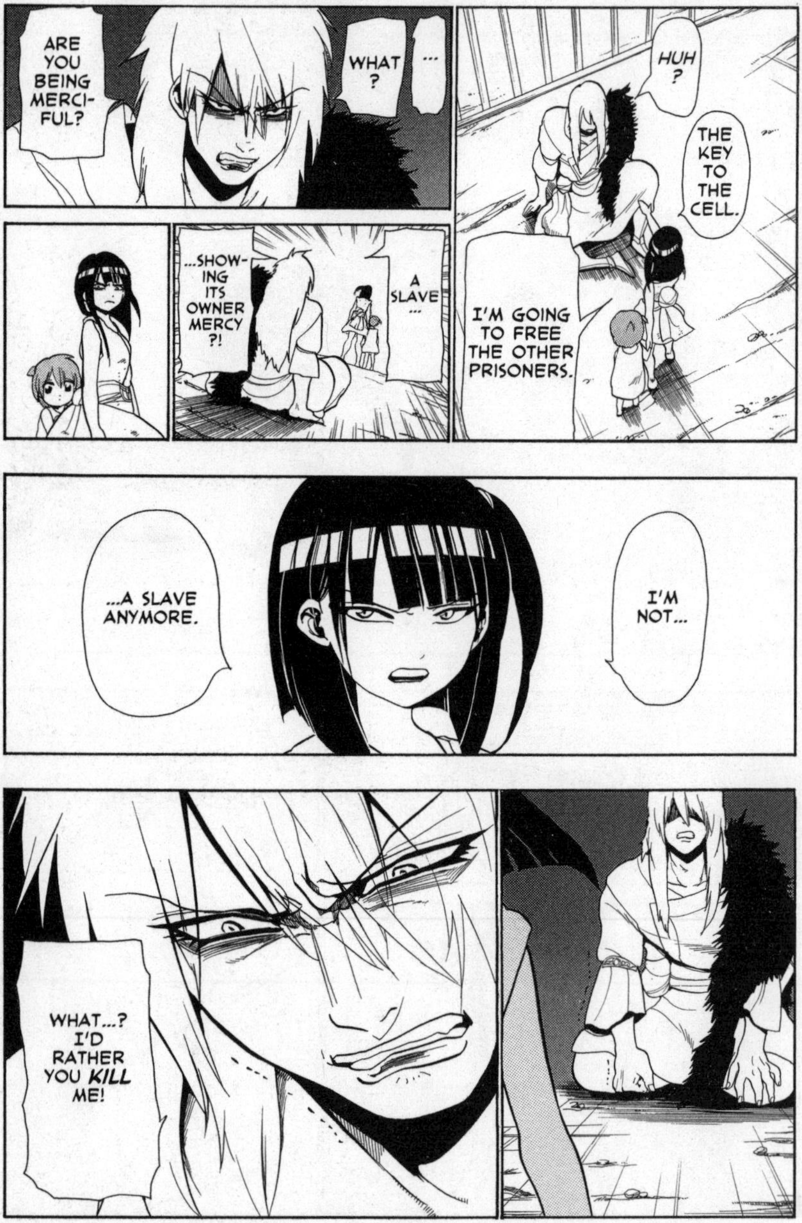
HUH?
THE KEY TO THE CELL.
I'M GOING TO FREE THE OTHER PRISONERS.
...
WHAT?
ARE YOU BEING MERCIFUL?
A SLAVE...
...SHOWING ITS OWNER MERCY?!
I'M NOT...
...A SLAVE ANYMORE.
WHAT...? I'D RATHER YOU *KILL* ME!

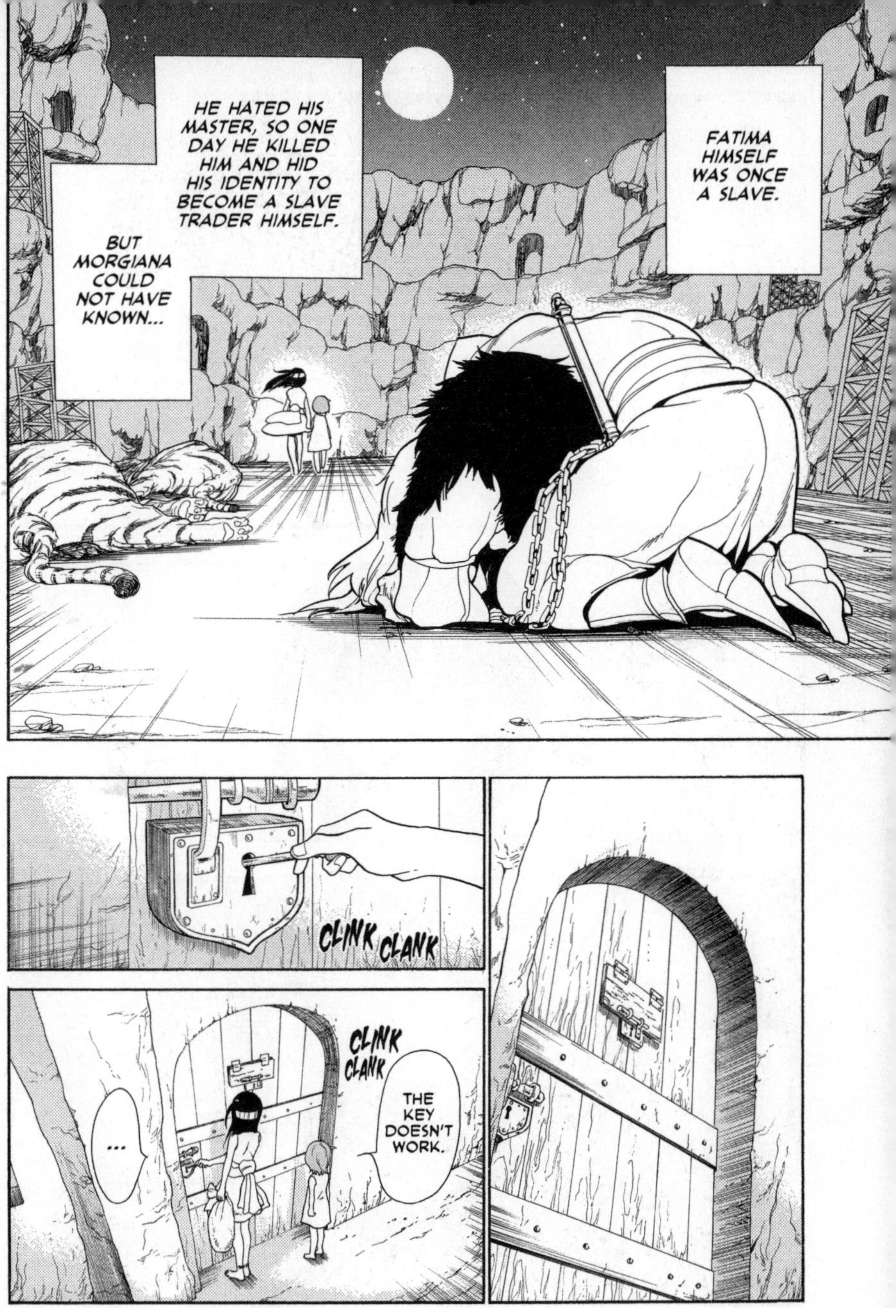
FATIMA HIMSELF WAS ONCE A SLAVE.
HE HATED HIS MASTER, SO ONE DAY HE KILLED HIM AND HID HIS IDENTITY TO BECOME A SLAVE TRADER HIMSELF.
BUT MORGIANA COULD NOT HAVE KNOWN...
CLINK CLANK
CLINK CLANK
THE KEY DOESN'T WORK.
...

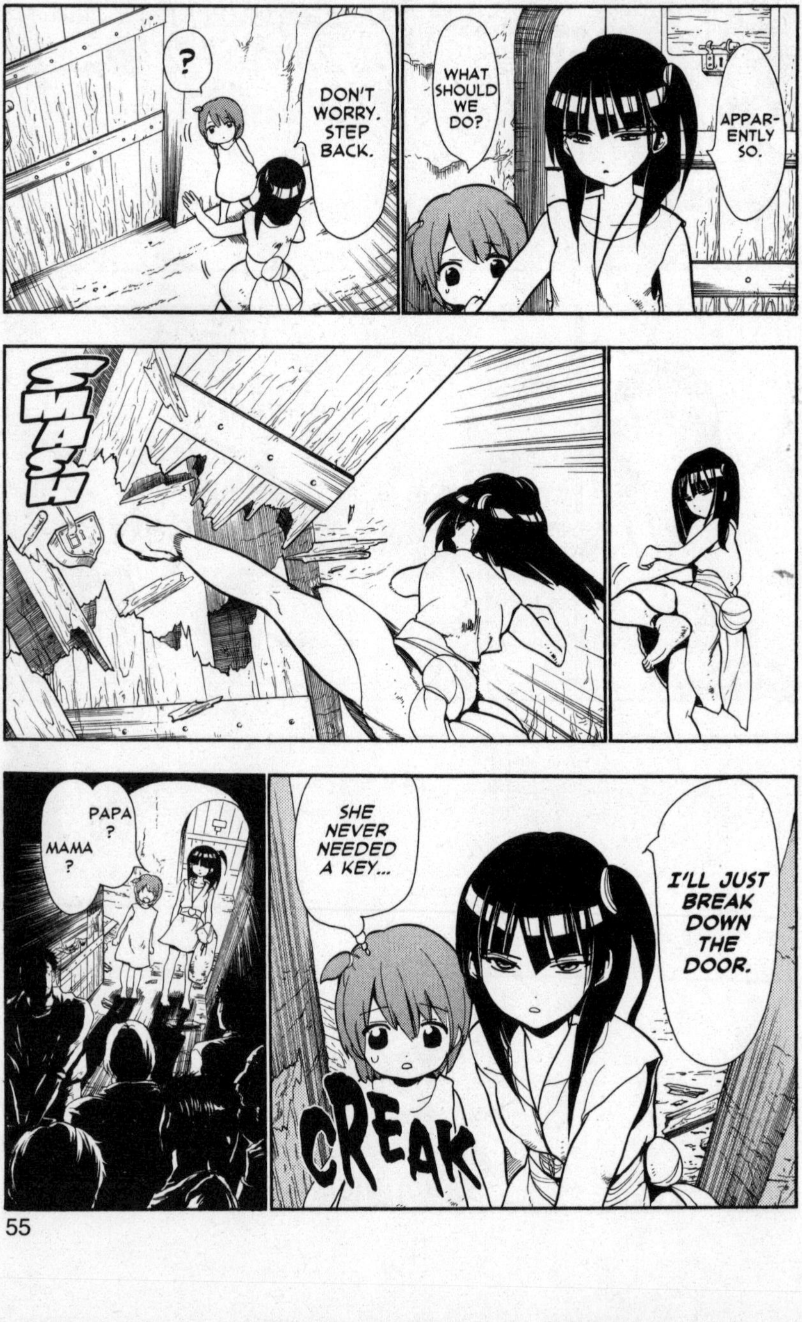
APPAR-ENTLY SO.
WHAT SHOULD WE DO?
DON'T WORRY. STEP BACK.
?
SMASH
I'LL JUST BREAK DOWN THE DOOR.
SHE NEVER NEEDED A KEY...
CREAK
PAPA?
MAMA?

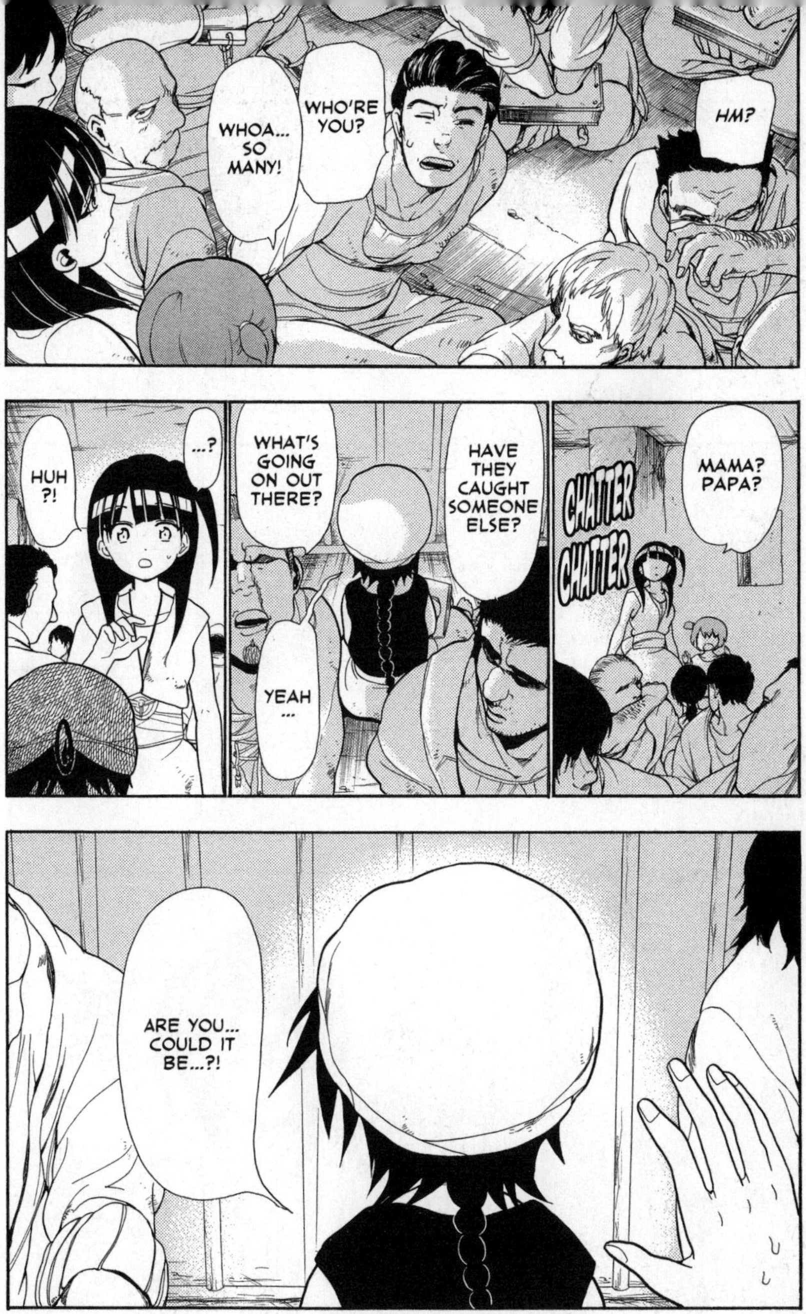
HM?
WHO'RE YOU?
WHOA... SO MANY!
MAMA? PAPA?
CHATTER CHATTER
HAVE THEY CAUGHT SOMEONE ELSE?
WHAT'S GOING ON OUT THERE?
YEAH ...
...?
HUH ?!
ARE YOU... COULD IT BE...?!

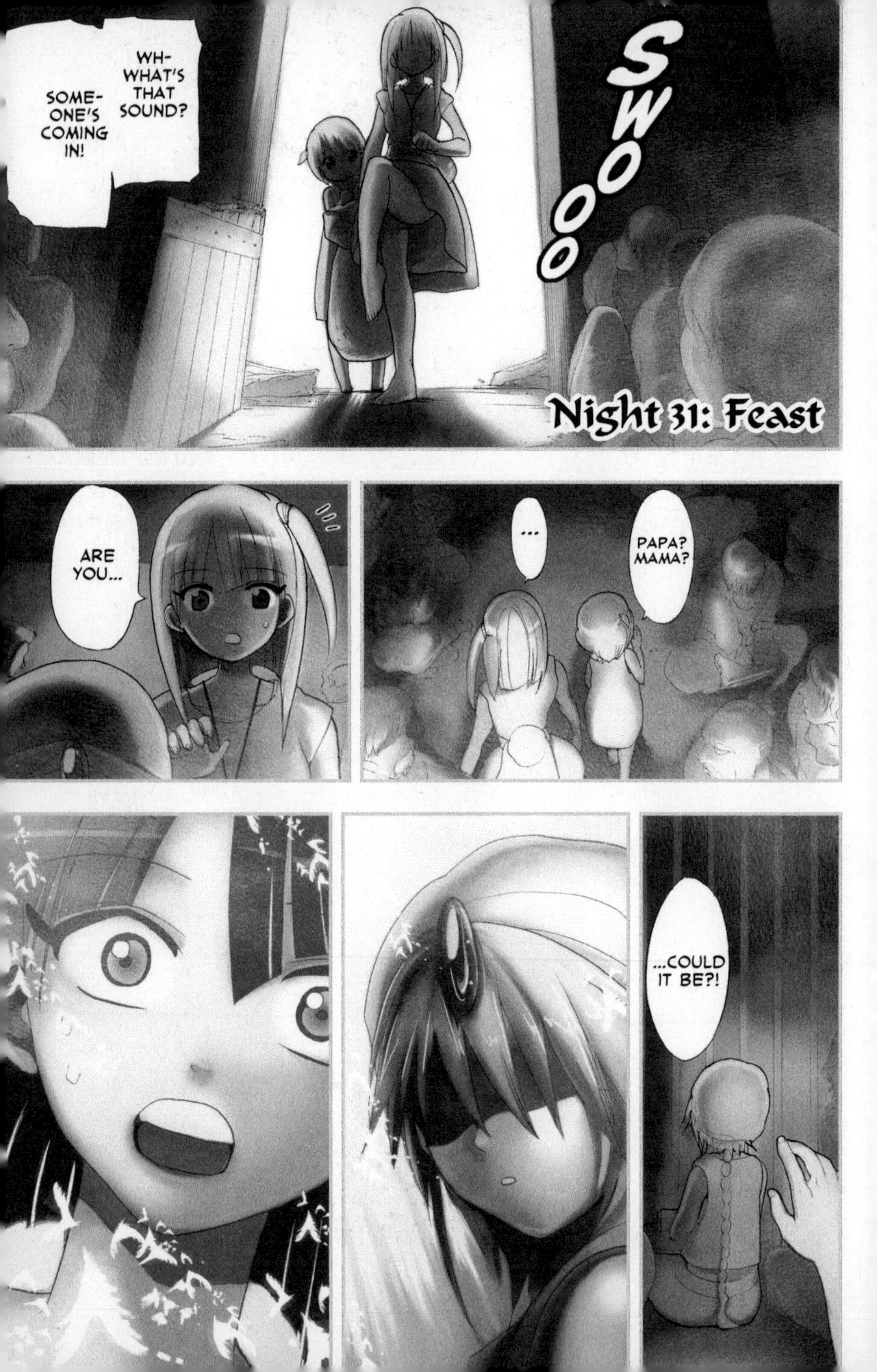
SWOOOO
WH- WHAT'S THAT SOUND?
SOME-ONE'S COMING IN!
Night 31: Feast
PAPA? MAMA?
...
ARE YOU...
...COULD IT BE?!

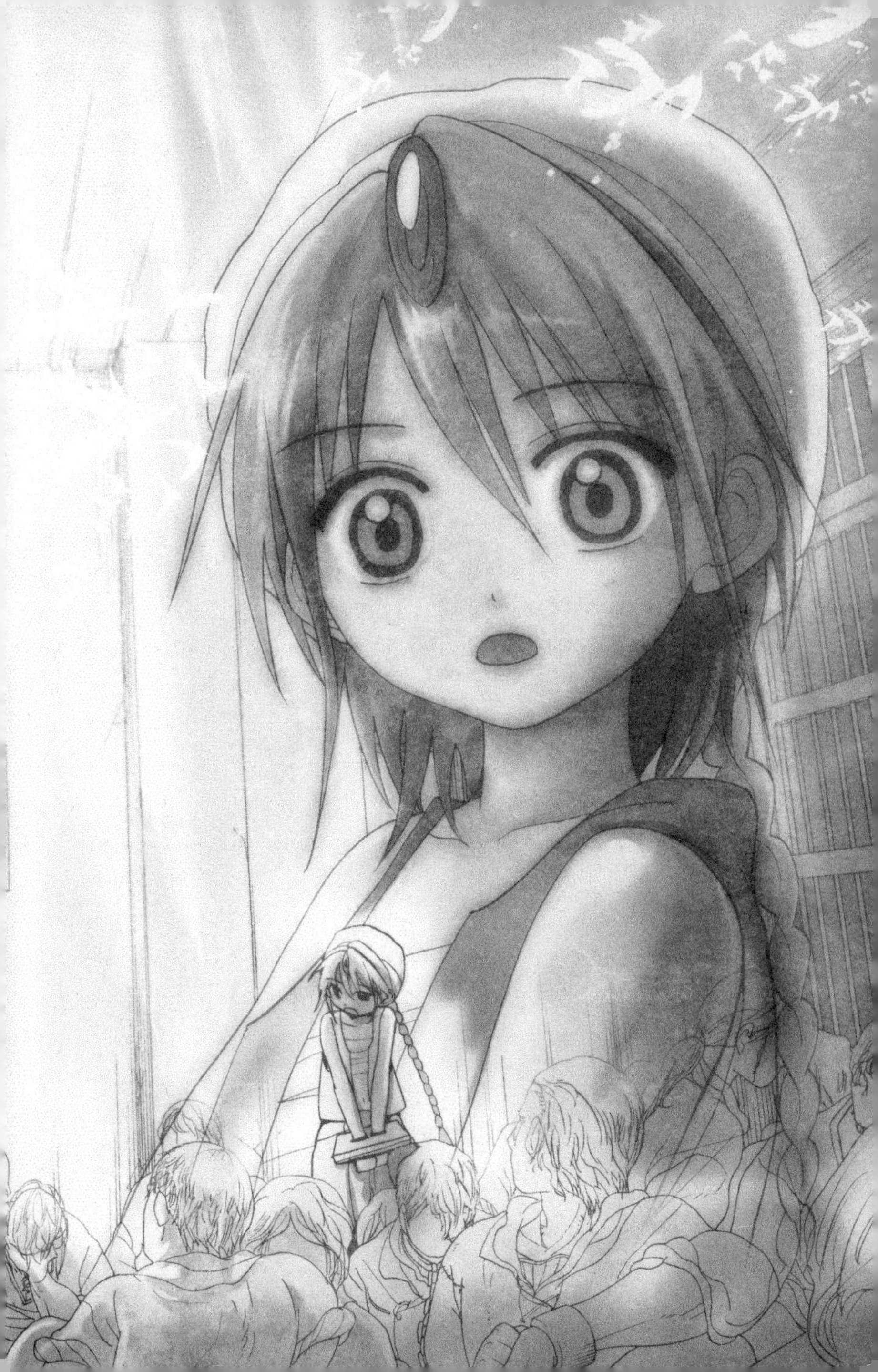

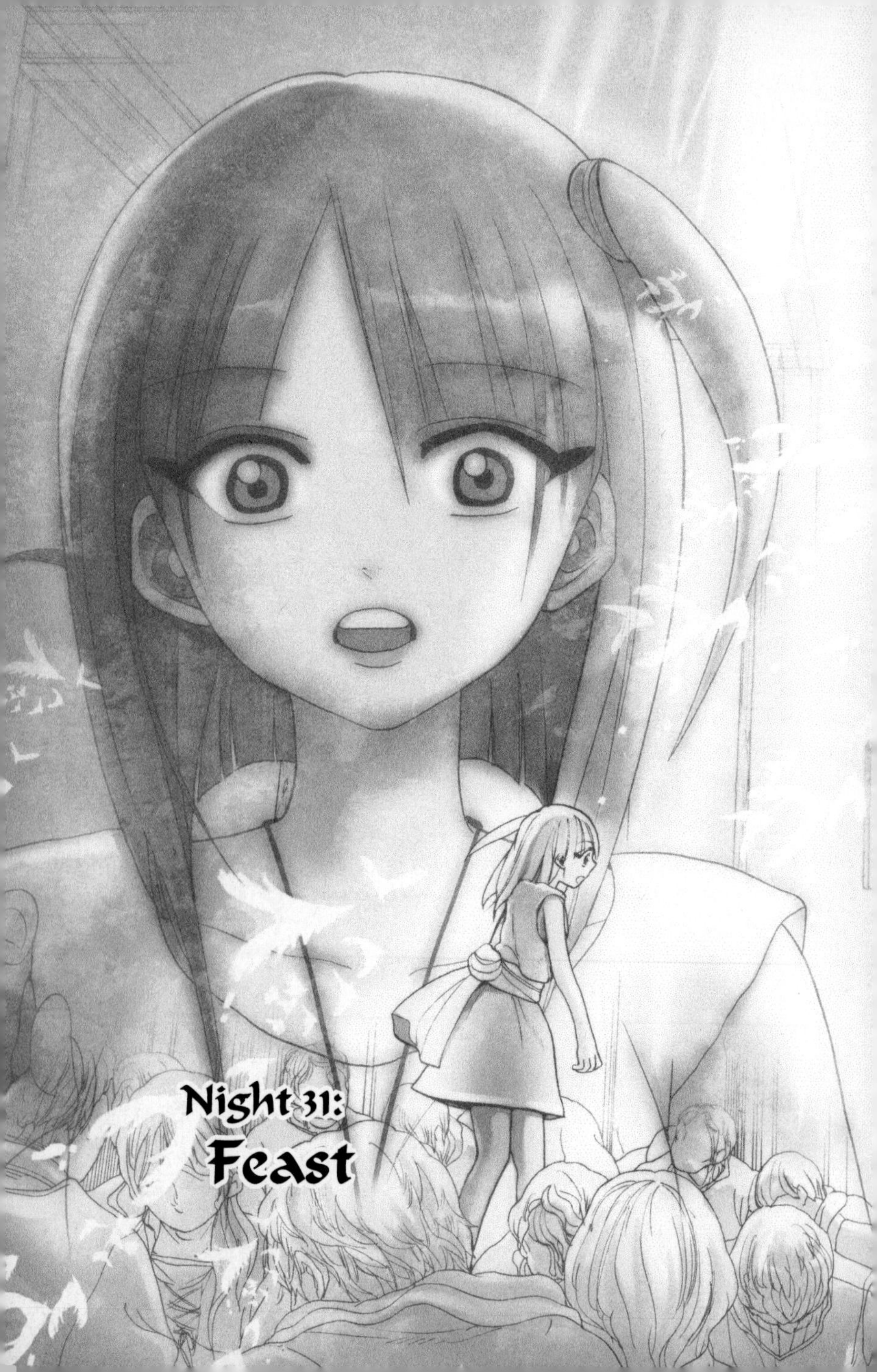
Night 31:
Feast

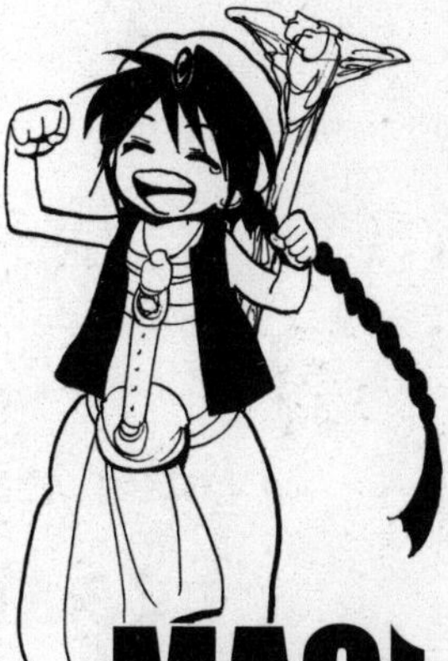

MAGI

The labyrinth of magic

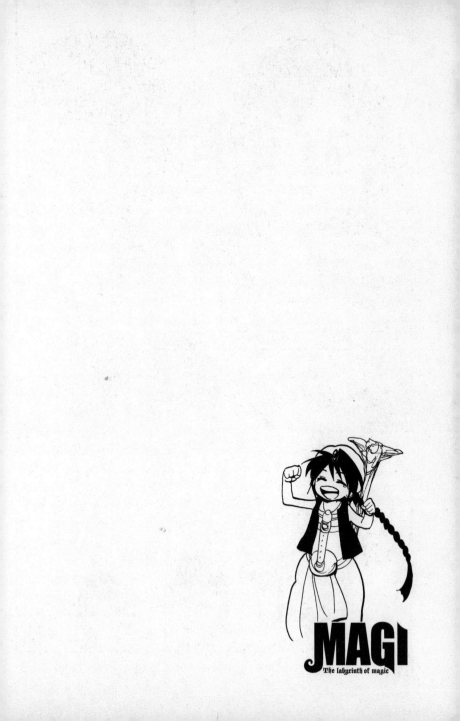

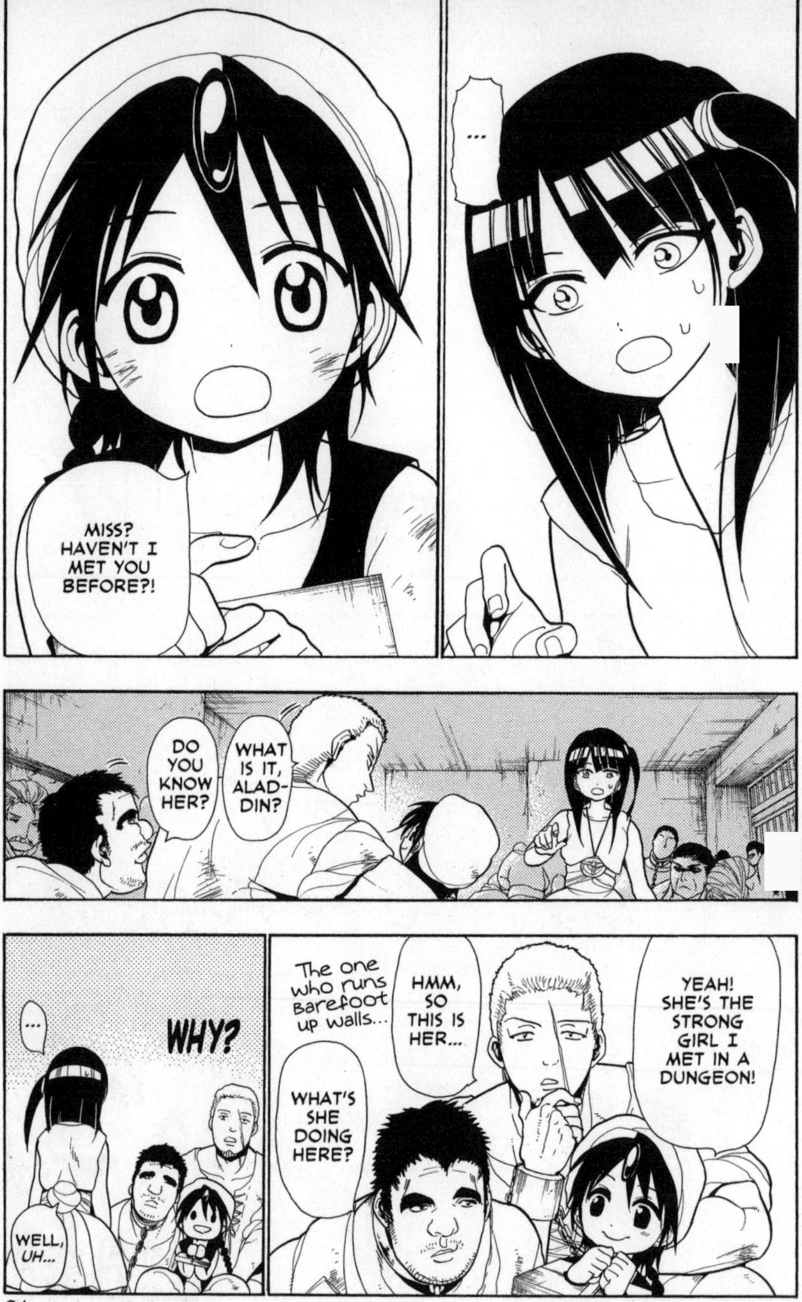
...
MISS? HAVEN'T I MET YOU BEFORE?!
WHAT IS IT, ALAD-DIN?
DO YOU KNOW HER?
YEAH! SHE'S THE STRONG GIRL I MET IN A DUNGEON!
HMM, SO THIS IS HER...
The one who runs Barefoot up walls...
WHAT'S SHE DOING HERE?
...
WHY?
WELL, UH...

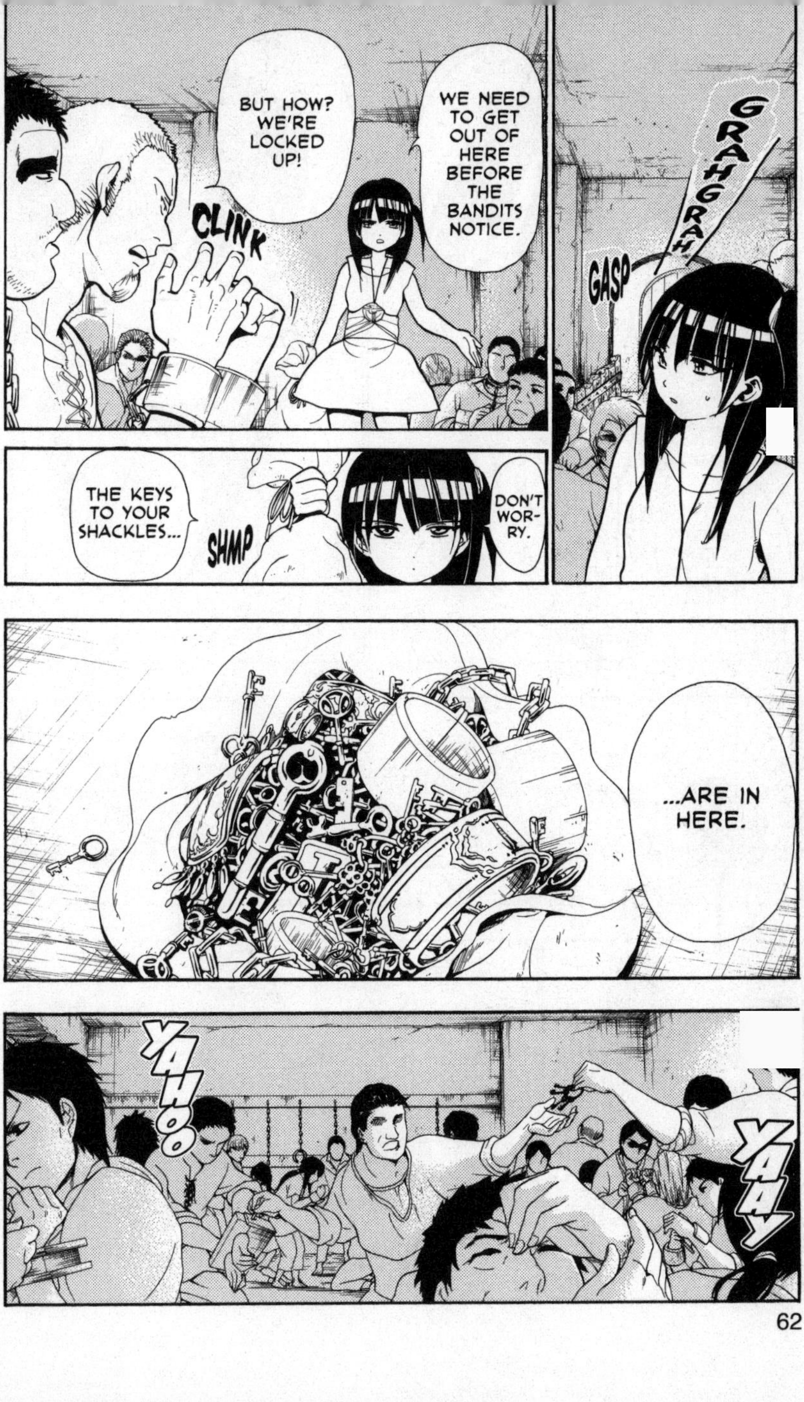
GRAHGRAH
GASP
WE NEED TO GET OUT OF HERE BEFORE THE BANDITS NOTICE.
BUT HOW? WE'RE LOCKED UP!
CLINK
DON'T WOR-RY.
SHMP
THE KEYS TO YOUR SHACKLES...
...ARE IN HERE.
YAAY
YAHOO

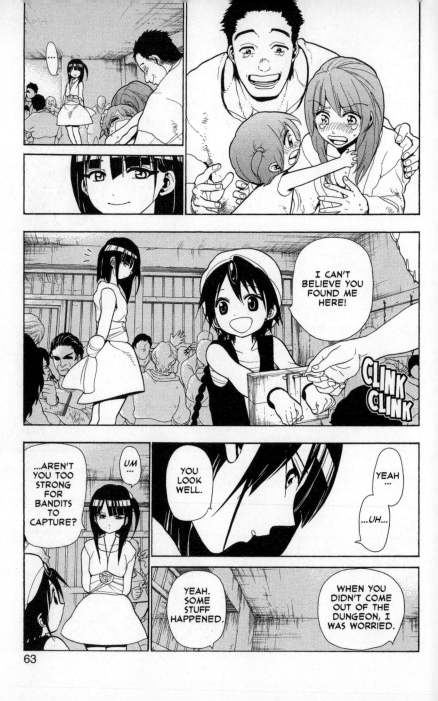

....
I CAN'T BELIEVE YOU FOUND ME HERE!
CLINK CLINK
YEAH ...
...UH...
YOU LOOK WELL.
WHEN YOU DIDN'T COME OUT OF THE DUNGEON, I WAS WORRIED.
YEAH. SOME STUFF HAPPENED.
UM ...
...AREN'T YOU TOO STRONG FOR BANDITS TO CAPTURE?

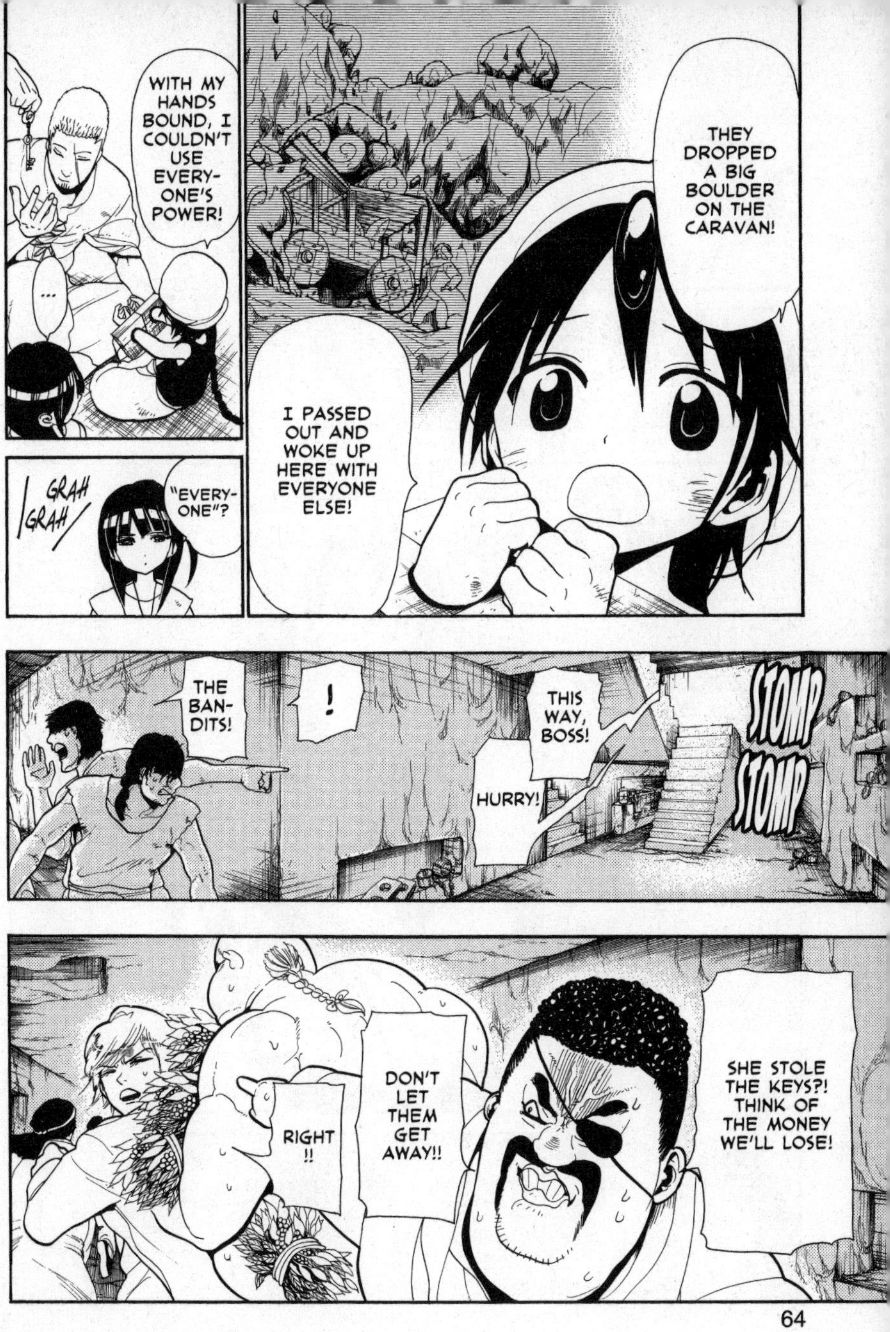
THEY DROPPED A BIG BOULDER ON THE CARAVAN!
I PASSED OUT AND WOKE UP HERE WITH EVERYONE ELSE!
WITH MY HANDS BOUND, I COULDN'T USE EVERY-ONE'S POWER!
...
"EVERY-ONE"?
GRAH GRAH
STOMP
STOMP
THIS WAY, BOSS!
HURRY!
!
THE BAN-DITS!
SHE STOLE THE KEYS?! THINK OF THE MONEY WE'LL LOSE!
DON'T LET THEM GET AWAY!!
RIGHT !!

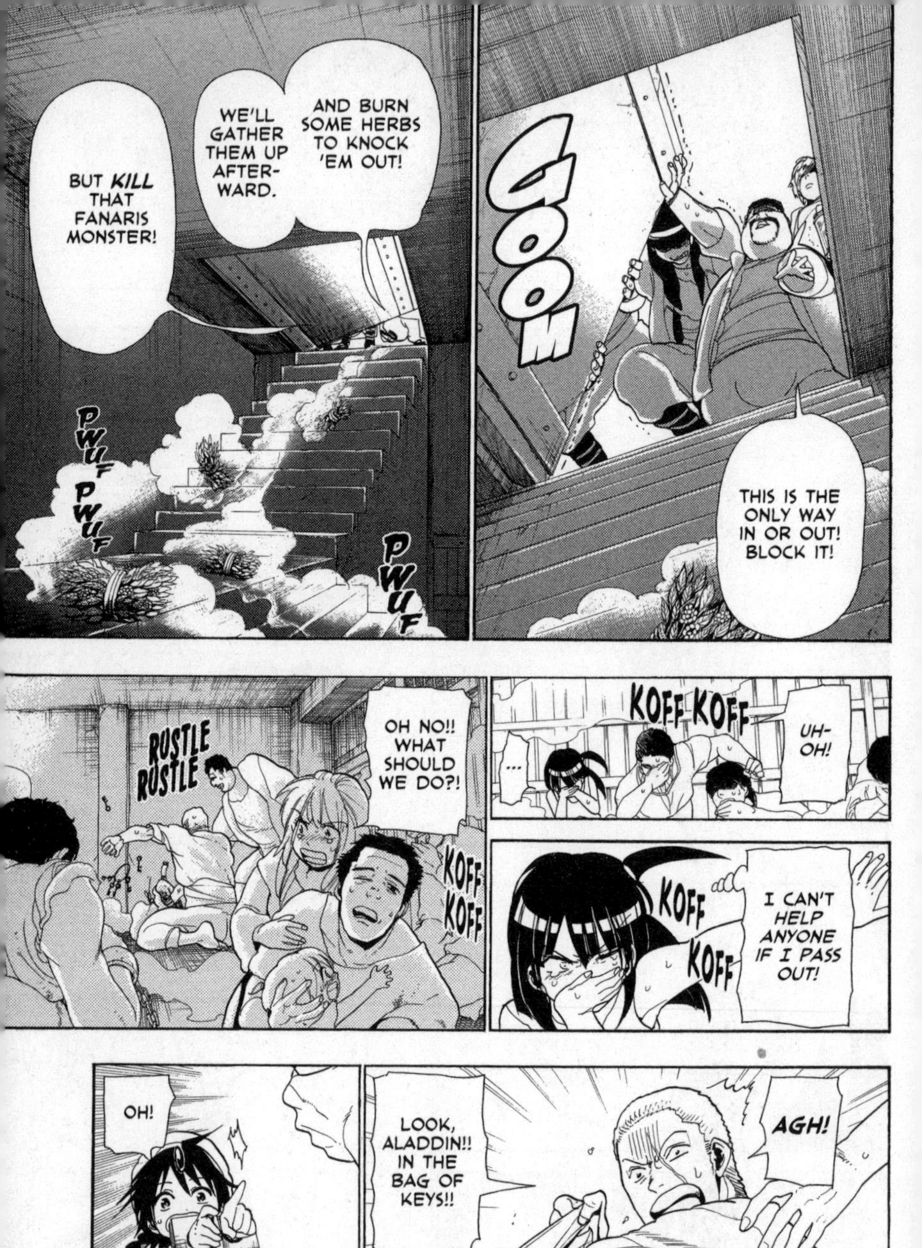
GOOOM
THIS IS THE ONLY WAY IN OR OUT! BLOCK IT!
AND BURN SOME HERBS TO KNOCK 'EM OUT!
WE'LL GATHER THEM UP AFTER-WARD.
BUT *KILL* THAT FANARIS MONSTER!
PWUF PWUF
PWUF
KOFF KOFF
UH-OH!
...
KOFF KOFF
I CAN'T HELP ANYONE IF I PASS OUT!
OH NO!! WHAT SHOULD WE DO?!
RUSTLE RUSTLE
KOFF KOFF
AGH!
LOOK, ALADDIN!! IN THE BAG OF KEYS!!
OH!

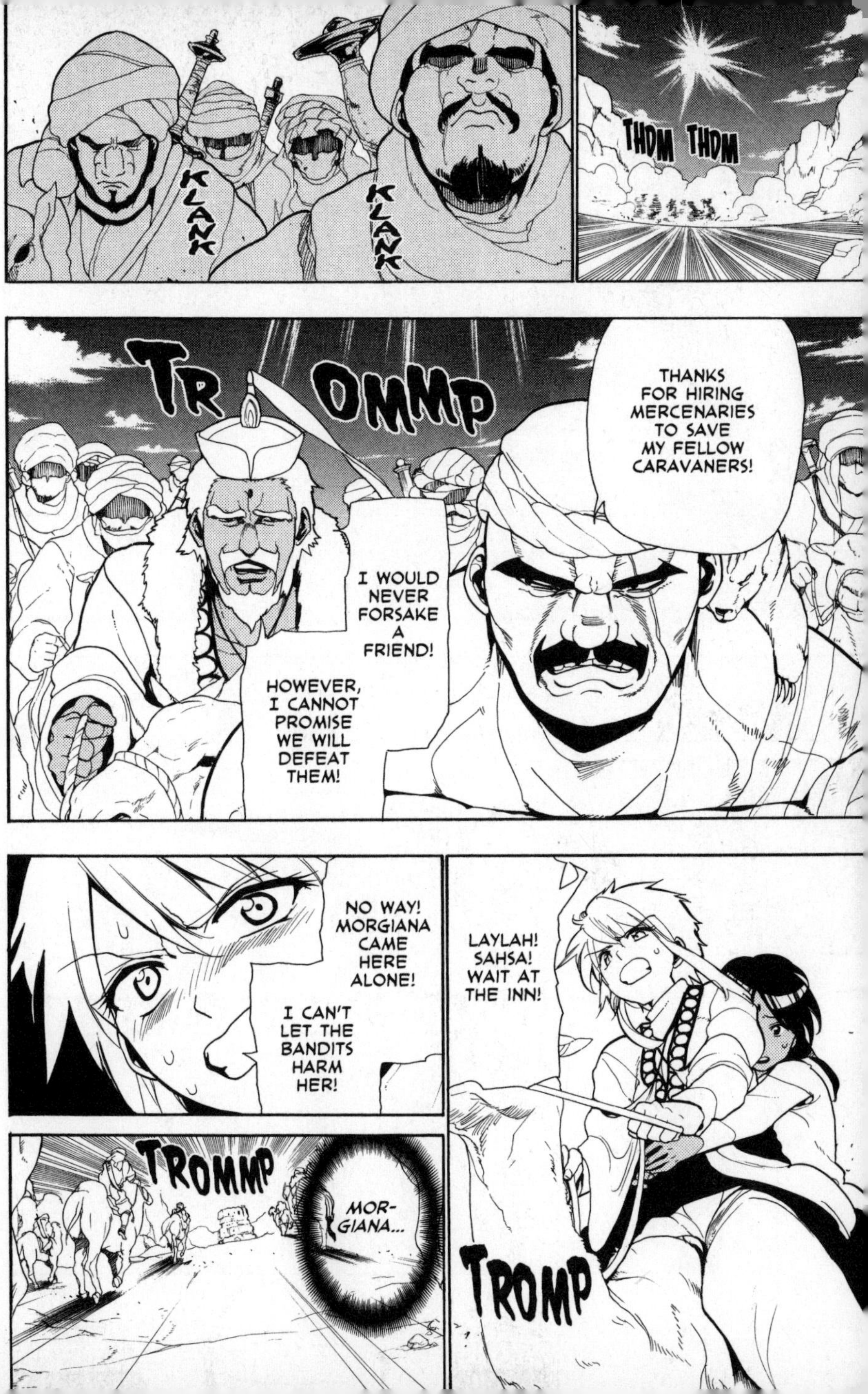
THDM THDM
KLANK
KLANK
TROMMP
THANKS FOR HIRING MERCENARIES TO SAVE MY FELLOW CARAVANERS!
I WOULD NEVER FORSAKE A FRIEND!
HOWEVER, I CANNOT PROMISE WE WILL DEFEAT THEM!
LAYLAH! SAHSA! WAIT AT THE INN!
TROMP
NO WAY! MORGIANA CAME HERE ALONE!
I CAN'T LET THE BANDITS HARM HER!
TROMMP
MOR-GIANA...

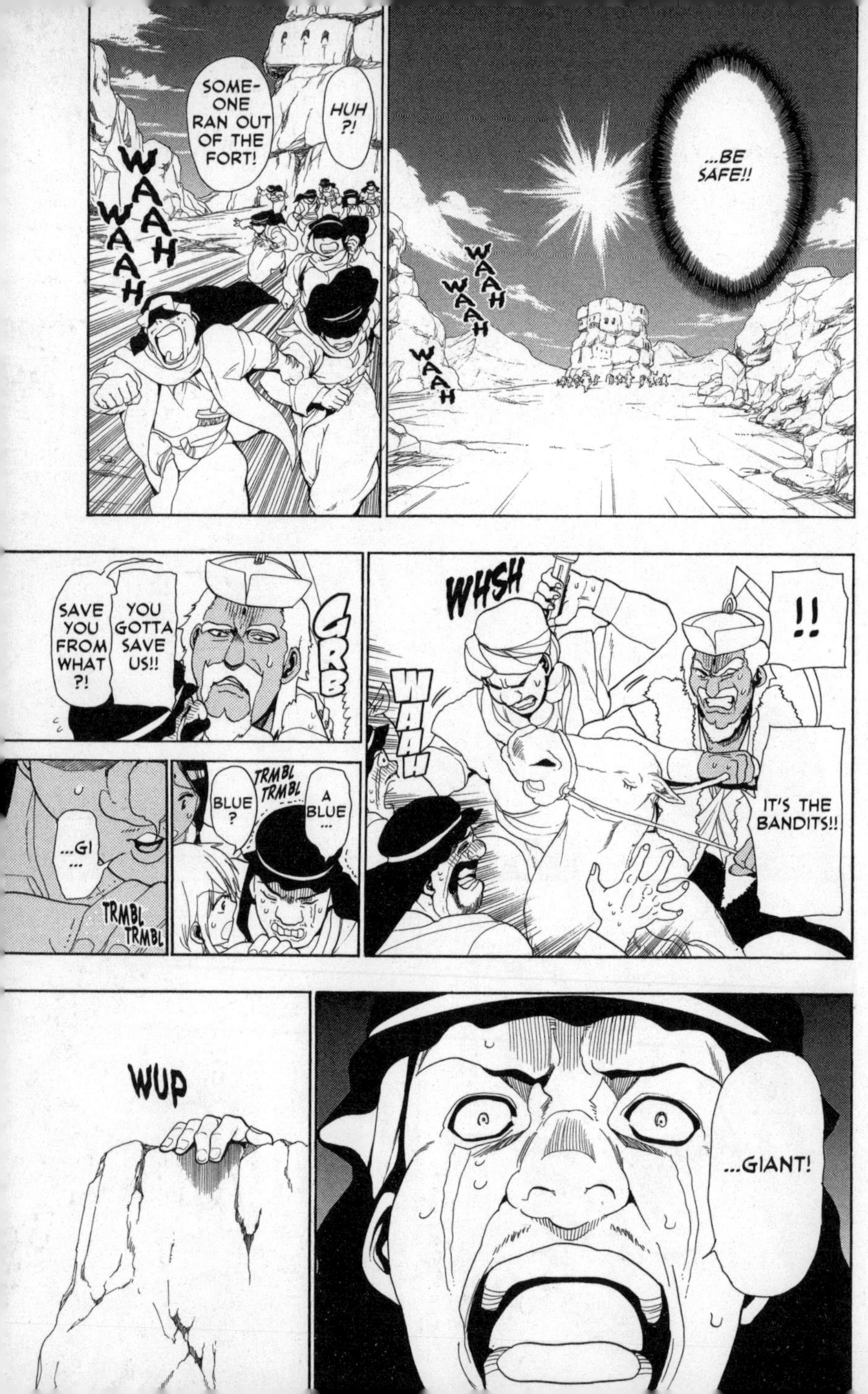
...BE SAFE!!
WAAH WAAH WAAH
HUH?!
SOME-ONE RAN OUT OF THE FORT!
WAAH WAAH WAAH
!!
WHSH
IT'S THE BANDITS!!
WAAH
GRB
YOU GOTTA SAVE US!!
SAVE YOU FROM WHAT?!
A BLUE...
TRMBL TRMBL
BLUE?
...GI...
TRMBL TRMBL
...GIANT!
WUP

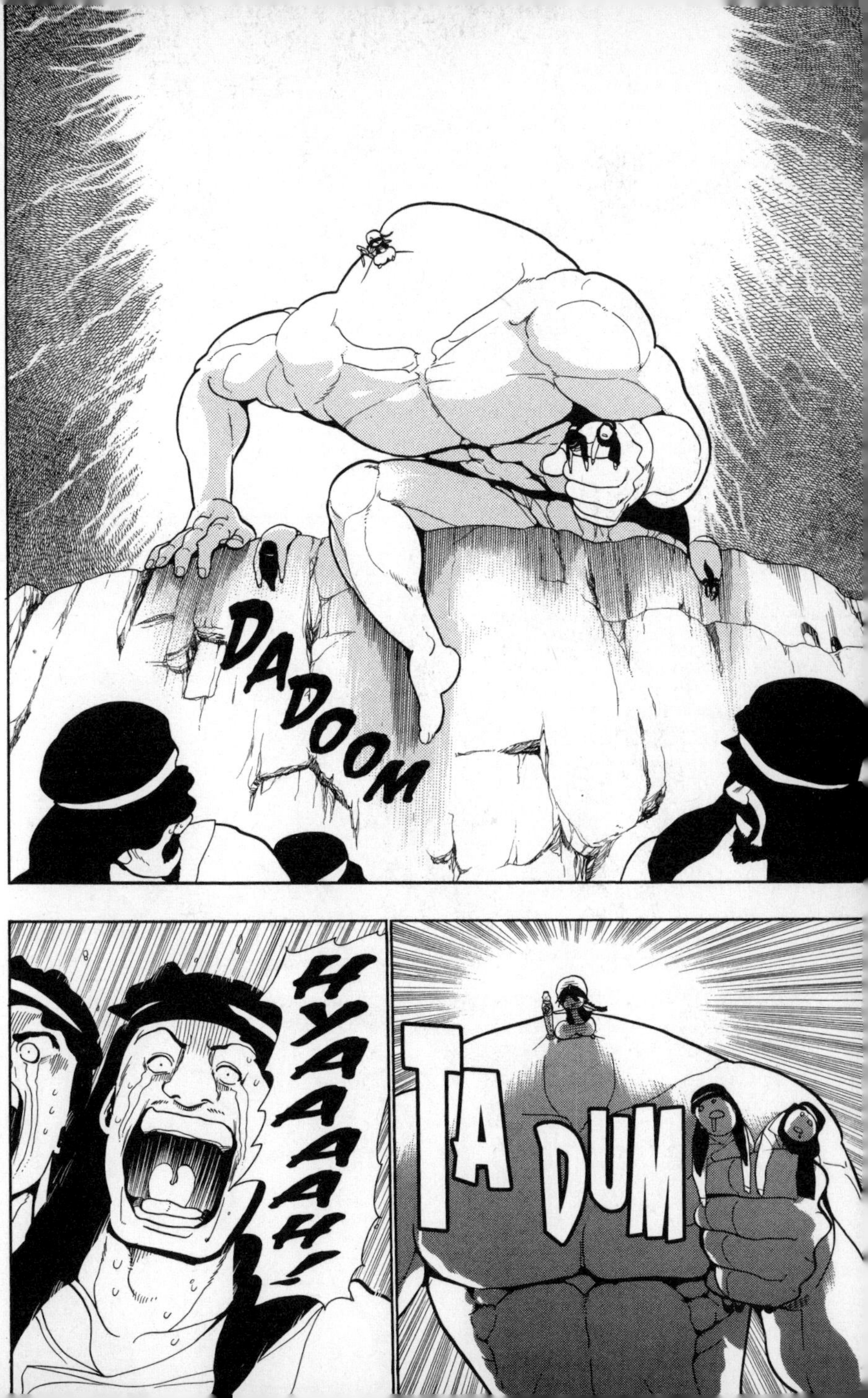
DADOOM
TA DUM
HYAAAAAH!

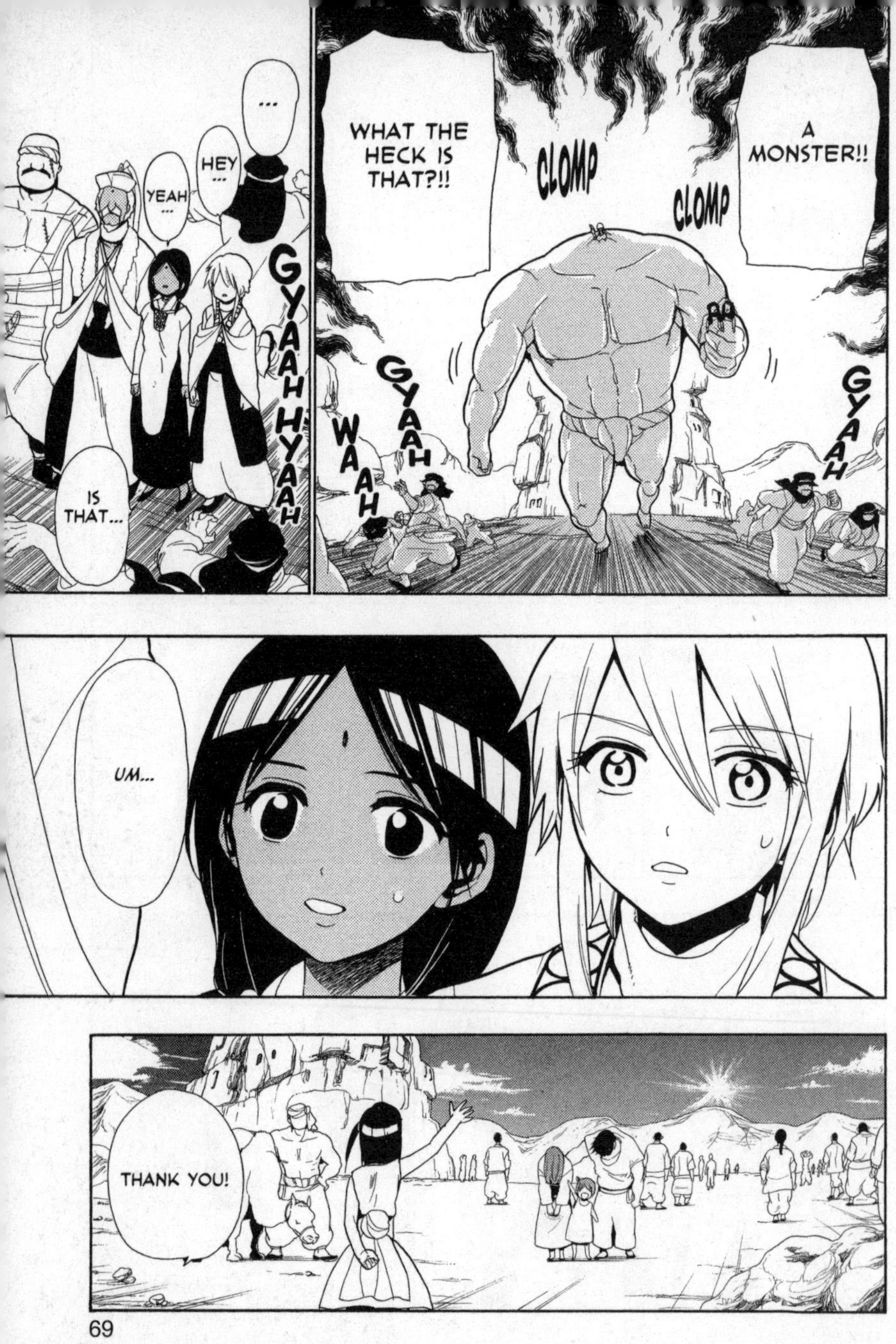
A MONSTER!!
WHAT THE HECK IS THAT?!!
CLOMP
CLOMP
GYAAH
GYAAH
WAAH
...
HEY...
YEAH...
GYAAHHYAAH
IS THAT...
UM...
THANK YOU!

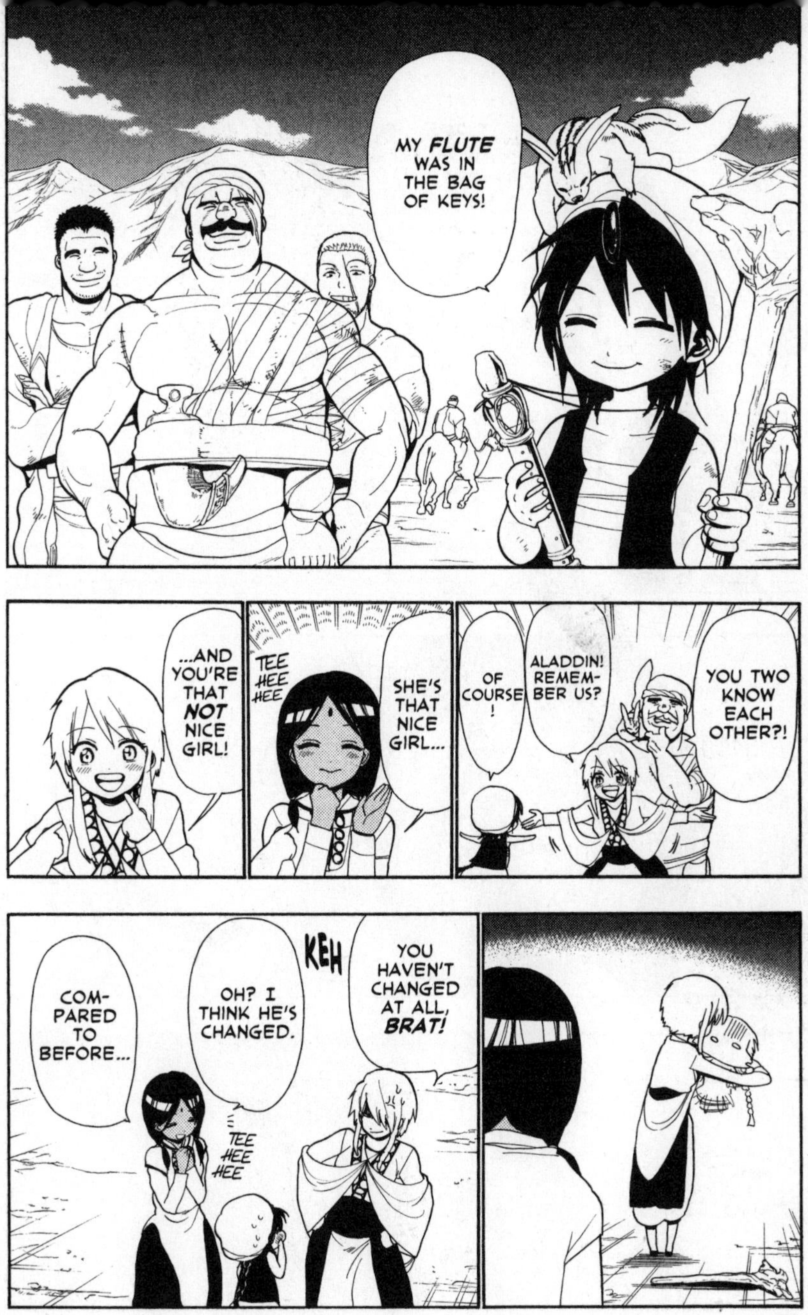
MY FLUTE WAS IN THE BAG OF KEYS!
YOU TWO KNOW EACH OTHER?!
ALADDIN! REMEMBER US?
OF COURSE!
SHE'S THAT NICE GIRL...
TEE HEE HEE
...AND YOU'RE THAT NOT NICE GIRL!
YOU HAVEN'T CHANGED AT ALL, BRAT!
KEH
OH? I THINK HE'S CHANGED.
COMPARED TO BEFORE...
TEE HEE HEE

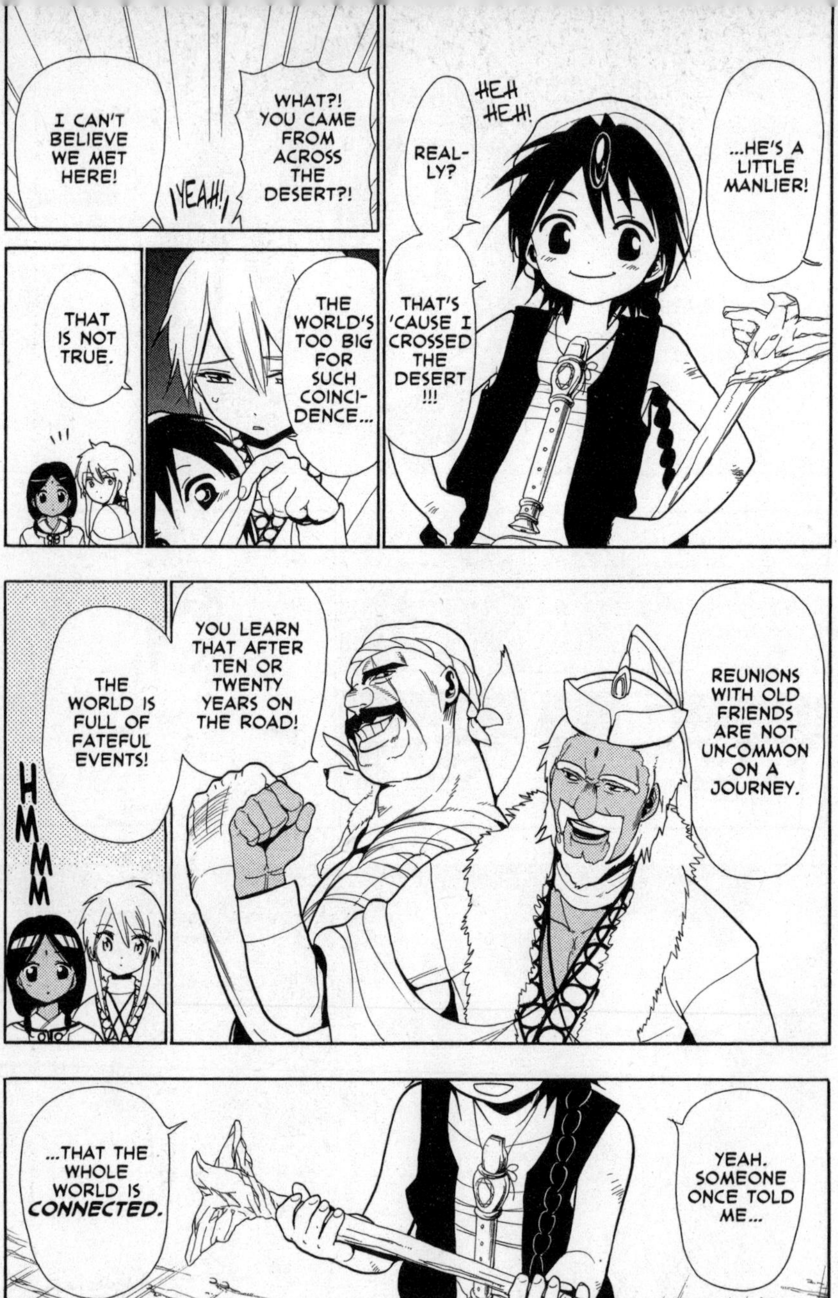
...HE'S A LITTLE MANLIER!
HEH HEH!
REAL-LY?
THAT'S 'CAUSE I CROSSED THE DESERT!!!
WHAT?! YOU CAME FROM ACROSS THE DESERT?!
YEAH!
I CAN'T BELIEVE WE MET HERE!
THE WORLD'S TOO BIG FOR SUCH COINCI-DENCE...
THAT IS NOT TRUE.
REUNIONS WITH OLD FRIENDS ARE NOT UNCOMMON ON A JOURNEY.
YOU LEARN THAT AFTER TEN OR TWENTY YEARS ON THE ROAD!
THE WORLD IS FULL OF FATEFUL EVENTS!
HMMM
YEAH. SOMEONE ONCE TOLD ME...
...THAT THE WHOLE WORLD IS ***CONNECTED.***

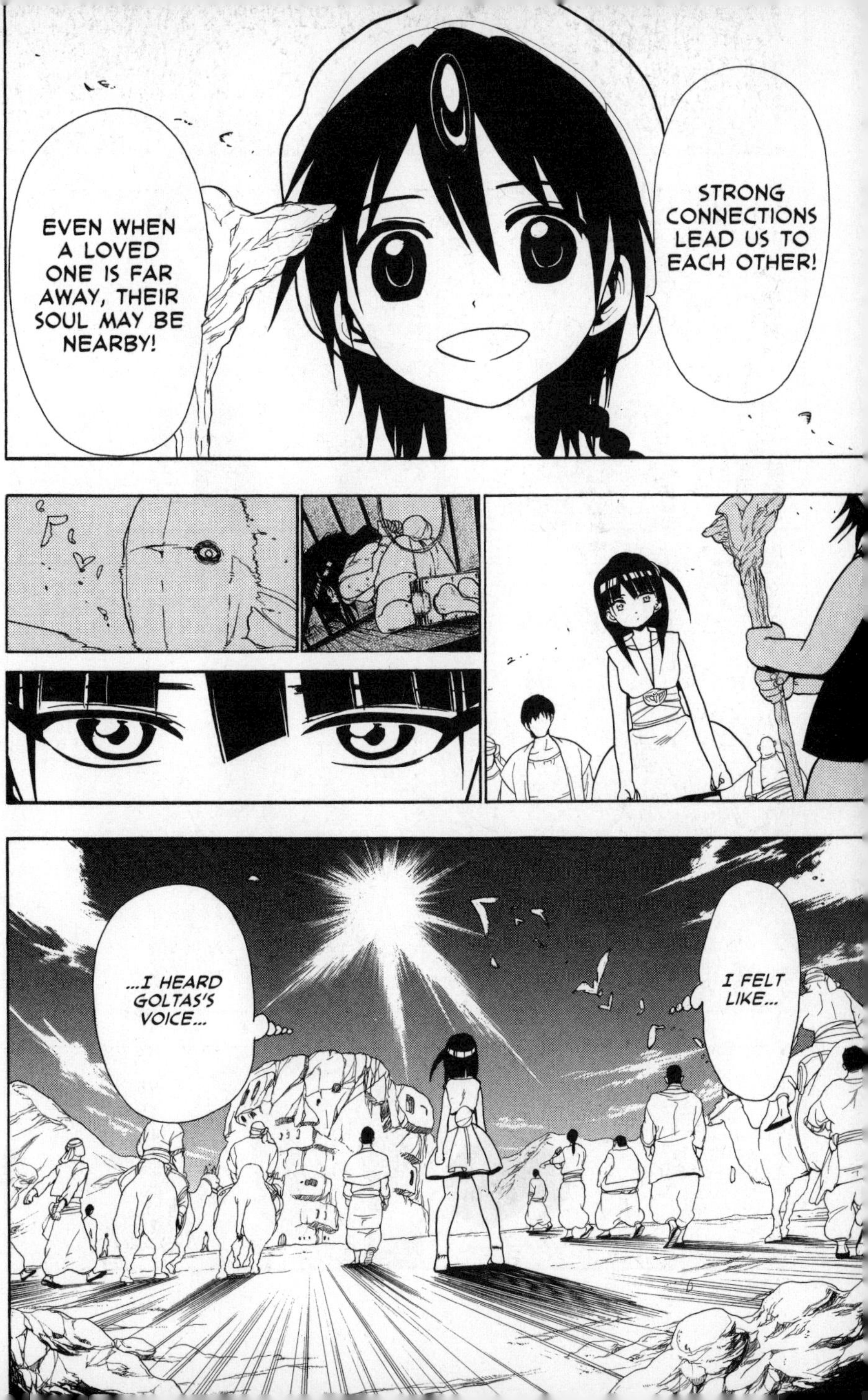
STRONG CONNECTIONS LEAD US TO EACH OTHER!
EVEN WHEN A LOVED ONE IS FAR AWAY, THEIR SOUL MAY BE NEARBY!
I FELT LIKE...
...I HEARD GOLTAS'S VOICE...

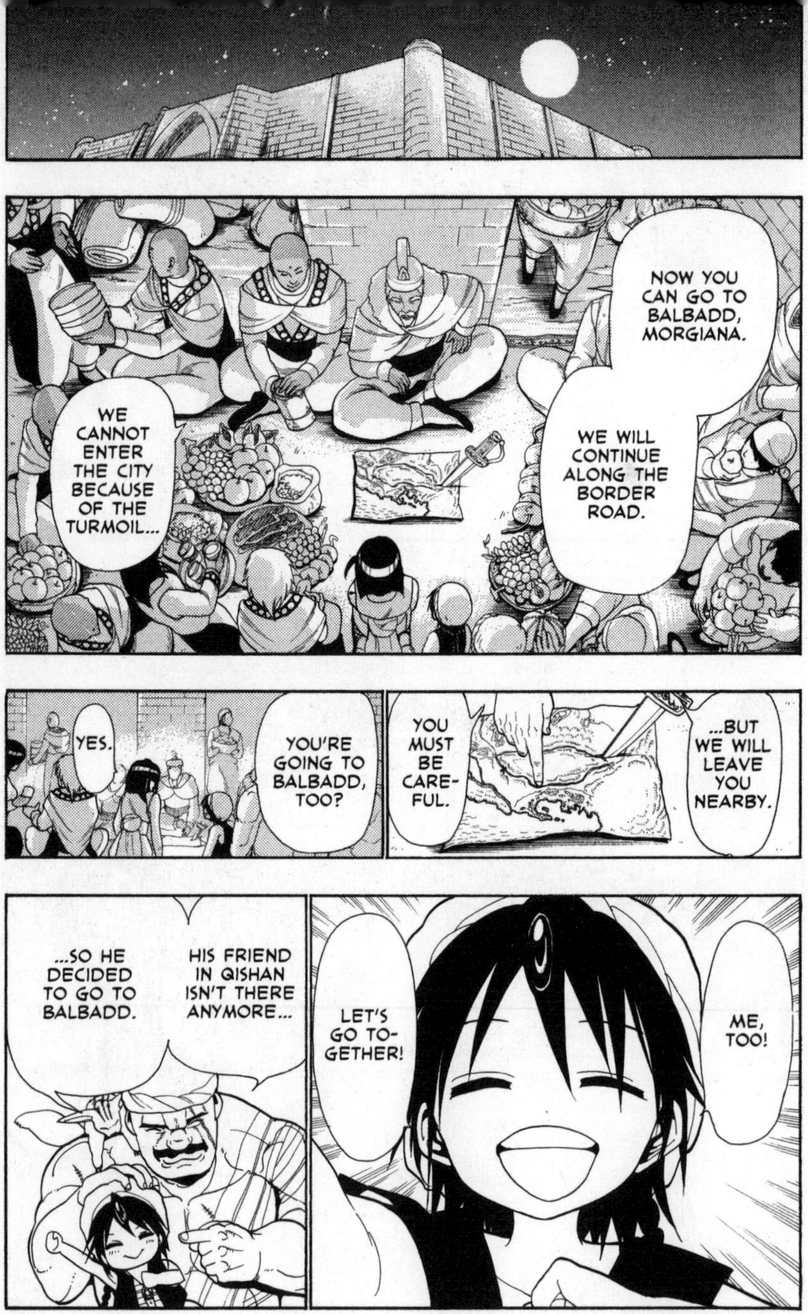
NOW YOU CAN GO TO BALBADD, MORGIANA.
WE WILL CONTINUE ALONG THE BORDER ROAD.
WE CANNOT ENTER THE CITY BECAUSE OF THE TURMOIL...
...BUT WE WILL LEAVE YOU NEARBY.
YOU MUST BE CARE-FUL.
YOU'RE GOING TO BALBADD, TOO?
YES.
ME, TOO!
LET'S GO TO-GETHER!
HIS FRIEND IN QISHAN ISN'T THERE ANYMORE...
...SO HE DECIDED TO GO TO BALBADD.

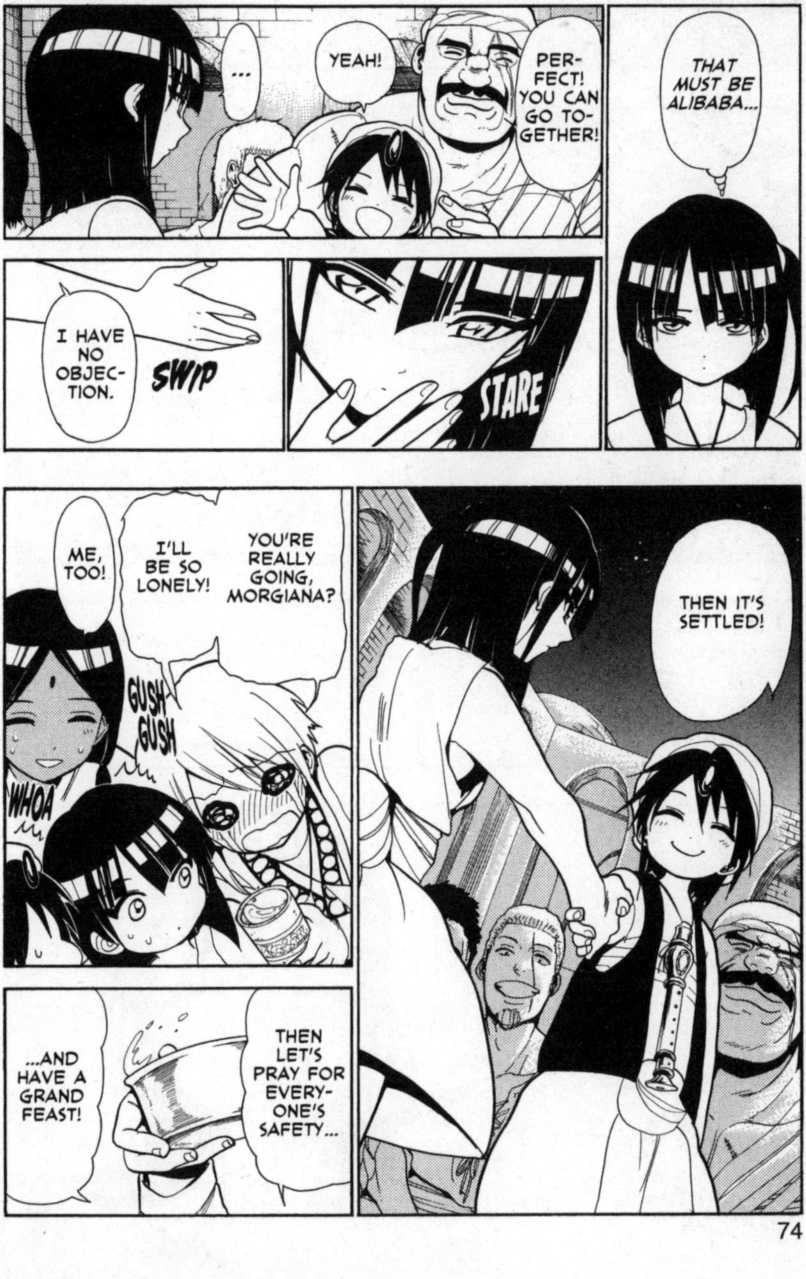
THAT MUST BE ALIBABA...
PER-FECT! YOU CAN GO TO-GETHER!
YEAH!
...
STARE
SWIP
I HAVE NO OBJEC-TION.
THEN IT'S SETTLED!
YOU'RE REALLY GOING, MORGIANA?
I'LL BE SO LONELY!
ME, TOO!
GUSH GUSH
WHOA
THEN LET'S PRAY FOR EVERY-ONE'S SAFETY...
...AND HAVE A GRAND FEAST!

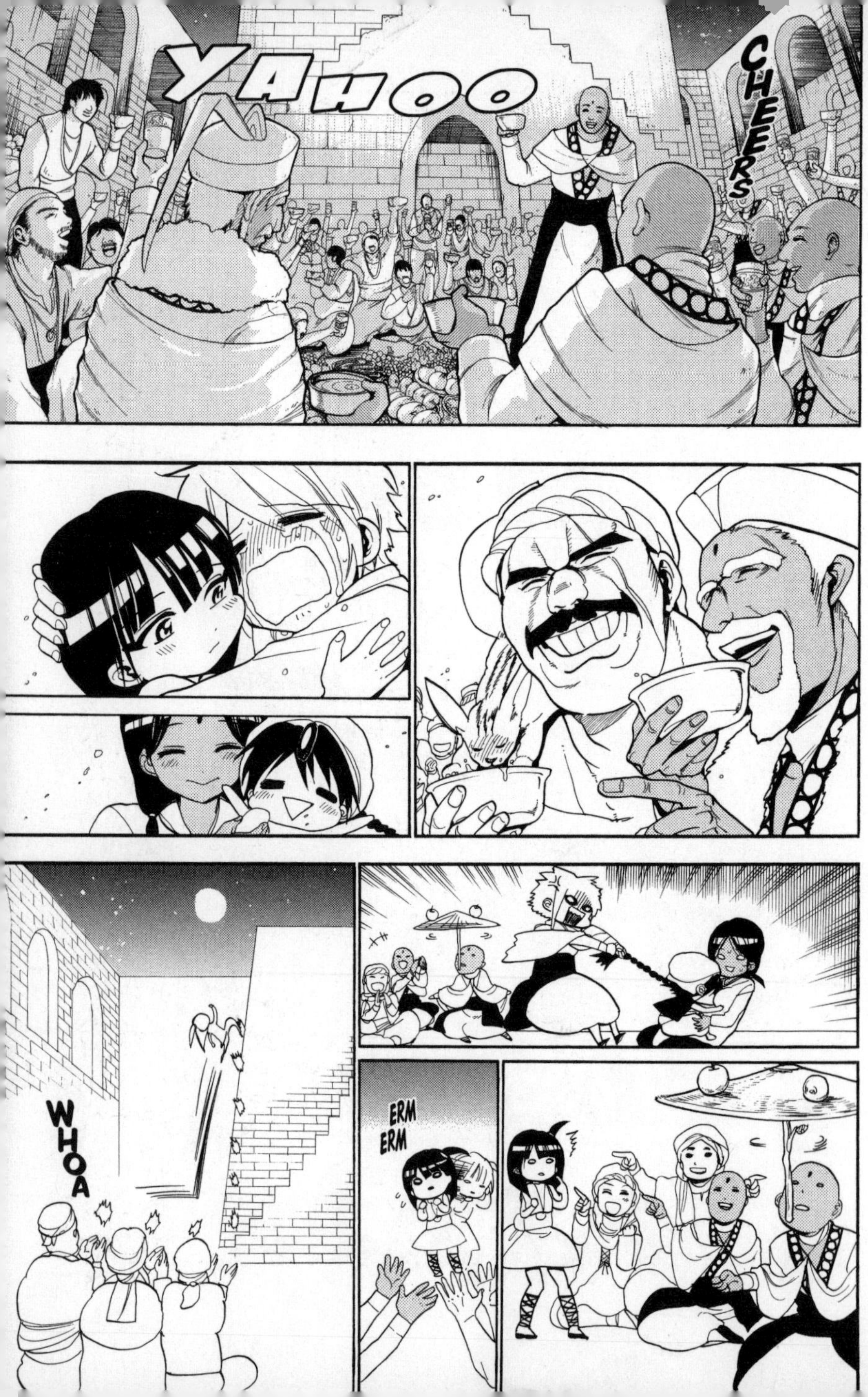
YAHOO
CHEERS
ERM ERM
WHOA

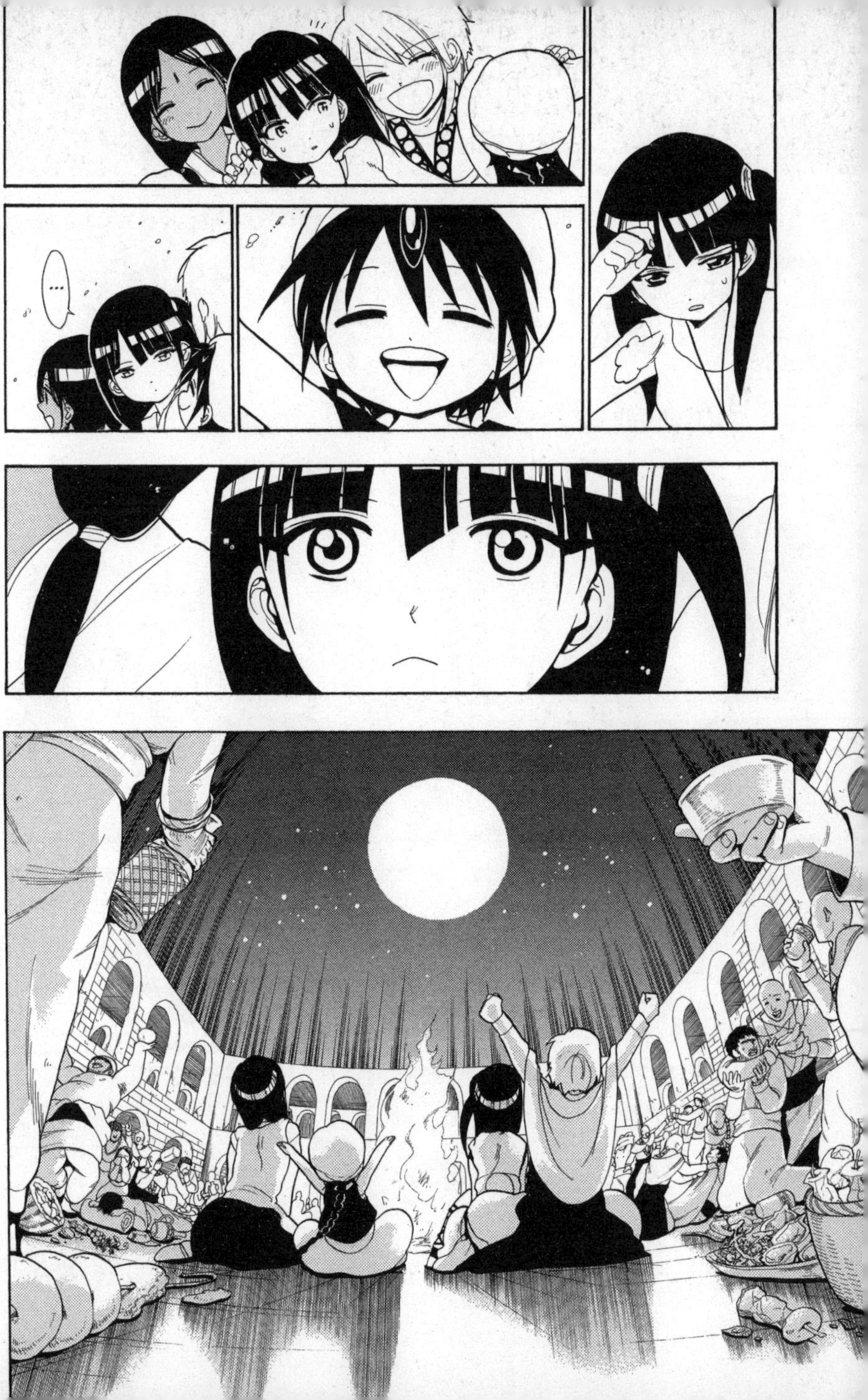
...

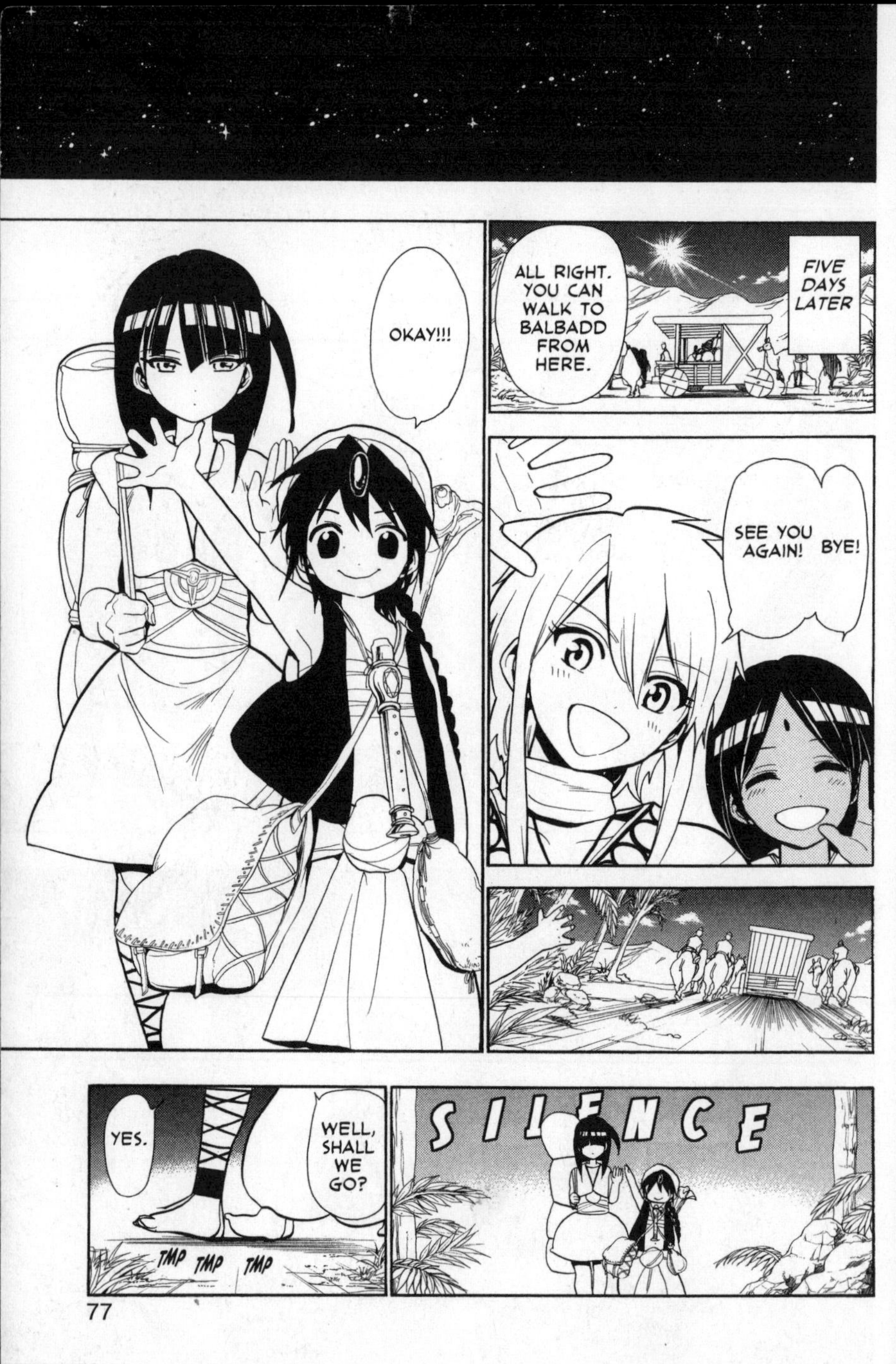
FIVE DAYS LATER
ALL RIGHT. YOU CAN WALK TO BALBADD FROM HERE.
SEE YOU AGAIN! BYE!
OKAY!!!
SILENCE
WELL, SHALL WE GO?
YES.
TMP TMP TMP

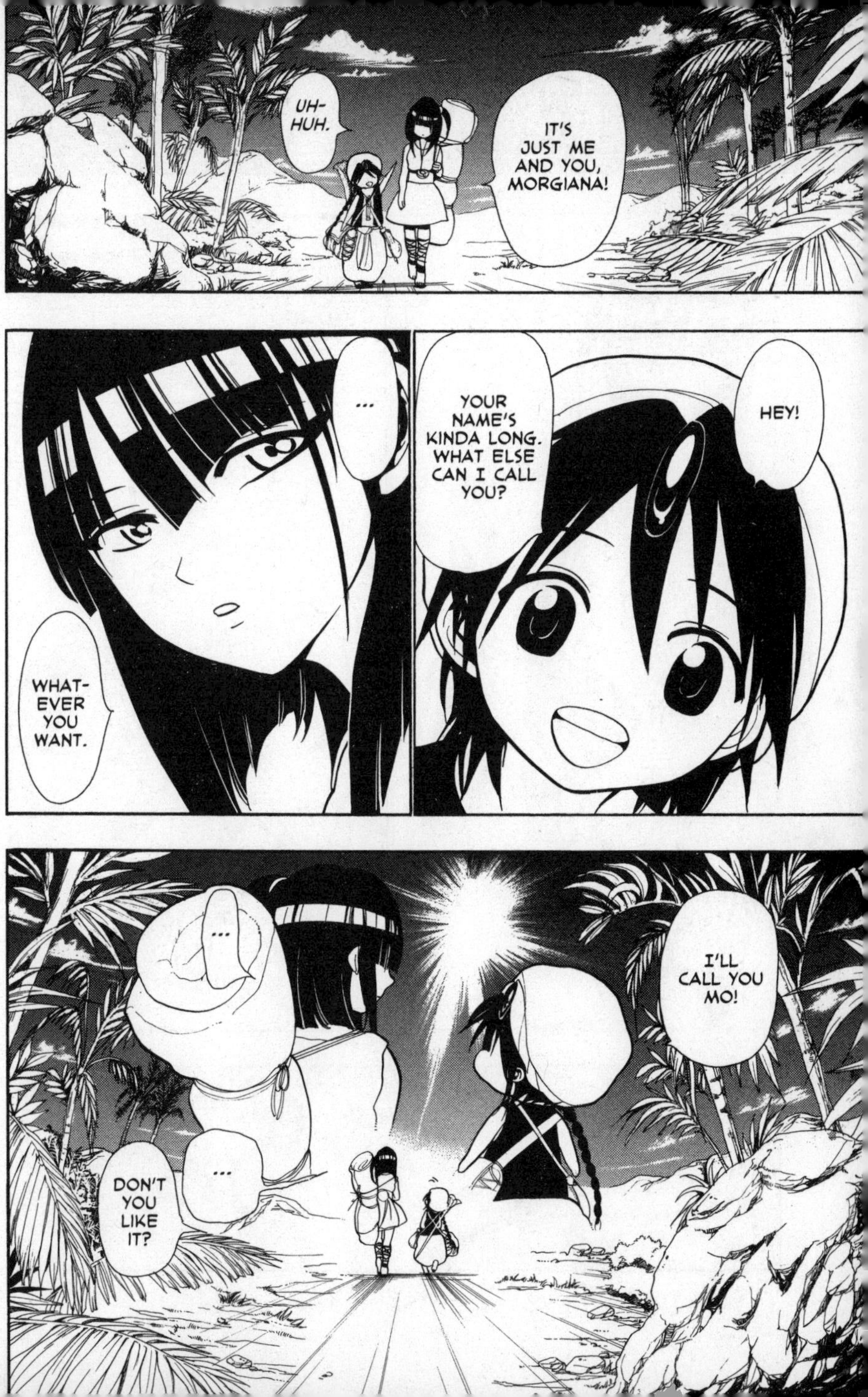
IT'S JUST ME AND YOU, MORGIANA!
UH-HUH.
HEY!
YOUR NAME'S KINDA LONG. WHAT ELSE CAN I CALL YOU?
...
WHAT-EVER YOU WANT.
I'LL CALL YOU MO!
...
...
DON'T YOU LIKE IT?

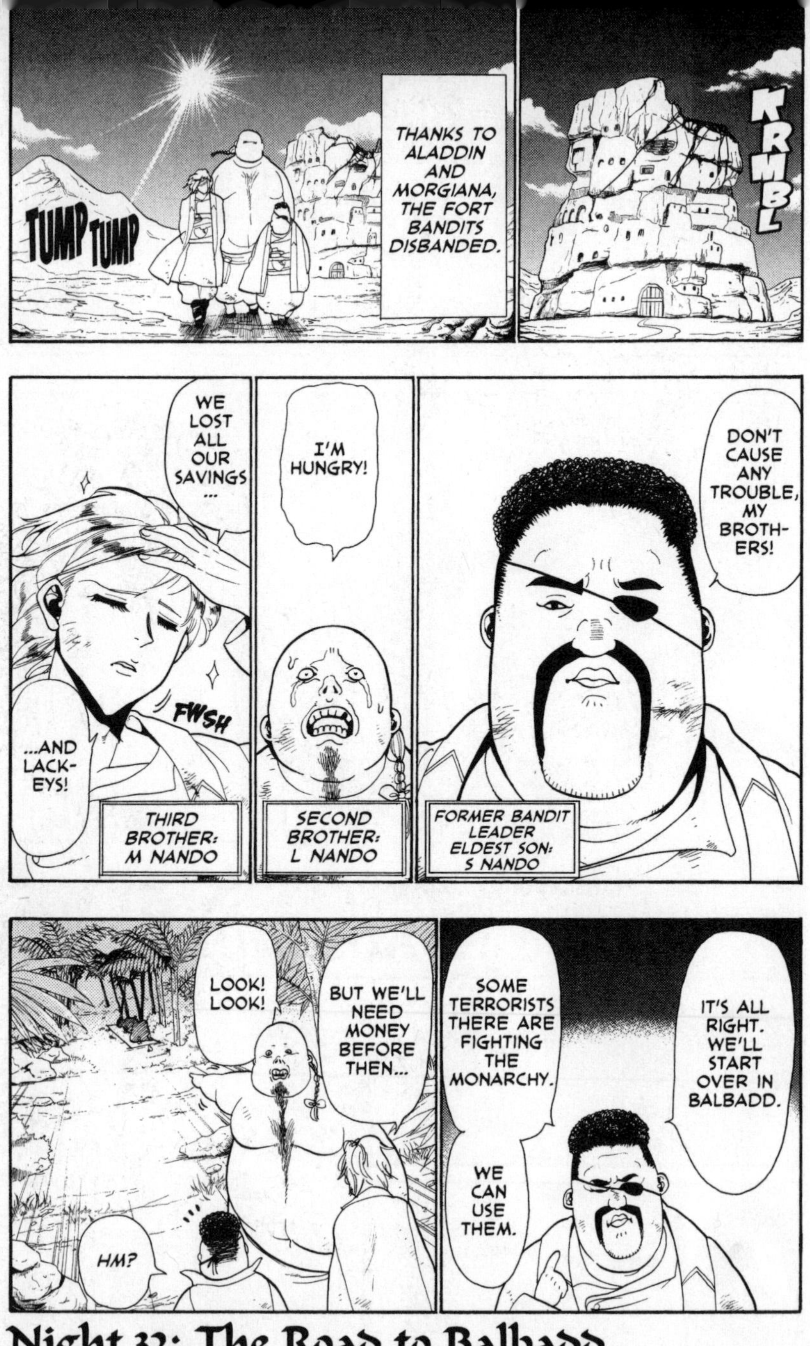
KRMBL
THANKS TO ALADDIN AND MORGIANA, THE FORT BANDITS DISBANDED.
TUMP TUMP
DON'T CAUSE ANY TROUBLE, MY BROTHERS!
FORMER BANDIT LEADER ELDEST SON: S NANDO
I'M HUNGRY!
SECOND BROTHER: L NANDO
WE LOST ALL OUR SAVINGS ...
FWSH
...AND LACKEYS!
THIRD BROTHER: M NANDO
IT'S ALL RIGHT. WE'LL START OVER IN BALBADD.
SOME TERRORISTS THERE ARE FIGHTING THE MONARCHY.
WE CAN USE THEM.
BUT WE'LL NEED MONEY BEFORE THEN...
LOOK! LOOK!
HM?

Night 32: The Road to Balbadd

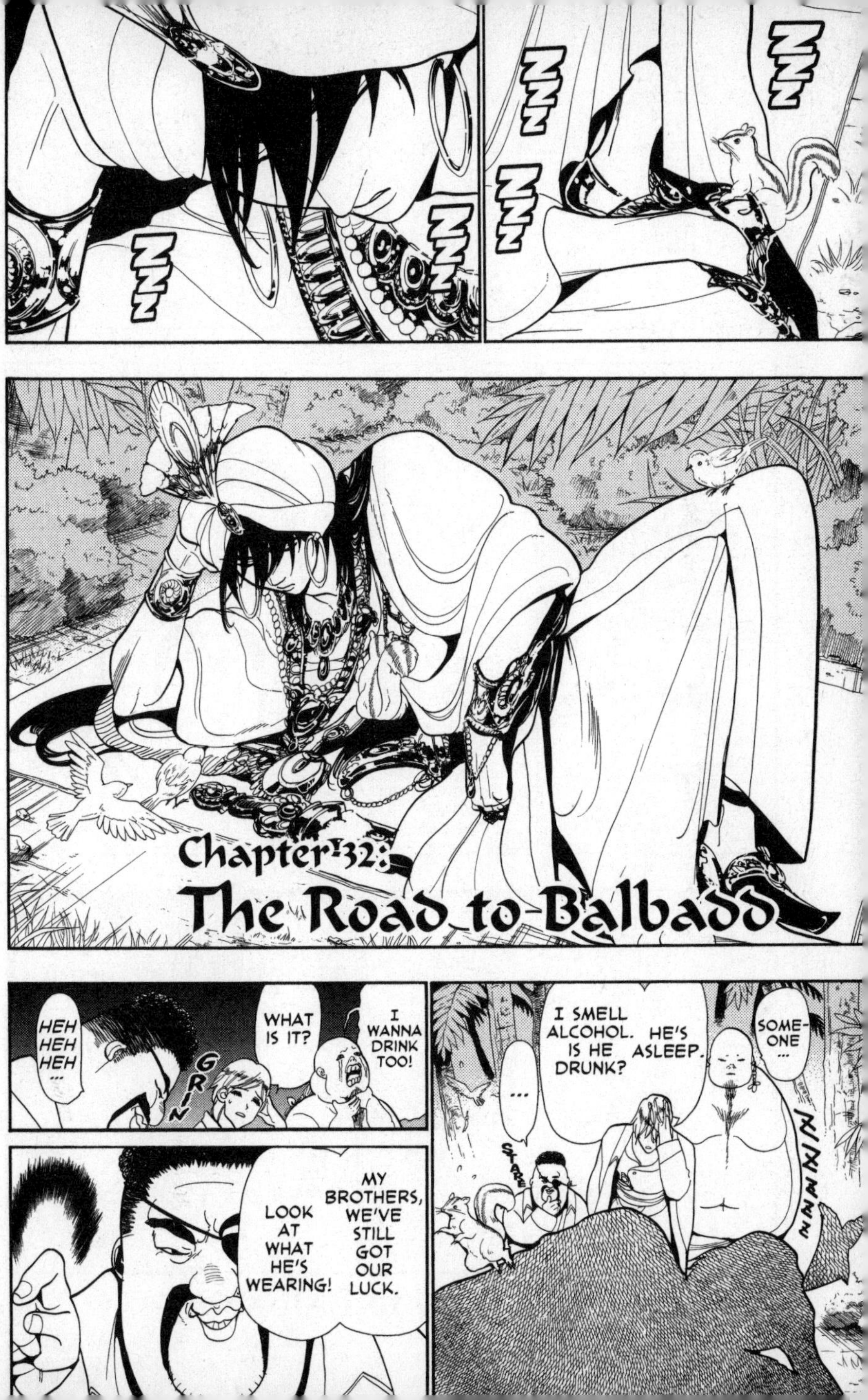
ZZZ
ZZZ
ZZZ
ZZZ
Chapter 32:
The Road to Balbadd
SOME-ONE ...
HE'S ASLEEP.
I SMELL ALCOHOL. IS HE DRUNK?
...
STARE
ZZZZZ
I WANNA DRINK TOO!
WHAT IS IT?
HEH HEH HEH ...
GRIN
MY BROTHERS, WE'VE STILL GOT OUR LUCK.
LOOK AT WHAT HE'S WEARING!

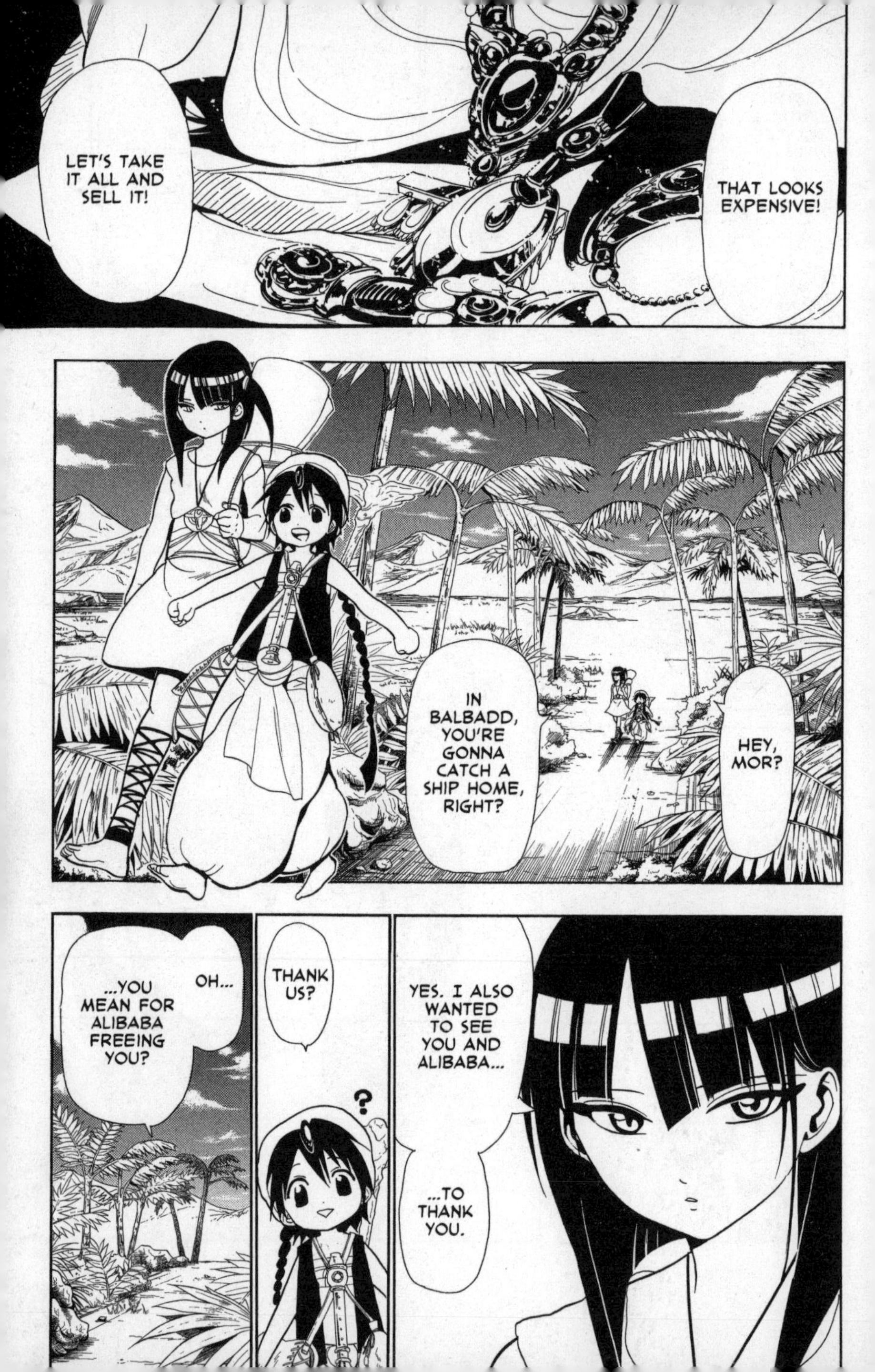
THAT LOOKS EXPENSIVE!
LET'S TAKE IT ALL AND SELL IT!
HEY, MOR?
IN BALBADD, YOU'RE GONNA CATCH A SHIP HOME, RIGHT?
YES. I ALSO WANTED TO SEE YOU AND ALIBABA...
...TO THANK YOU.
THANK US?
?
OH...
...YOU MEAN FOR ALIBABA FREEING YOU?

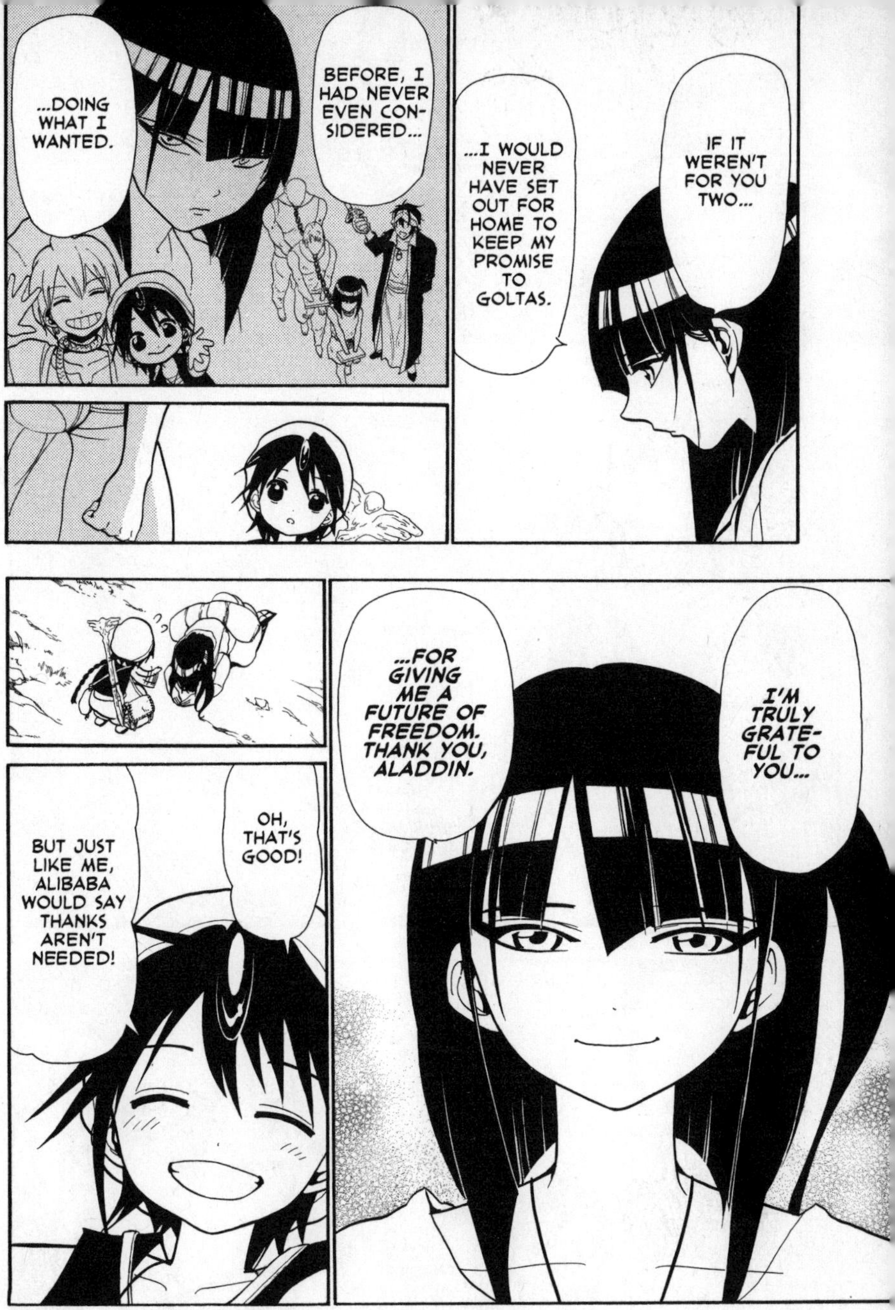
IF IT WEREN'T FOR YOU TWO...
...I WOULD NEVER HAVE SET OUT FOR HOME TO KEEP MY PROMISE TO GOLTAS.
BEFORE, I HAD NEVER EVEN CONSIDERED...
...DOING WHAT I WANTED.
I'M TRULY GRATEFUL TO YOU...
...FOR GIVING ME A FUTURE OF FREEDOM. THANK YOU, ALADDIN.
OH, THAT'S GOOD!
BUT JUST LIKE ME, ALIBABA WOULD SAY THANKS AREN'T NEEDED!

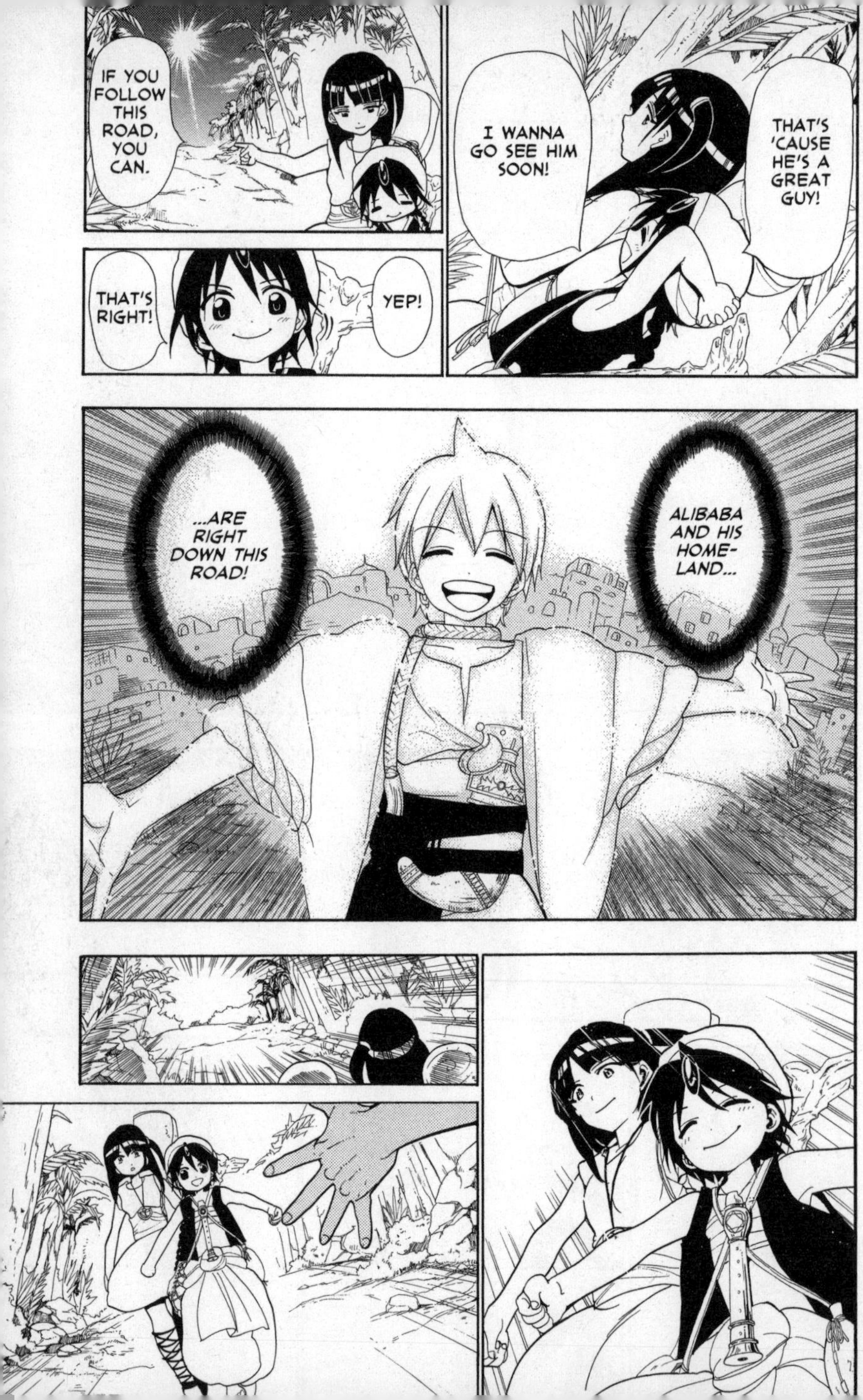
THAT'S 'CAUSE HE'S A GREAT GUY!
I WANNA GO SEE HIM SOON!
IF YOU FOLLOW THIS ROAD, YOU CAN.
YEP!
THAT'S RIGHT!
ALIBABA AND HIS HOME-LAND...
...ARE RIGHT DOWN THIS ROAD!

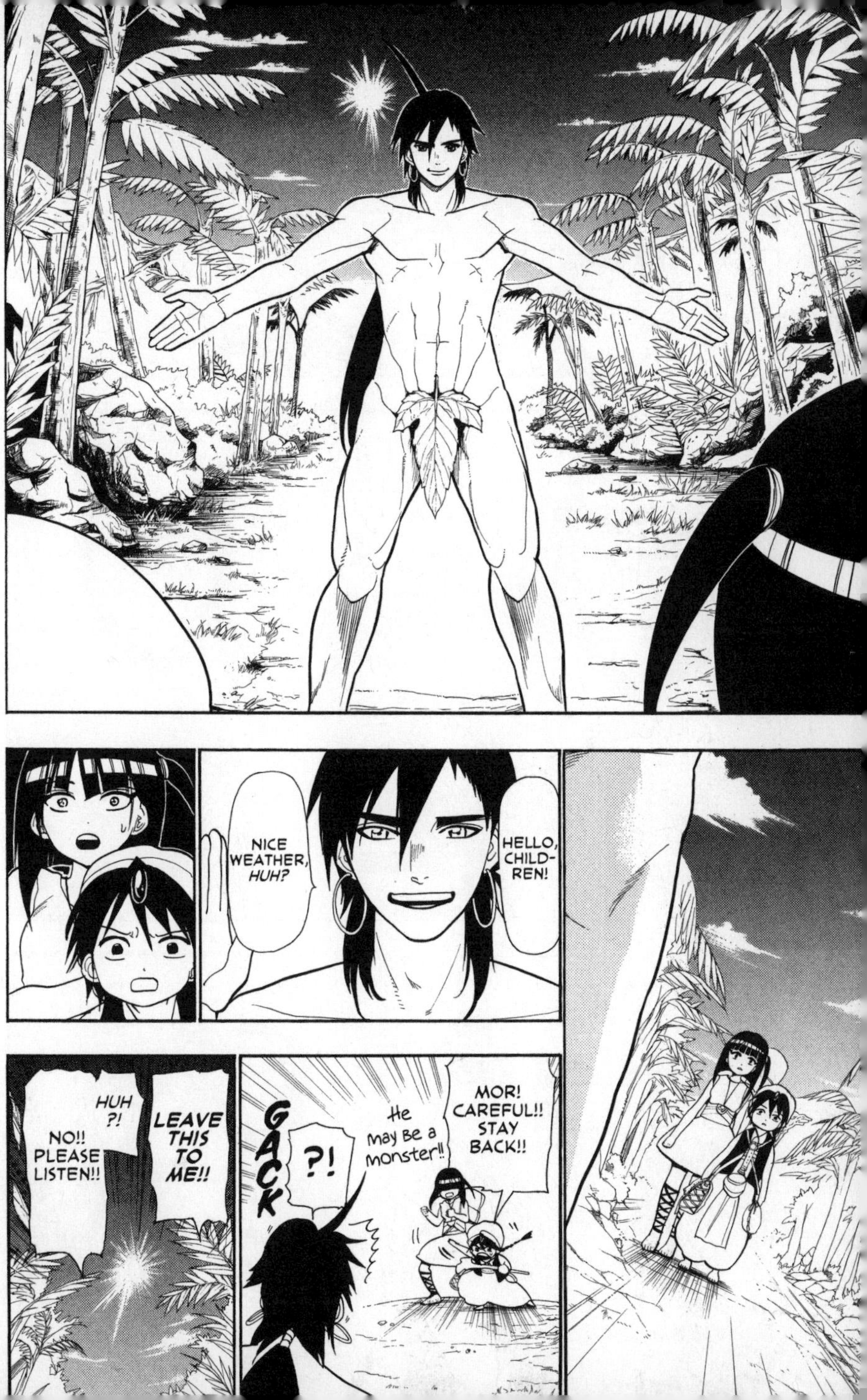
HELLO, CHILD-REN!
NICE WEATHER, HUH?
MOR! CAREFUL!! STAY BACK!!
He May Be a monster!!
?!
GACK
LEAVE THIS TO ME!!
HUH ?!
NO!! PLEASE LISTEN!!

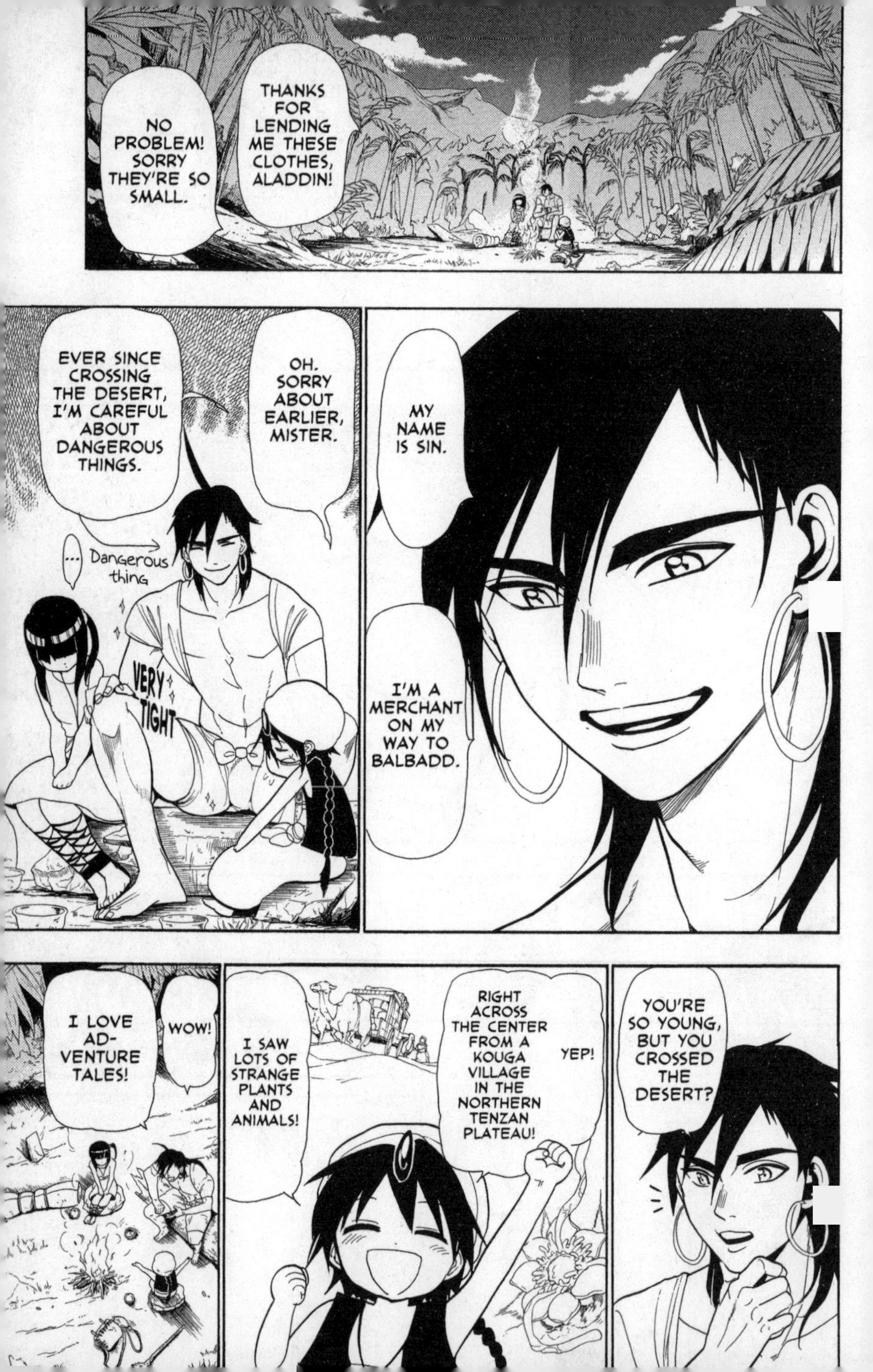
THANKS FOR LENDING ME THESE CLOTHES, ALADDIN!
NO PROBLEM! SORRY THEY'RE SO SMALL.
MY NAME IS SIN.
I'M A MERCHANT ON MY WAY TO BALBADD.
OH. SORRY ABOUT EARLIER, MISTER.
EVER SINCE CROSSING THE DESERT, I'M CAREFUL ABOUT DANGEROUS THINGS.
...
Dangerous thing
VERY TIGHT
YOU'RE SO YOUNG, BUT YOU CROSSED THE DESERT?
YEP!
RIGHT ACROSS THE CENTER FROM A KOUGA VILLAGE IN THE NORTHERN TENZAN PLATEAU!
I SAW LOTS OF STRANGE PLANTS AND ANIMALS!
WOW!
I LOVE AD-VENTURE TALES!

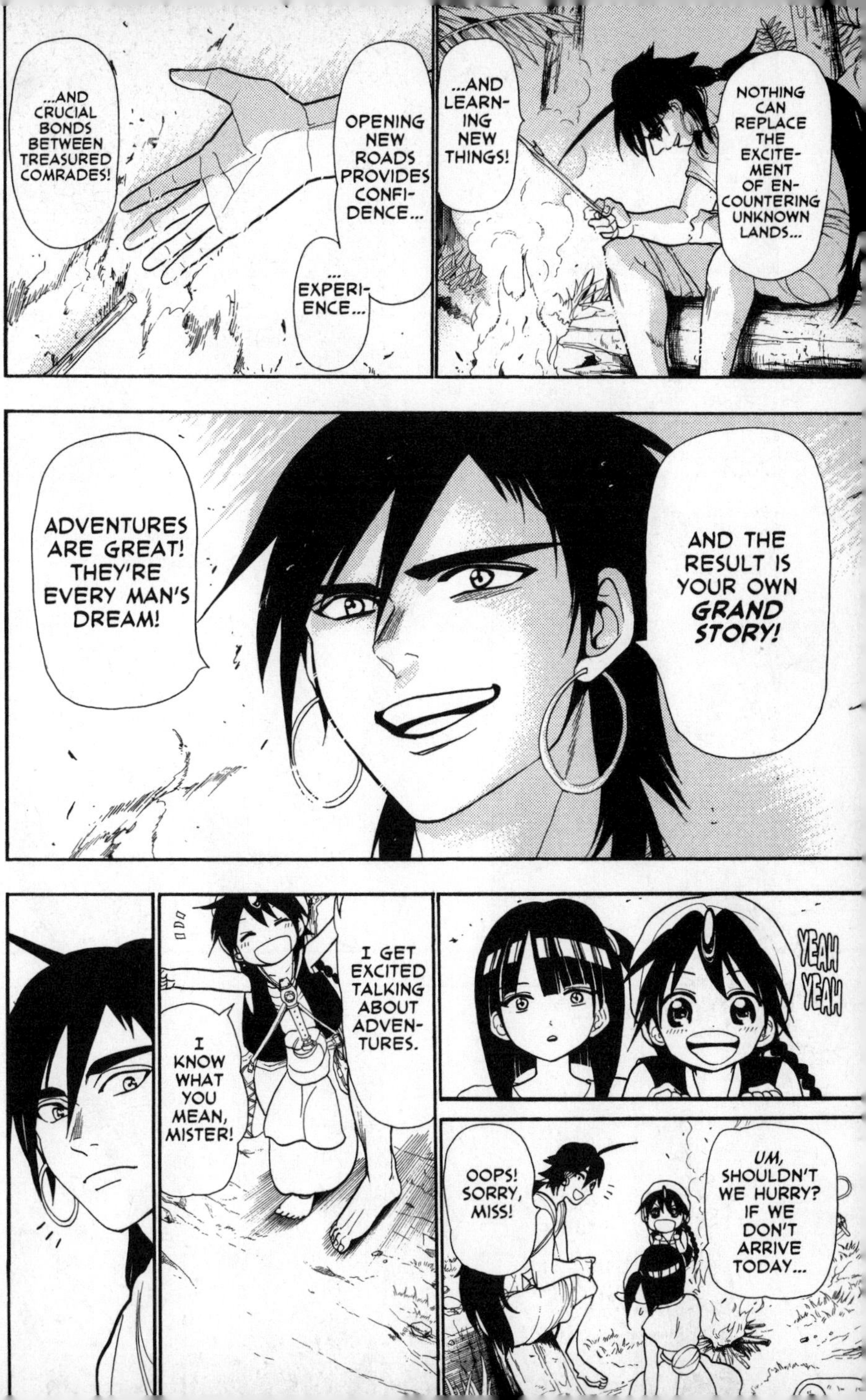
NOTHING CAN REPLACE THE EXCITEMENT OF ENCOUNTERING UNKNOWN LANDS...
...AND LEARNING NEW THINGS!
OPENING NEW ROADS PROVIDES CONFIDENCE...
...EXPERIENCE...
...AND CRUCIAL BONDS BETWEEN TREASURED COMRADES!
AND THE RESULT IS YOUR OWN *GRAND STORY!*
ADVENTURES ARE GREAT! THEY'RE EVERY MAN'S DREAM!
YEAH YEAH
UM, SHOULDN'T WE HURRY? IF WE DON'T ARRIVE TODAY...
OOPS! SORRY, MISS!
I GET EXCITED TALKING ABOUT ADVENTURES.
I KNOW WHAT YOU MEAN, MISTER!

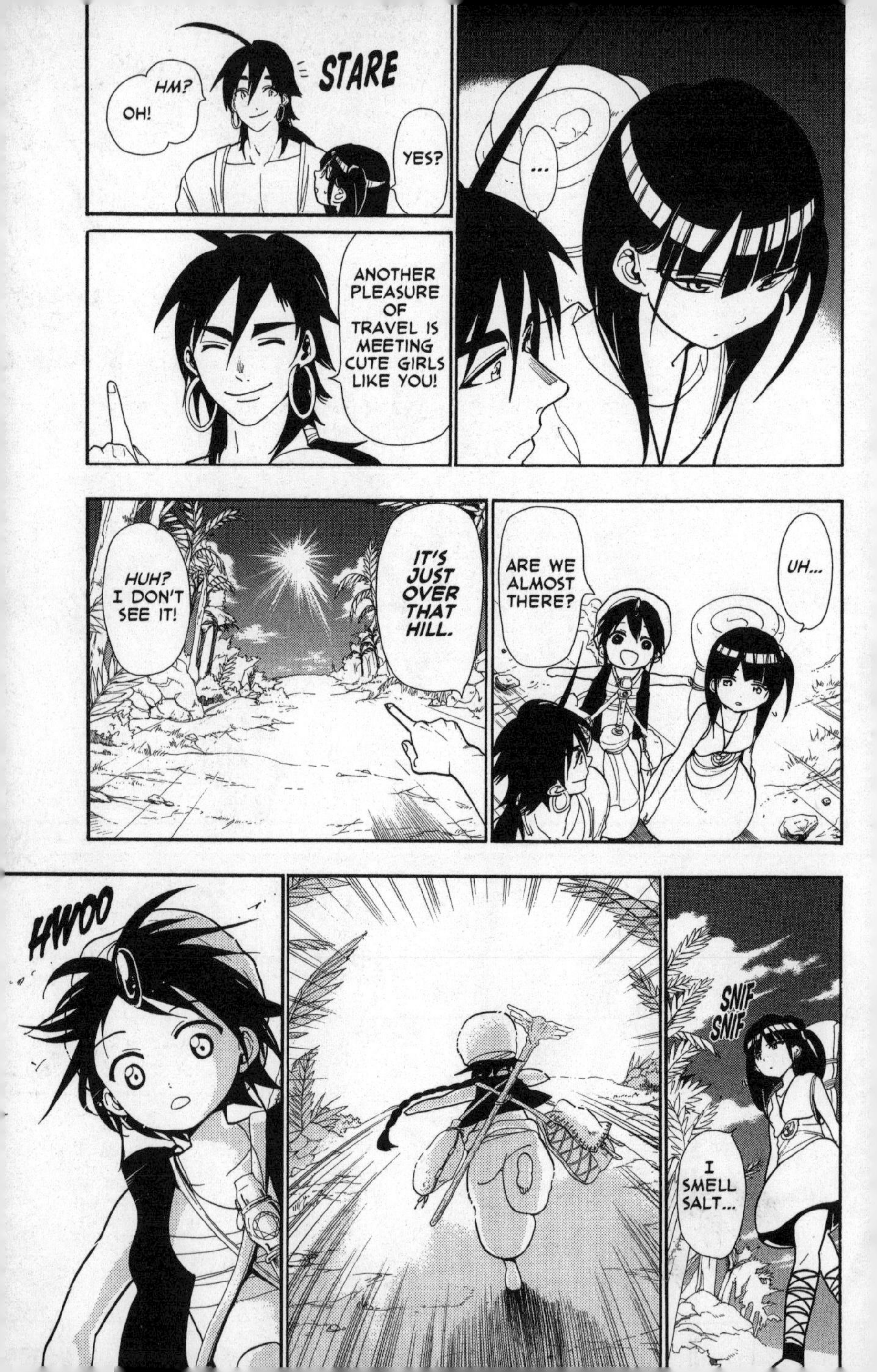
...
STARE
HM?
OH!
YES?
ANOTHER PLEASURE OF TRAVEL IS MEETING CUTE GIRLS LIKE YOU!
UH...
ARE WE ALMOST THERE?
IT'S JUST OVER THAT HILL.
HUH? I DON'T SEE IT!
SNIF SNIF
I SMELL SALT...
HWOO

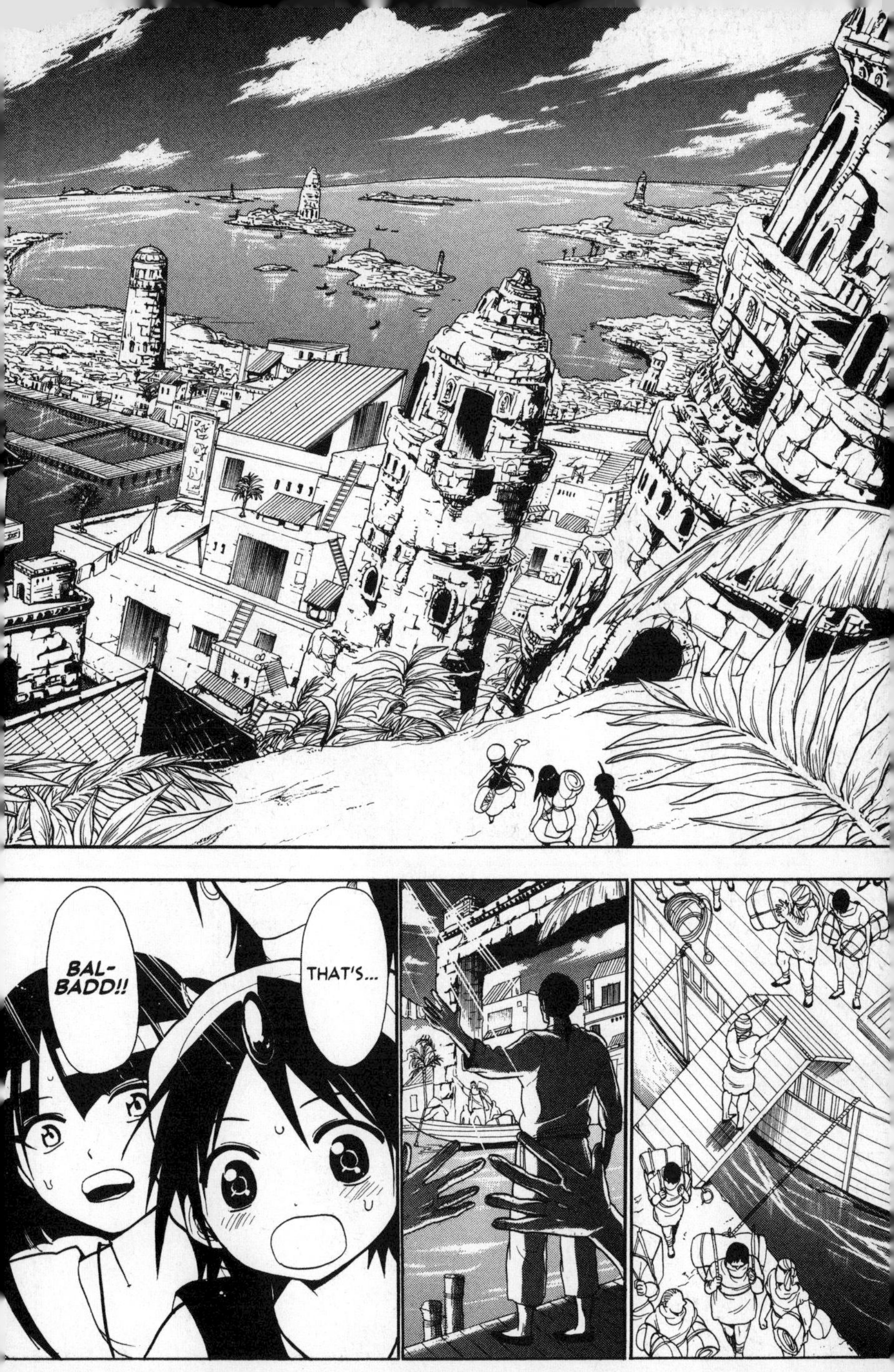
THAT'S...
BAL-
BADD!!

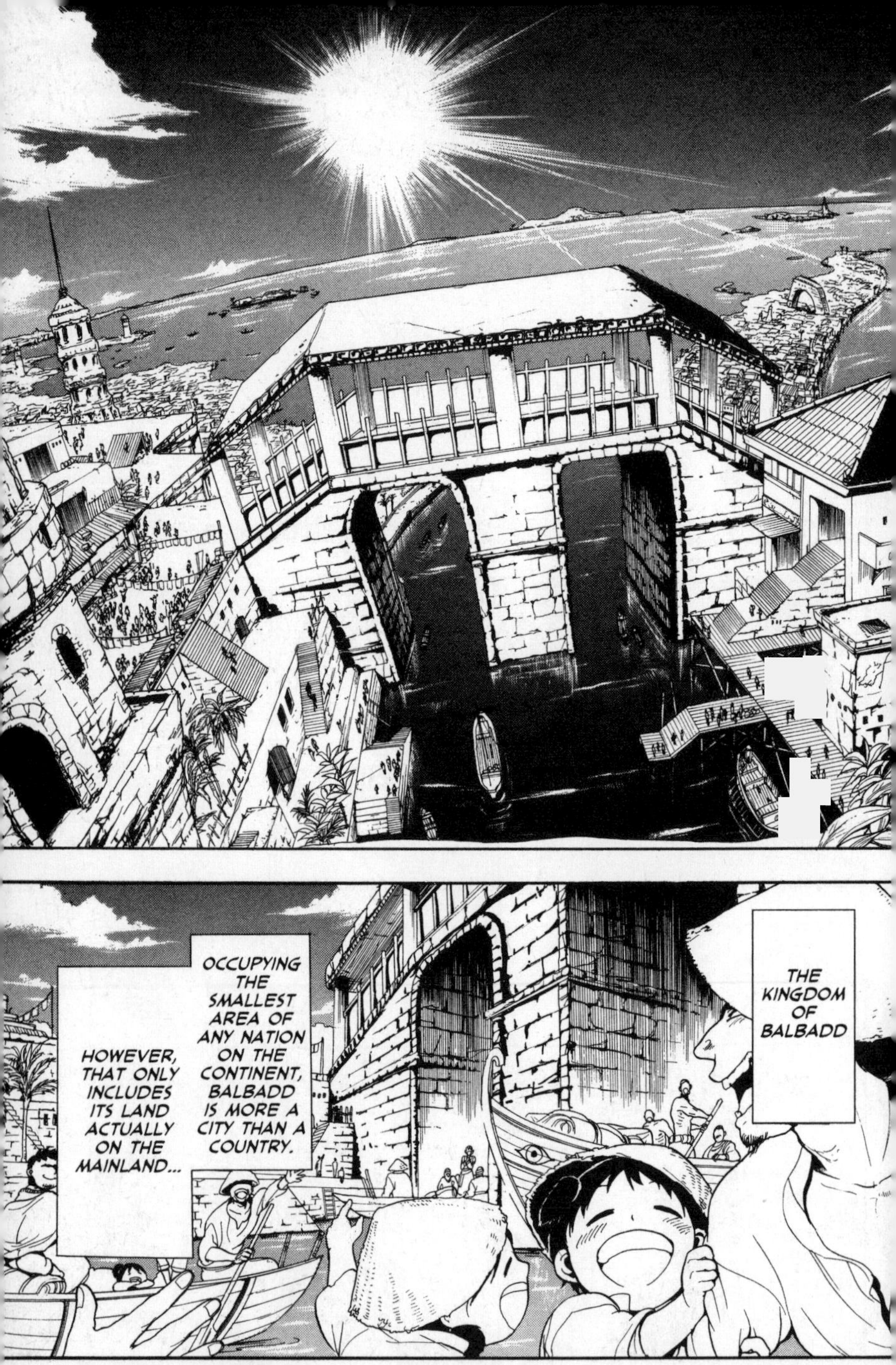
THE KINGDOM OF BALBADD
OCCUPYING THE SMALLEST AREA OF ANY NATION ON THE CONTINENT, BALBADD IS MORE A CITY THAN A COUNTRY.
HOWEVER, THAT ONLY INCLUDES ITS LAND ACTUALLY ON THE MAINLAND...

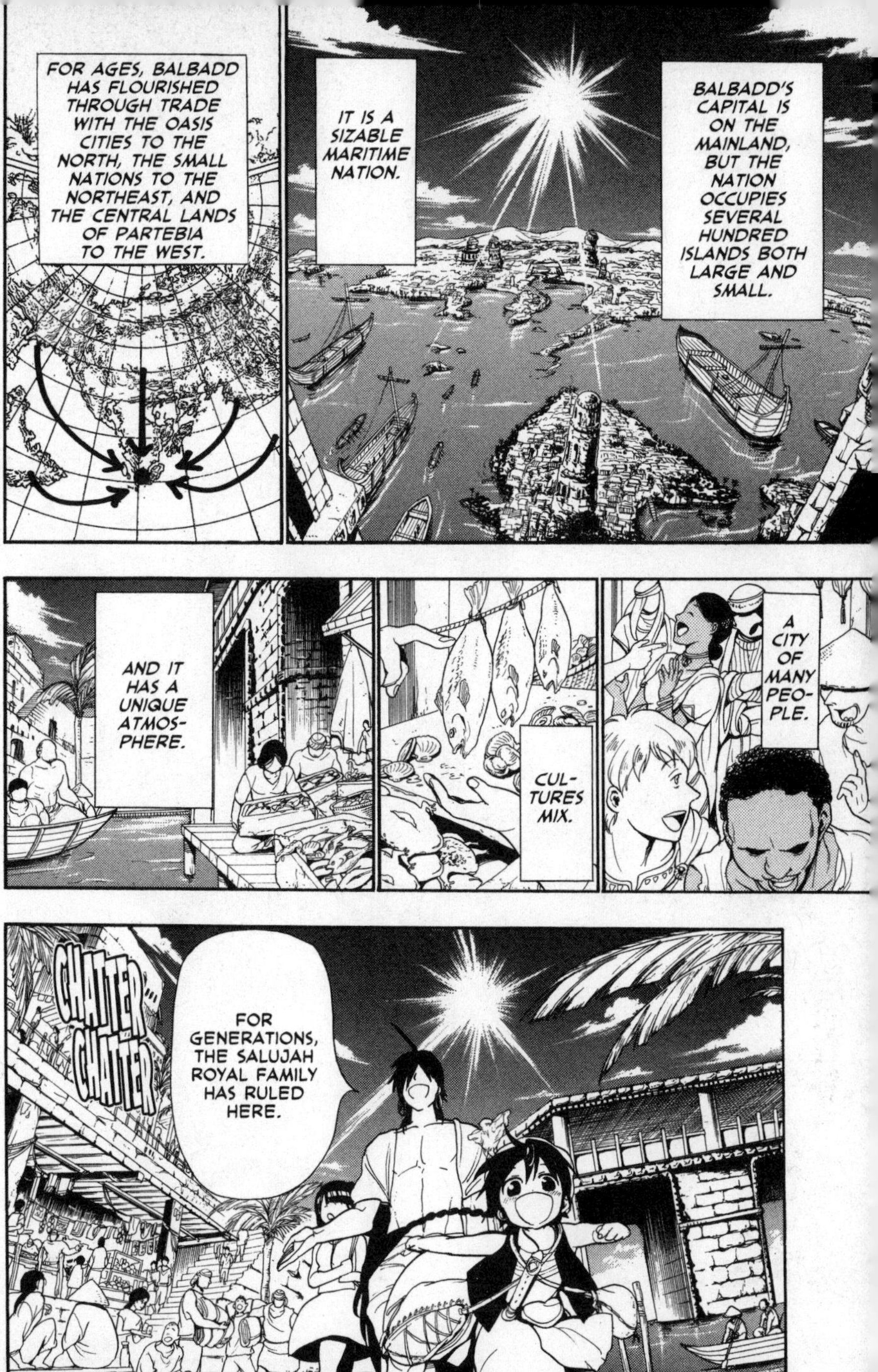
BALBADD'S CAPITAL IS ON THE MAINLAND, BUT THE NATION OCCUPIES SEVERAL HUNDRED ISLANDS BOTH LARGE AND SMALL.
IT IS A SIZABLE MARITIME NATION.
FOR AGES, BALBADD HAS FLOURISHED THROUGH TRADE WITH THE OASIS CITIES TO THE NORTH, THE SMALL NATIONS TO THE NORTHEAST, AND THE CENTRAL LANDS OF PARTEBIA TO THE WEST.
A CITY OF MANY PEO-PLE.
CUL-TURES MIX.
AND IT HAS A UNIQUE ATMOS-PHERE.
FOR GENERATIONS, THE SALUJAH ROYAL FAMILY HAS RULED HERE.
CHATTER CHATTER

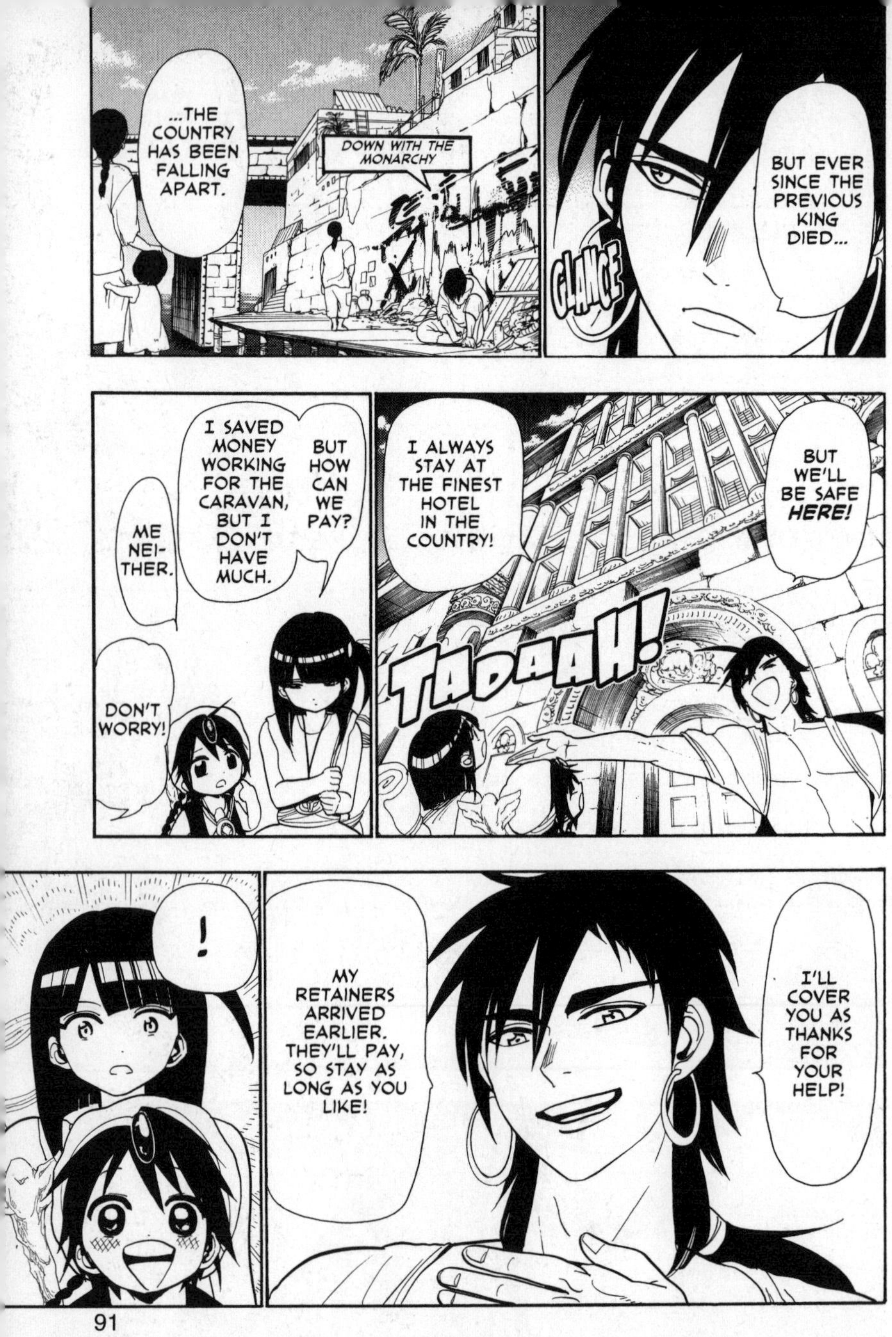
BUT EVER SINCE THE PREVIOUS KING DIED...
GLANCE
...THE COUNTRY HAS BEEN FALLING APART.
DOWN WITH THE MONARCHY
BUT WE'LL BE SAFE *HERE!*
I ALWAYS STAY AT THE FINEST HOTEL IN THE COUNTRY!
TADAAH!
BUT HOW CAN WE PAY?
I SAVED MONEY WORKING FOR THE CARAVAN, BUT I DON'T HAVE MUCH.
ME NEI-THER.
DON'T WORRY!
I'LL COVER YOU AS THANKS FOR YOUR HELP!
MY RETAINERS ARRIVED EARLIER. THEY'LL PAY, SO STAY AS LONG AS YOU LIKE!
!

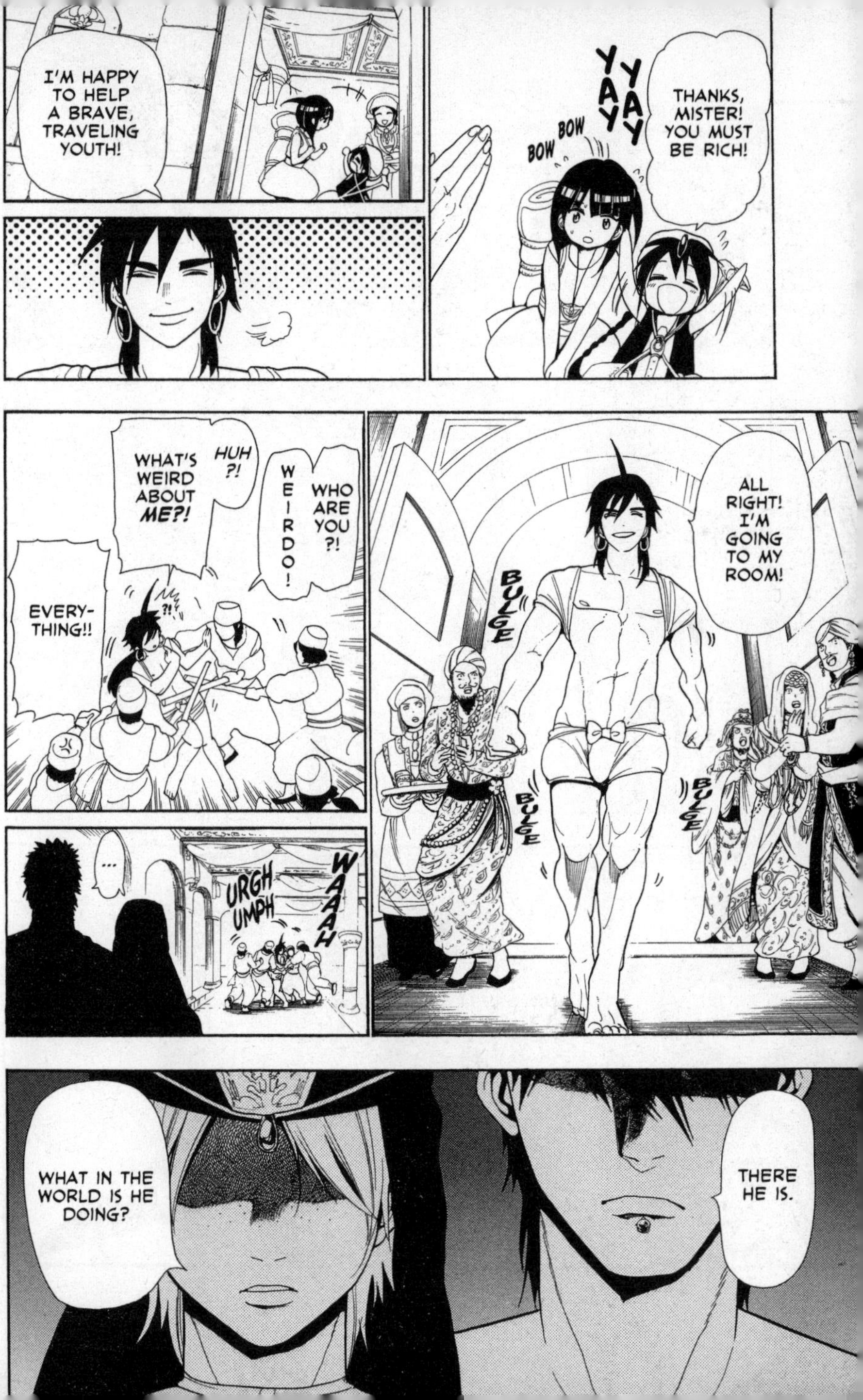
YAY YAY
BOW BOW
THANKS, MISTER! YOU MUST BE RICH!
I'M HAPPY TO HELP A BRAVE, TRAVELING YOUTH!
ALL RIGHT! I'M GOING TO MY ROOM!
BULGE
BULGE
BULGE
WHO ARE YOU?!
WEIRDO!
HUH?!
WHAT'S WEIRD ABOUT *ME?!*
EVERY-THING!!
...
WAAAH
URGH
UMPH
THERE HE IS.
WHAT IN THE WORLD IS HE DOING?

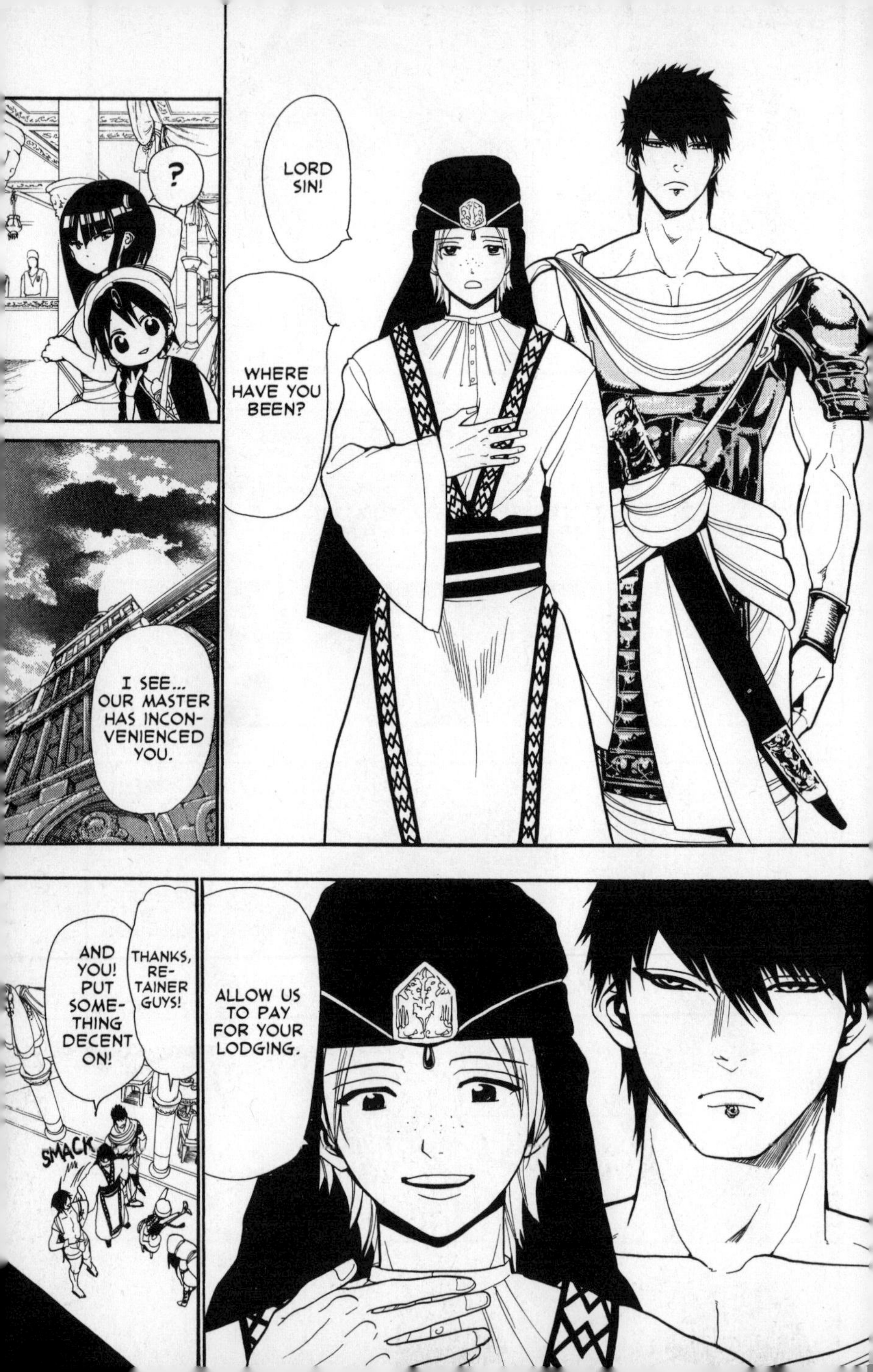
LORD SIN!
WHERE HAVE YOU BEEN?
?
I SEE... OUR MASTER HAS INCON-VENIENCED YOU.
ALLOW US TO PAY FOR YOUR LODGING.
THANKS, RE-TAINER GUYS!
AND YOU! PUT SOME-THING DECENT ON!
SMACK

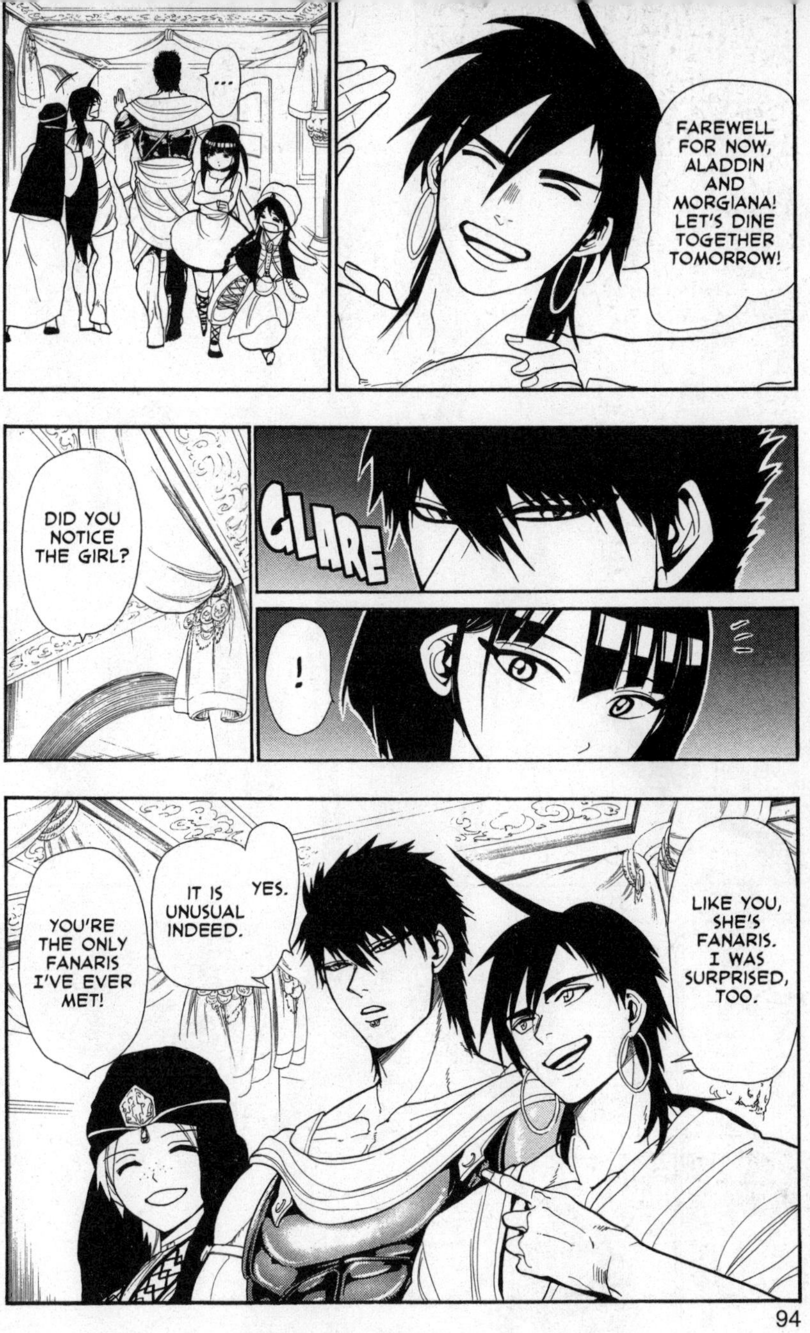
FAREWELL FOR NOW, ALADDIN AND MORGIANA! LET'S DINE TOGETHER TOMORROW!
...
GLARE
!
DID YOU NOTICE THE GIRL?
LIKE YOU, SHE'S FANARIS. I WAS SURPRISED, TOO.
YES.
IT IS UNUSUAL INDEED.
YOU'RE THE ONLY FANARIS I'VE EVER MET!

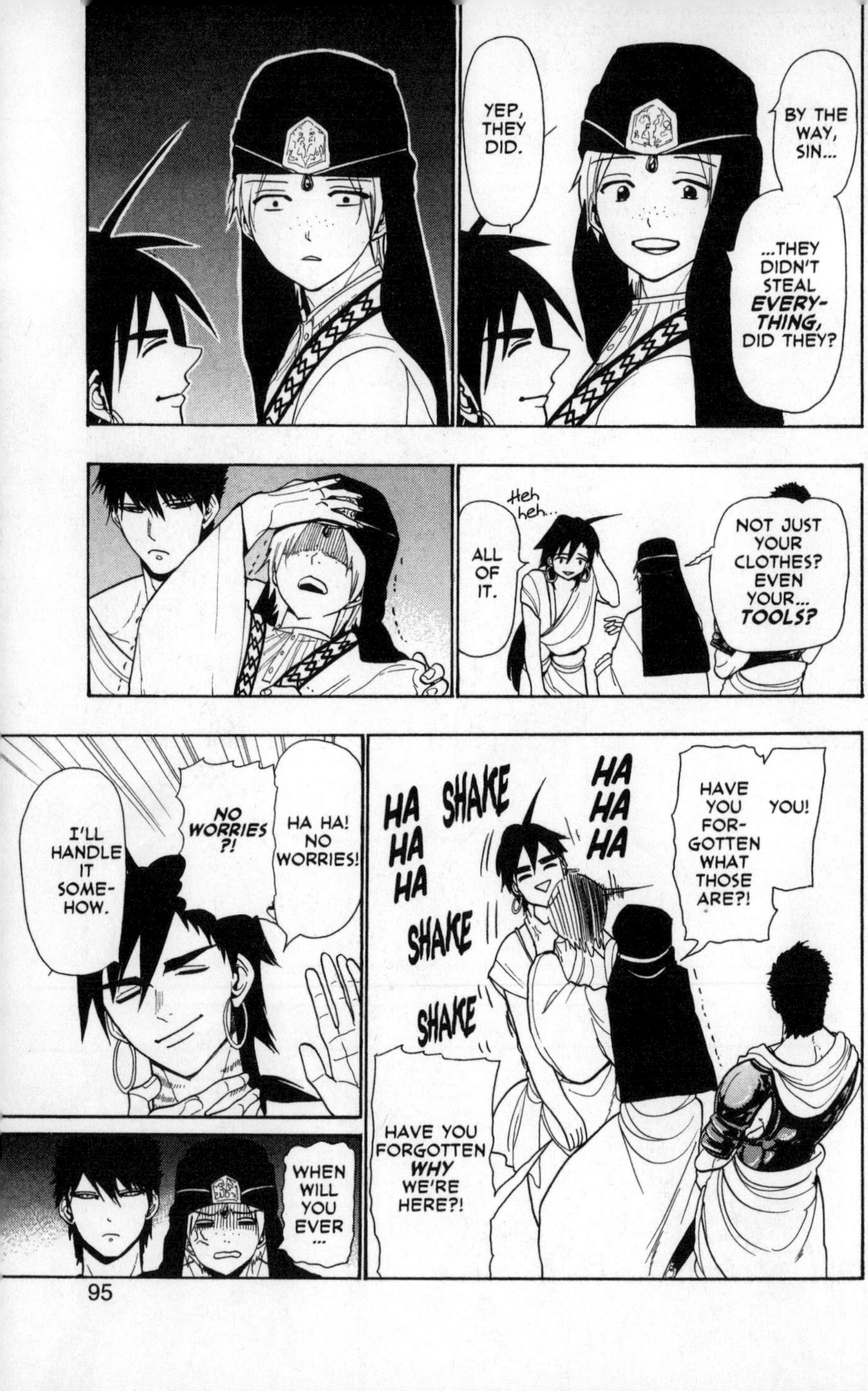
BY THE WAY, SIN...
...THEY DIDN'T STEAL *EVERYTHING*, DID THEY?
YEP, THEY DID.
NOT JUST YOUR CLOTHES? EVEN YOUR... *TOOLS?*
Heh heh...
ALL OF IT.
YOU!
HAVE YOU FORGOTTEN WHAT THOSE ARE?!
HA HA HA
SHAKE
HA HA HA
SHAKE
SHAKE
HAVE YOU FORGOTTEN *WHY* WE'RE HERE?!
HA HA! NO WORRIES!
NO WORRIES?!
I'LL HANDLE IT SOMEHOW.
WHEN WILL YOU EVER ...

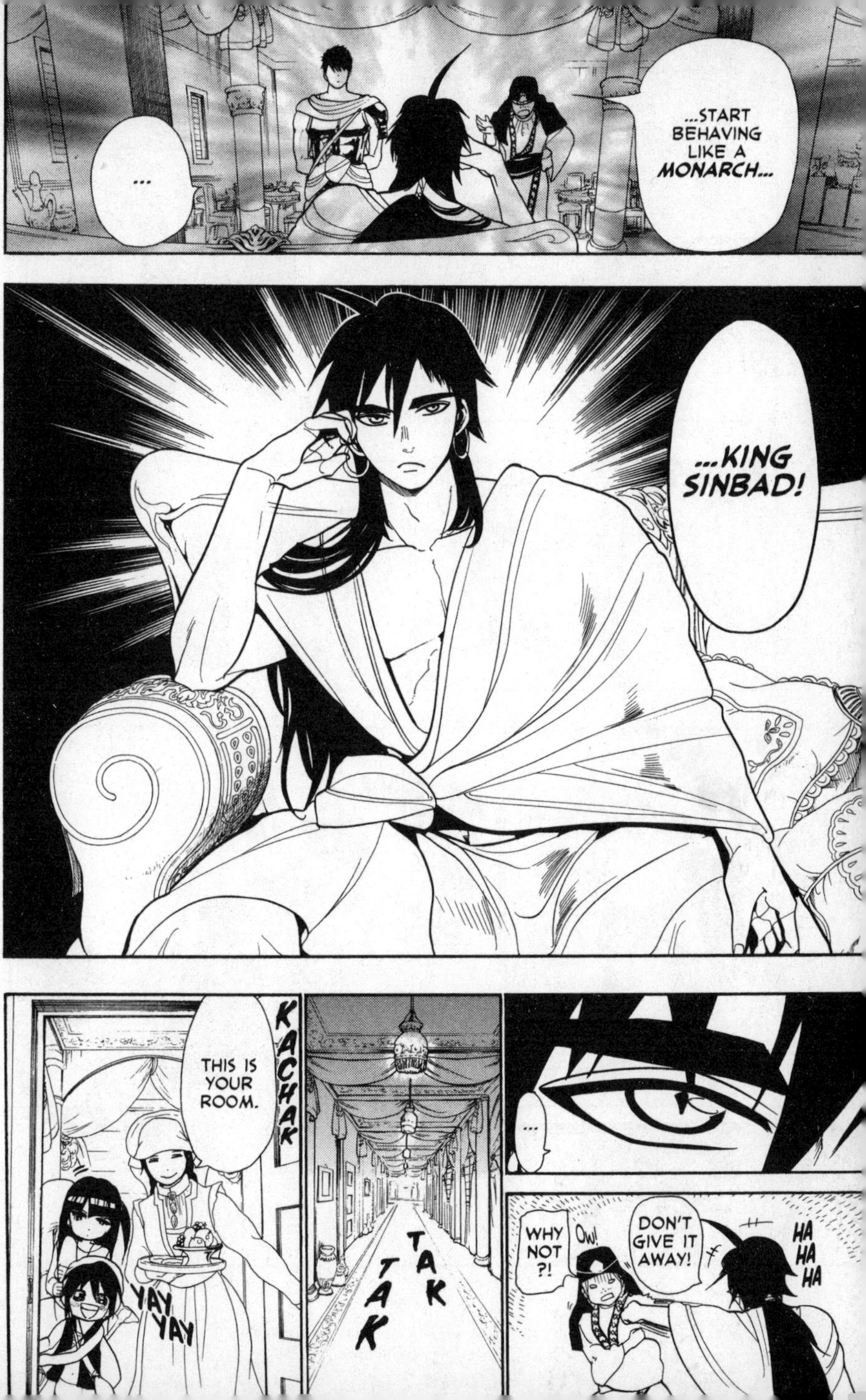
...START BEHAVING LIKE A MONARCH...
...
...KING SINBAD!
...
HA HA HA
DON'T GIVE IT AWAY!
OW!
WHY NOT ?!
TAK TAK TAK
KACHAK
THIS IS YOUR ROOM.
YAY YAY

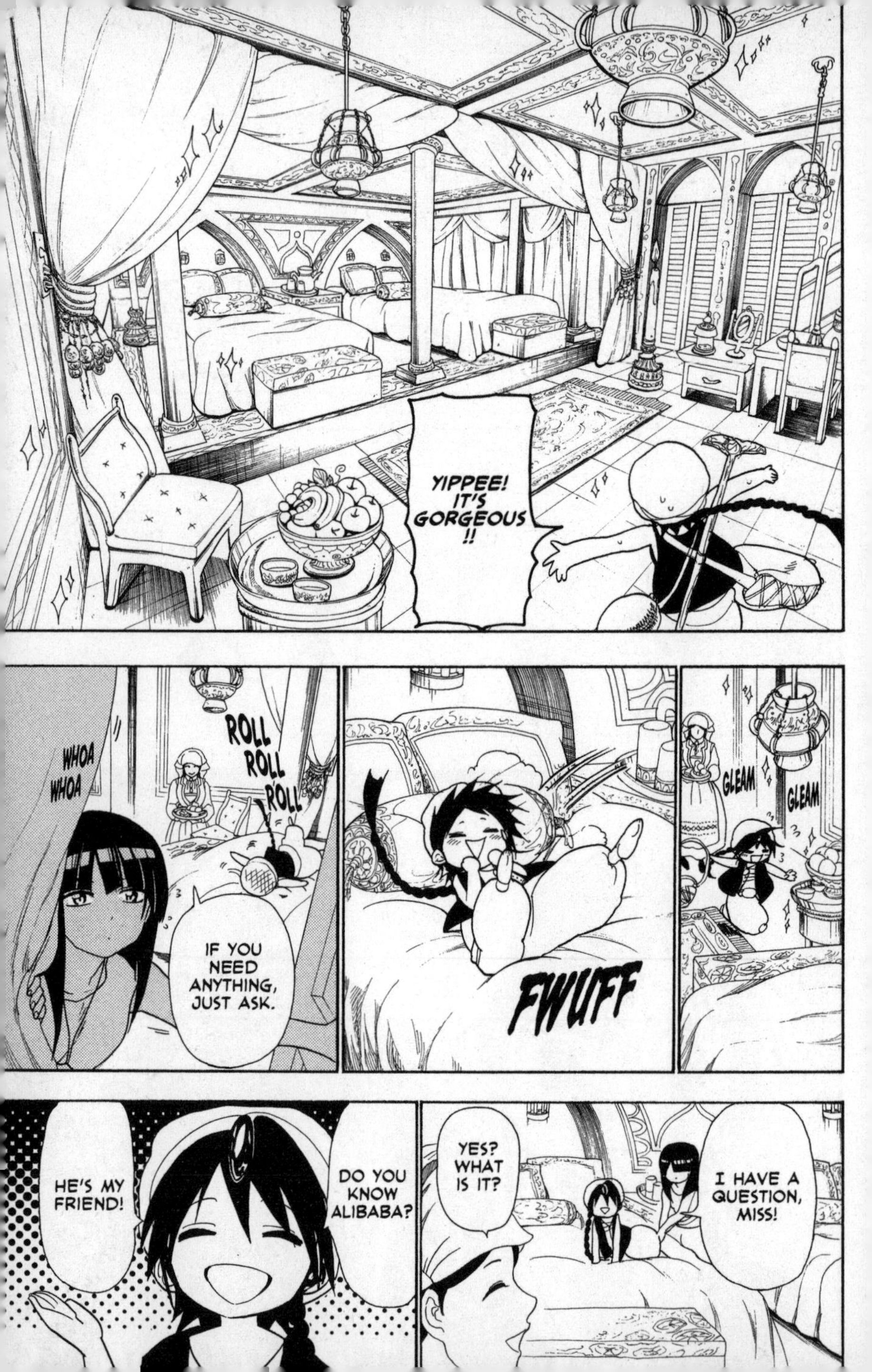
YIPPEE! IT'S GORGEOUS !!
GLEAM GLEAM
FWUFF
ROLL ROLL ROLL
WHOA WHOA
IF YOU NEED ANYTHING, JUST ASK.
I HAVE A QUESTION, MISS!
YES? WHAT IS IT?
DO YOU KNOW ALIBABA?
HE'S MY FRIEND!

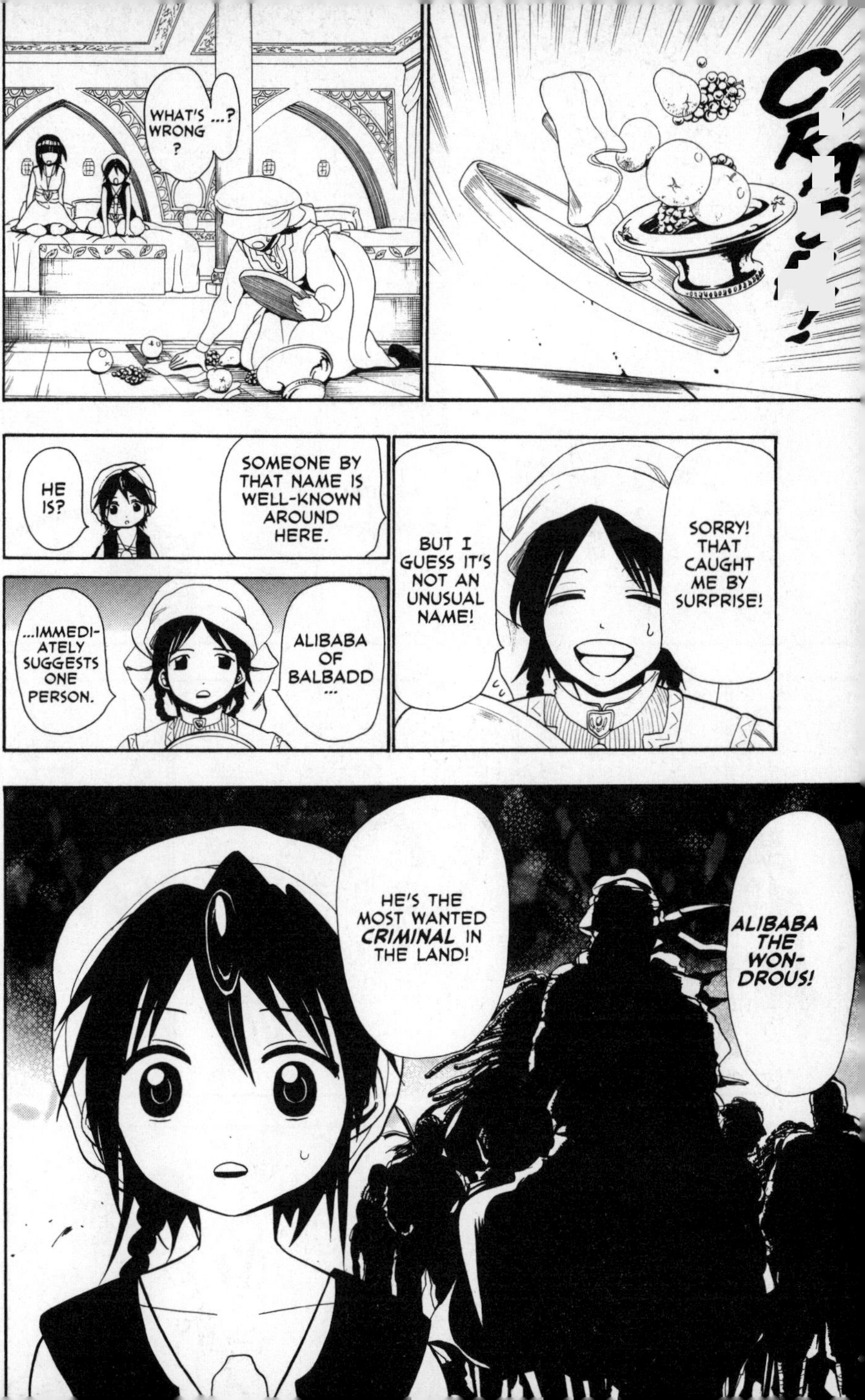
WHAT'S ...? WRONG ?
SORRY! THAT CAUGHT ME BY SURPRISE!
BUT I GUESS IT'S NOT AN UNUSUAL NAME!
SOMEONE BY THAT NAME IS WELL-KNOWN AROUND HERE.
HE IS?
ALIBABA OF BALBADD ...
...IMMEDI-ATELY SUGGESTS ONE PERSON.
ALIBABA THE WON-DROUS!
HE'S THE MOST WANTED CRIMINAL IN THE LAND!

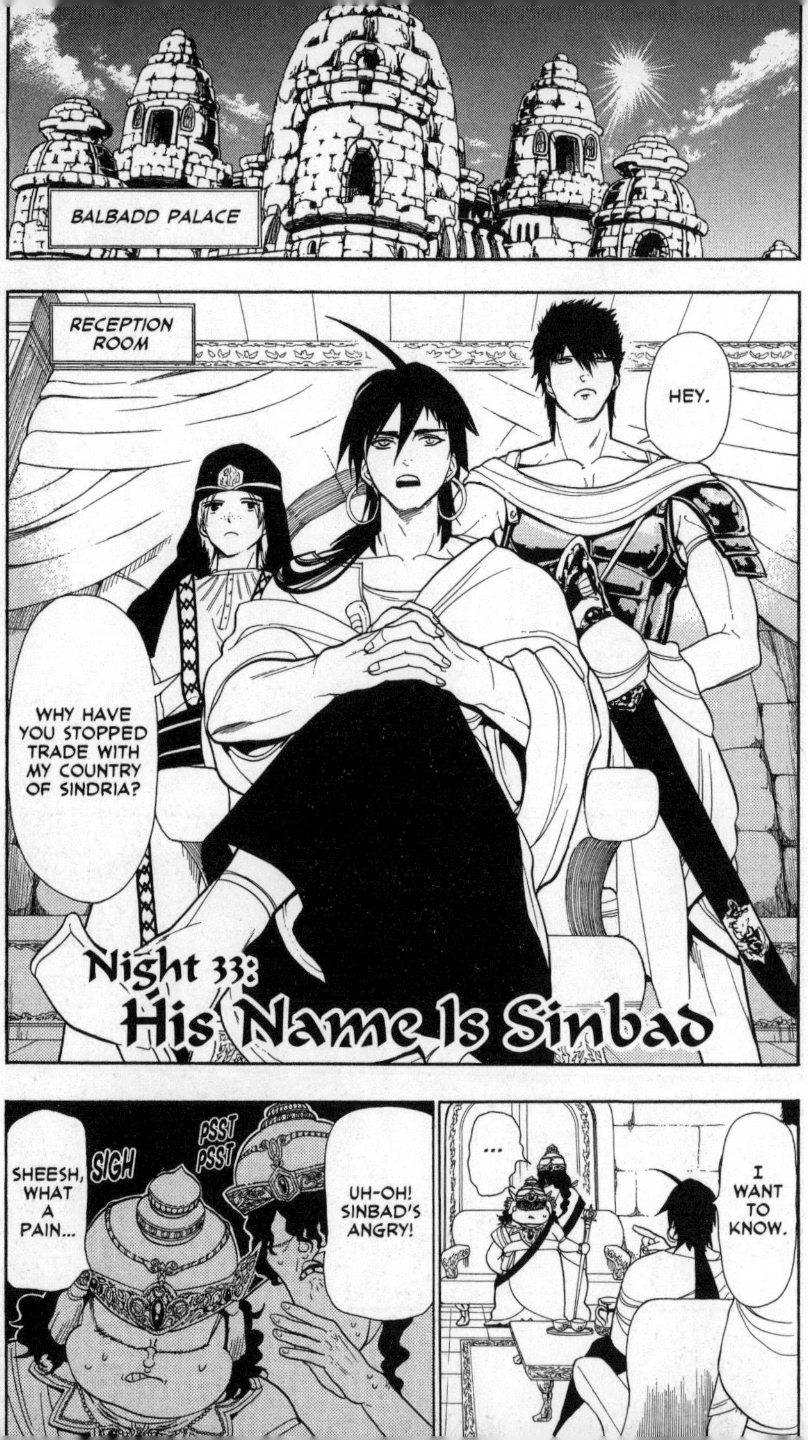
BALBADD PALACE
RECEPTION ROOM
HEY.
WHY HAVE YOU STOPPED TRADE WITH MY COUNTRY OF SINDRIA?
Night 33: His Name Is Sinbad
I WANT TO KNOW.
...
UH-OH! SINBAD'S ANGRY!
PSST PSST
SIGH
SHEESH, WHAT A PAIN...

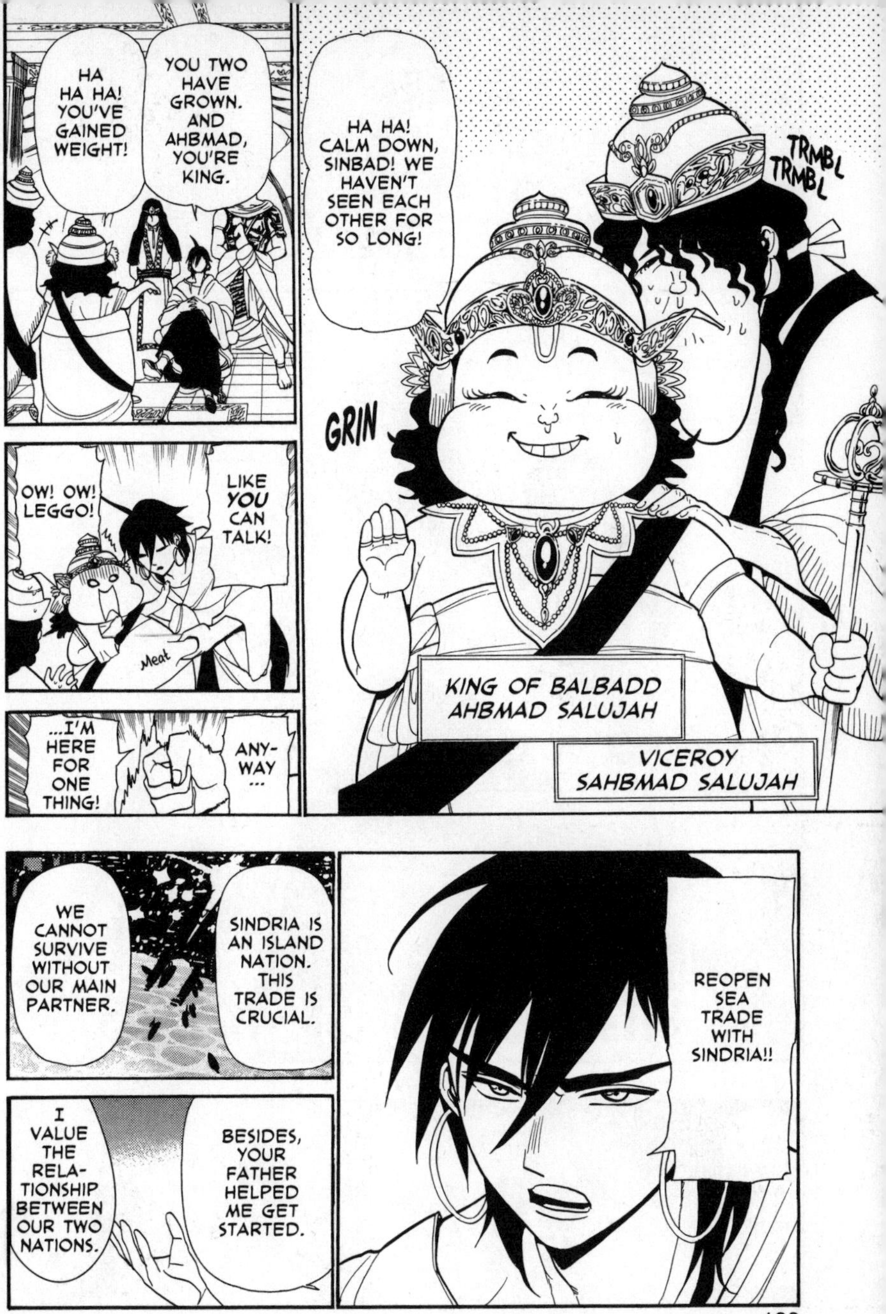
HA HA! CALM DOWN, SINBAD! WE HAVEN'T SEEN EACH OTHER FOR SO LONG!
TRMBL TRMBL
GRIN
KING OF BALBADD AHBMAD SALUJAH
VICEROY SAHBMAD SALUJAH
YOU TWO HAVE GROWN. AND AHBMAD, YOU'RE KING.
HA HA HA! YOU'VE GAINED WEIGHT!
LIKE YOU CAN TALK!
OW! OW! LEGGO!
Meat
ANY-WAY...
...I'M HERE FOR ONE THING!
REOPEN SEA TRADE WITH SINDRIA!!
SINDRIA IS AN ISLAND NATION. THIS TRADE IS CRUCIAL.
WE CANNOT SURVIVE WITHOUT OUR MAIN PARTNER.
BESIDES, YOUR FATHER HELPED ME GET STARTED.
I VALUE THE RELA-TIONSHIP BETWEEN OUR TWO NATIONS.

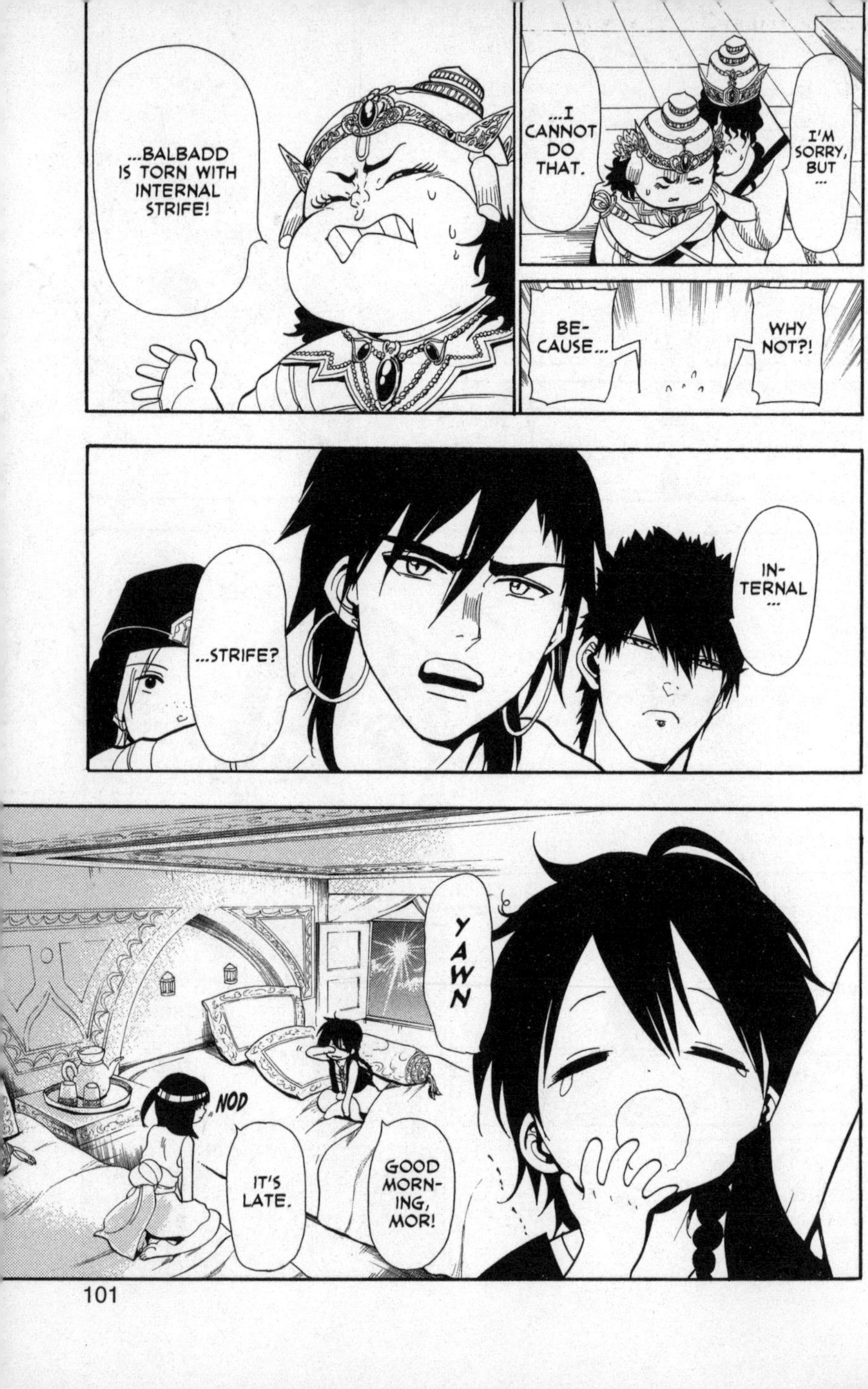
I'M SORRY, BUT ...
...I CANNOT DO THAT.
WHY NOT?!
BE-CAUSE...
...BALBADD IS TORN WITH INTERNAL STRIFE!
IN-TERNAL ...
...STRIFE?
YAWN
GOOD MORN-ING, MOR!
IT'S LATE.
NOD

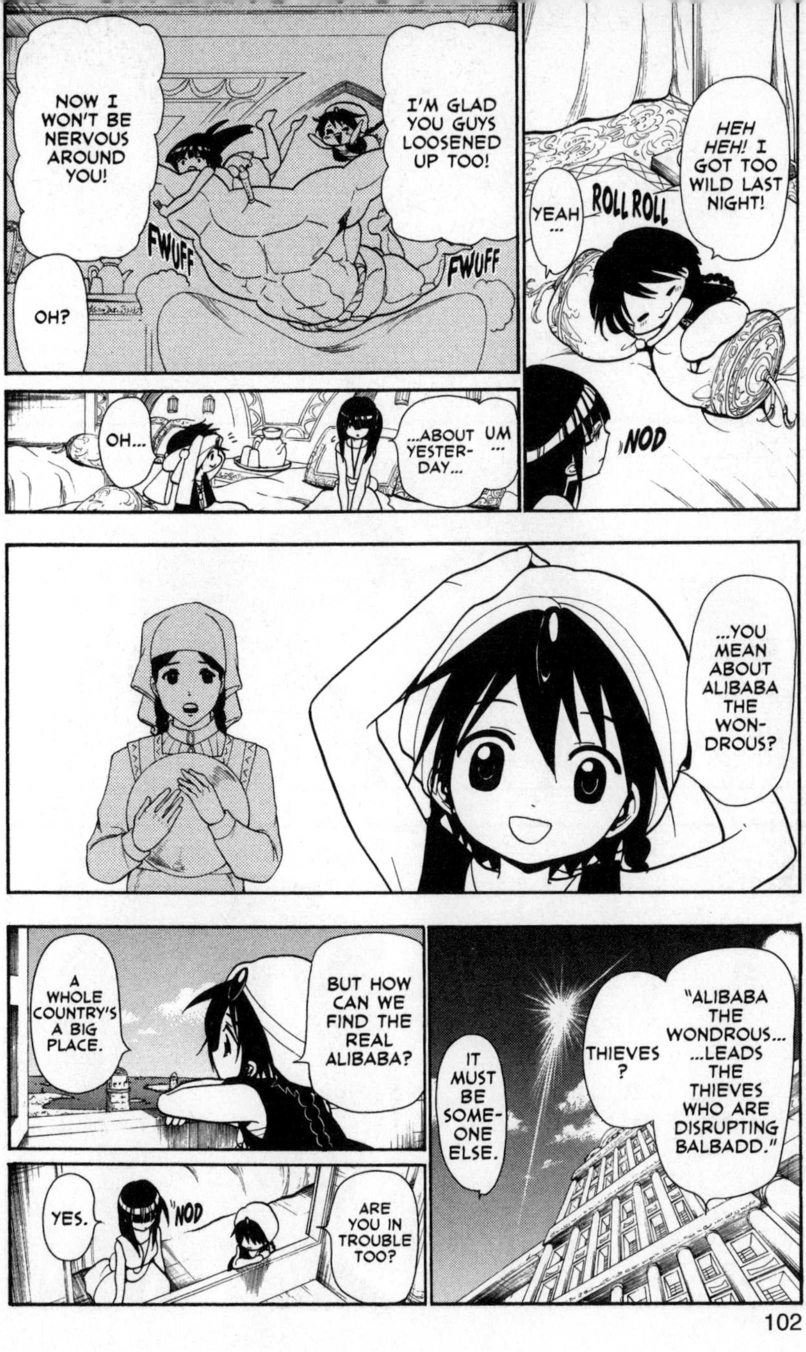
HEH HEH! I GOT TOO WILD LAST NIGHT!
ROLL ROLL
YEAH...
NOD
I'M GLAD YOU GUYS LOOSENED UP TOO!
NOW I WON'T BE NERVOUS AROUND YOU!
FWUFF
FWUFF
OH?
UM...
...ABOUT YESTERDAY...
OH...
...YOU MEAN ABOUT ALIBABA THE WONDROUS?
"ALIBABA THE WONDROUS... ...LEADS THE THIEVES WHO ARE DISRUPTING BALBADD."
THIEVES?
IT MUST BE SOMEONE ELSE.
BUT HOW CAN WE FIND THE REAL ALIBABA?
A WHOLE COUNTRY'S A BIG PLACE.
ARE YOU IN TROUBLE TOO?
NOD
YES.

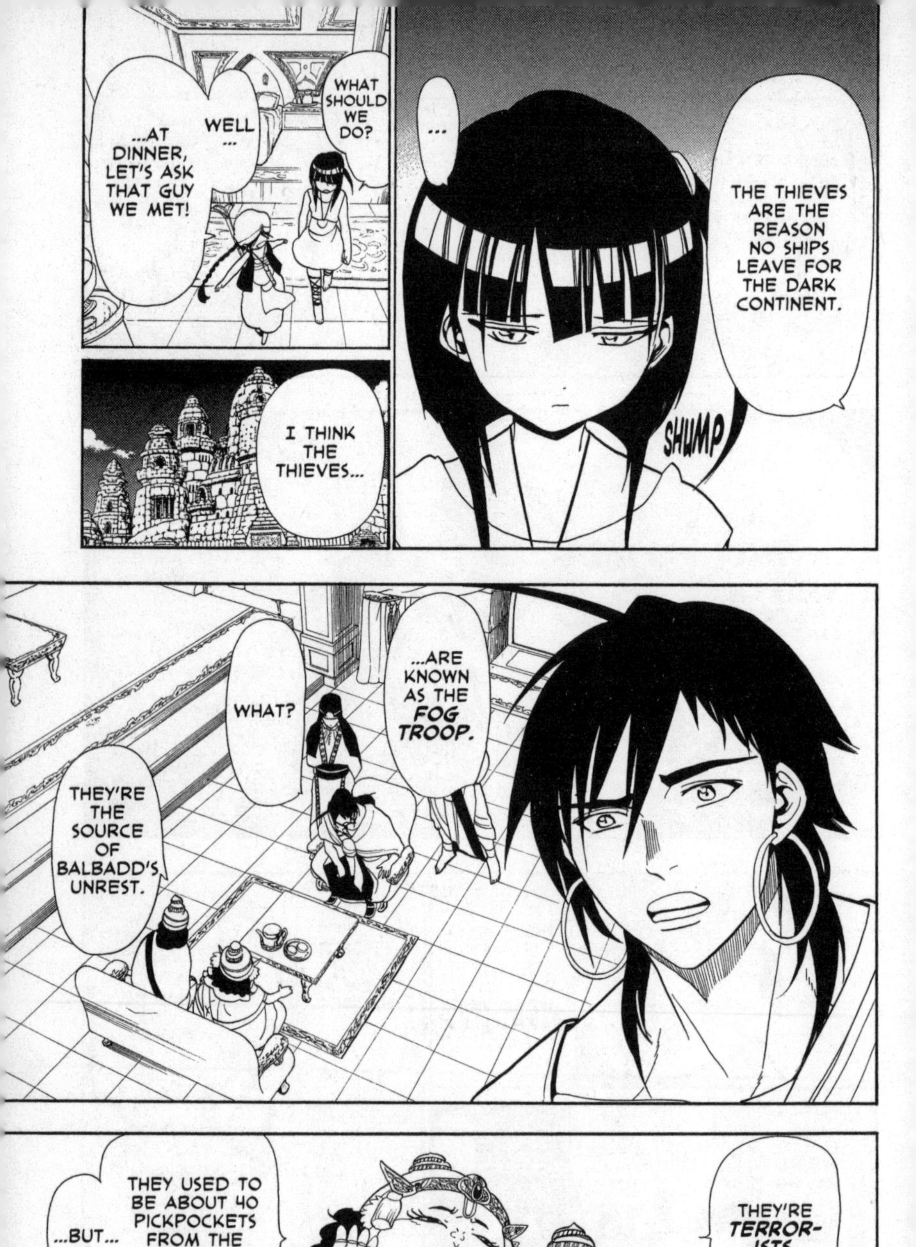

...
THE THIEVES ARE THE REASON NO SHIPS LEAVE FOR THE DARK CONTINENT.
SHUMP
WHAT SHOULD WE DO?
WELL ...
...AT DINNER, LET'S ASK THAT GUY WE MET!
I THINK THE THIEVES...
...ARE KNOWN AS THE FOG TROOP.
WHAT?
THEY'RE THE SOURCE OF BALBADD'S UNREST.
THEY'RE TERRORISTS.
THEY USED TO BE ABOUT 40 PICKPOCKETS FROM THE SLUMS...
...BUT...

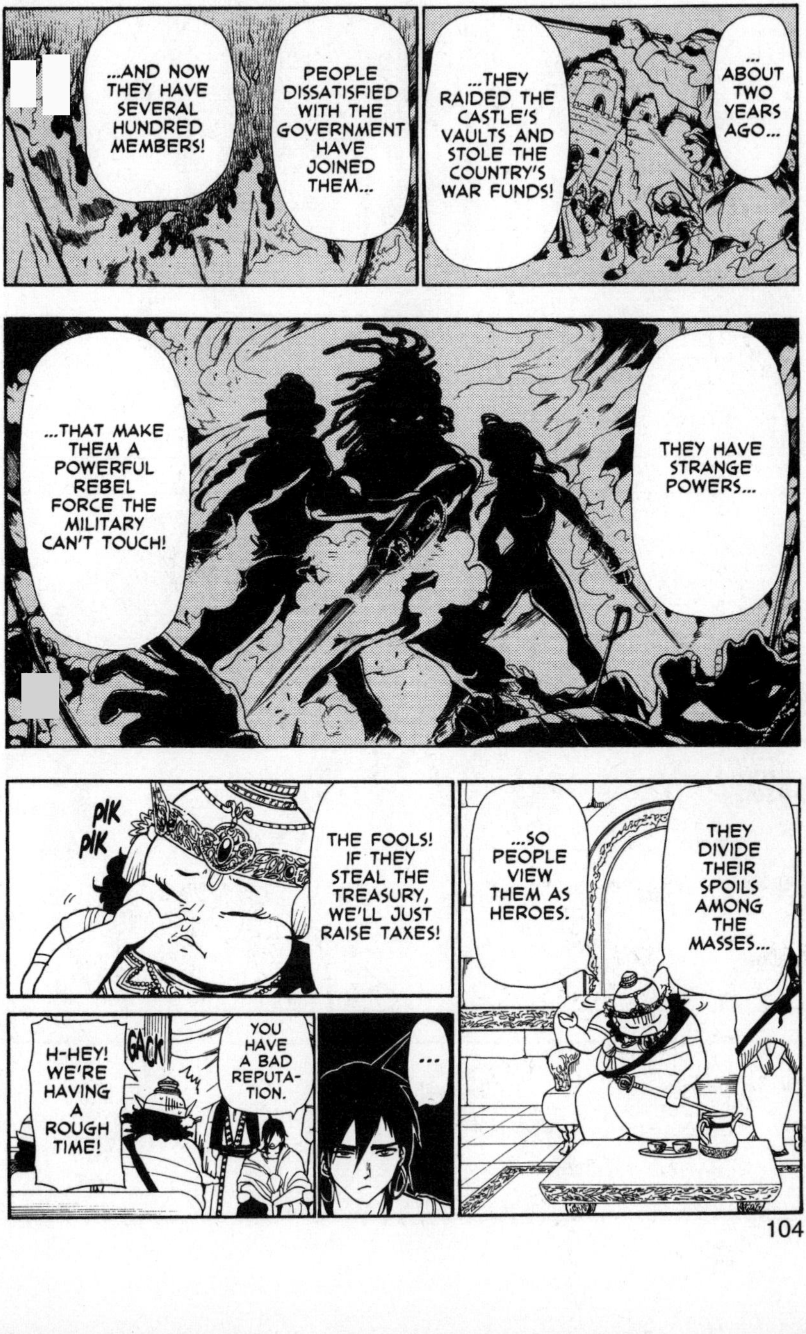
...ABOUT TWO YEARS AGO...
...THEY RAIDED THE CASTLE'S VAULTS AND STOLE THE COUNTRY'S WAR FUNDS!
PEOPLE DISSATISFIED WITH THE GOVERNMENT HAVE JOINED THEM...
...AND NOW THEY HAVE SEVERAL HUNDRED MEMBERS!
THEY HAVE STRANGE POWERS...
...THAT MAKE THEM A POWERFUL REBEL FORCE THE MILITARY CAN'T TOUCH!
THEY DIVIDE THEIR SPOILS AMONG THE MASSES...
...SO PEOPLE VIEW THEM AS HEROES.
THE FOOLS! IF THEY STEAL THE TREASURY, WE'LL JUST RAISE TAXES!
PIK PIK
...
YOU HAVE A BAD REPUTATION.
GACK
H-HEY! WE'RE HAVING A ROUGH TIME!

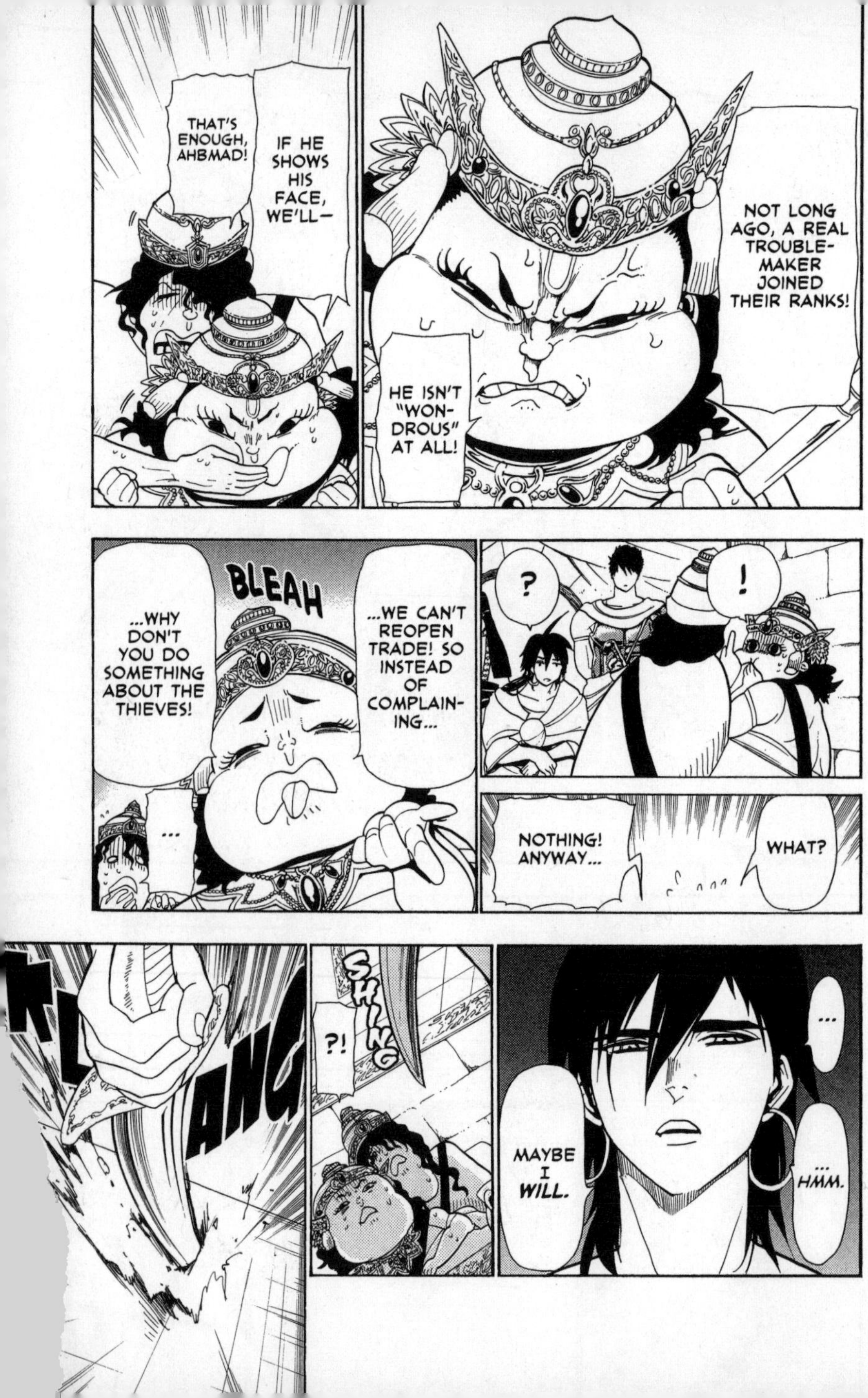
NOT LONG AGO, A REAL TROUBLE-MAKER JOINED THEIR RANKS!
HE ISN'T "WONDROUS" AT ALL!
IF HE SHOWS HIS FACE, WE'LL—
THAT'S ENOUGH, AHBMAD!
!
?
WHAT?
NOTHING! ANYWAY...
...WE CAN'T REOPEN TRADE! SO INSTEAD OF COMPLAIN-ING...
BLEAH
...WHY DON'T YOU DO SOMETHING ABOUT THE THIEVES!
...
...
... HMM.
MAYBE I WILL.
SHING
?!

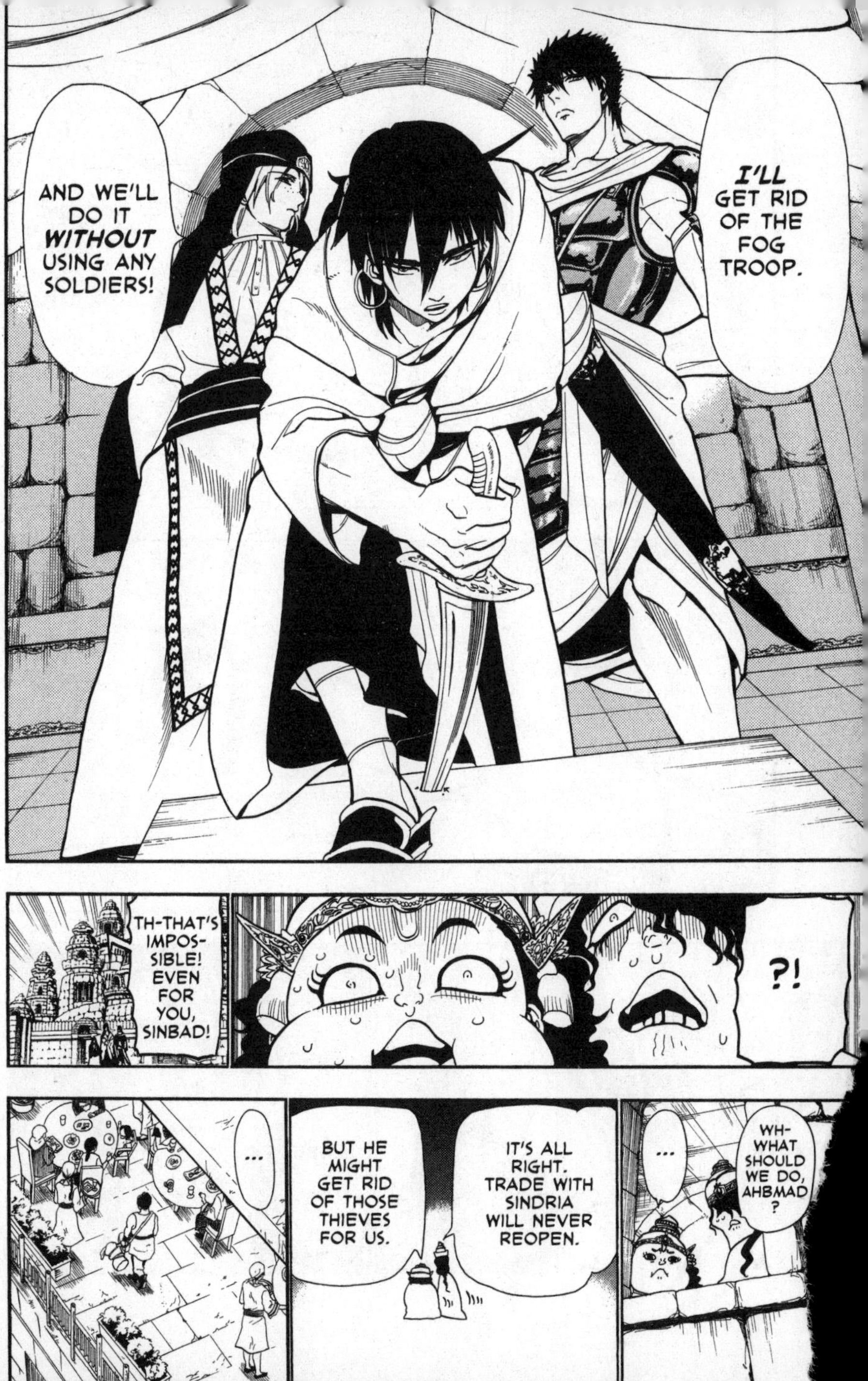
I'LL GET RID OF THE FOG TROOP.
AND WE'LL DO IT WITHOUT USING ANY SOLDIERS!
?!
TH-THAT'S IMPOSSIBLE! EVEN FOR YOU, SINBAD!
WH-WHAT SHOULD WE DO, AHBMAD?
...
IT'S ALL RIGHT. TRADE WITH SINDRIA WILL NEVER REOPEN.
BUT HE MIGHT GET RID OF THOSE THIEVES FOR US.
...

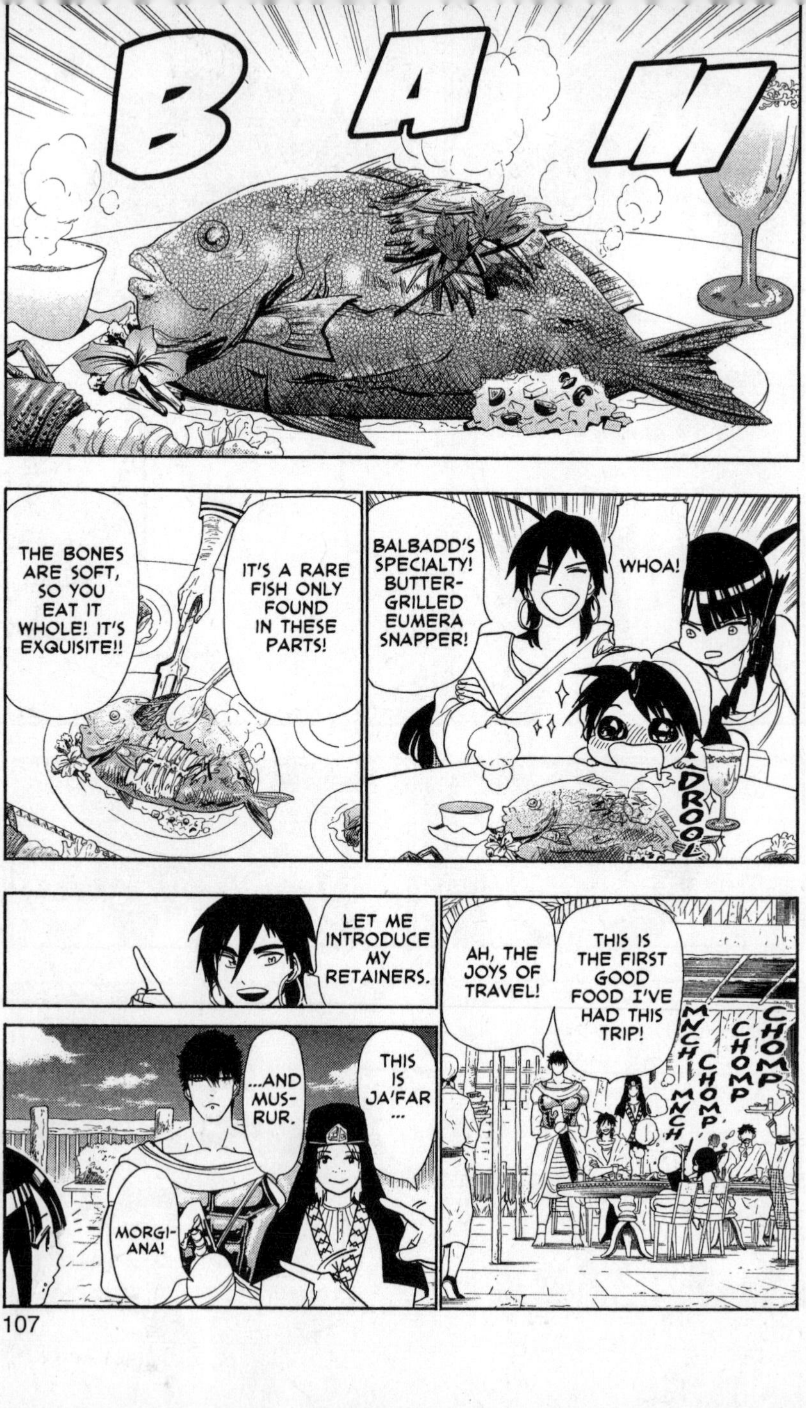
BAM
WHOA!
BALBADD'S SPECIALTY! BUTTER-GRILLED EUMERA SNAPPER!
DROOL
IT'S A RARE FISH ONLY FOUND IN THESE PARTS!
THE BONES ARE SOFT, SO YOU EAT IT WHOLE! IT'S EXQUISITE!!
THIS IS THE FIRST GOOD FOOD I'VE HAD THIS TRIP!
AH, THE JOYS OF TRAVEL!
CHOMP CHOMP
CHOMP, MNCH MNCH
LET ME INTRODUCE MY RETAINERS.
THIS IS JA'FAR...
...AND MUS-RUR.
MORGI-ANA!

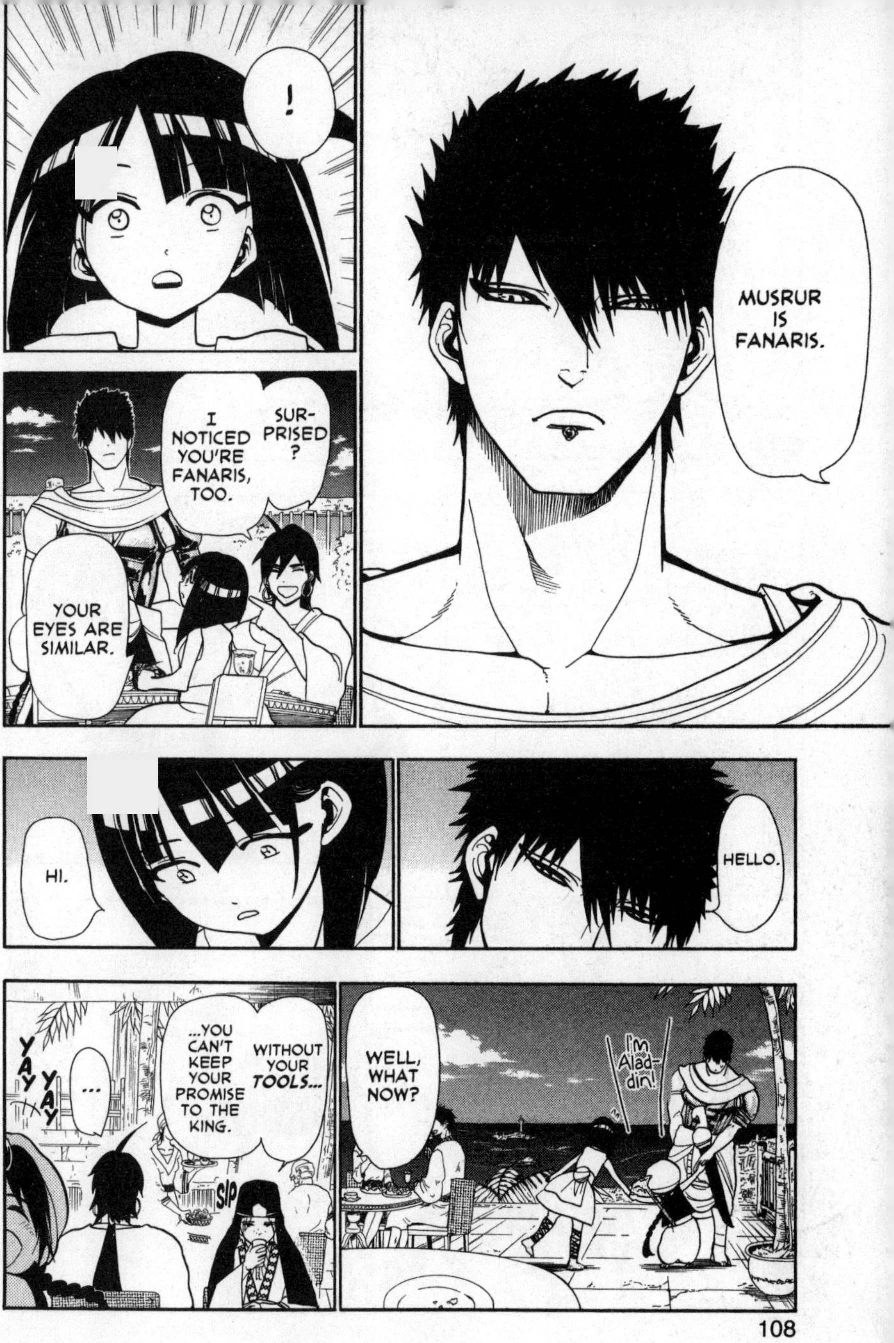
MUSRUR IS FANARIS.
!
SUR-PRISED?
I NOTICED YOU'RE FANARIS, TOO.
YOUR EYES ARE SIMILAR.
HELLO.
HI.
WELL, WHAT NOW?
I'm Aladdin!
WITHOUT YOUR TOOLS...
...YOU CAN'T KEEP YOUR PROMISE TO THE KING.
...
YAY YAY
SIP

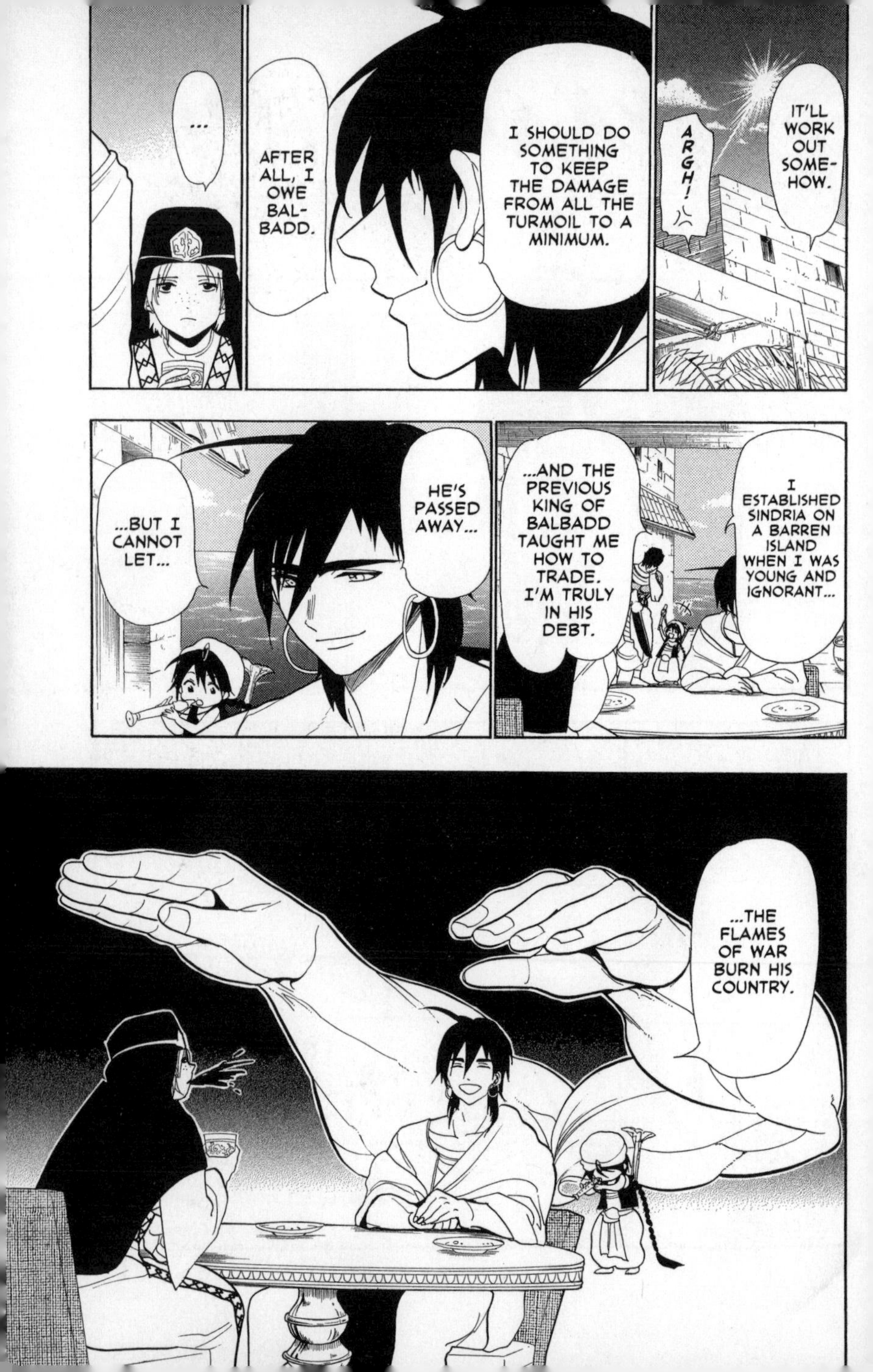
IT'LL WORK OUT SOMEHOW.
ARGH!
I SHOULD DO SOMETHING TO KEEP THE DAMAGE FROM ALL THE TURMOIL TO A MINIMUM.
AFTER ALL, I OWE BALBADD.
...
I ESTABLISHED SINDRIA ON A BARREN ISLAND WHEN I WAS YOUNG AND IGNORANT...
...AND THE PREVIOUS KING OF BALBADD TAUGHT ME HOW TO TRADE. I'M TRULY IN HIS DEBT.
HE'S PASSED AWAY...
...BUT I CANNOT LET...
...THE FLAMES OF WAR BURN HIS COUNTRY.

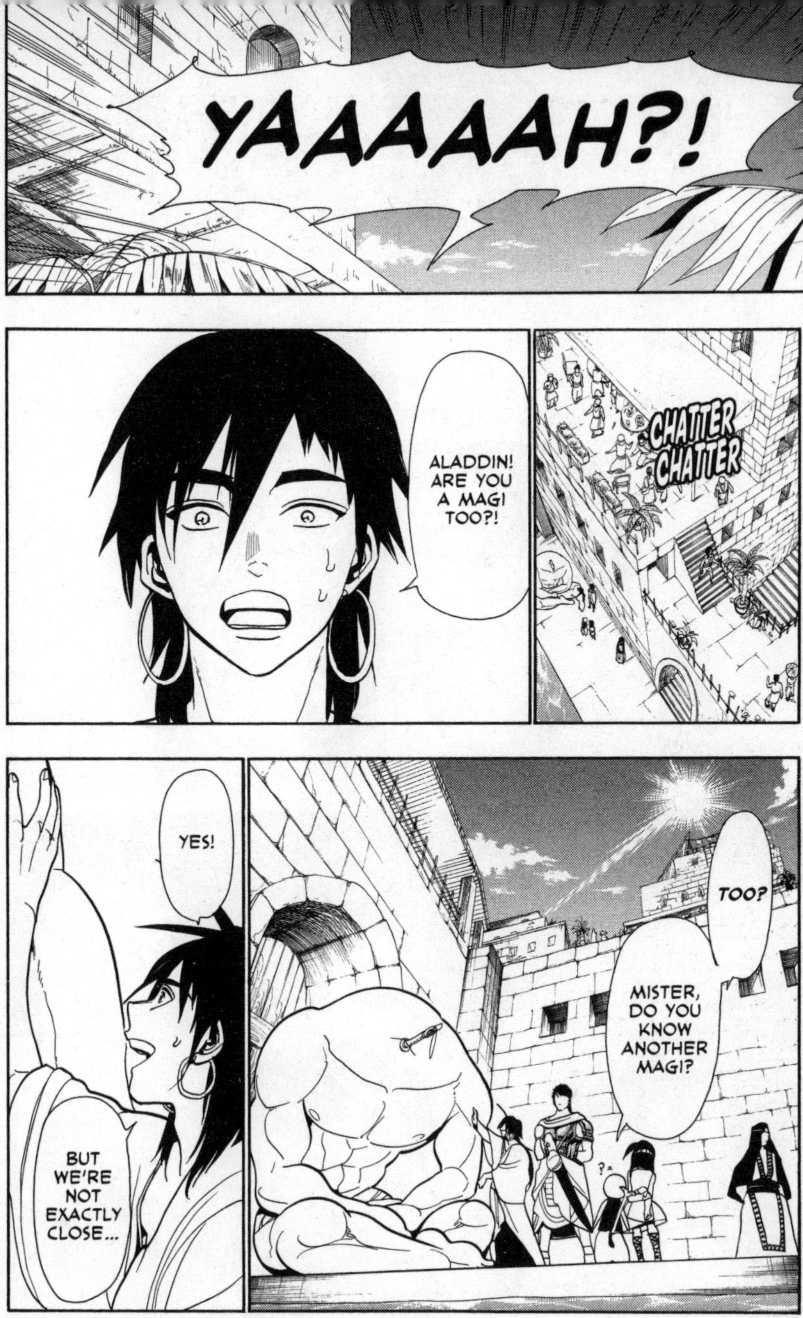
YAAAAAH?!
CHATTER CHATTER
ALADDIN! ARE YOU A MAGI TOO?!
TOO?
MISTER, DO YOU KNOW ANOTHER MAGI?
YES!
BUT WE'RE NOT EXACTLY CLOSE...

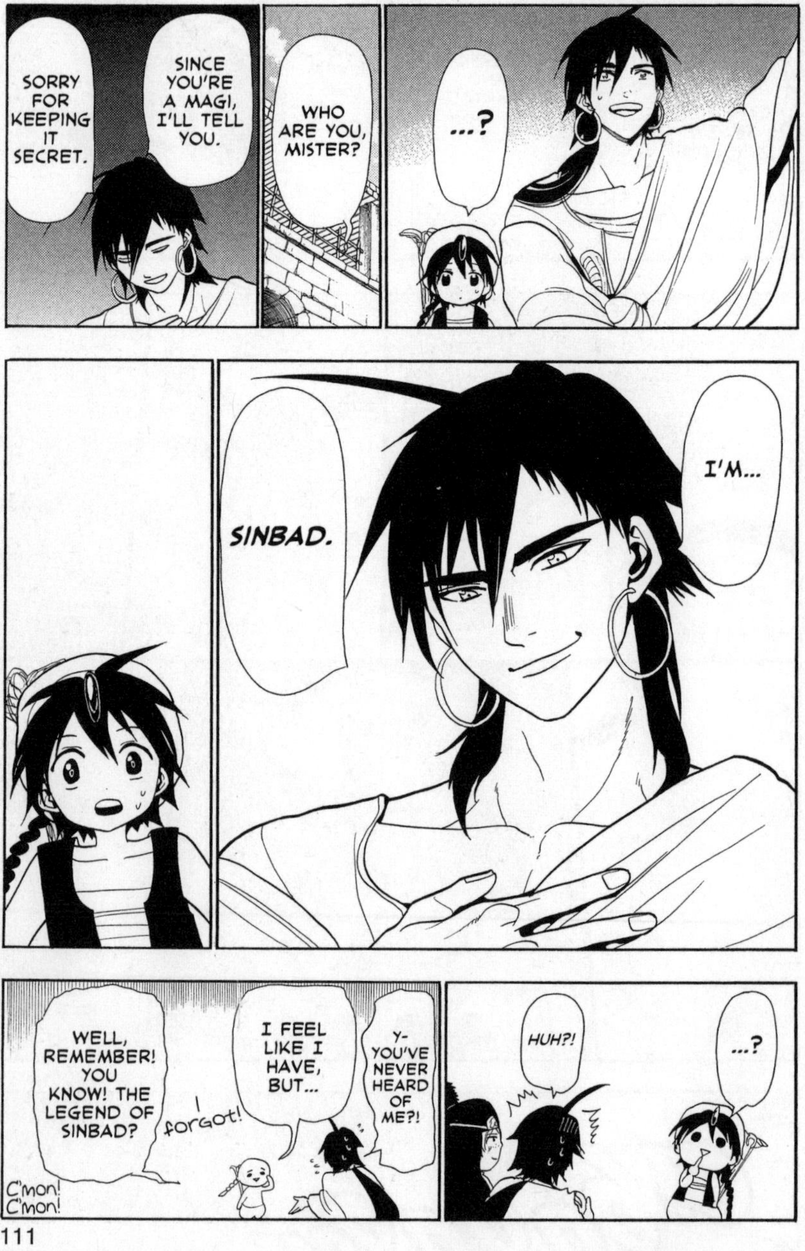
...?
WHO ARE YOU, MISTER?
SINCE YOU'RE A MAGI, I'LL TELL YOU.
SORRY FOR KEEPING IT SECRET.
I'M...
SINBAD.
...?
HUH?!
Y-YOU'VE NEVER HEARD OF ME?!
I FEEL LIKE I HAVE, BUT...
I forgot!
WELL, REMEMBER! YOU KNOW! THE LEGEND OF SINBAD?
C'mon! C'mon!

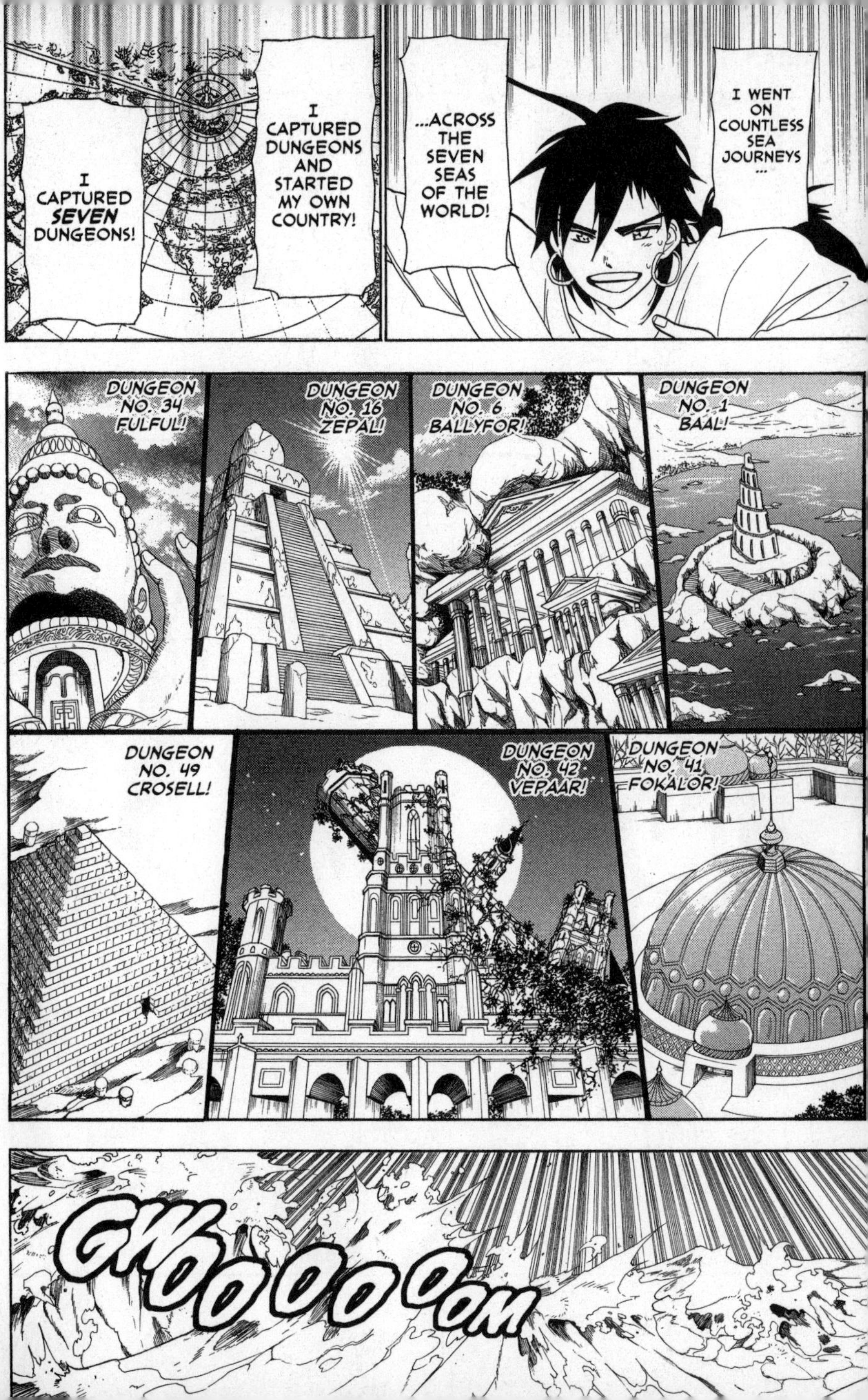
I WENT ON COUNTLESS SEA JOURNEYS...
...ACROSS THE SEVEN SEAS OF THE WORLD!
I CAPTURED DUNGEONS AND STARTED MY OWN COUNTRY!
I CAPTURED SEVEN DUNGEONS!
DUNGEON NO. 1 BAAL!
DUNGEON NO. 6 BALLYFOR!
DUNGEON NO. 16 ZEPAL!
DUNGEON NO. 34 FULFUL!
DUNGEON NO. 41 FOKALOR!
DUNGEON NO. 42 VEPAAR!
DUNGEON NO. 49 CROSELL!
GWOOOOOOOM

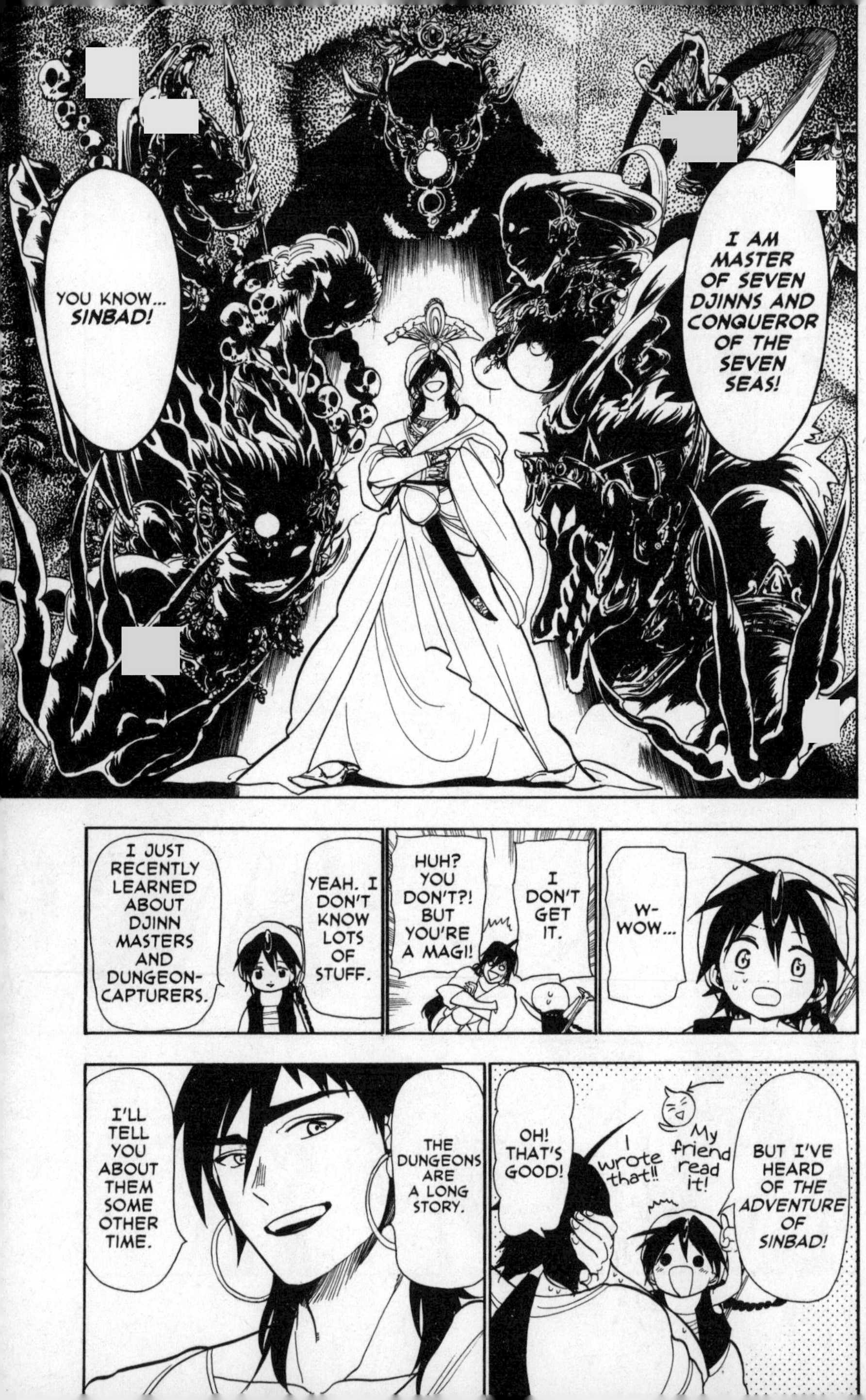
I AM MASTER OF SEVEN DJINNS AND CONQUEROR OF THE SEVEN SEAS!
YOU KNOW... SINBAD!
W-WOW...
I DON'T GET IT.
HUH? YOU DON'T?! BUT YOU'RE A MAGI!
YEAH. I DON'T KNOW LOTS OF STUFF.
I JUST RECENTLY LEARNED ABOUT DJINN MASTERS AND DUNGEON-CAPTURERS.
BUT I'VE HEARD OF THE ADVENTURE OF SINBAD!
My friend read it!
I wrote that!!
OH! THAT'S GOOD!
THE DUNGEONS ARE A LONG STORY.
I'LL TELL YOU ABOUT THEM SOME OTHER TIME.

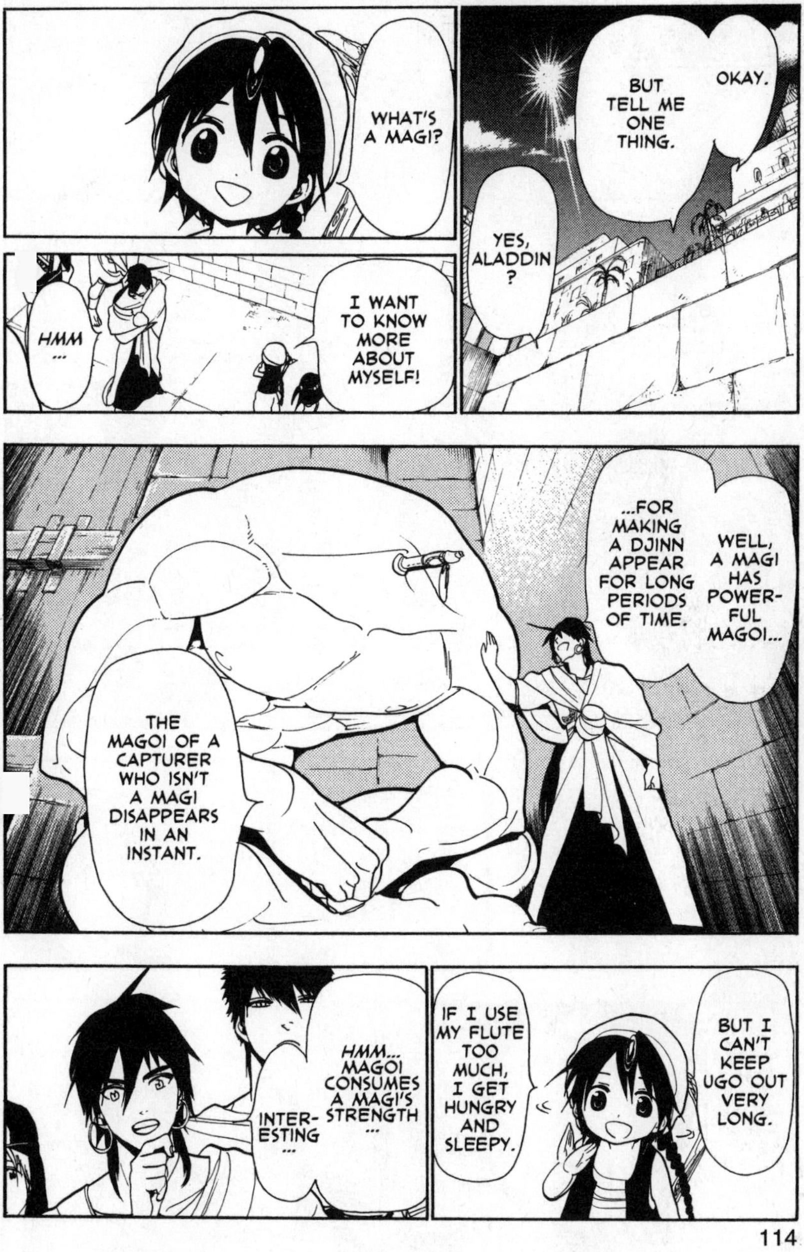
OKAY.
BUT TELL ME ONE THING.
YES, ALADDIN?
WHAT'S A MAGI?
I WANT TO KNOW MORE ABOUT MYSELF!
HMM...
WELL, A MAGI HAS POWERFUL MAGOI...
...FOR MAKING A DJINN APPEAR FOR LONG PERIODS OF TIME.
THE MAGOI OF A CAPTURER WHO ISN'T A MAGI DISAPPEARS IN AN INSTANT.
BUT I CAN'T KEEP UGO OUT VERY LONG.
IF I USE MY FLUTE TOO MUCH, I GET HUNGRY AND SLEEPY.
HMM... MAGOI CONSUMES A MAGI'S STRENGTH...
INTERESTING...

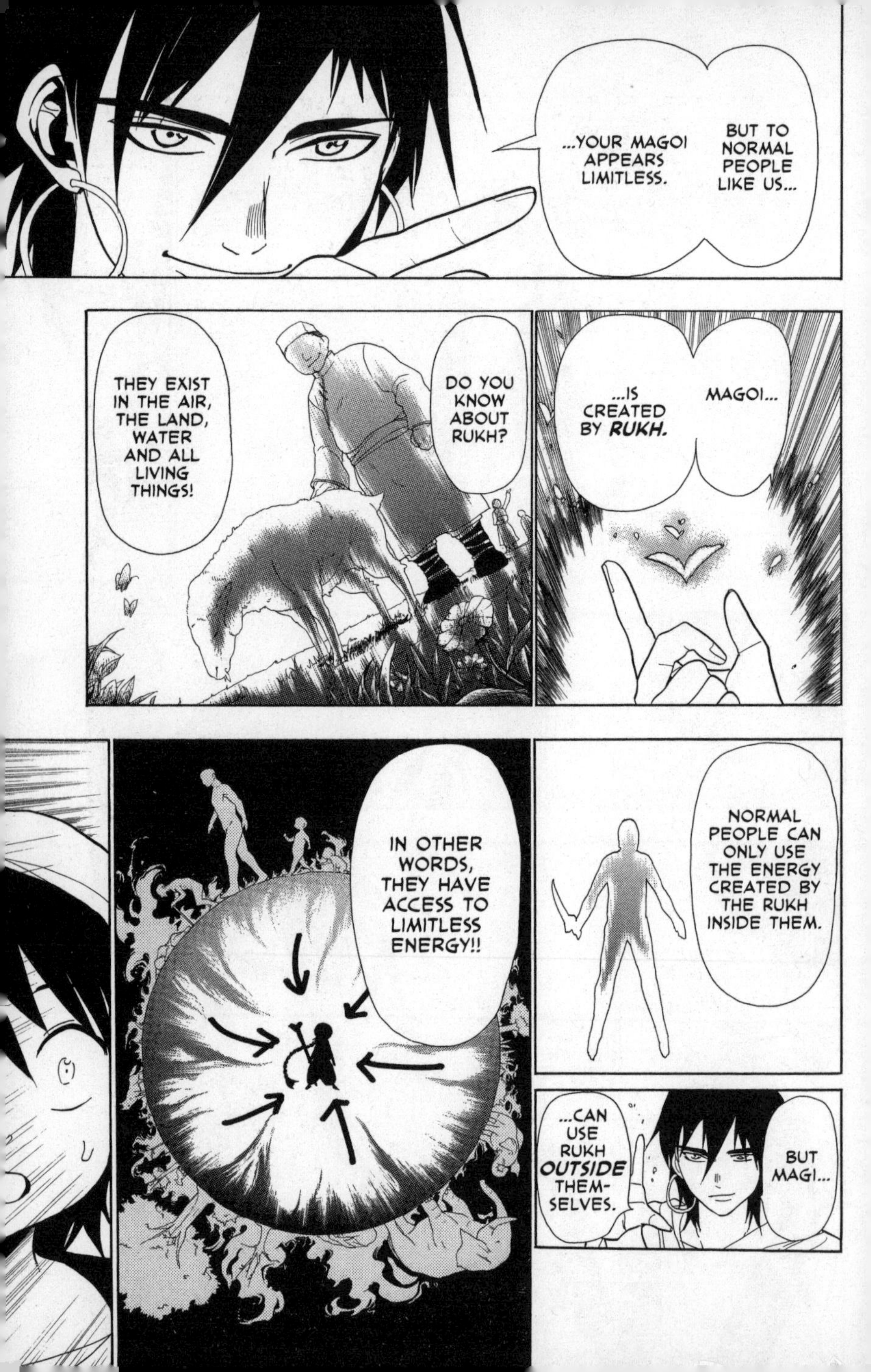
BUT TO NORMAL PEOPLE LIKE US...
...YOUR MAGOI APPEARS LIMITLESS.
MAGOI...
...IS CREATED BY **RUKH.**
DO YOU KNOW ABOUT RUKH?
THEY EXIST IN THE AIR, THE LAND, WATER AND ALL LIVING THINGS!
NORMAL PEOPLE CAN ONLY USE THE ENERGY CREATED BY THE RUKH INSIDE THEM.
BUT MAGI...
...CAN USE RUKH **OUTSIDE** THEM-SELVES.
IN OTHER WORDS, THEY HAVE ACCESS TO LIMITLESS ENERGY!!

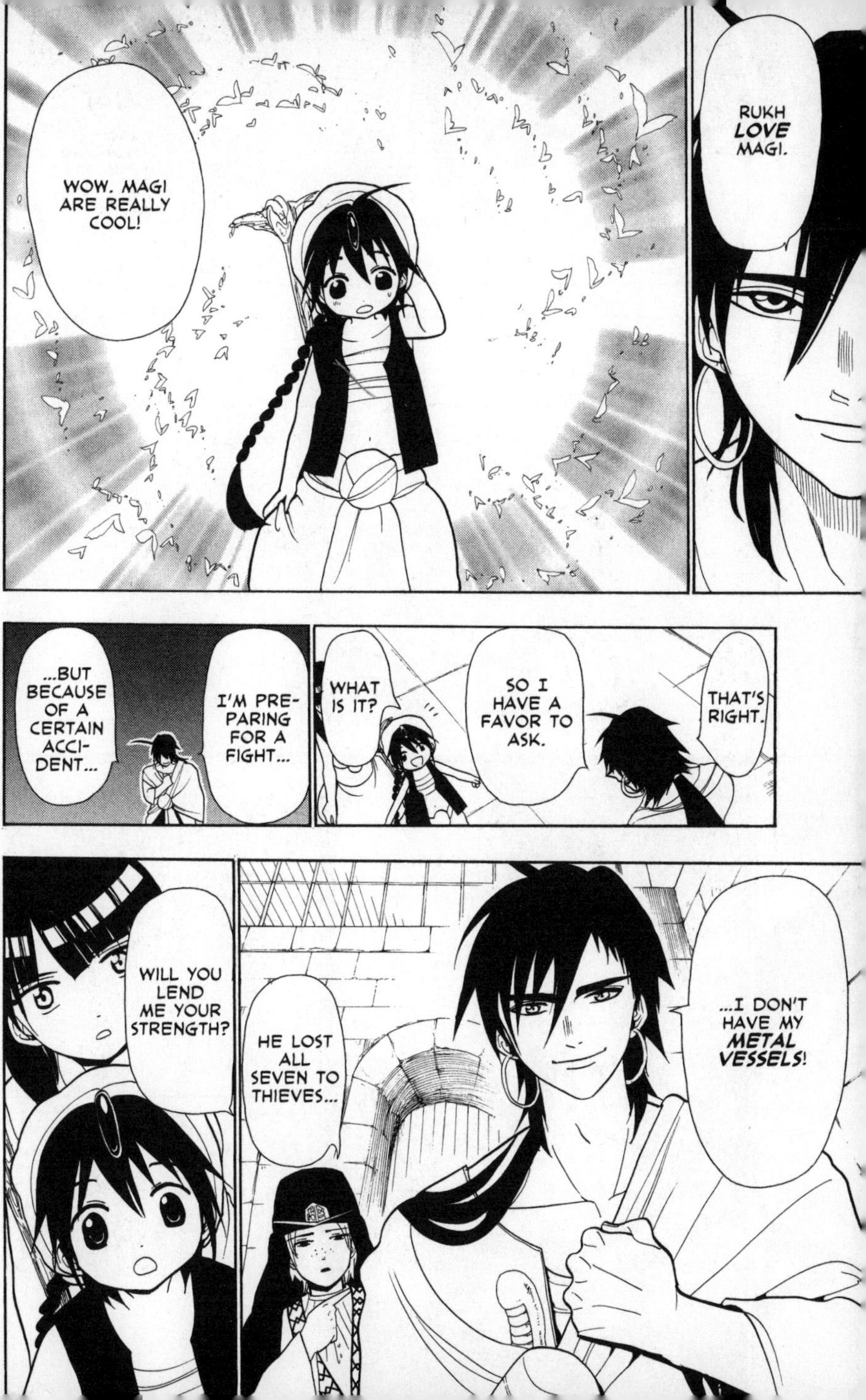
RUKH LOVE MAGI.
WOW. MAGI ARE REALLY COOL!
THAT'S RIGHT.
SO I HAVE A FAVOR TO ASK.
WHAT IS IT?
I'M PRE-PARING FOR A FIGHT...
...BUT BECAUSE OF A CERTAIN ACCI-DENT...
...I DON'T HAVE MY METAL VESSELS!
HE LOST ALL SEVEN TO THIEVES...
WILL YOU LEND ME YOUR STRENGTH?

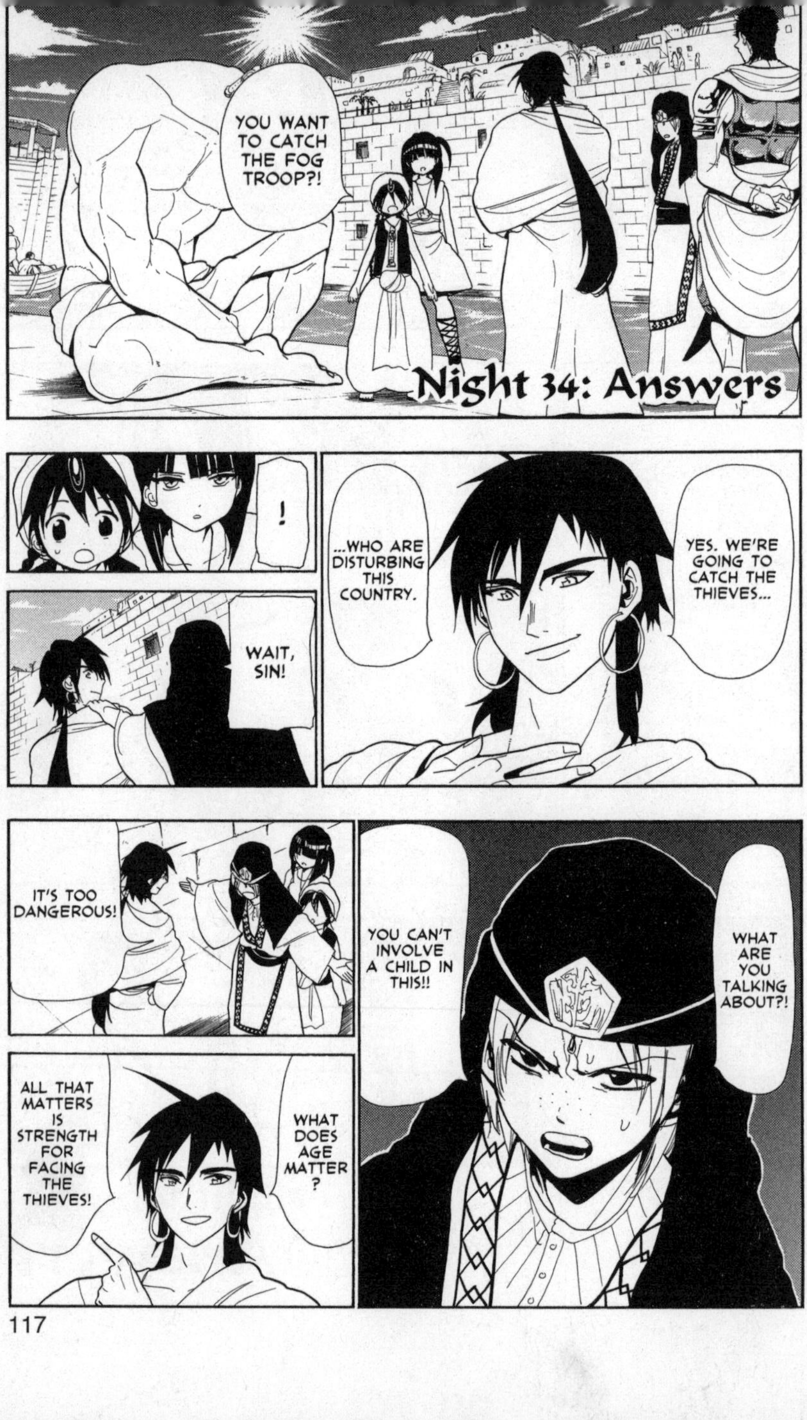
YOU WANT TO CATCH THE FOG TROOP?!
Night 34: Answers
YES. WE'RE GOING TO CATCH THE THIEVES...
...WHO ARE DISTURBING THIS COUNTRY.
!
WAIT, SIN!
WHAT ARE YOU TALKING ABOUT?!
YOU CAN'T INVOLVE A CHILD IN THIS!!
IT'S TOO DANGEROUS!
WHAT DOES AGE MATTER?
ALL THAT MATTERS IS STRENGTH FOR FACING THE THIEVES!

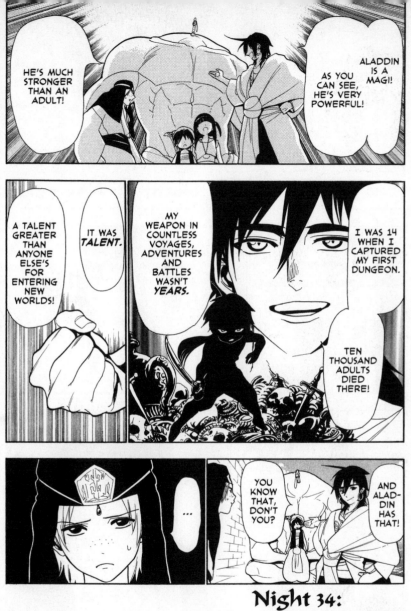

ALADDIN IS A MAGI!
AS YOU CAN SEE, HE'S VERY POWERFUL!
HE'S MUCH STRONGER THAN AN ADULT!
I WAS 14 WHEN I CAPTURED MY FIRST DUNGEON.
TEN THOUSAND ADULTS DIED THERE!
MY WEAPON IN COUNTLESS VOYAGES, ADVENTURES AND BATTLES WASN'T *YEARS.*
IT WAS *TALENT.*
A TALENT GREATER THAN ANYONE ELSE'S FOR ENTERING NEW WORLDS!
AND ALADDIN HAS THAT!
YOU KNOW THAT, DON'T YOU?
...

Night 34: Answers

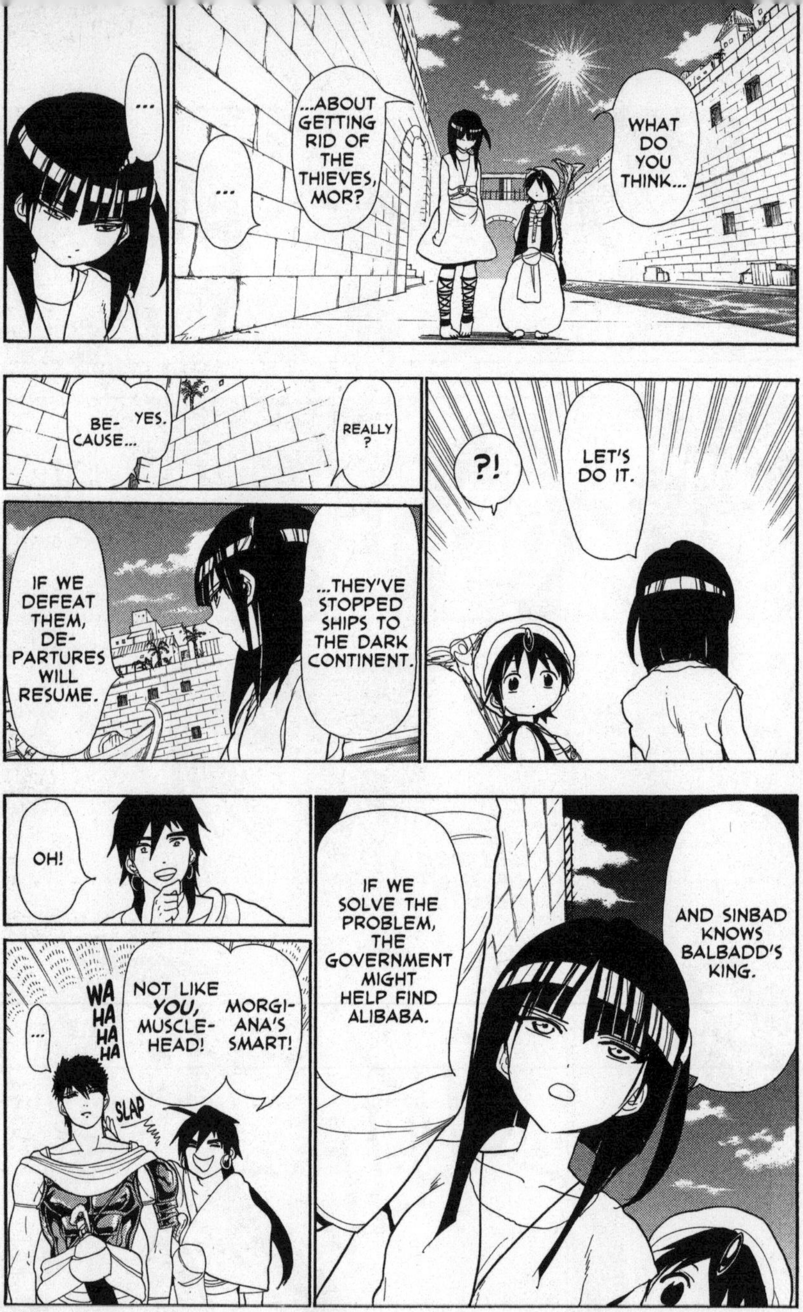
WHAT DO YOU THINK...
...ABOUT GETTING RID OF THE THIEVES, MOR?
...
...
LET'S DO IT.
?!
REALLY?
YES. BE-CAUSE...
...THEY'VE STOPPED SHIPS TO THE DARK CONTINENT.
IF WE DEFEAT THEM, DE-PARTURES WILL RESUME.
AND SINBAD KNOWS BALBADD'S KING.
IF WE SOLVE THE PROBLEM, THE GOVERNMENT MIGHT HELP FIND ALIBABA.
OH!
MORGI-ANA'S SMART!
NOT LIKE *YOU*, MUSCLE-HEAD!
WA HA HA HA HA
...
SLAP

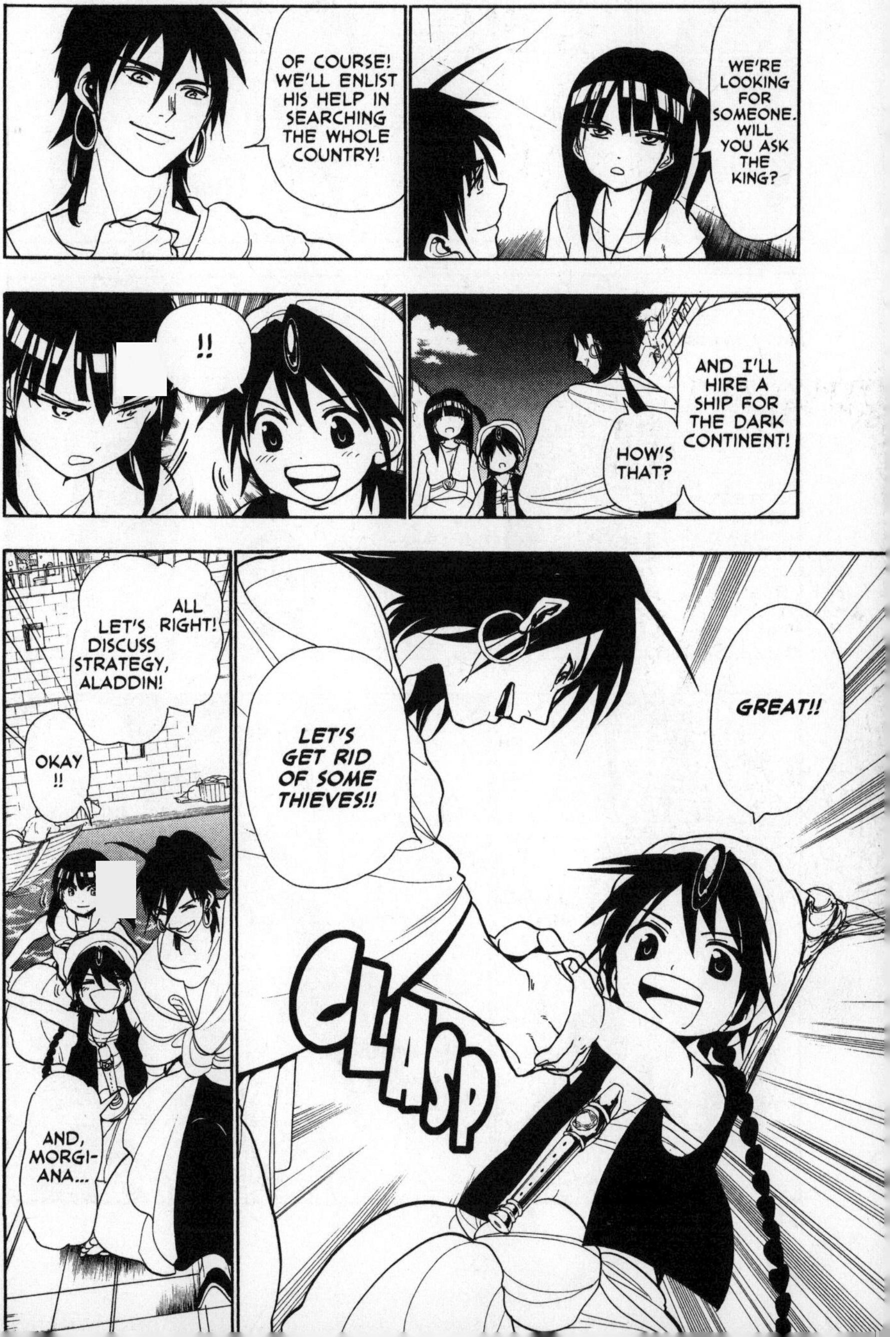
WE'RE LOOKING FOR SOMEONE. WILL YOU ASK THE KING?
OF COURSE! WE'LL ENLIST HIS HELP IN SEARCHING THE WHOLE COUNTRY!
AND I'LL HIRE A SHIP FOR THE DARK CONTINENT!
HOW'S THAT?
!!
GREAT!!
LET'S GET RID OF SOME THIEVES!!
CLASP
ALL RIGHT! LET'S DISCUSS STRATEGY, ALADDIN!
OKAY!!
AND, MORGIANA...

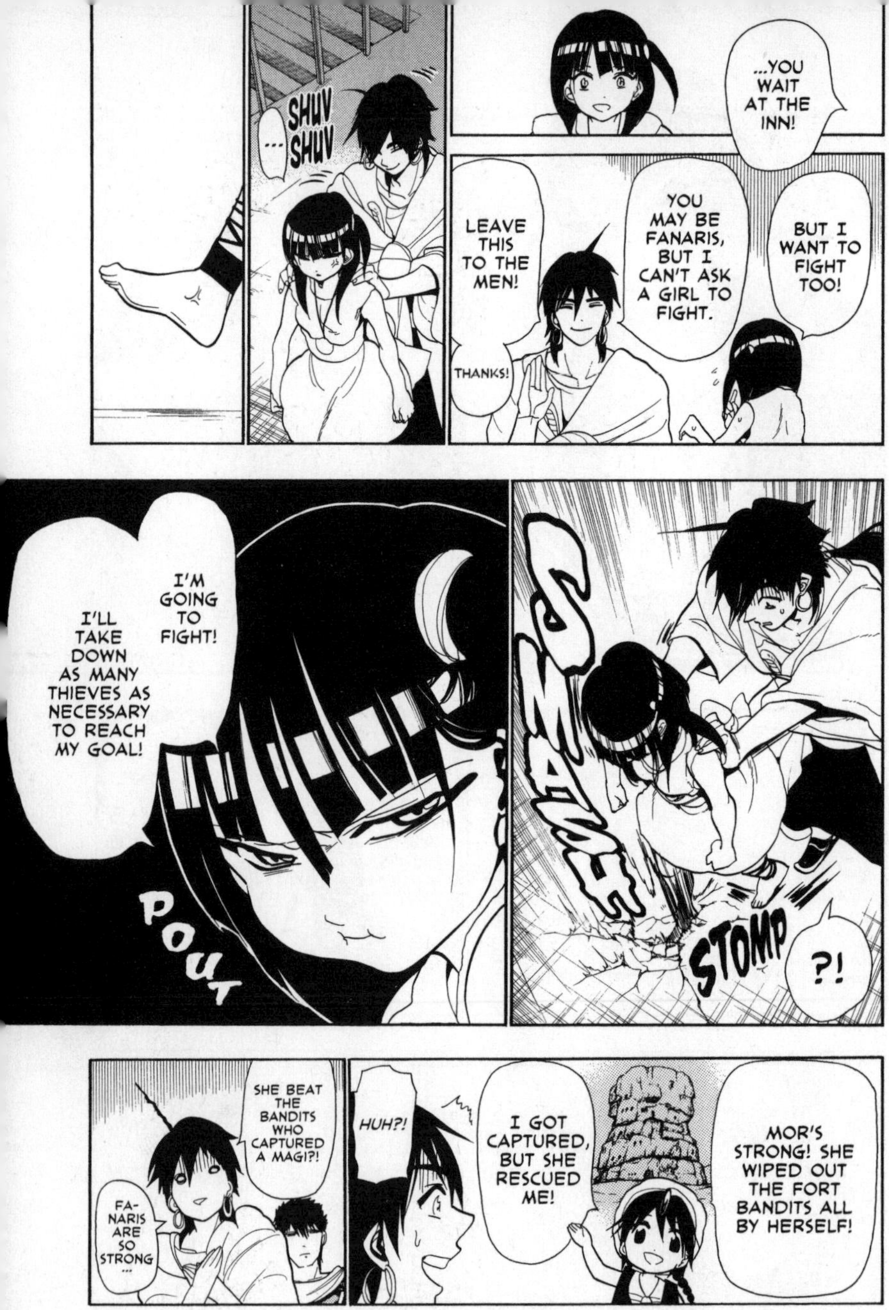
...YOU WAIT AT THE INN!
BUT I WANT TO FIGHT TOO!
YOU MAY BE FANARIS, BUT I CAN'T ASK A GIRL TO FIGHT.
LEAVE THIS TO THE MEN!
THANKS!
SHUV SHUV
...
SMASH
STOMP
?!
I'M GOING TO FIGHT!
I'LL TAKE DOWN AS MANY THIEVES AS NECESSARY TO REACH MY GOAL!
POUT
MOR'S STRONG! SHE WIPED OUT THE FORT BANDITS ALL BY HERSELF!
I GOT CAPTURED, BUT SHE RESCUED ME!
HUH?!
SHE BEAT THE BANDITS WHO CAPTURED A MAGI?!
FA-NARIS ARE SO STRONG...

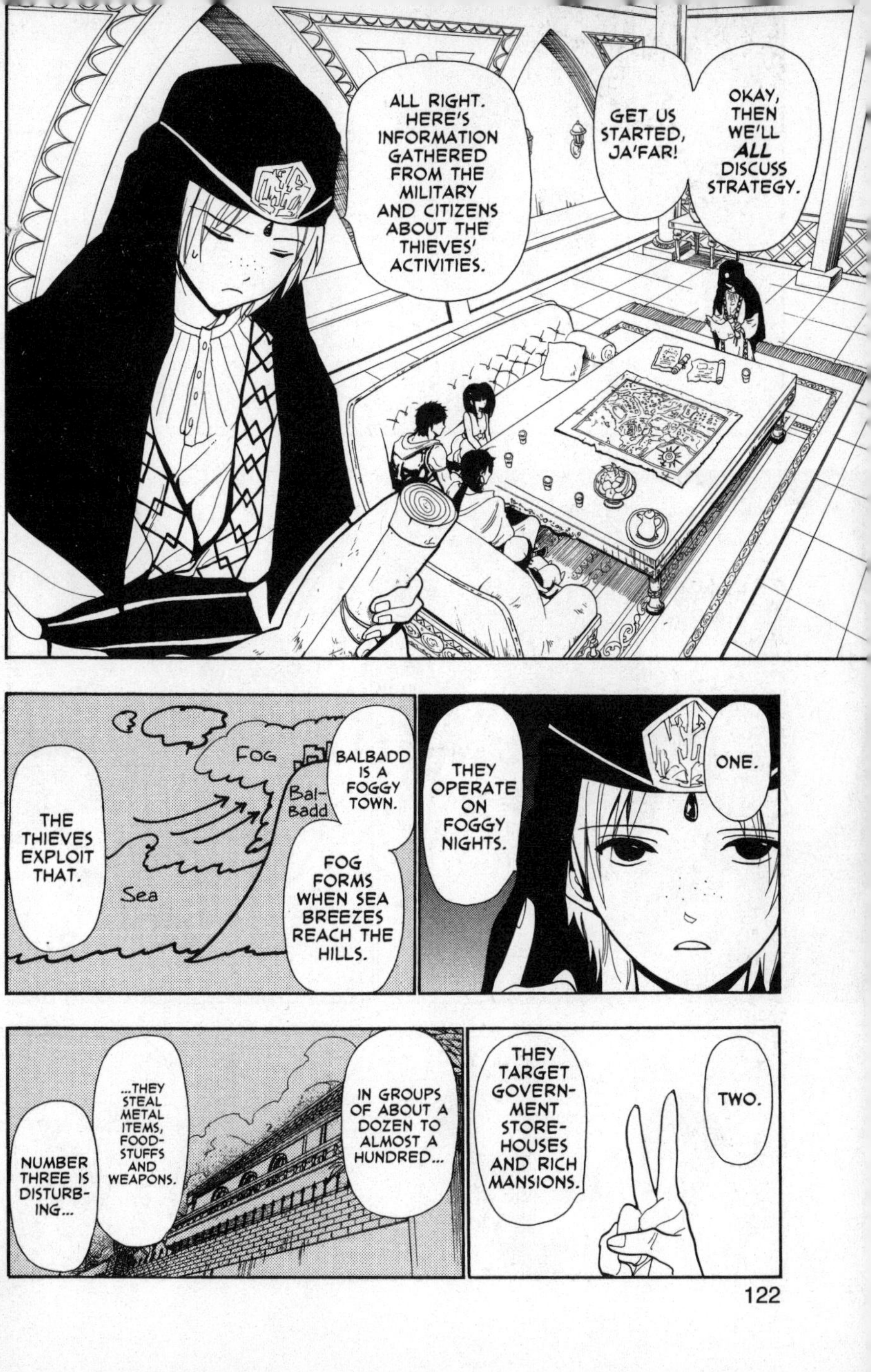
OKAY, THEN WE'LL **ALL** DISCUSS STRATEGY.
GET US STARTED, JA'FAR!
ALL RIGHT. HERE'S INFORMATION GATHERED FROM THE MILITARY AND CITIZENS ABOUT THE THIEVES' ACTIVITIES.
ONE.
THEY OPERATE ON FOGGY NIGHTS.
BALBADD IS A FOGGY TOWN.
FOG FORMS WHEN SEA BREEZES REACH THE HILLS.
Fog
Bal-badd
Sea
THE THIEVES EXPLOIT THAT.
TWO.
THEY TARGET GOVERN-MENT STORE-HOUSES AND RICH MANSIONS.
IN GROUPS OF ABOUT A DOZEN TO ALMOST A HUNDRED...
...THEY STEAL METAL ITEMS, FOOD-STUFFS AND WEAPONS.
NUMBER THREE IS DISTURB-ING...

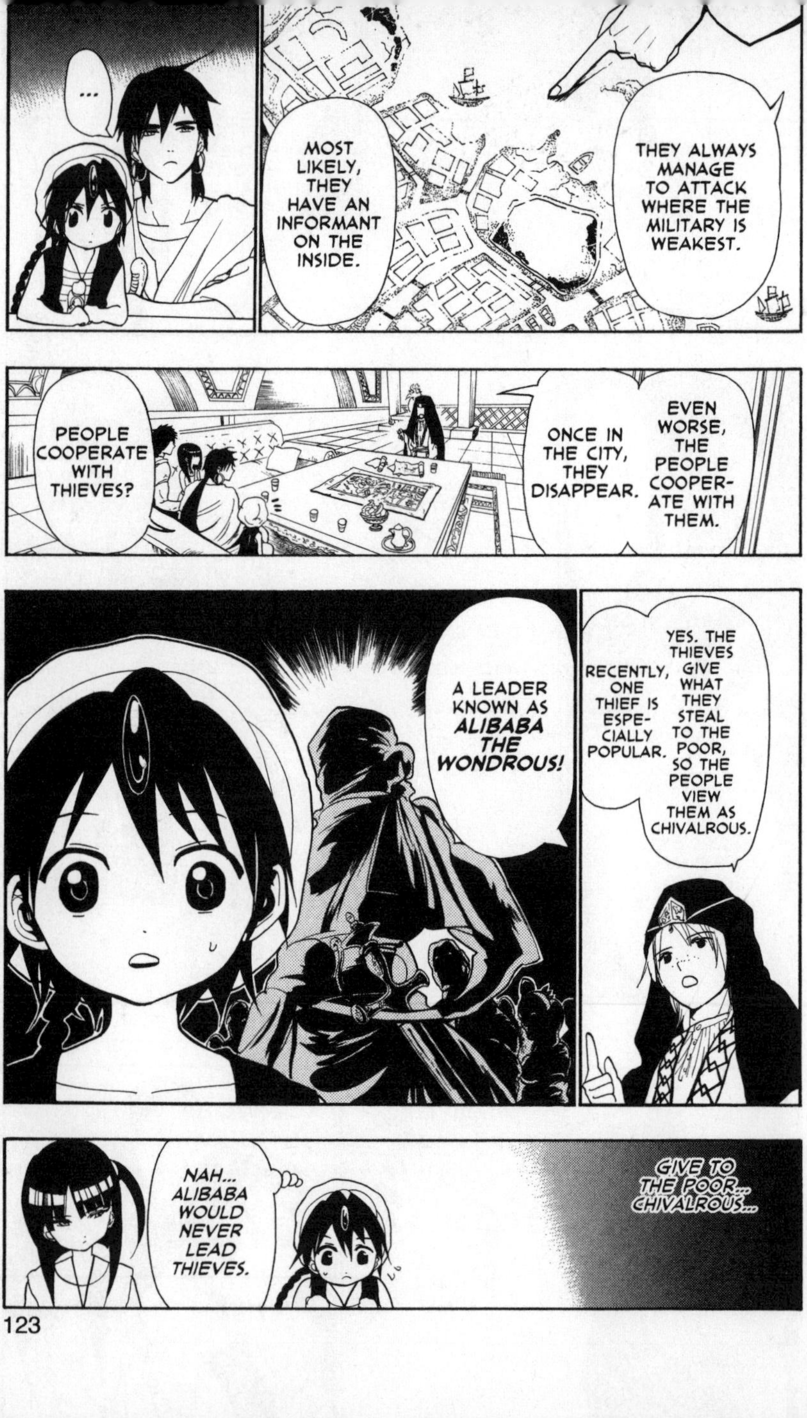
THEY ALWAYS MANAGE TO ATTACK WHERE THE MILITARY IS WEAKEST.
MOST LIKELY, THEY HAVE AN INFORMANT ON THE INSIDE.
...
ONCE IN THE CITY, THEY DISAPPEAR.
EVEN WORSE, THE PEOPLE COOPERATE WITH THEM.
PEOPLE COOPERATE WITH THIEVES?
YES. THE THIEVES GIVE WHAT THEY STEAL TO THE POOR, SO THE PEOPLE VIEW THEM AS CHIVALROUS.
RECENTLY, ONE THIEF IS ESPECIALLY POPULAR.
A LEADER KNOWN AS *ALIBABA THE WONDROUS!*
GIVE TO THE POOR... CHIVALROUS...
NAH... ALIBABA WOULD NEVER LEAD THIEVES.

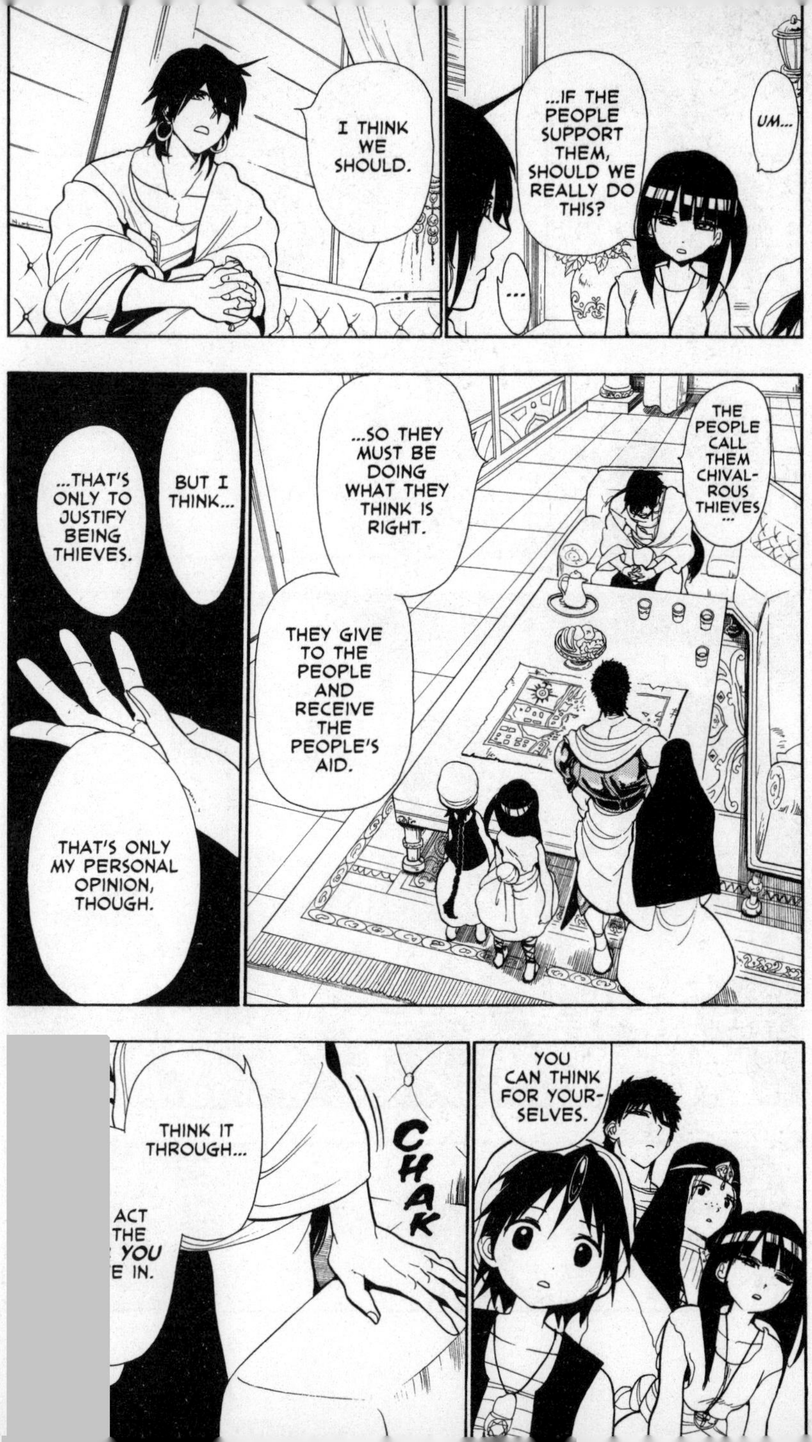
UM...
...IF THE PEOPLE SUPPORT THEM, SHOULD WE REALLY DO THIS?
...
I THINK WE SHOULD.
THE PEOPLE CALL THEM CHIVAL-ROUS THIEVES...
...SO THEY MUST BE DOING WHAT THEY THINK IS RIGHT.
THEY GIVE TO THE PEOPLE AND RECEIVE THE PEOPLE'S AID.
BUT I THINK...
...THAT'S ONLY TO JUSTIFY BEING THIEVES.
THAT'S ONLY MY PERSONAL OPINION, THOUGH.
YOU CAN THINK FOR YOUR-SELVES.
CHAK
THINK IT THROUGH...
ACT
THE
YOU
E IN.

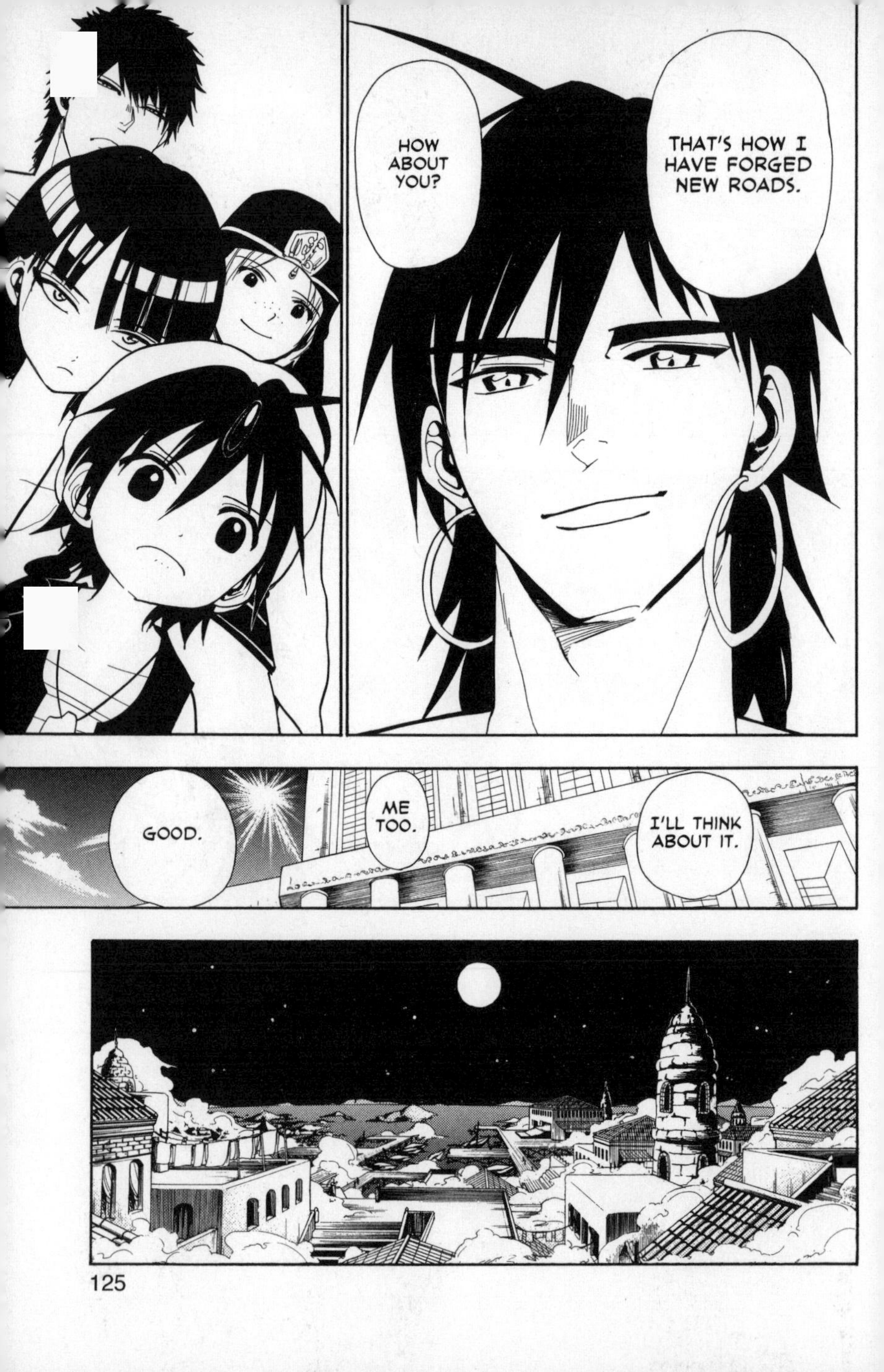
THAT'S HOW I HAVE FORGED NEW ROADS.
HOW ABOUT YOU?
I'LL THINK ABOUT IT.
ME TOO.
GOOD.

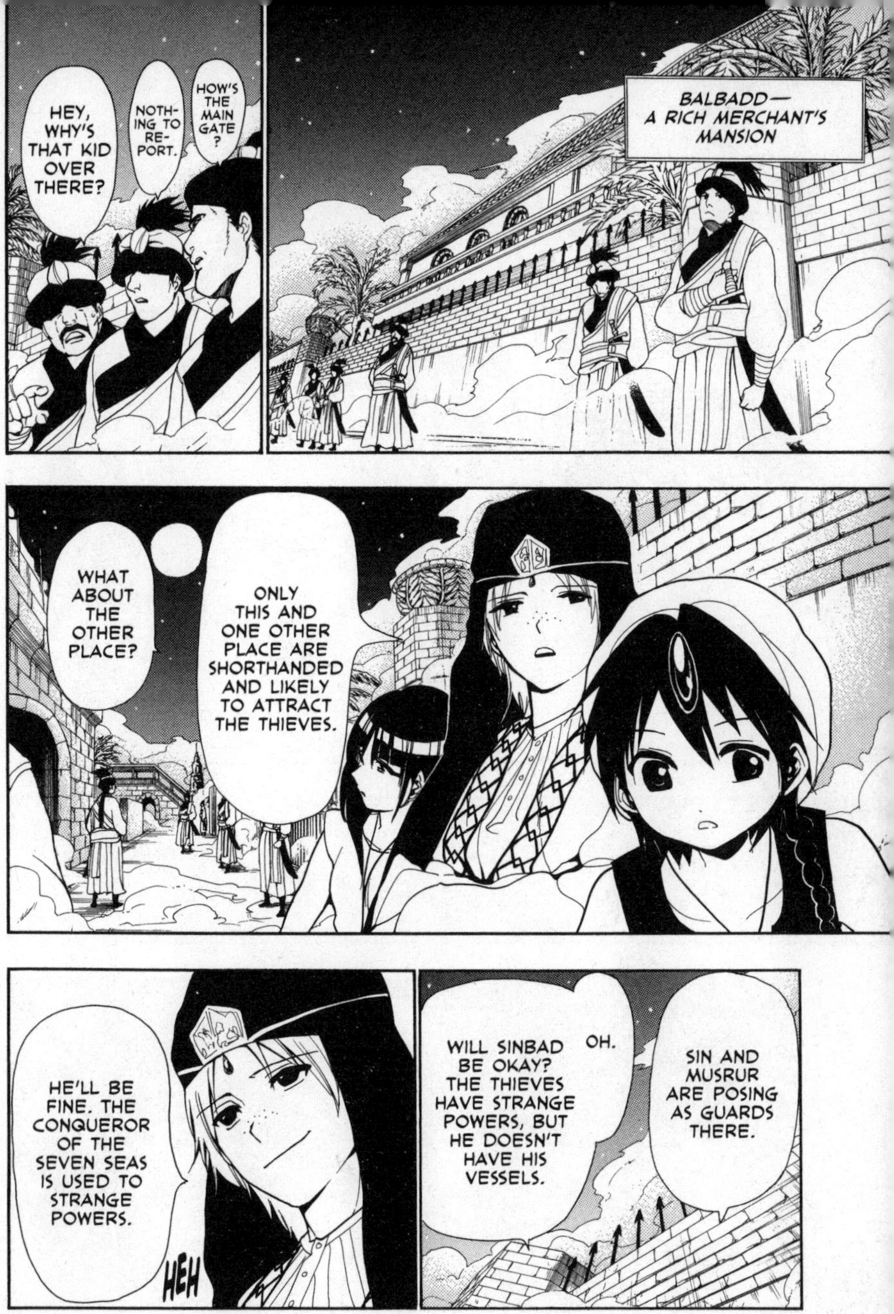
BALBADD— A RICH MERCHANT'S MANSION
HOW'S THE MAIN GATE?
NOTHING TO REPORT.
HEY, WHY'S THAT KID OVER THERE?
ONLY THIS AND ONE OTHER PLACE ARE SHORTHANDED AND LIKELY TO ATTRACT THE THIEVES.
WHAT ABOUT THE OTHER PLACE?
SIN AND MUSRUR ARE POSING AS GUARDS THERE.
OH.
WILL SINBAD BE OKAY? THE THIEVES HAVE STRANGE POWERS, BUT HE DOESN'T HAVE HIS VESSELS.
HE'LL BE FINE. THE CONQUEROR OF THE SEVEN SEAS IS USED TO STRANGE POWERS.
HEH

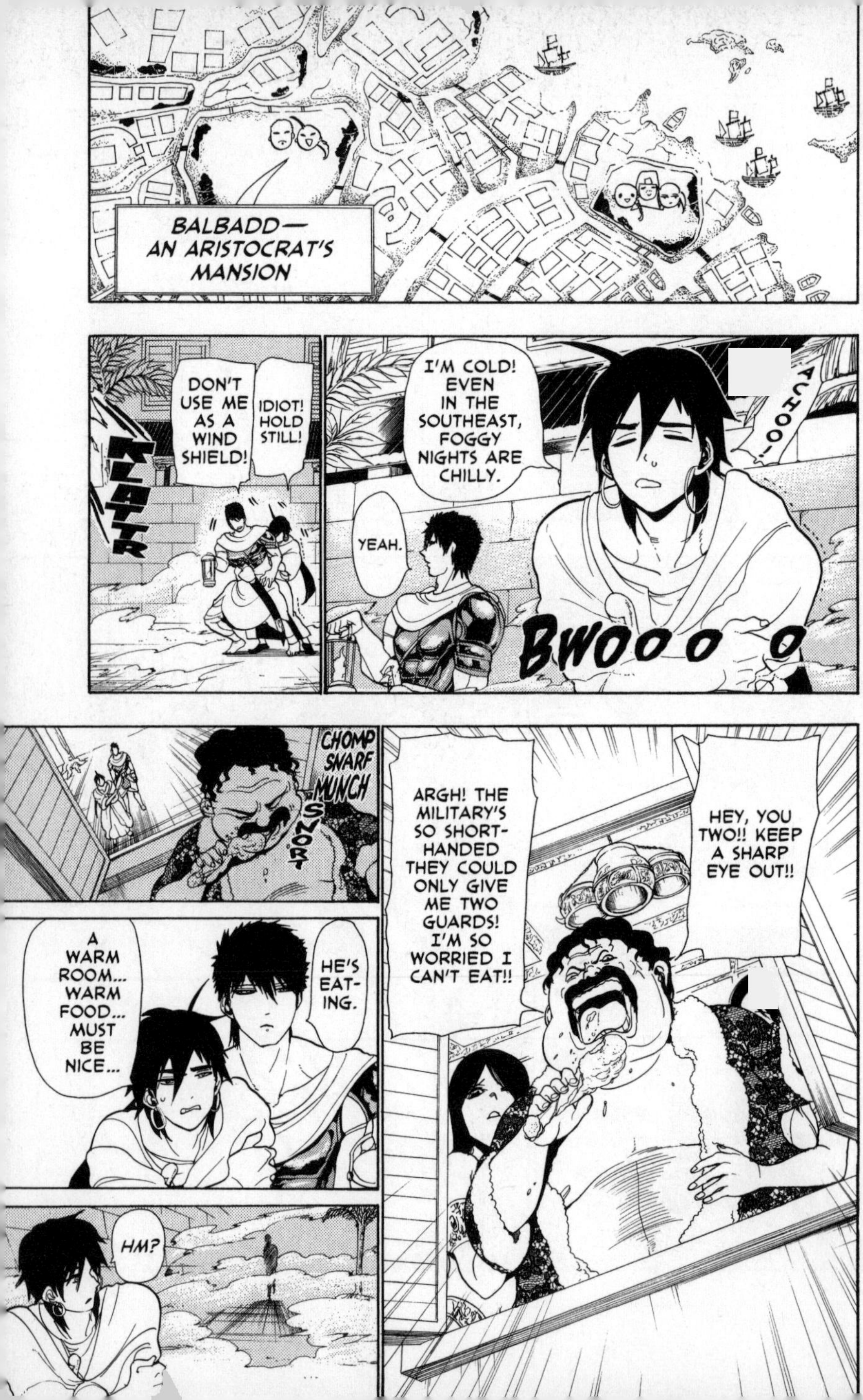
BALBADD—
AN ARISTOCRAT'S
MANSION
ACHOO!
I'M COLD! EVEN IN THE SOUTHEAST, FOGGY NIGHTS ARE CHILLY.
YEAH.
BWOOO O O
IDIOT! HOLD STILL!
DON'T USE ME AS A WIND SHIELD!
KLATTR
HEY, YOU TWO!! KEEP A SHARP EYE OUT!!
ARGH! THE MILITARY'S SO SHORT-HANDED THEY COULD ONLY GIVE ME TWO GUARDS! I'M SO WORRIED I CAN'T EAT!!
CHOMP SNARF MUNCH
SNORT
HE'S EAT-ING.
A WARM ROOM... WARM FOOD... MUST BE NICE...
HM?

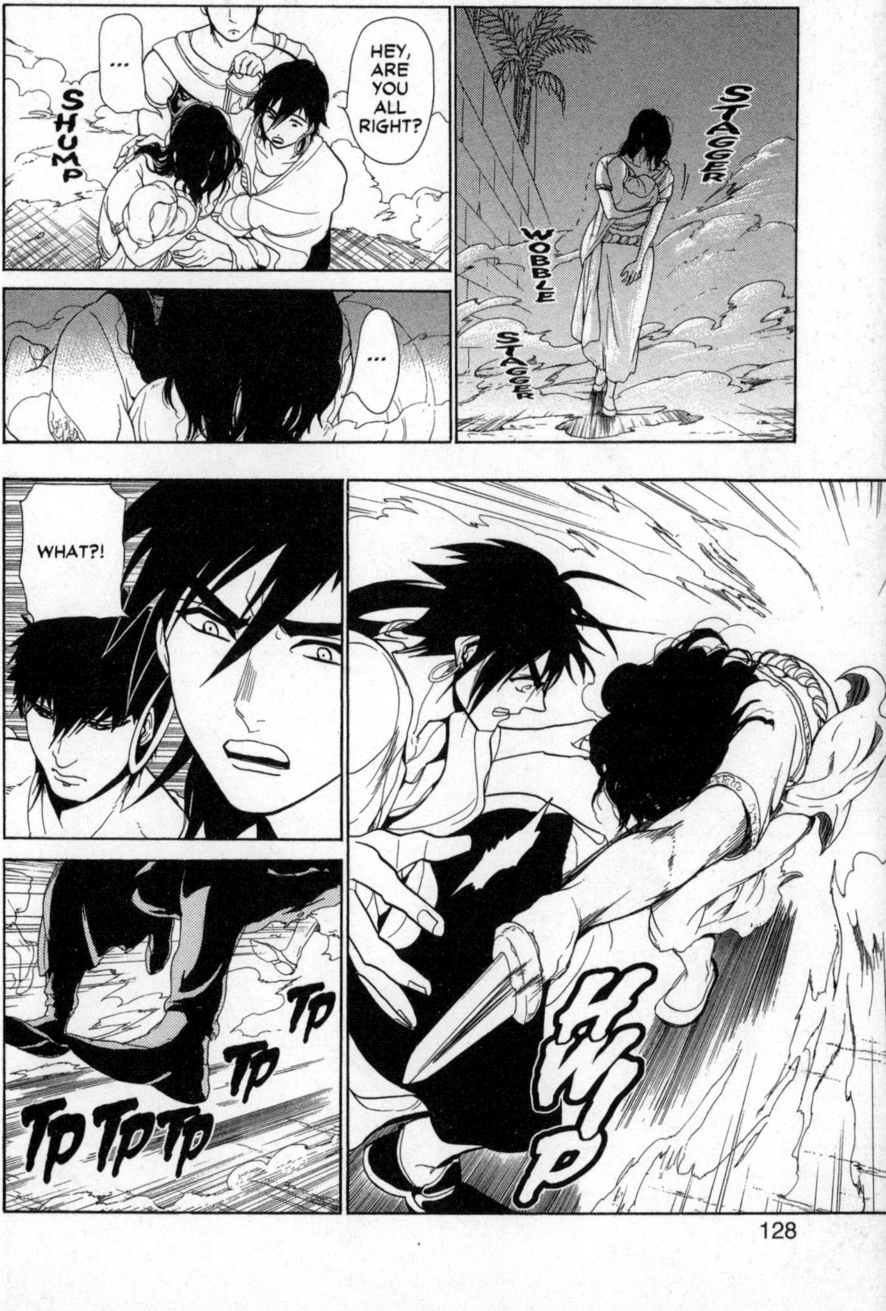
STAGGER
WOBBLE
STAGGER
HEY, ARE YOU ALL RIGHT?
...
SHUMP
...
HWIP
WHAT?!
Tp
Tp
Tp Tp Tp Tp

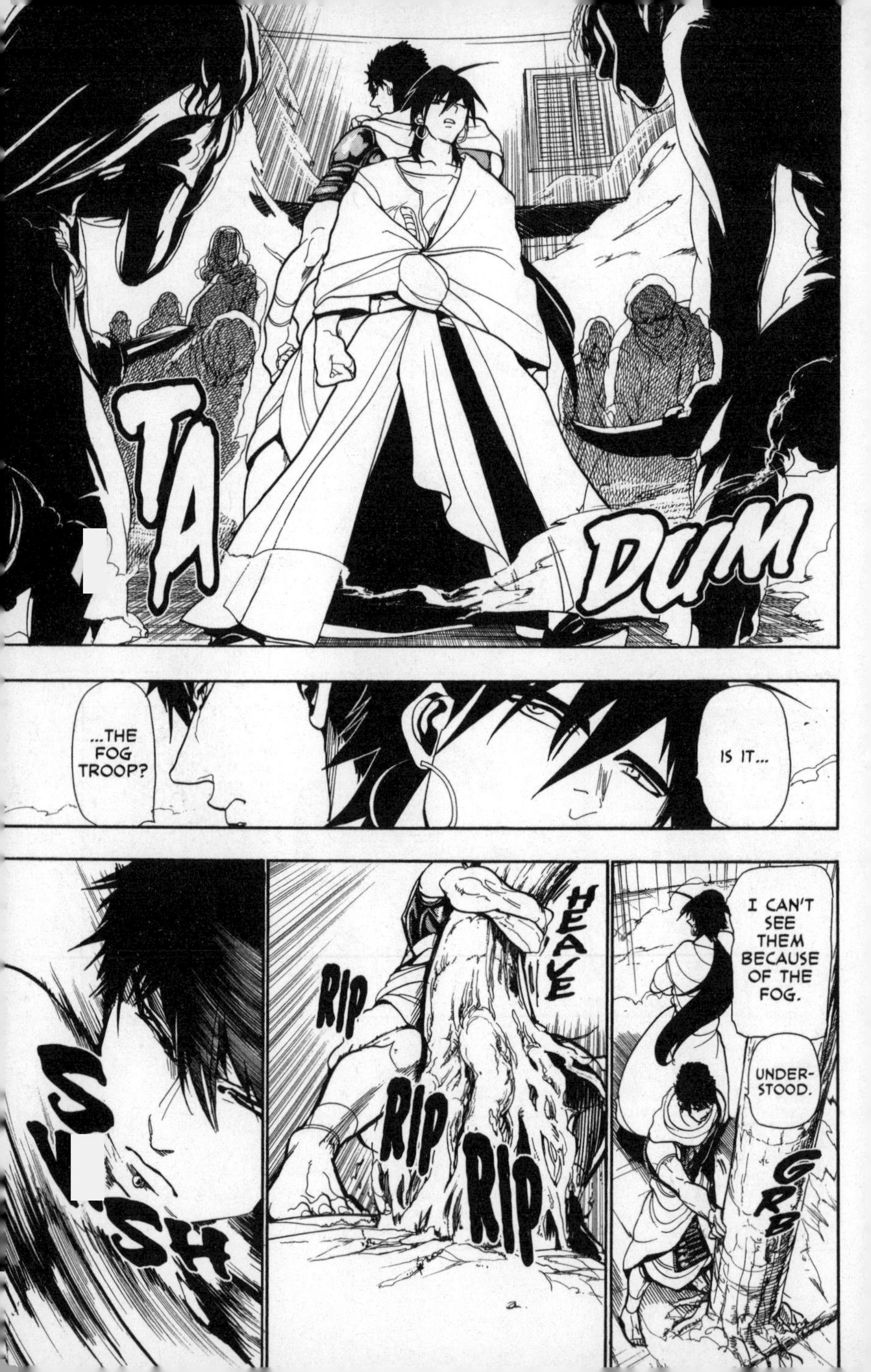
TA
DUM
IS IT...
...THE FOG TROOP?
I CAN'T SEE THEM BECAUSE OF THE FOG.
UNDER-STOOD.
GRB
HEAVE
RIP
RIP
RIP
RIP
SV
SH

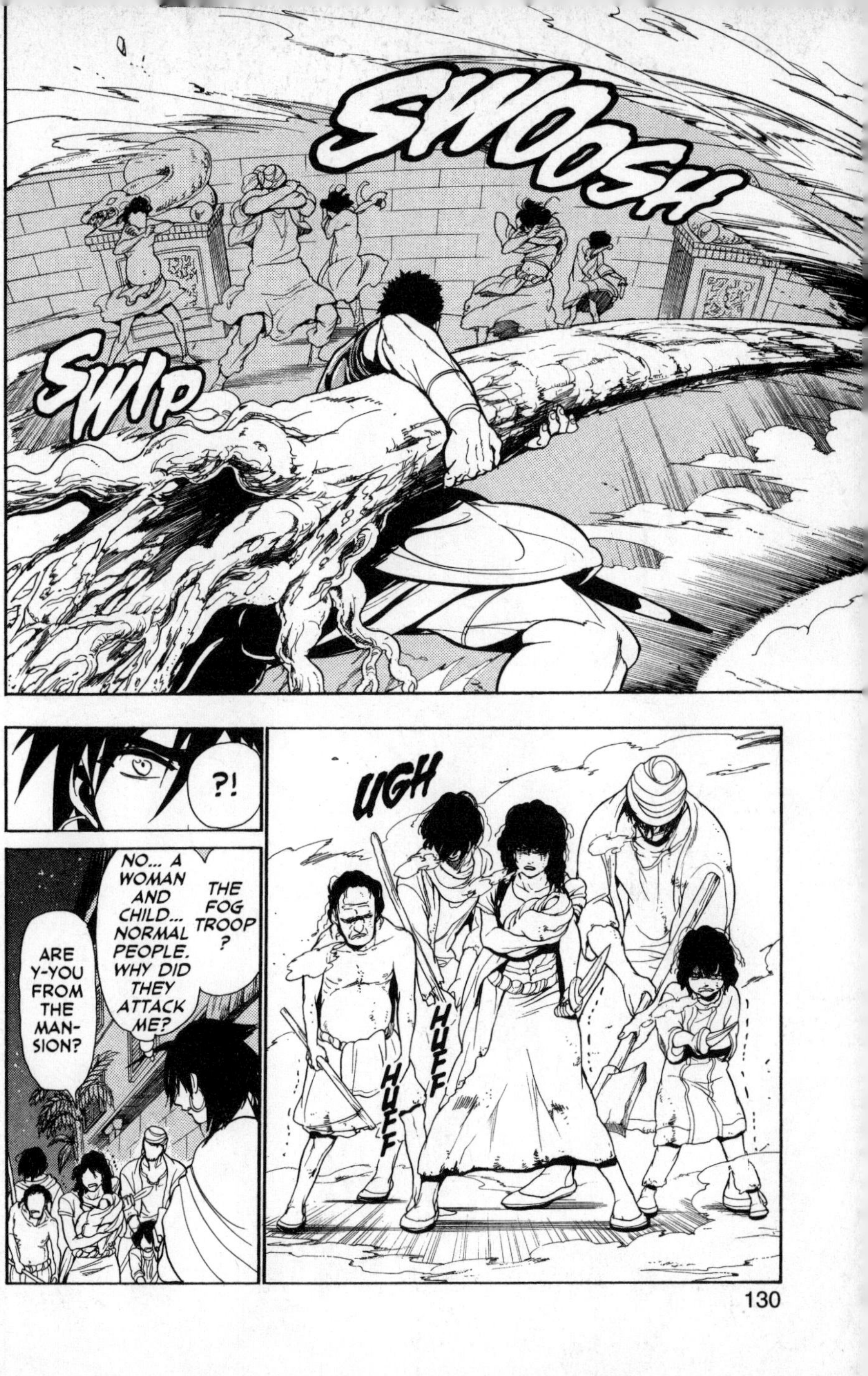
SWOOSH
SWIP
UGH
HUFF
HUFF
?!
THE FOG TROOP?
NO... A WOMAN AND CHILD... NORMAL PEOPLE. WHY DID THEY ATTACK ME?
ARE Y-YOU FROM THE MAN-SION?

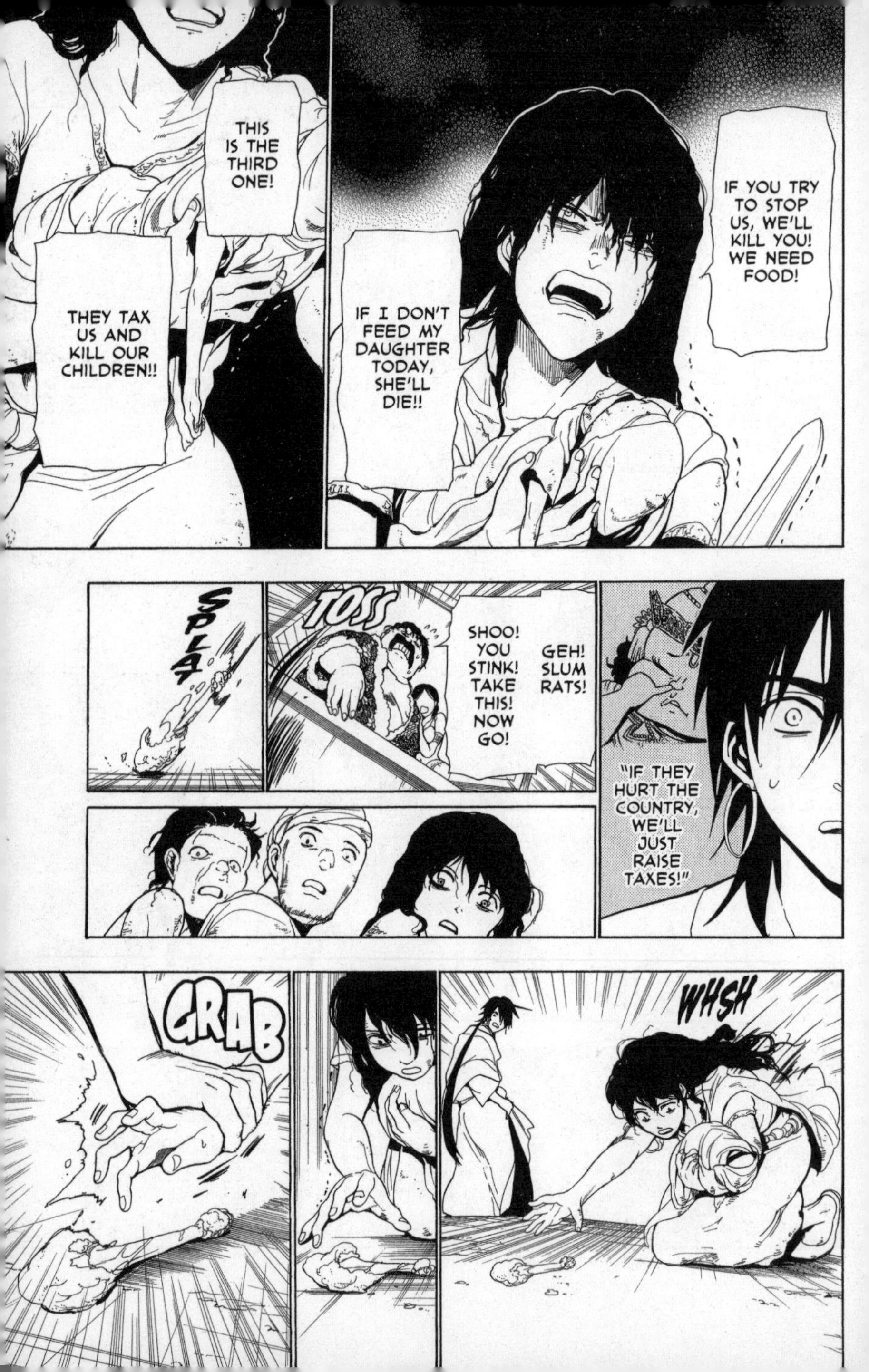
IF YOU TRY TO STOP US, WE'LL KILL YOU! WE NEED FOOD!
IF I DON'T FEED MY DAUGHTER TODAY, SHE'LL DIE!!
THIS IS THE THIRD ONE!
THEY TAX US AND KILL OUR CHILDREN!!
"IF THEY HURT THE COUNTRY, WE'LL JUST RAISE TAXES!"
TOSS
GEH! SLUM RATS!
SHOO! YOU STINK! TAKE THIS! NOW GO!
SPLAT
WHSH
GRAB

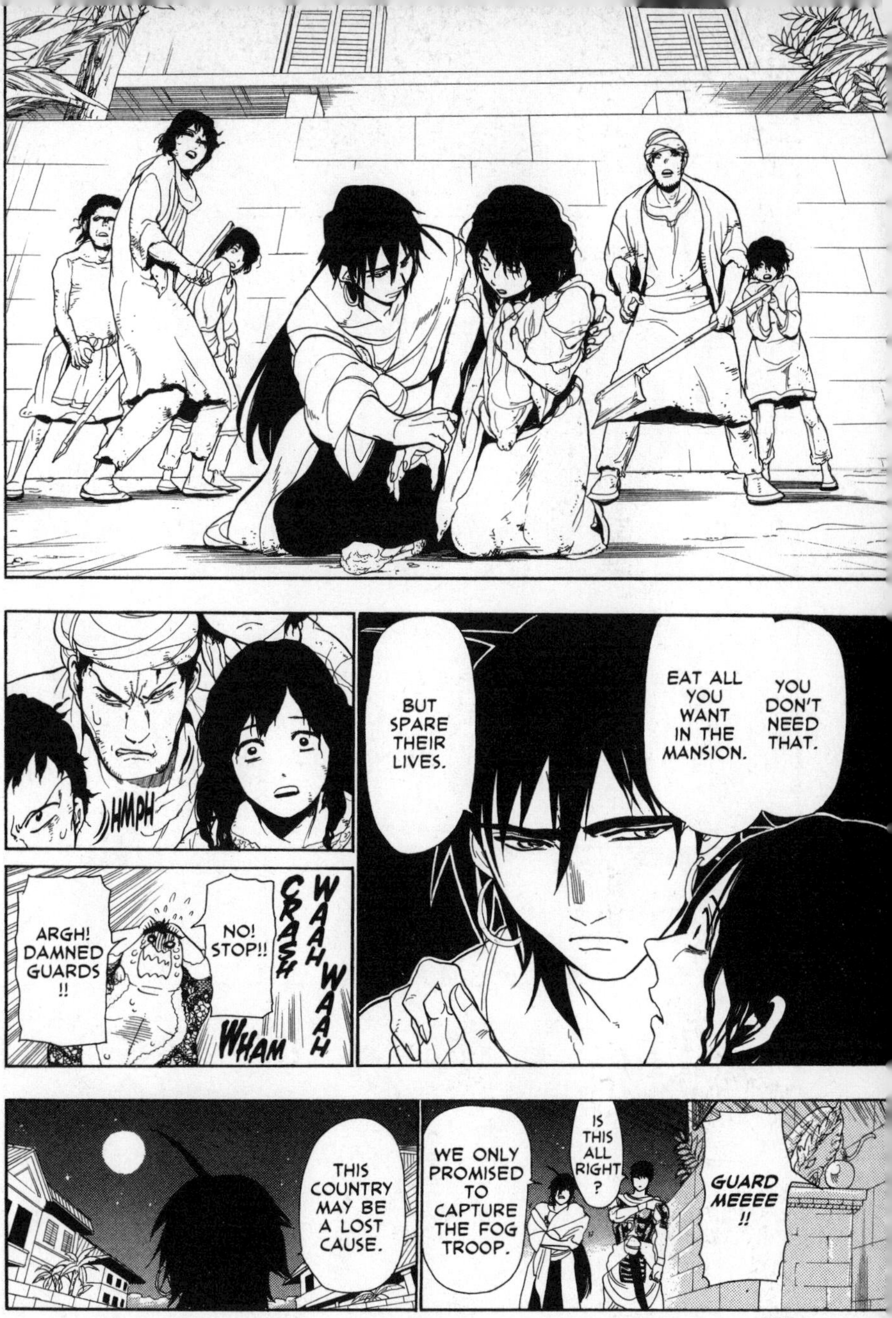

YOU DON'T NEED THAT.
EAT ALL YOU WANT IN THE MANSION.
BUT SPARE THEIR LIVES.
HMPH
CRASH
WAAH WAAH WAAH
NO! STOP!!
ARGH! DAMNED GUARDS !!
WHAM
GUARD MEEEE !!
IS THIS ALL RIGHT?
WE ONLY PROMISED TO CAPTURE THE FOG TROOP.
THIS COUNTRY MAY BE A LOST CAUSE.

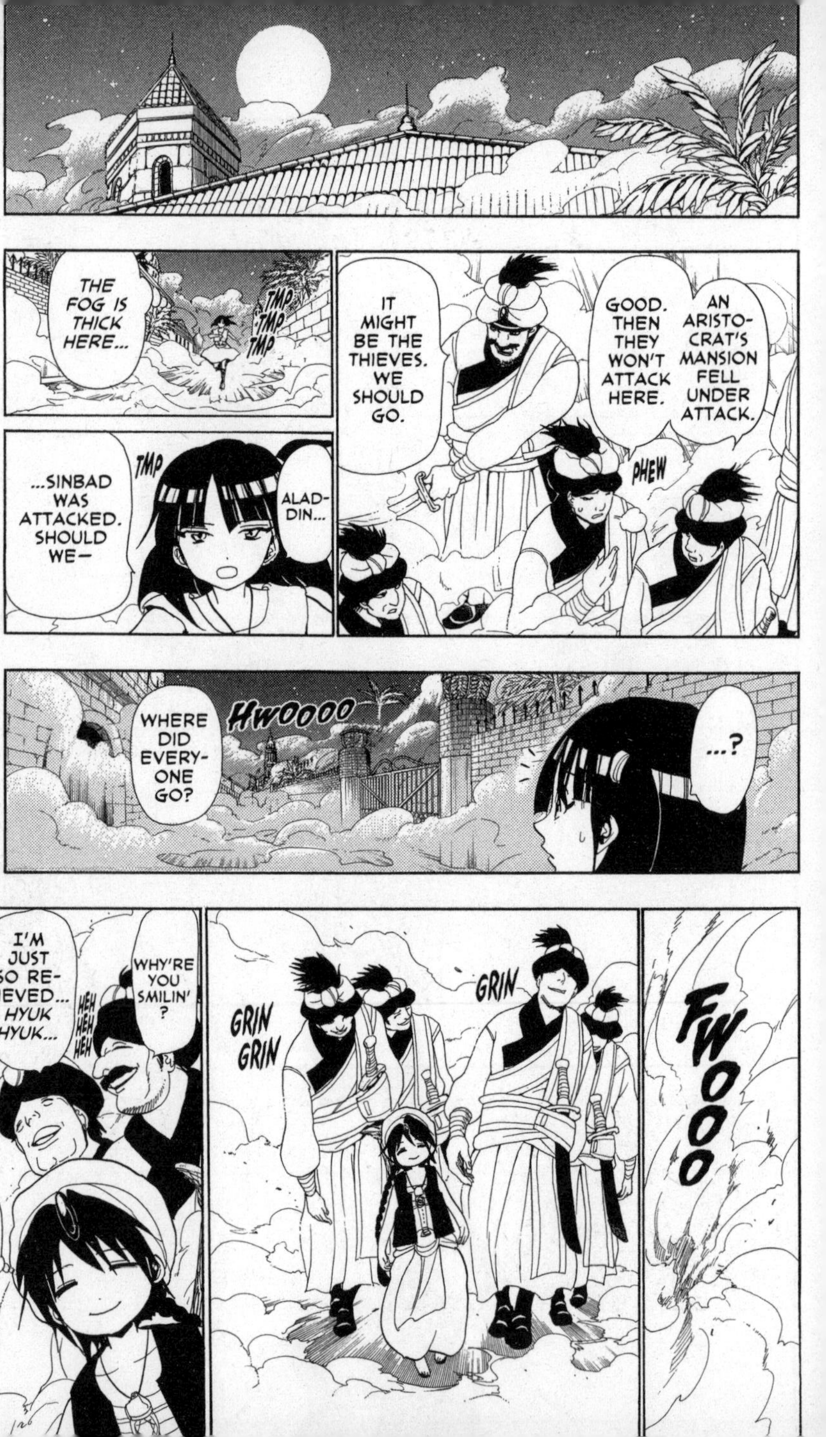

AN ARISTOCRAT'S MANSION FELL UNDER ATTACK.
GOOD. THEN THEY WON'T ATTACK HERE.
PHEW
IT MIGHT BE THE THIEVES. WE SHOULD GO.
TMP TMP TMP
THE FOG IS THICK HERE...
ALADDIN...
TMP
...SINBAD WAS ATTACKED. SHOULD WE—
...?
HWOOOO
WHERE DID EVERYONE GO?
FWOOOO
GRIN
GRIN GRIN
WHY'RE YOU SMILIN'?
HEH HEH HEH
I'M JUST SO RELIEVED... HYUK HYUK...
STAGGER STAGGER
...

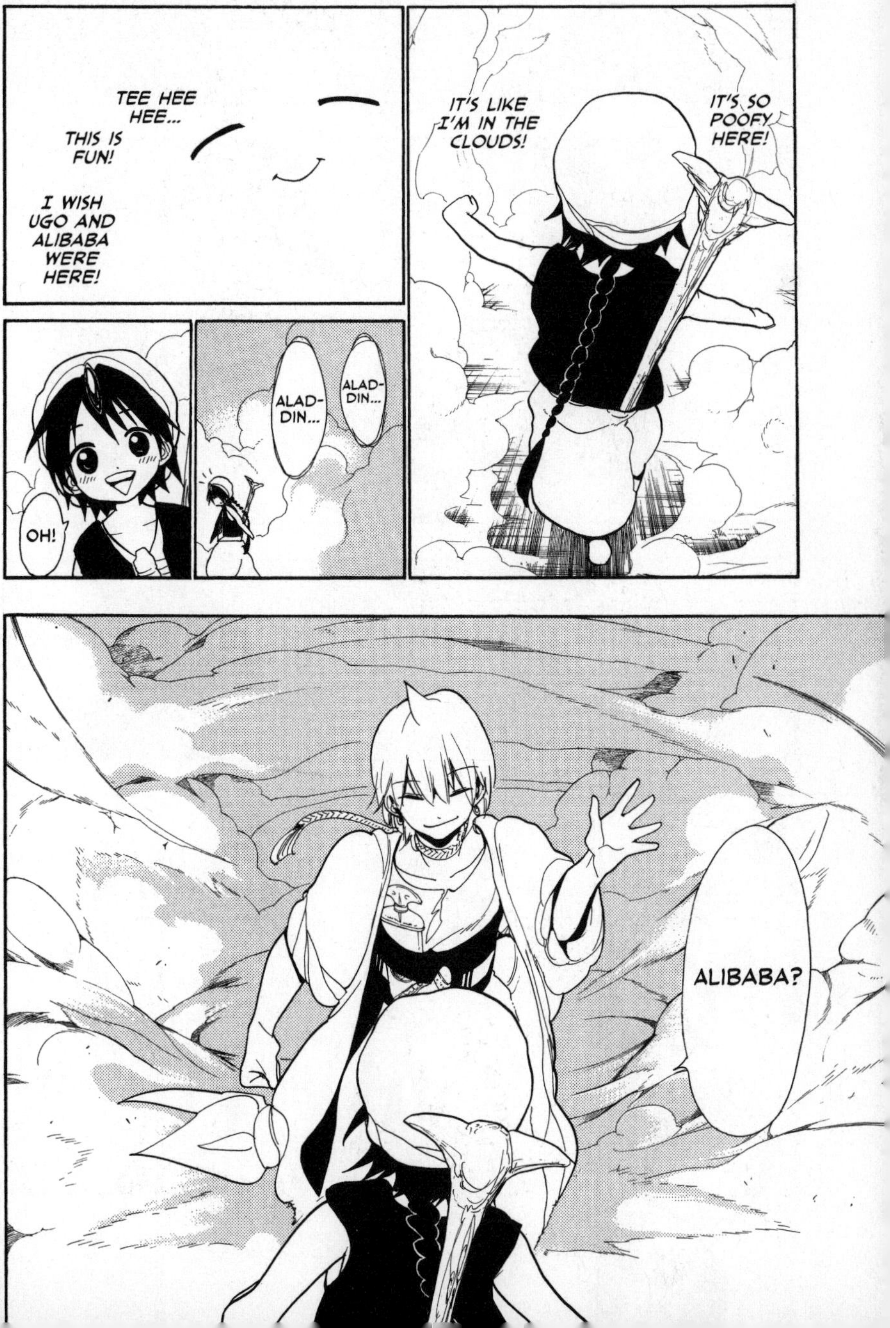
IT'S SO POOFY HERE!
IT'S LIKE I'M IN THE CLOUDS!
TEE HEE HEE... THIS IS FUN!
I WISH UGO AND ALIBABA WERE HERE!
ALAD-DIN...
ALAD-DIN...
OH!
ALIBABA?

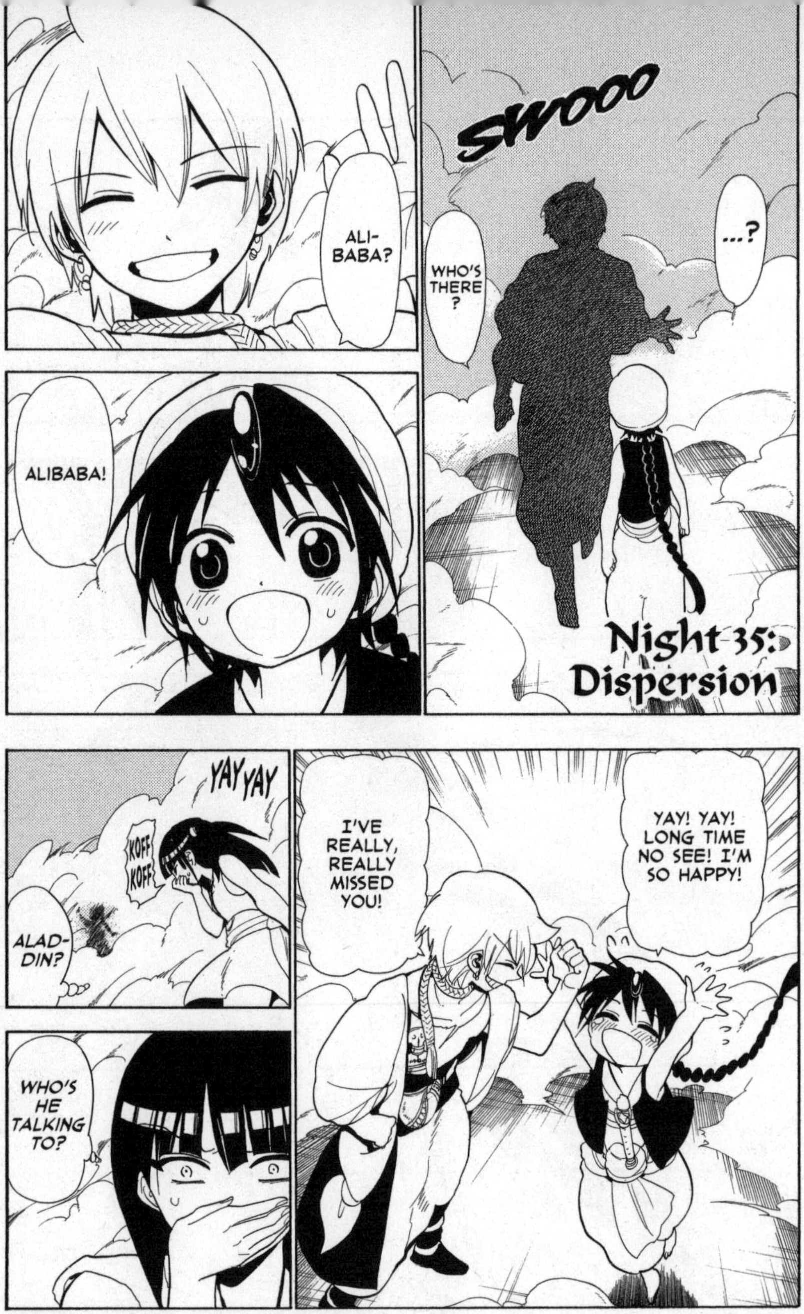
SWOOO
...?
WHO'S THERE?
Night 35: Dispersion
ALI-BABA?
ALIBABA!
YAY! YAY! LONG TIME NO SEE! I'M SO HAPPY!
I'VE REALLY, REALLY MISSED YOU!
YAY YAY
KOFF KOFF
ALAD-DIN?
WHO'S HE TALKING TO?

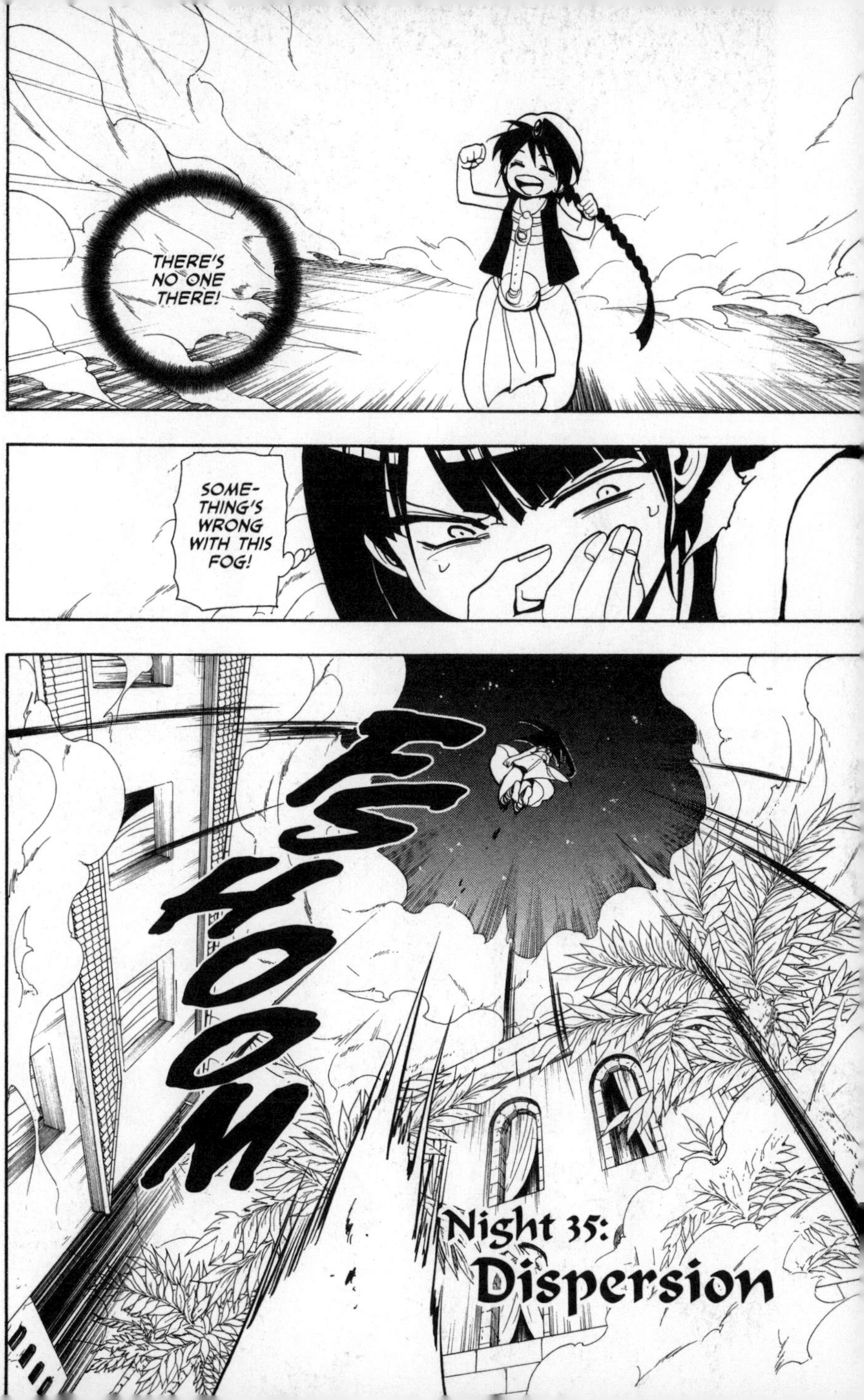
THERE'S NO ONE THERE!
SOME-THING'S WRONG WITH THIS FOG!
FSHOOOM
Night 35: Dispersion

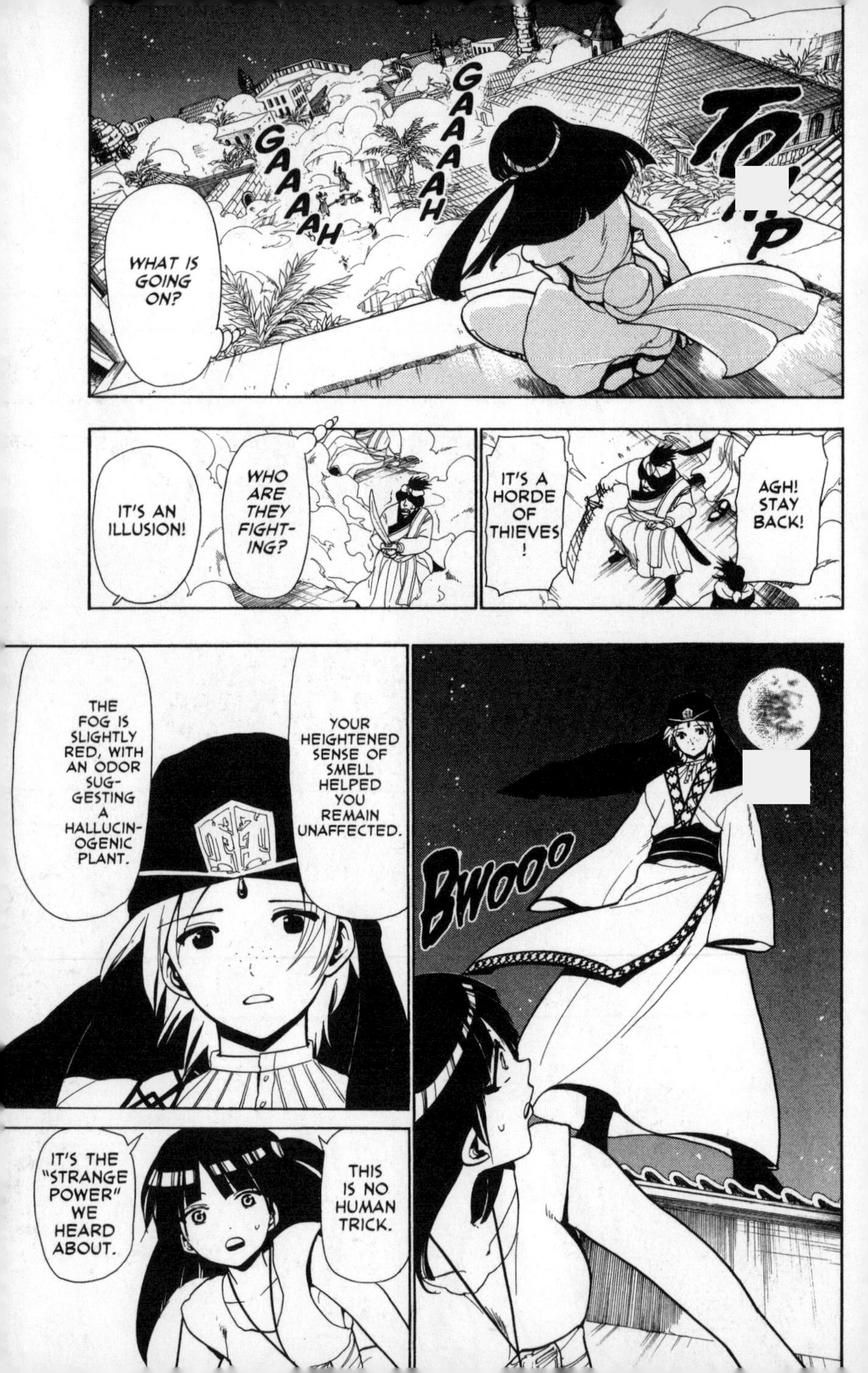
GAAAAH
GAAAAH
WHAT IS GOING ON?
AGH! STAY BACK!
IT'S A HORDE OF THIEVES!
WHO ARE THEY FIGHTING?
IT'S AN ILLUSION!
BWOOO
YOUR HEIGHTENED SENSE OF SMELL HELPED YOU REMAIN UNAFFECTED.
THE FOG IS SLIGHTLY RED, WITH AN ODOR SUGGESTING A HALLUCINOGENIC PLANT.
THIS IS NO HUMAN TRICK.
IT'S THE "STRANGE POWER" WE HEARD ABOUT.

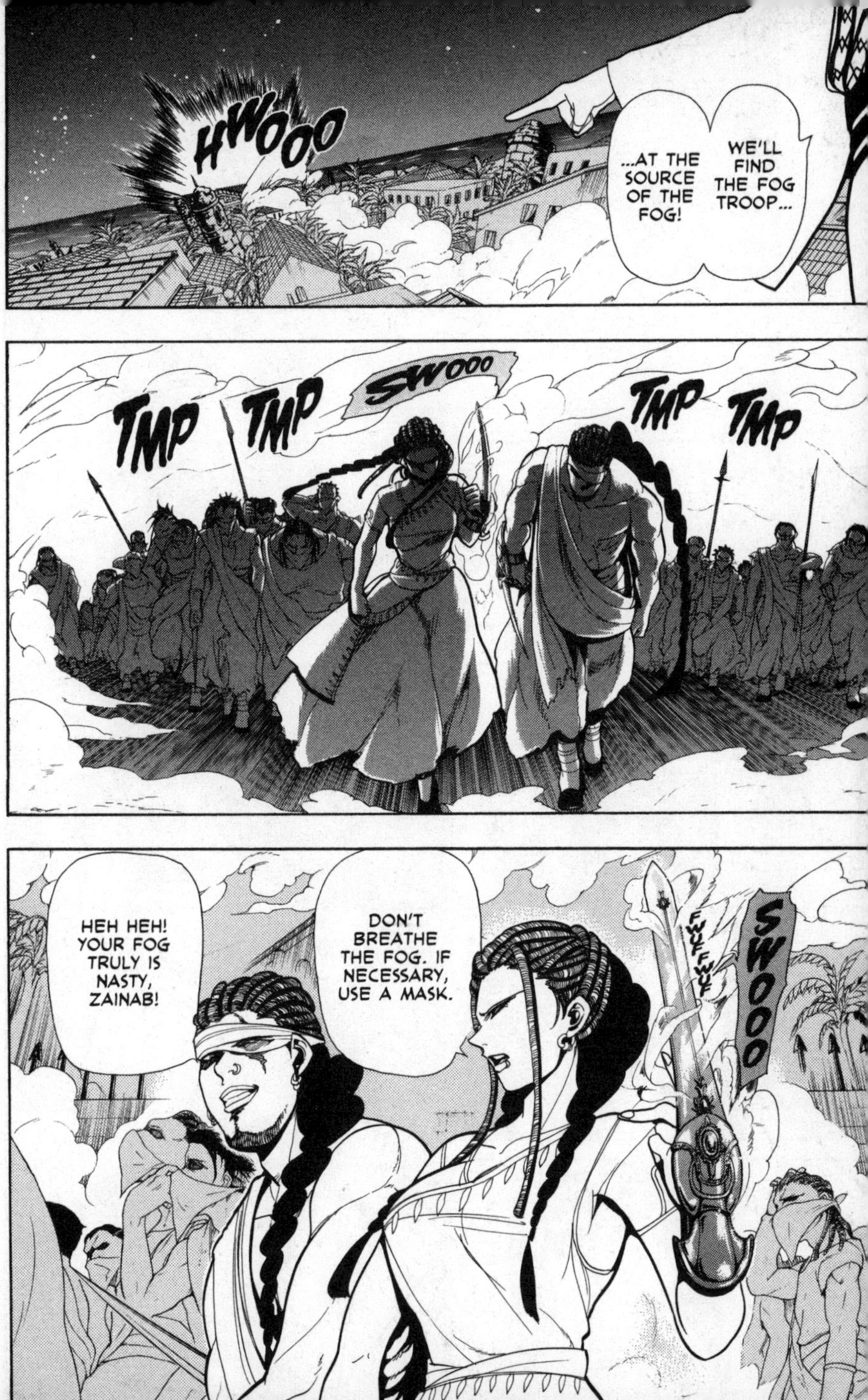
WE'LL FIND THE FOG TROOP...
...AT THE SOURCE OF THE FOG!
HWOOO
TMP TMP
TMP TMP
SWOOO
SWOOO
FWUF FWUF
DON'T BREATHE THE FOG. IF NECESSARY, USE A MASK.
HEH HEH! YOUR FOG TRULY IS NASTY, ZAINAB!

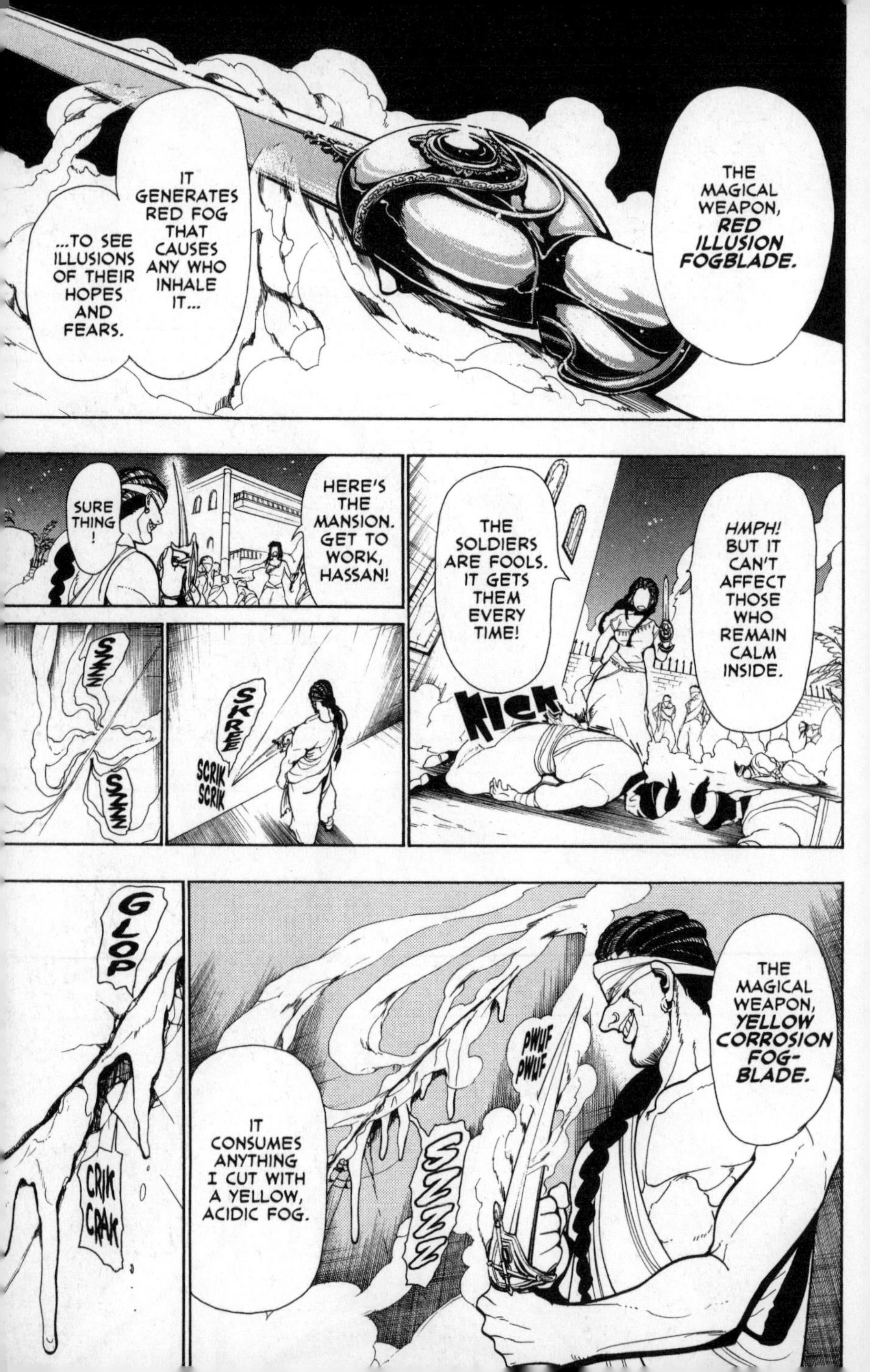
THE MAGICAL WEAPON, RED ILLUSION FOGBLADE.
IT GENERATES RED FOG THAT CAUSES ANY WHO INHALE IT...
...TO SEE ILLUSIONS OF THEIR HOPES AND FEARS.
HMPH! BUT IT CAN'T AFFECT THOSE WHO REMAIN CALM INSIDE.
THE SOLDIERS ARE FOOLS. IT GETS THEM EVERY TIME!
KICK
HERE'S THE MANSION. GET TO WORK, HASSAN!
SURE THING!
SKREE
SCRIK SCRIK
SZZZ
SZZZ
THE MAGICAL WEAPON, YELLOW CORROSION FOG-BLADE.
PWUF PWUF
SZZZZ
IT CONSUMES ANYTHING I CUT WITH A YELLOW, ACIDIC FOG.
GLOP
CRIK CRAK

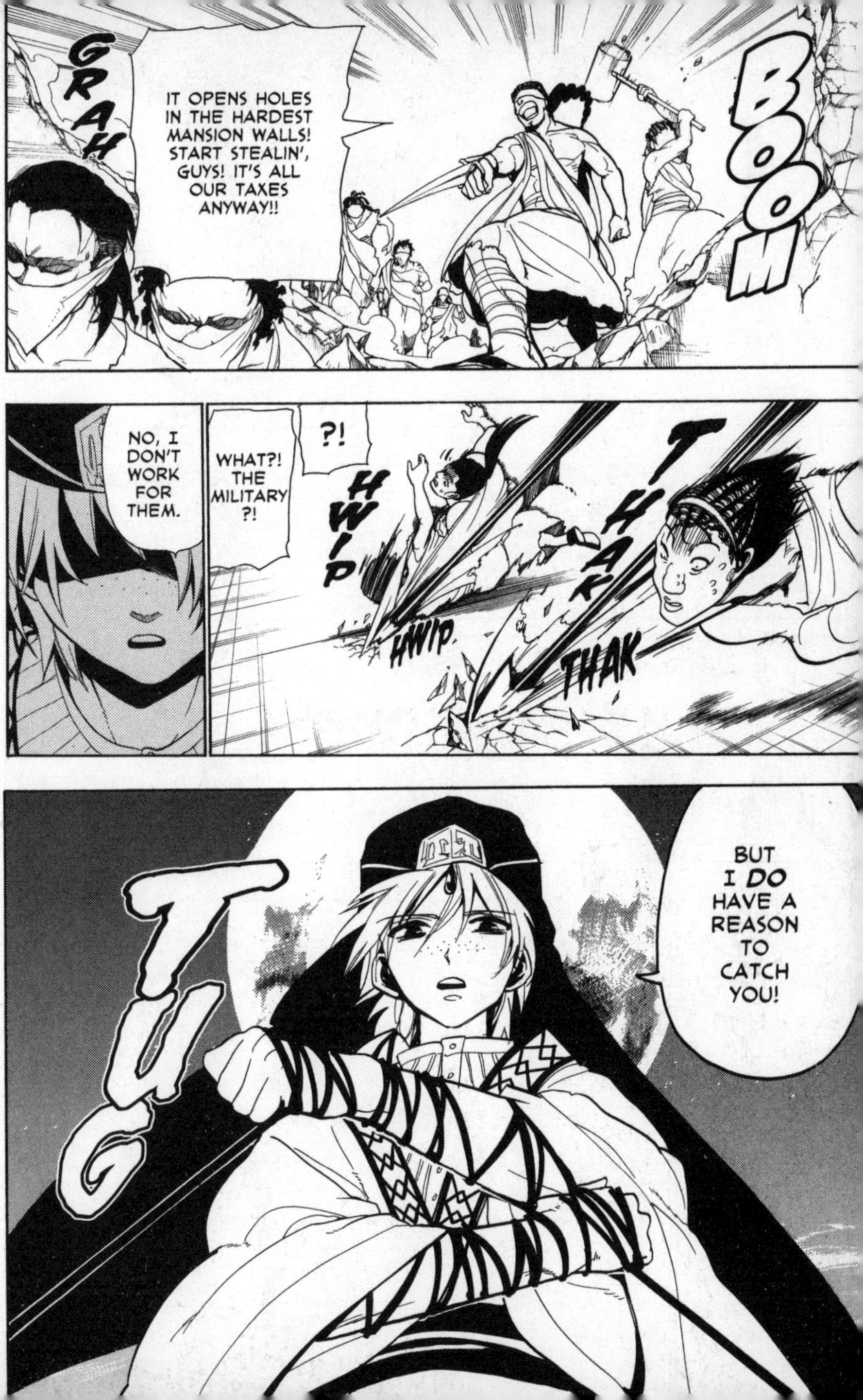
BOOOM
IT OPENS HOLES IN THE HARDEST MANSION WALLS! START STEALIN', GUYS! IT'S ALL OUR TAXES ANYWAY!!
GRAH
THAK
?!
HWIP
WHAT?! THE MILITARY?!
HWIP
THAK
NO, I DON'T WORK FOR THEM.
BUT I DO HAVE A REASON TO CATCH YOU!
TUG

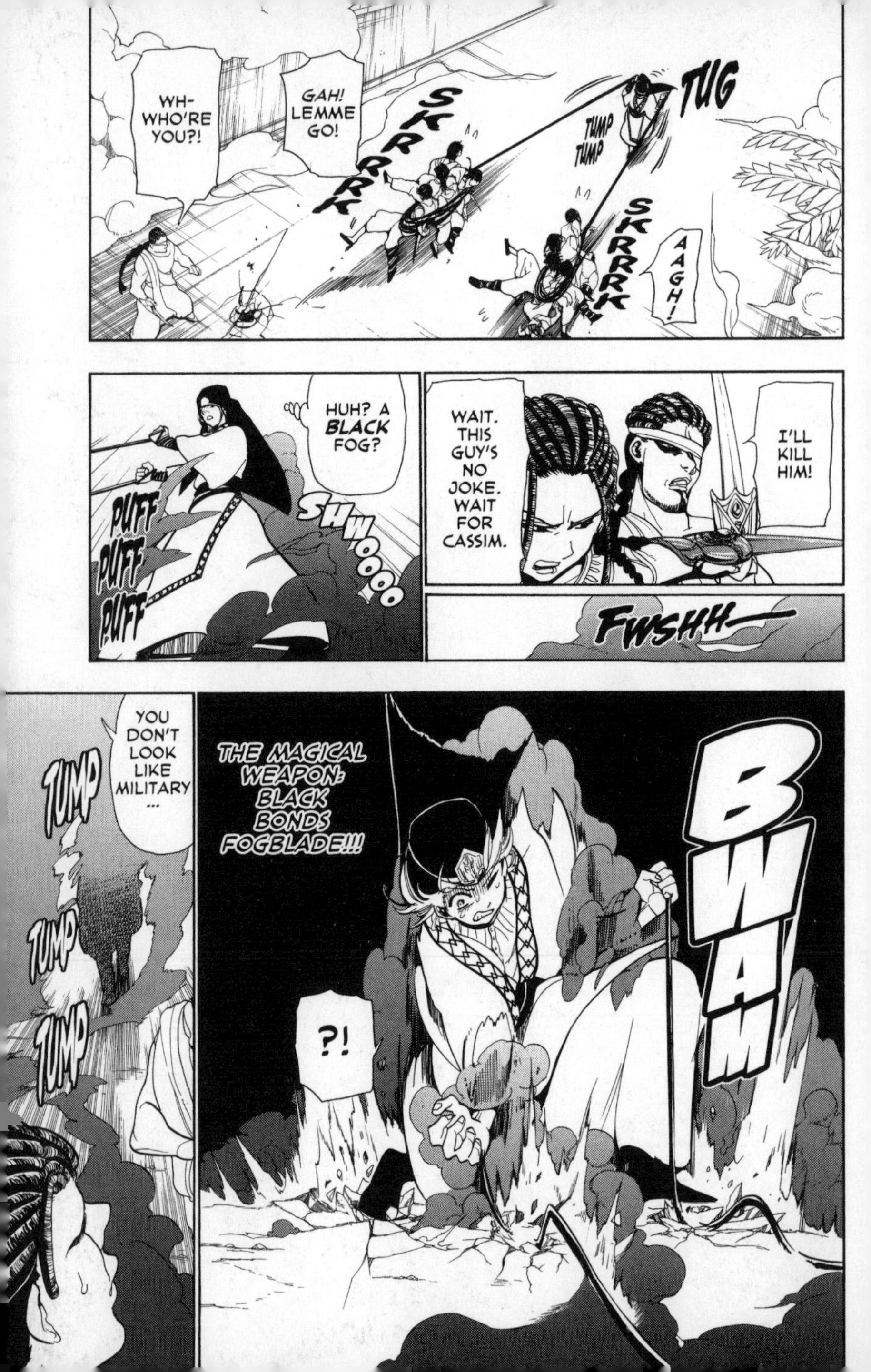
TUG
TUMP TUMP
SKRRRK
AAGH!
SKRRRK
GAH! LEMME GO!
WH- WHO'RE YOU?!
I'LL KILL HIM!
WAIT. THIS GUY'S NO JOKE. WAIT FOR CASSIM.
FWSHH
HUH? A BLACK FOG?
SHWOOOO
PUFF PUFF PUFF
BWAM
THE MAGICAL WEAPON: BLACK BONDS FOGBLADE!!!
?!
YOU DON'T LOOK LIKE MILITARY...
TUMP
TUMP
TUMP

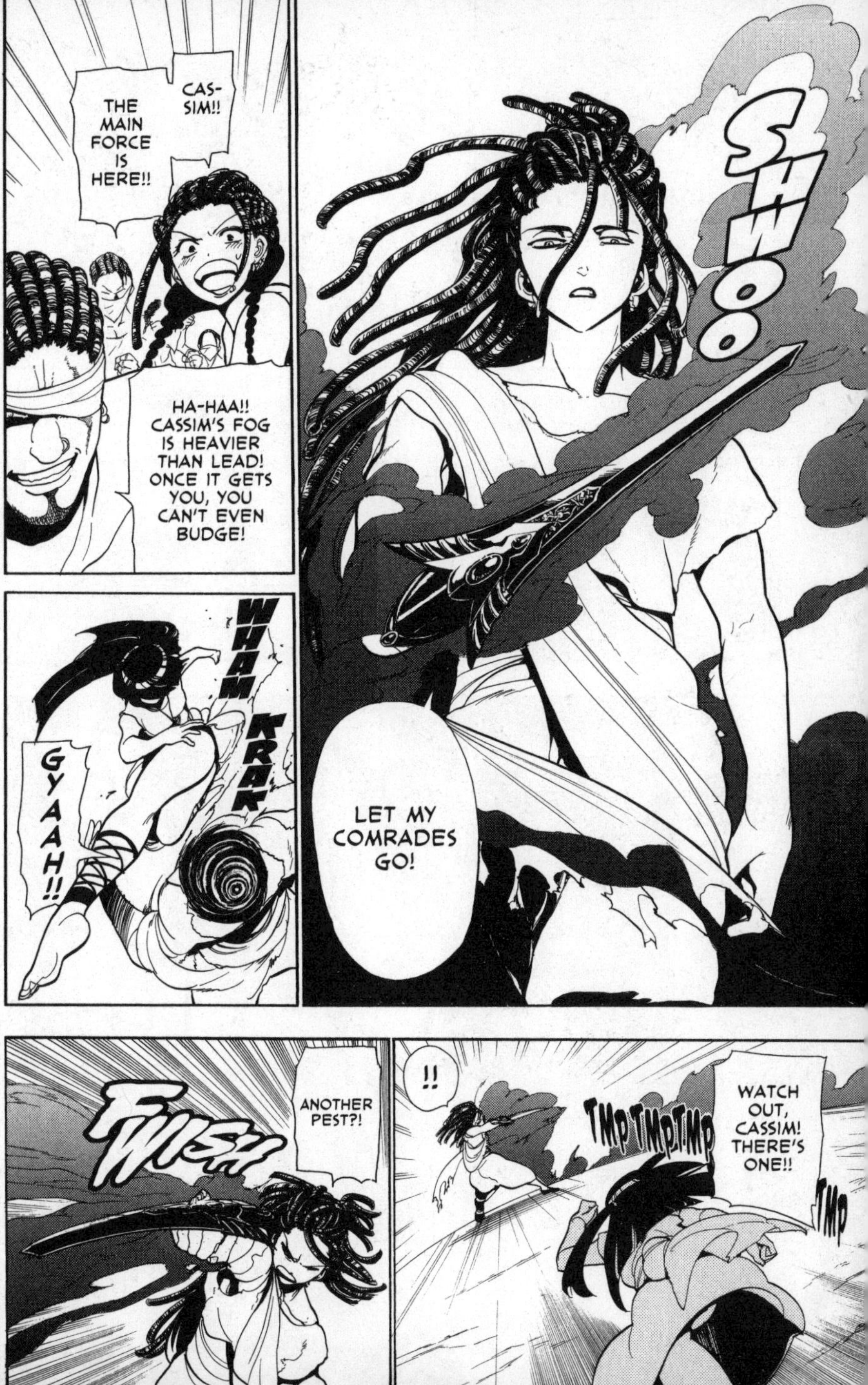
SHWOOO
LET MY COMRADES GO!
CAS-SIM!!
THE MAIN FORCE IS HERE!!
HA-HAA!! CASSIM'S FOG IS HEAVIER THAN LEAD! ONCE IT GETS YOU, YOU CAN'T EVEN BUDGE!
WHAM KRAK
GYAAH!!
WATCH OUT, CASSIM! THERE'S ONE!!
!!
TMP TMP TMP
TMP
ANOTHER PEST?!
FWISH

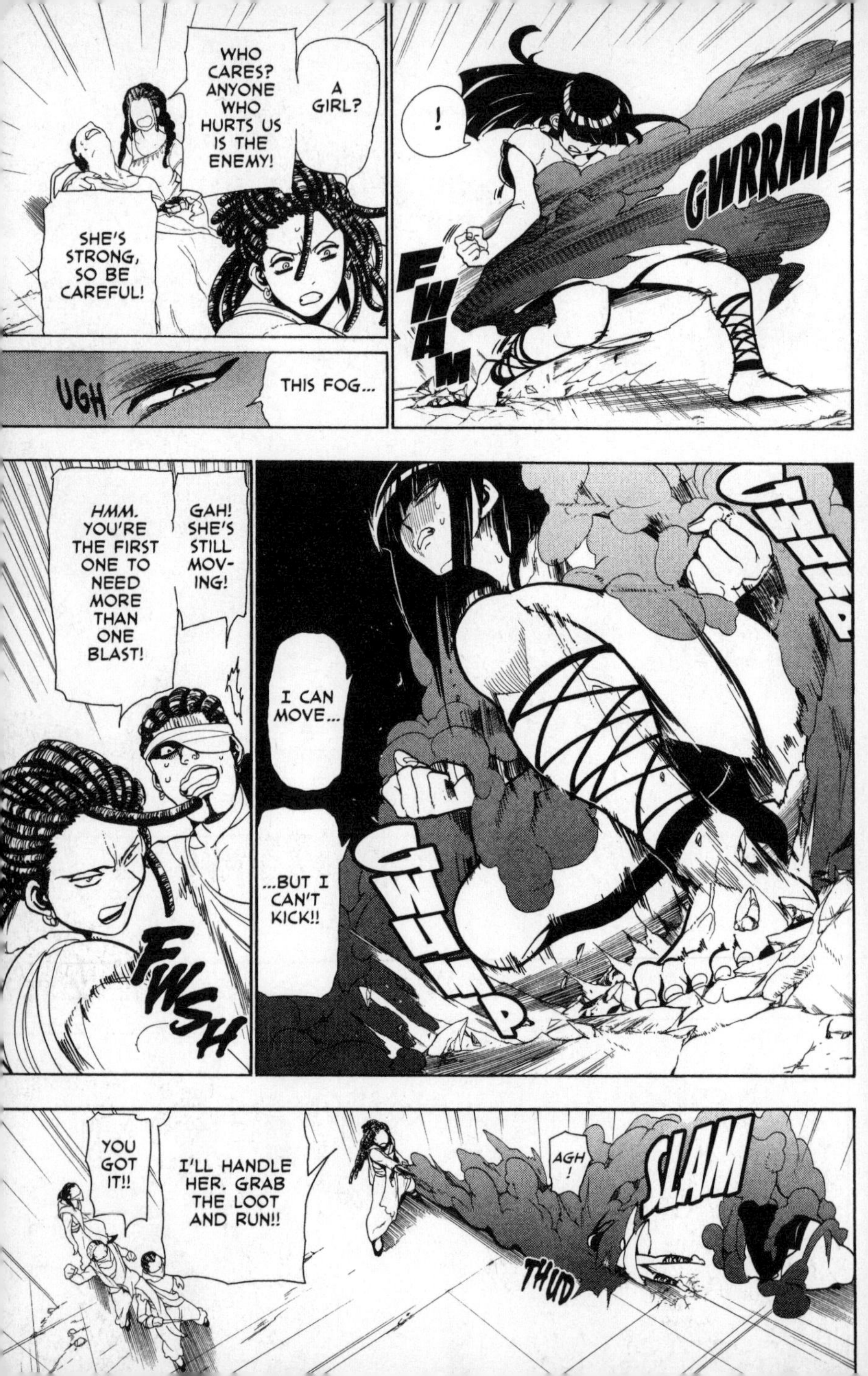
!
GWRRMP
FWAM
A GIRL?
WHO CARES? ANYONE WHO HURTS US IS THE ENEMY!
SHE'S STRONG, SO BE CAREFUL!
THIS FOG...
UGH
GWHUMP
I CAN MOVE...
...BUT I CAN'T KICK!!
GWHUMP
GAH! SHE'S STILL MOV-ING!
HMM. YOU'RE THE FIRST ONE TO NEED MORE THAN ONE BLAST!
FWSH
SLAM
AGH!
THUD
I'LL HANDLE HER. GRAB THE LOOT AND RUN!!
YOU GOT IT!!

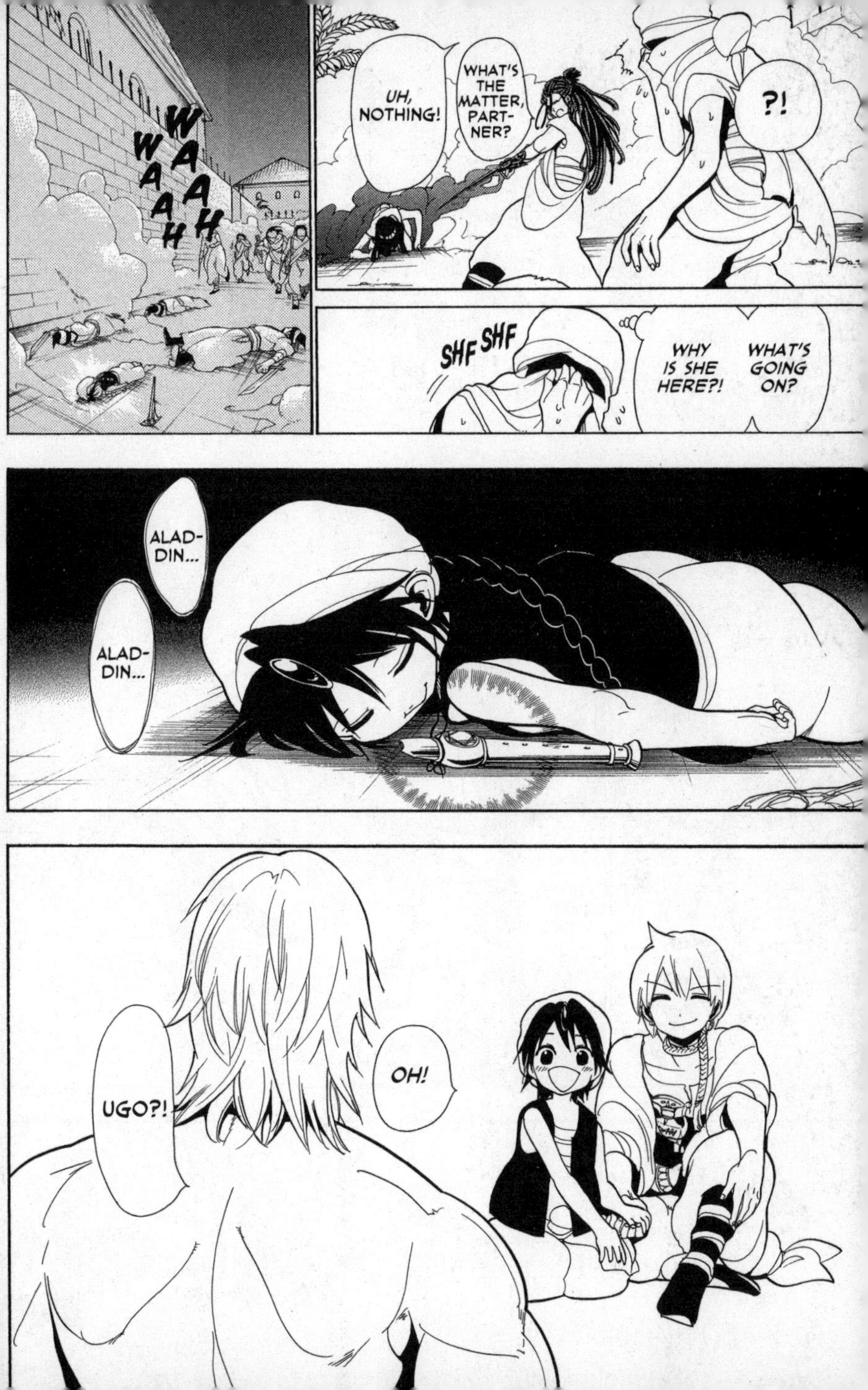
?!
WHAT'S THE MATTER, PARTNER?
UH, NOTHING!
WHAT'S GOING ON?
WHY IS SHE HERE?!
SHF SHF
WAAAH
WAAAH
ALAD-DIN...
ALAD-DIN...
OH!
UGO?!

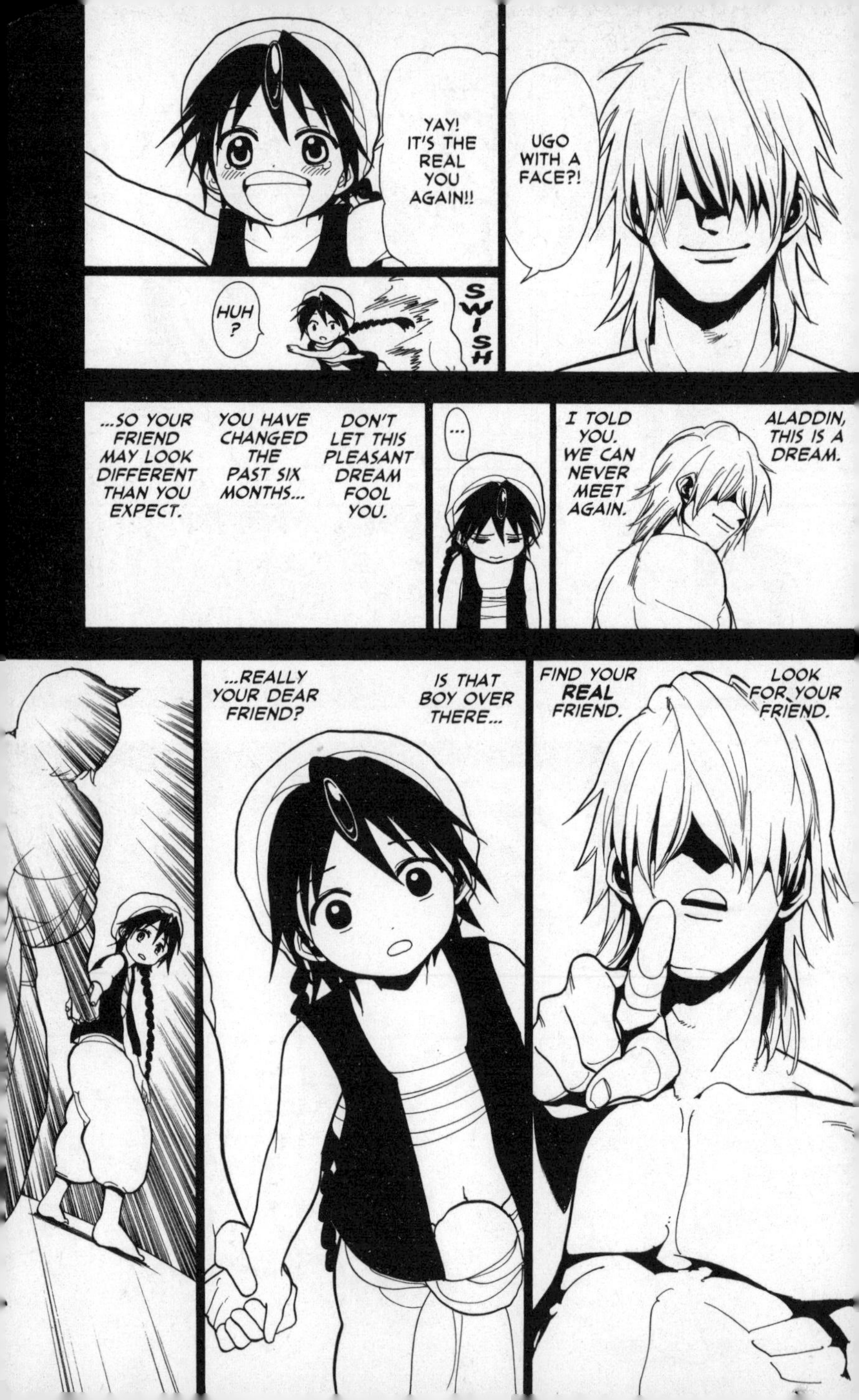
UGO WITH A FACE?!
YAY! IT'S THE REAL YOU AGAIN!!
HUH?
SWISH
ALADDIN, THIS IS A DREAM.
I TOLD YOU. WE CAN NEVER MEET AGAIN.
...
DON'T LET THIS PLEASANT DREAM FOOL YOU.
YOU HAVE CHANGED THE PAST SIX MONTHS...
...SO YOUR FRIEND MAY LOOK DIFFERENT THAN YOU EXPECT.
LOOK FOR YOUR FRIEND.
FIND YOUR **REAL** FRIEND.
IS THAT BOY OVER THERE...
...REALLY YOUR DEAR FRIEND?

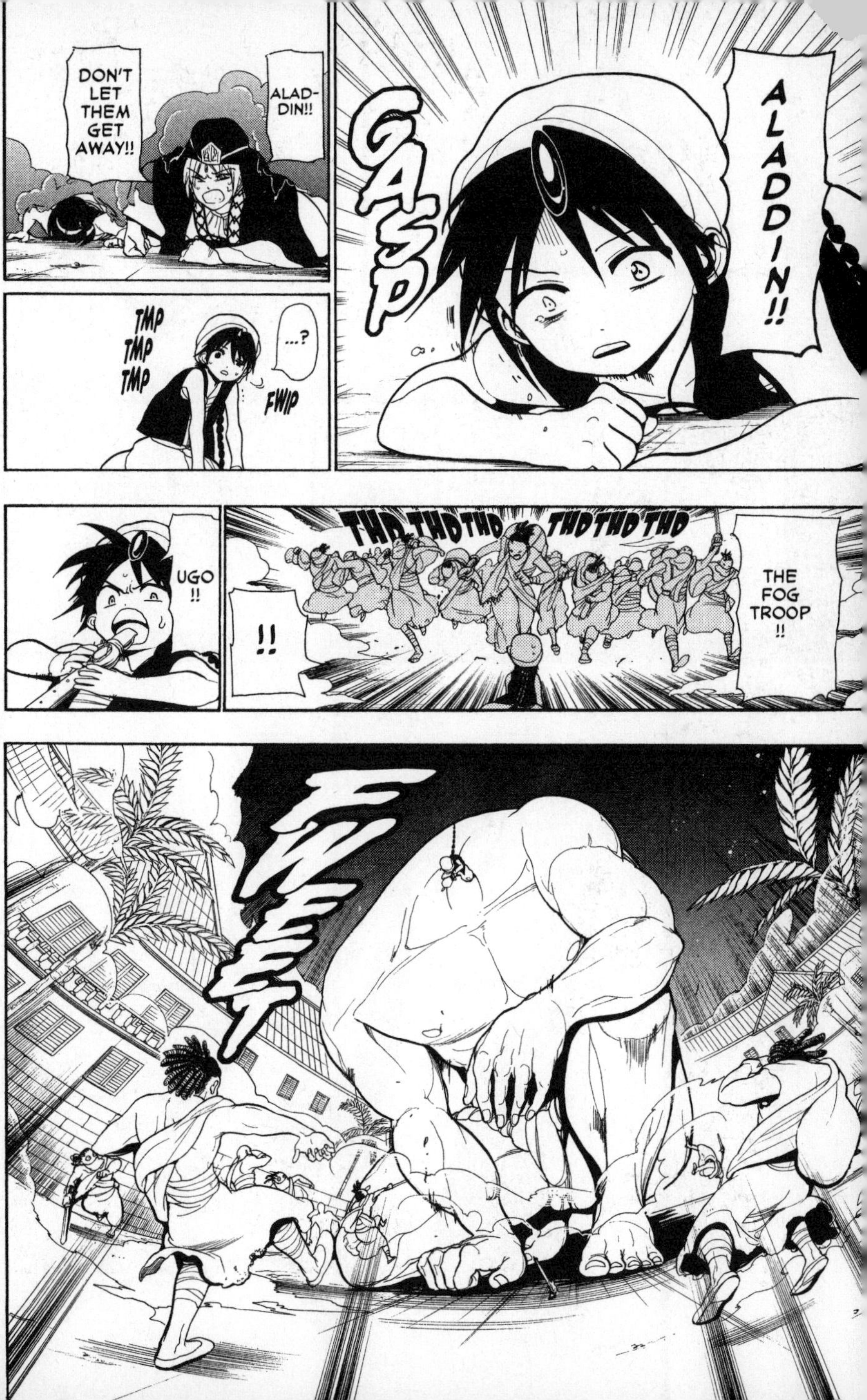
ALADDIN!!
GASP
ALAD-DIN!!
DON'T LET THEM GET AWAY!!
...?
FWIP
TMP TMP TMP
THE FOG TROOP!!
THD THD THD THD THD THD
!!
UGO!!
FWEEET

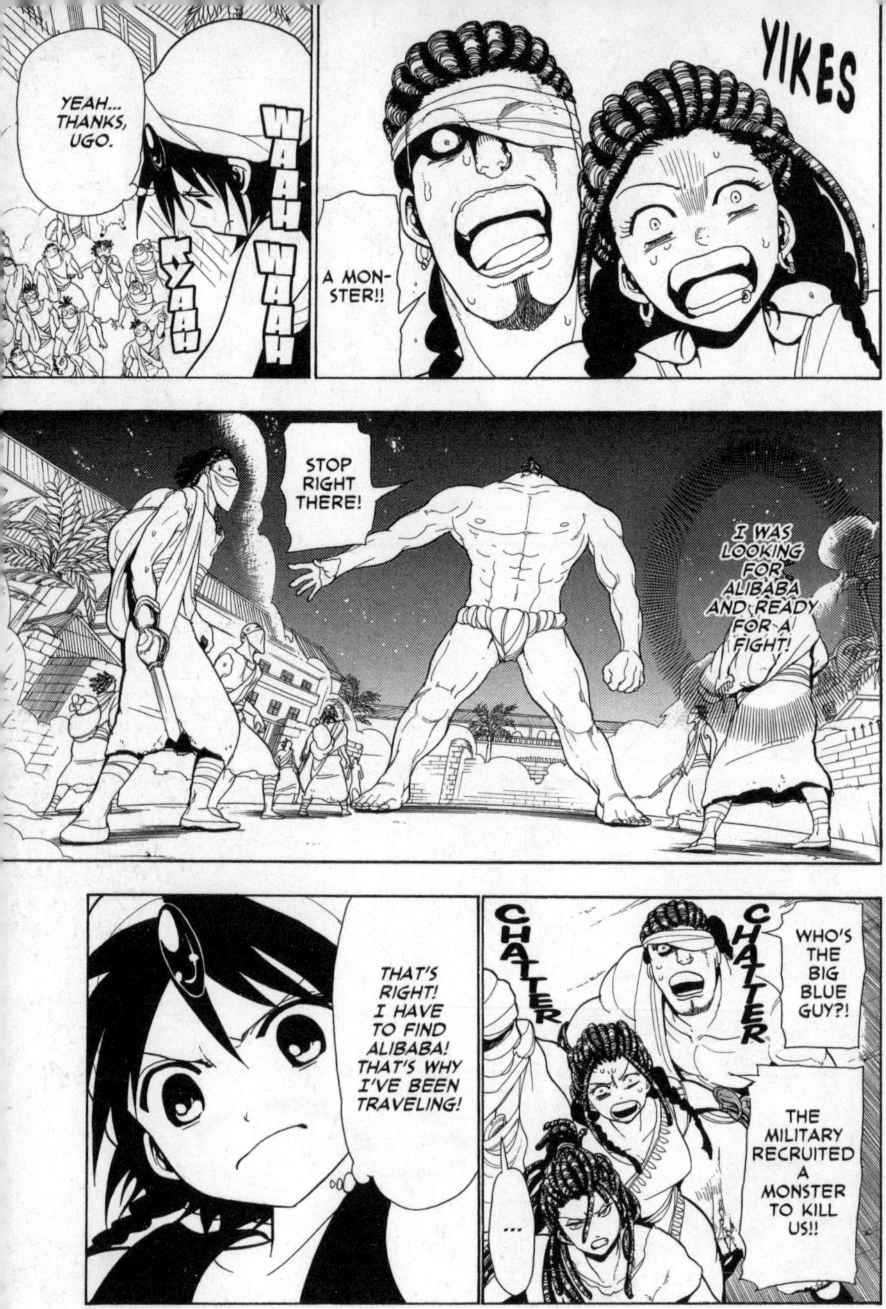
YIKES
A MON-STER!!
YEAH... THANKS, UGO.
WAAH WAAH
KYAAH
STOP RIGHT THERE!
I WAS LOOKING FOR ALIBABA AND READY FOR A FIGHT!
...
CHATTER CHATTER
WHO'S THE BIG BLUE GUY?!
THE MILITARY RECRUITED A MONSTER TO KILL US!!
...
THAT'S RIGHT! I HAVE TO FIND ALIBABA! THAT'S WHY I'VE BEEN TRAVELING!

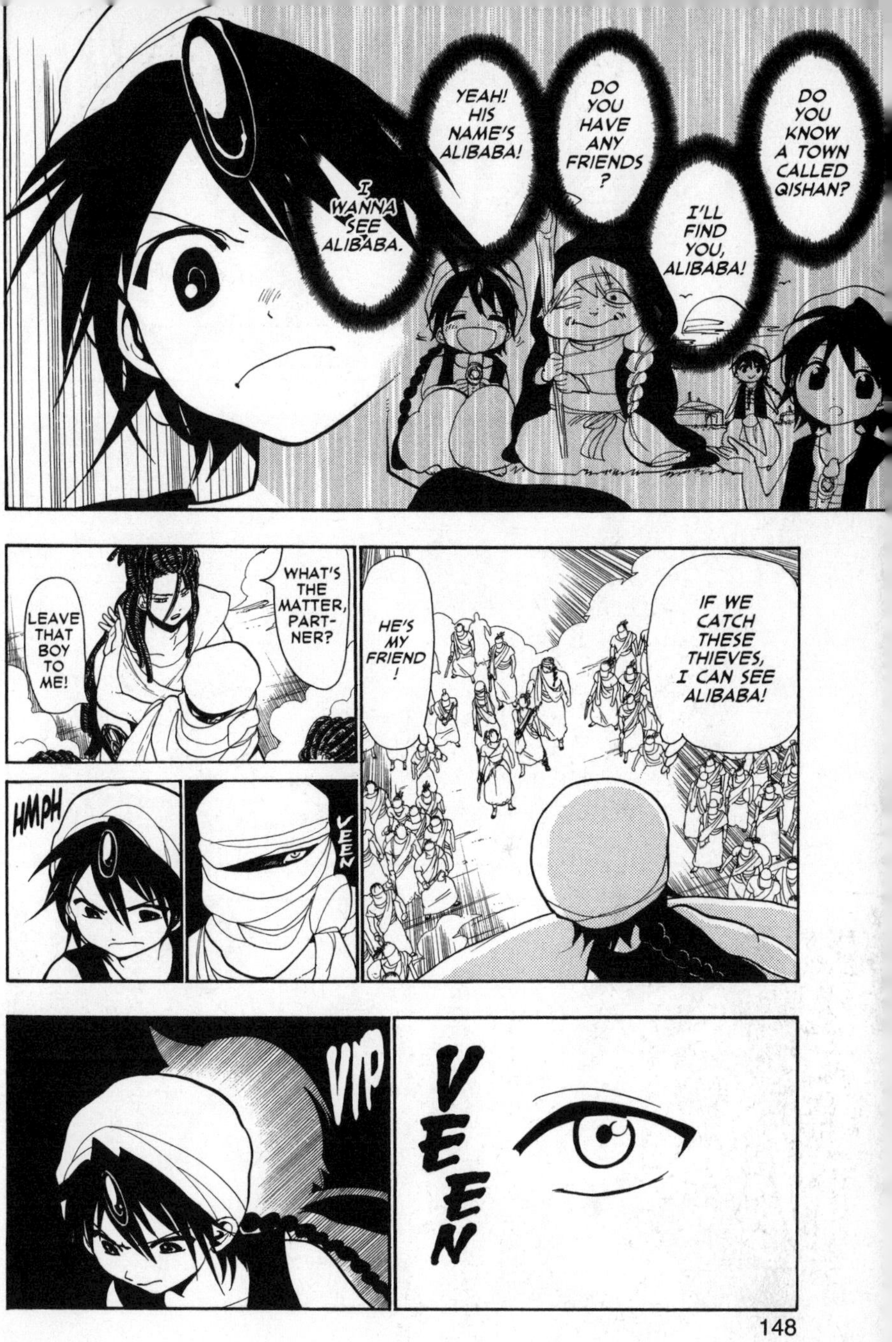
DO YOU KNOW A TOWN CALLED QISHAN?
I'LL FIND YOU, ALIBABA!
DO YOU HAVE ANY FRIENDS?
YEAH! HIS NAME'S ALIBABA!
I WANNA SEE ALIBABA.
IF WE CATCH THESE THIEVES, I CAN SEE ALIBABA!
HE'S MY FRIEND!
WHAT'S THE MATTER, PARTNER?
LEAVE THAT BOY TO ME!
VEEN
HMPH
VEEN
VIP

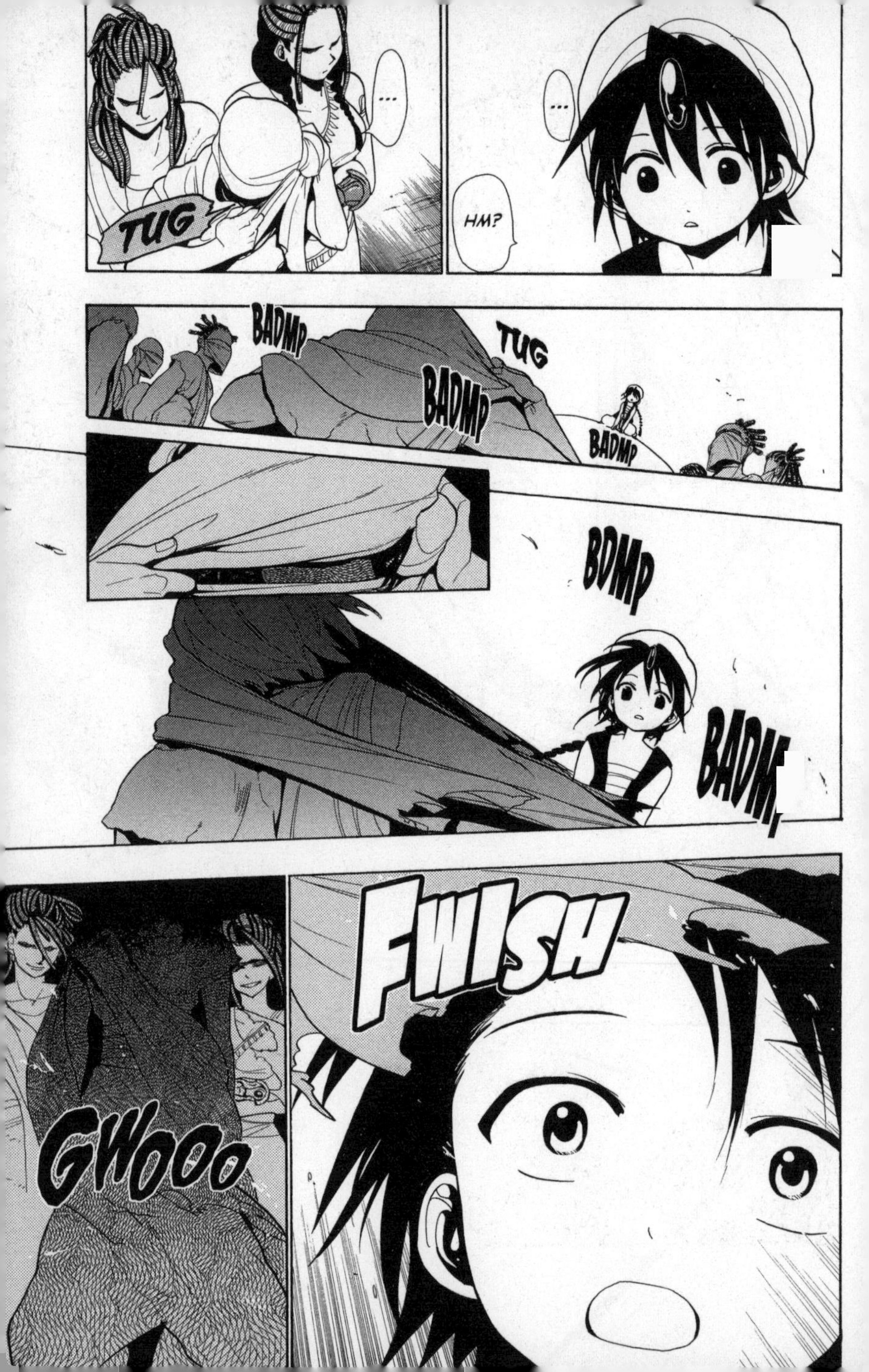
...
HM?
...
TUG
BADMP
TUG
BADMP
BADMP
BDMP
FWISH
GWOOO

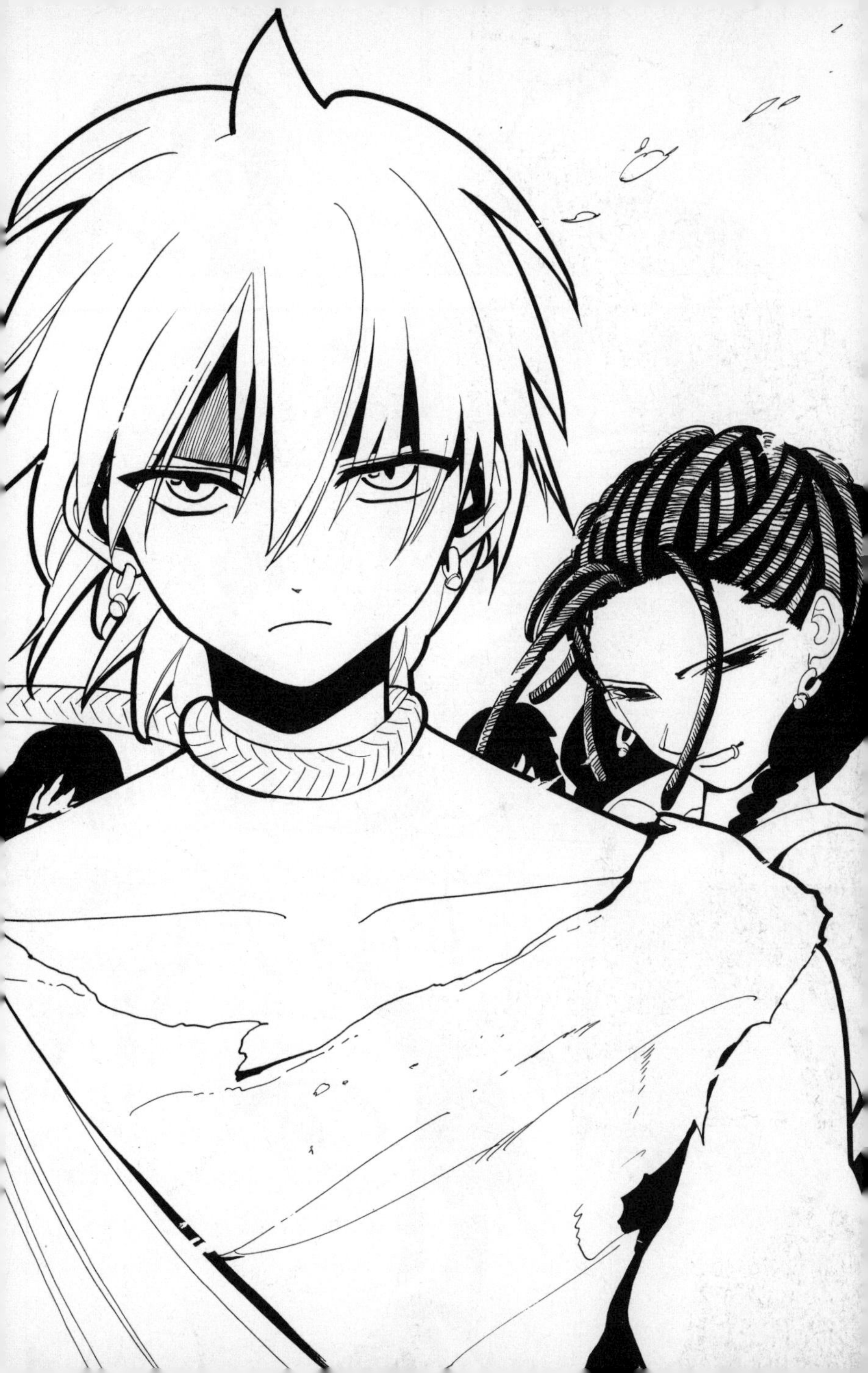

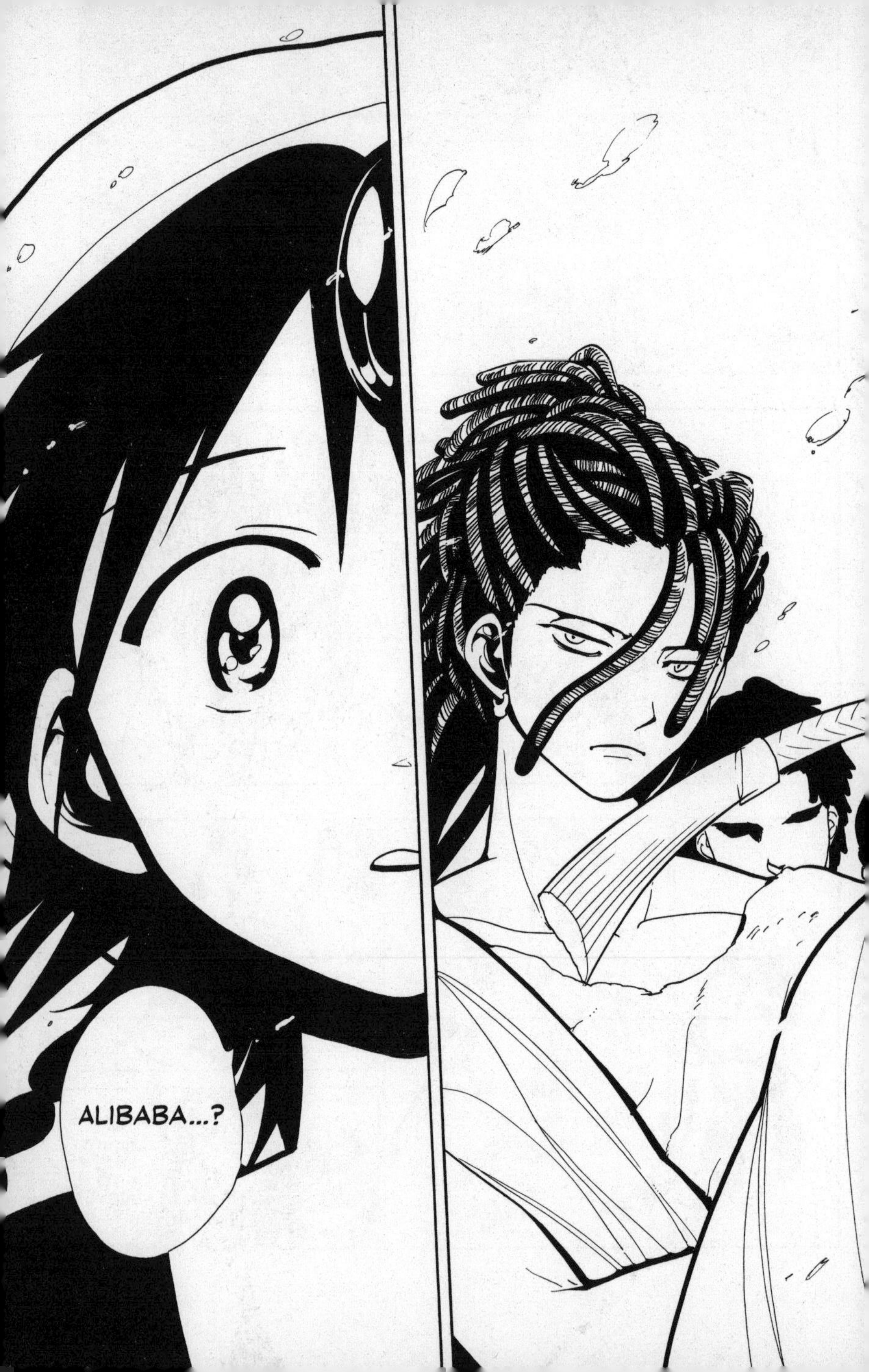
ALIBABA...?

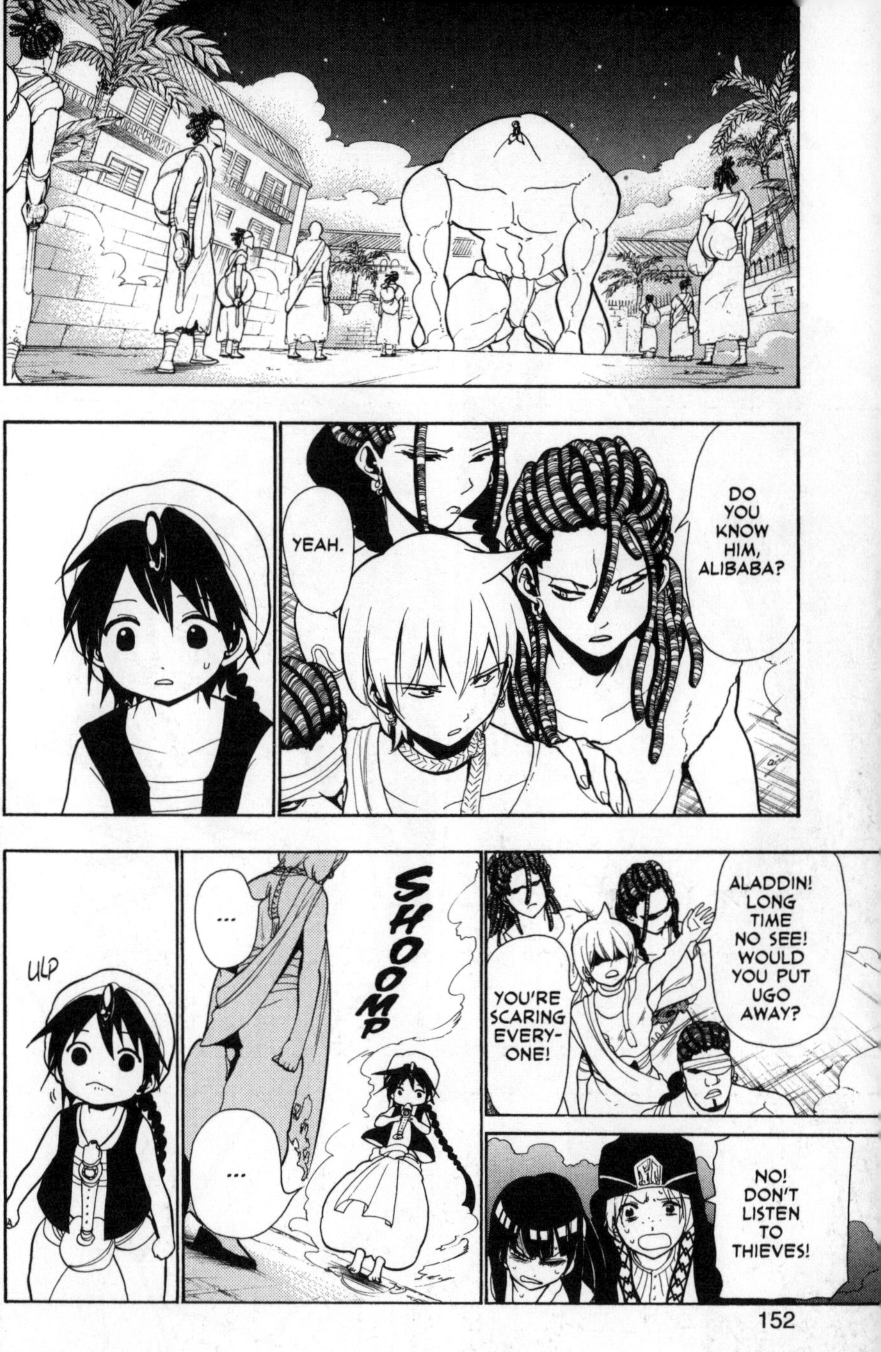
DO YOU KNOW HIM, ALIBABA?
YEAH.
ALADDIN! LONG TIME NO SEE! WOULD YOU PUT UGO AWAY?
YOU'RE SCARING EVERY-ONE!
NO! DON'T LISTEN TO THIEVES!
SHOOOMP
...
...
ULP

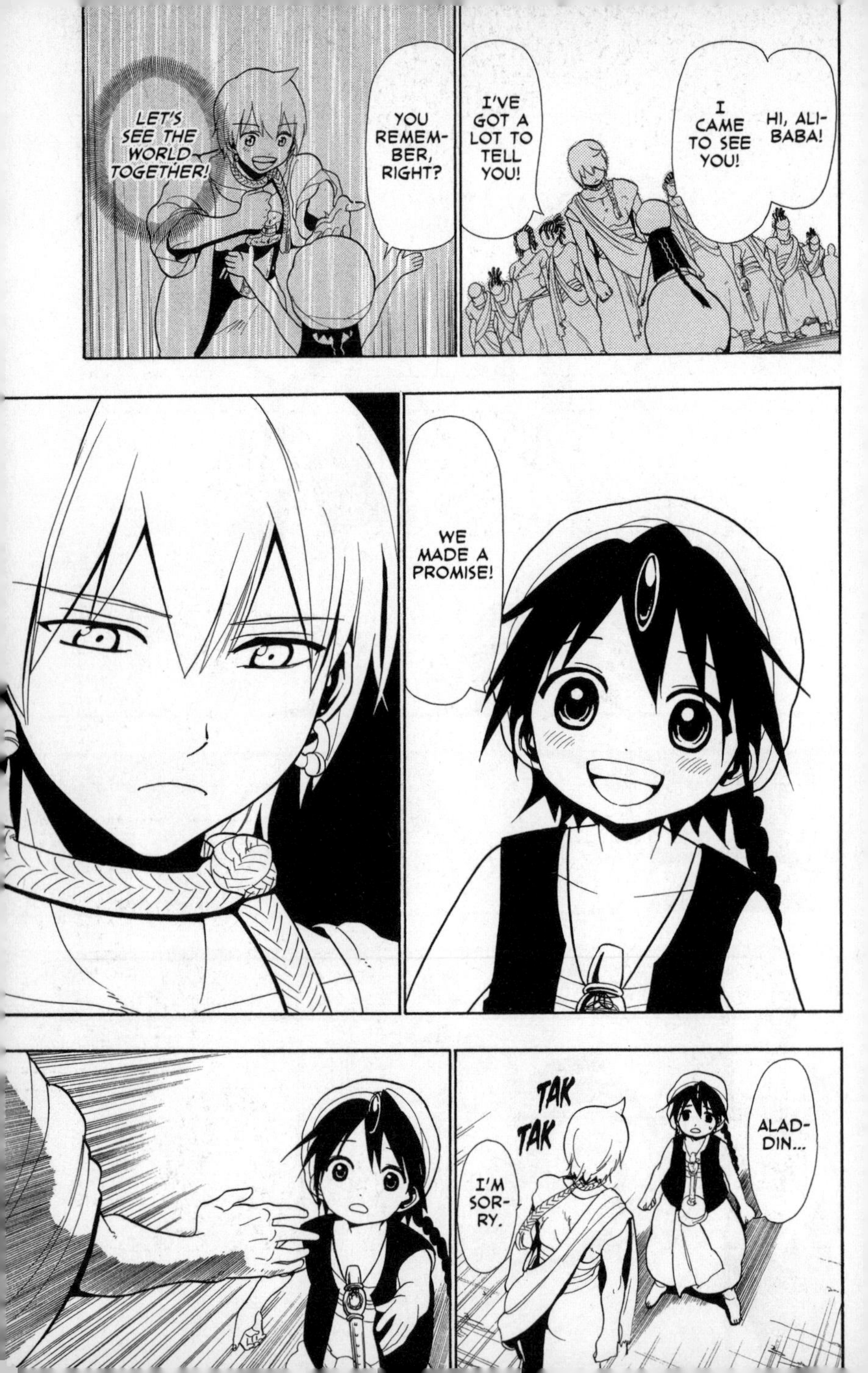
HI, ALI-BABA!
I CAME TO SEE YOU!
I'VE GOT A LOT TO TELL YOU!
YOU REMEMBER, RIGHT?
LET'S SEE THE WORLD TOGETHER!
WE MADE A PROMISE!
ALAD-DIN...
TAK TAK
I'M SOR-RY.

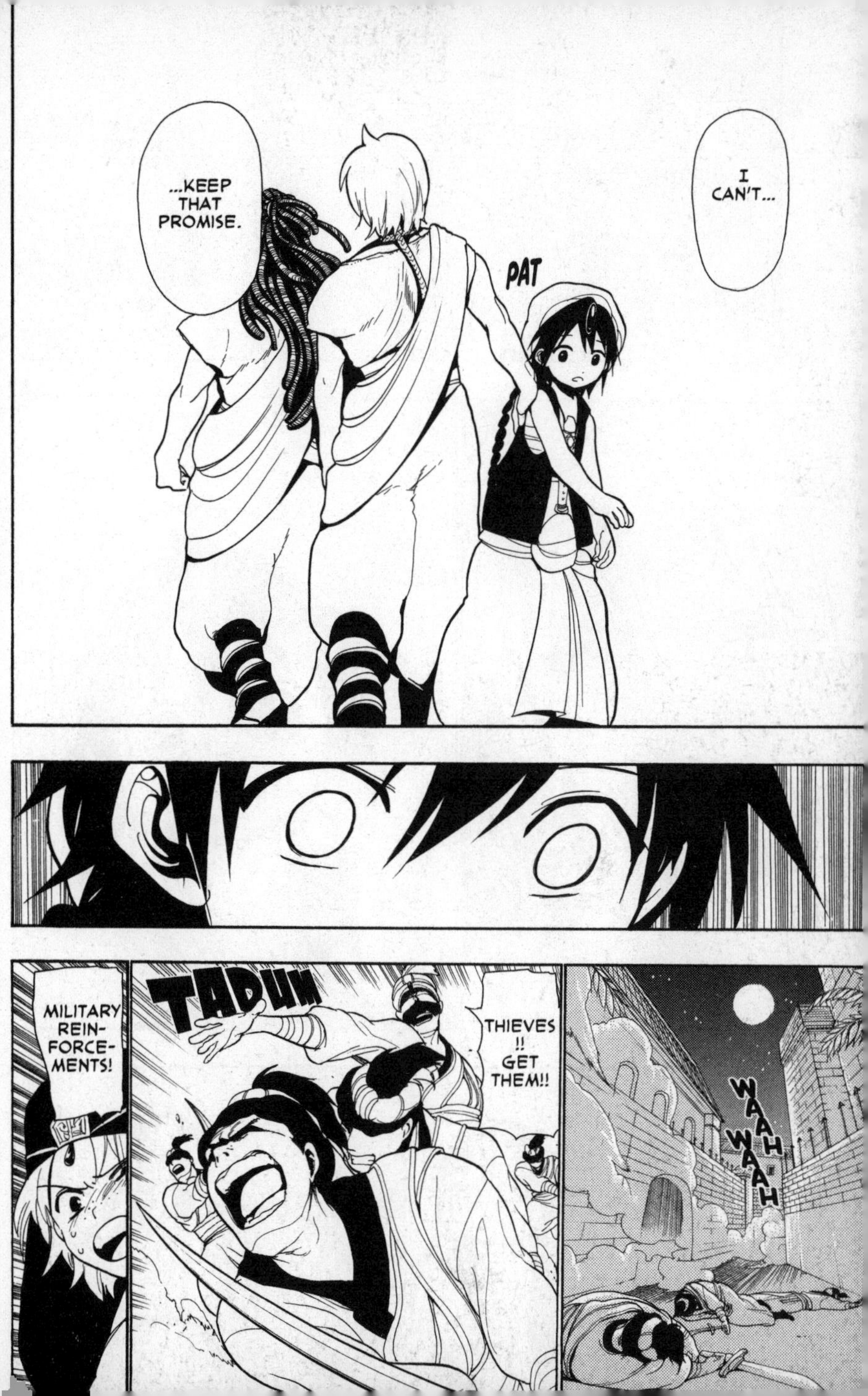
I CAN'T...
PAT
...KEEP THAT PROMISE.
WAAH WAAH
THIEVES!! GET THEM!!
TADUM
MILITARY REIN-FORCEMENTS!

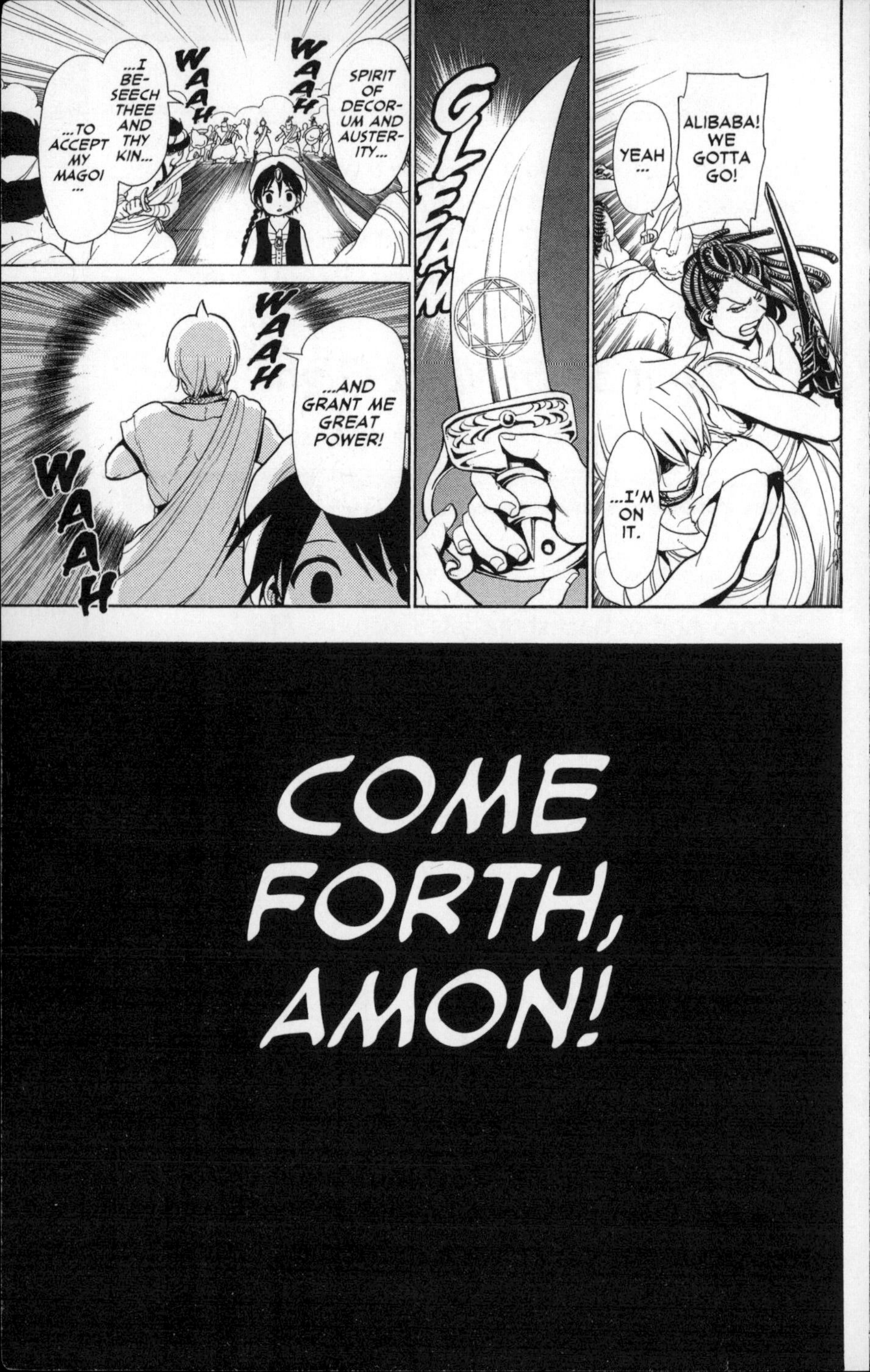
ALIBABA! WE GOTTA GO!
YEAH...
...I'M ON IT.
GLEAM
SPIRIT OF DECORUM AND AUSTERITY...
WAAH
...I BESEECH THEE AND THY KIN...
WAAH
...TO ACCEPT MY MAGOI...
WAAH
...AND GRANT ME GREAT POWER!
WAAH
COME FORTH, AMON!

message from Shinobu Ohtaka

There's actually a ***hidden episode*** that takes place between Night 36 and Night 37, which are found in this volume. On March 10, 2010, it was posted in the ***"Manga Author Backstage Shinobu Ohtaka Corner"*** on *Shonen Sunday's* homepage *Web Sunday:*

Night 36.5: Night Flight

You can read "Night Flight" at the ***address below.****

http://websunday.net/backstage/ootaka/033.html

"Manga Author Backstage" also includes ***Magi production secrets*** and ***little episodes*** from work and so on. I try to update it ***every Wednesday,*** so please ***check it out!***

http://websunday.net/backstage/

You can also read the most recent Backstage

on cell phones!!

Mobile Sunday

http://mobasun.com

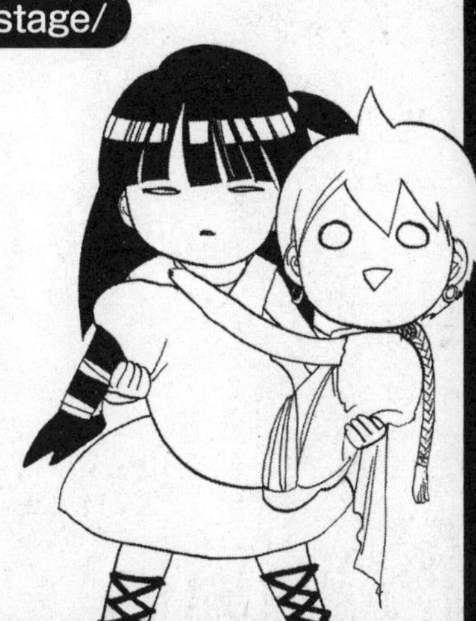

*Links to *Shonen Sunday* (Japanese). Current as of June 2010. Backstage content may be removed without advance notice. Thank you for your understanding.

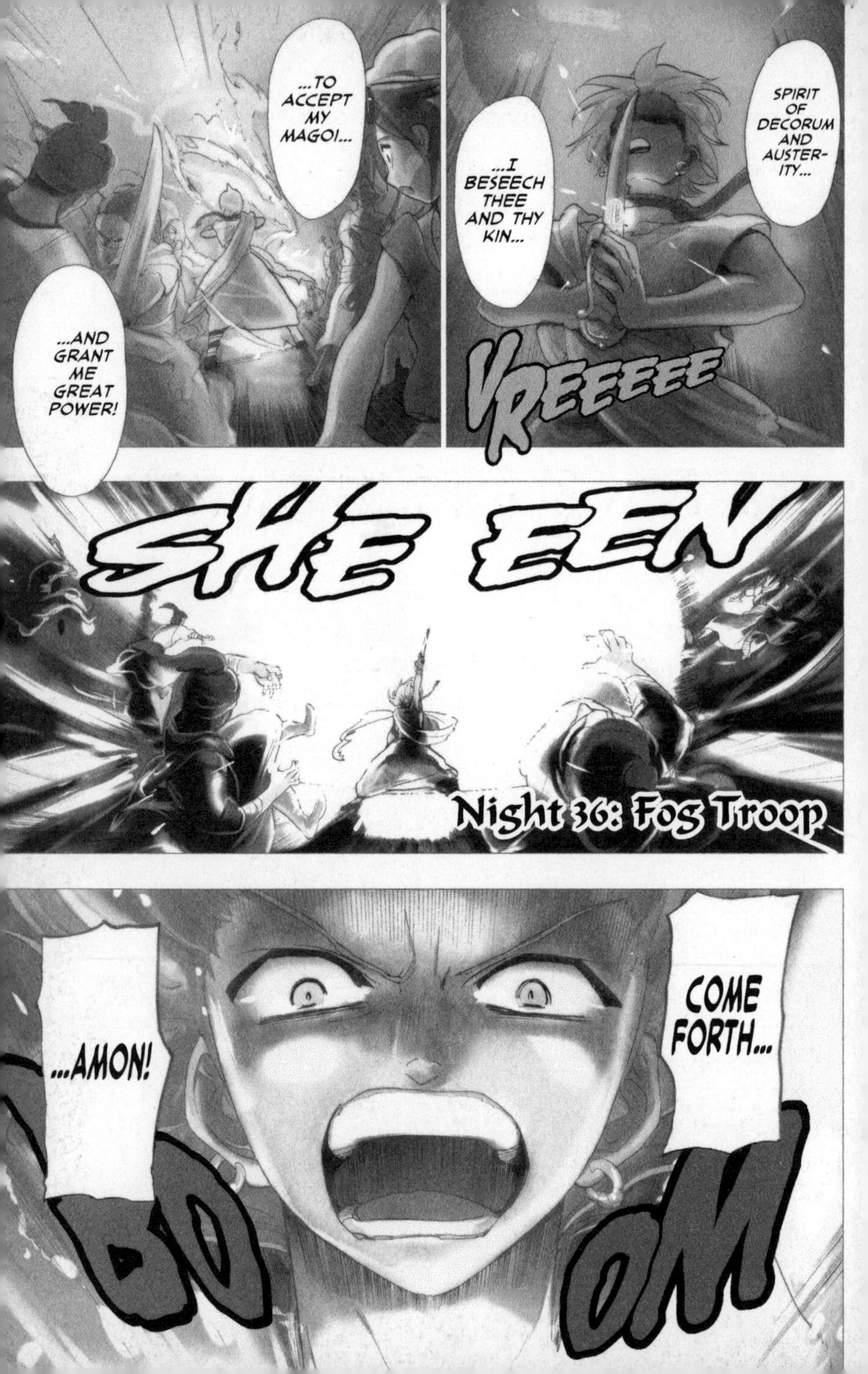
SPIRIT OF DECORUM AND AUSTERITY...
...I BESEECH THEE AND THY KIN...
VREEEEEE
...TO ACCEPT MY MAGOI...
...AND GRANT ME GREAT POWER!
SHEEEN
Night 36: Fog Troop
COME FORTH...
...AMON!
BOOOM

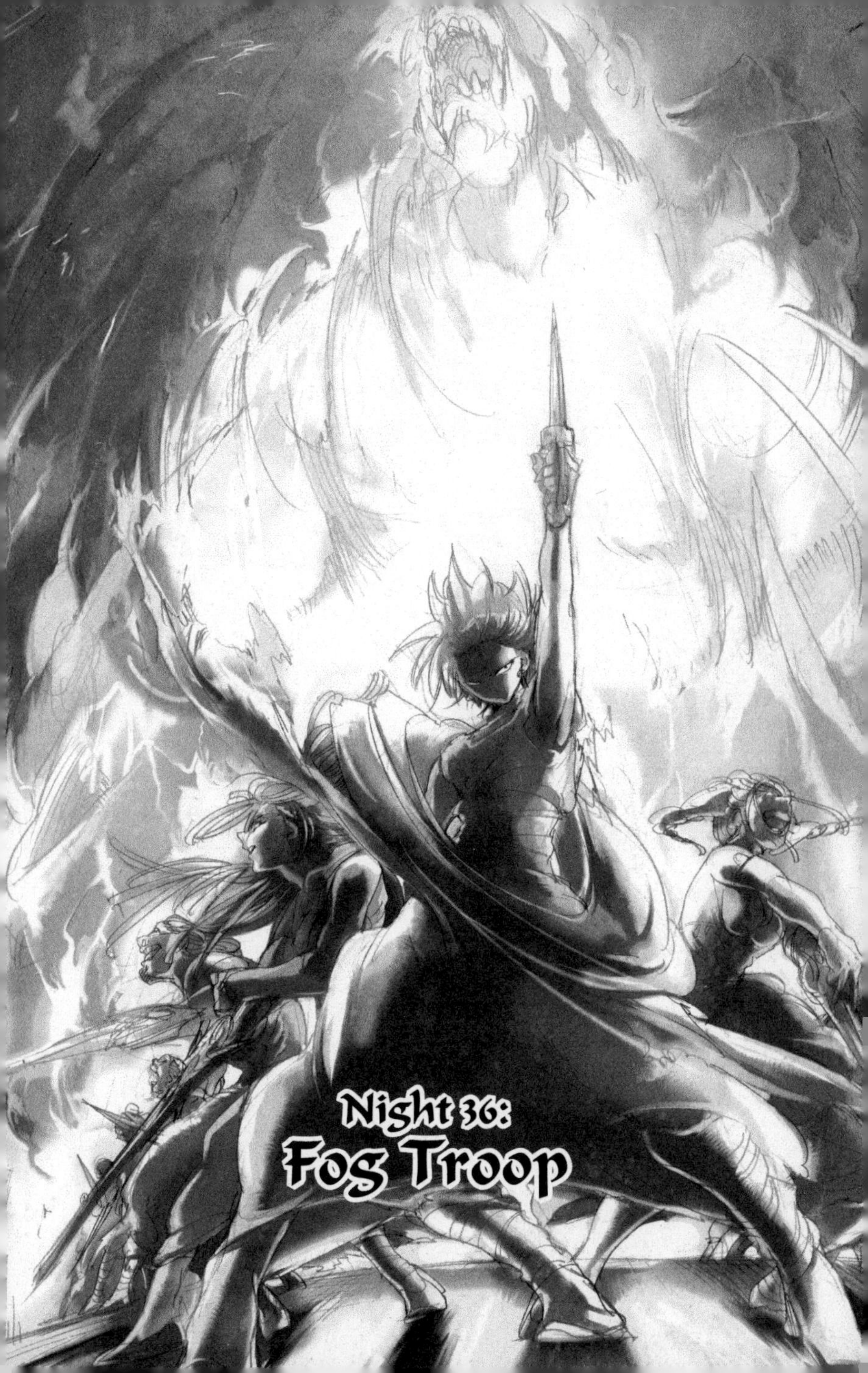
Night 36:
Fog Troop

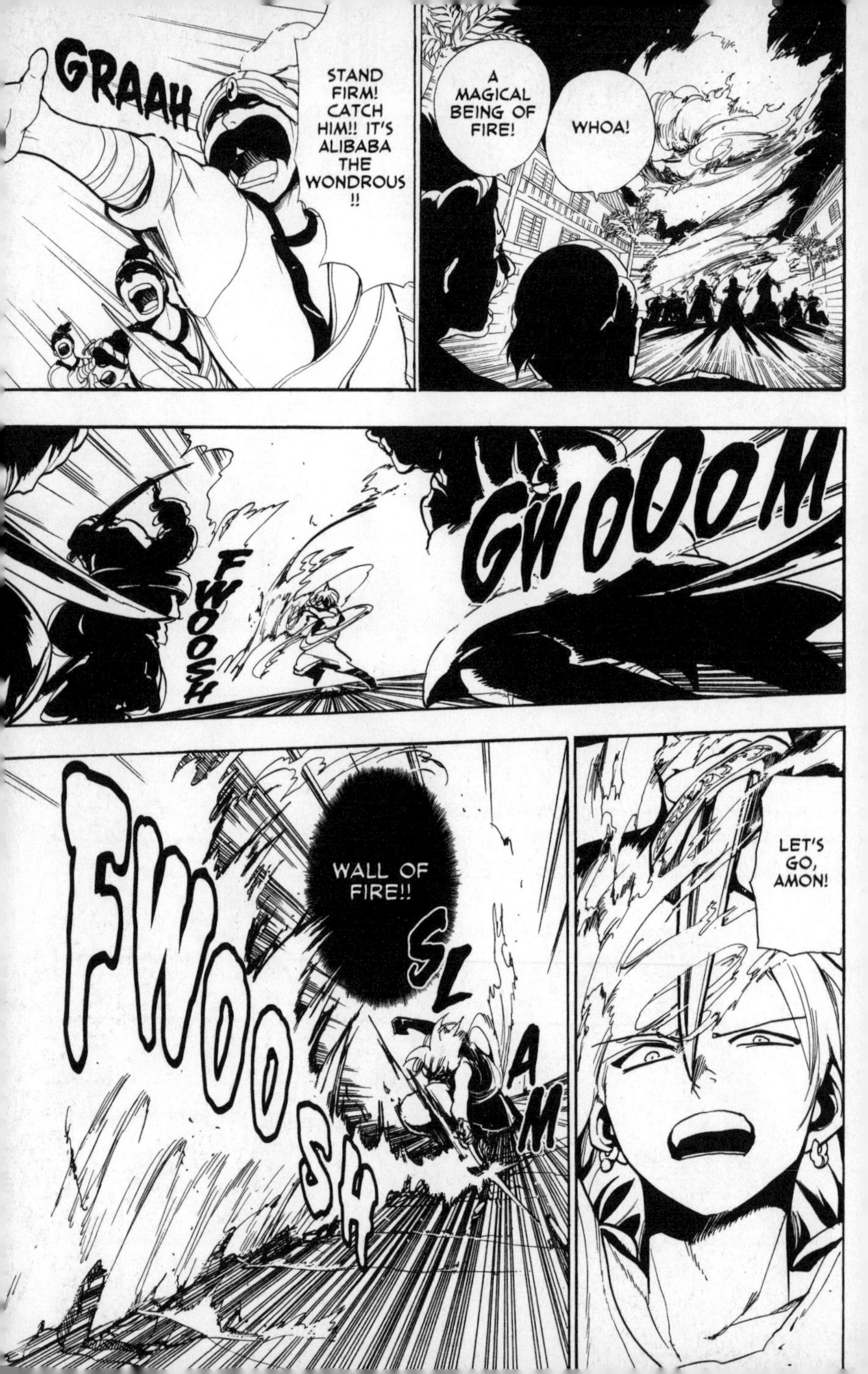
WHOA!
A MAGICAL BEING OF FIRE!
STAND FIRM! CATCH HIM!! IT'S ALIBABA THE WONDROUS!!
GRAAH
GWOOOM
FWOOSH
LET'S GO, AMON!
WALL OF FIRE!!
SLAM
FWOOSH

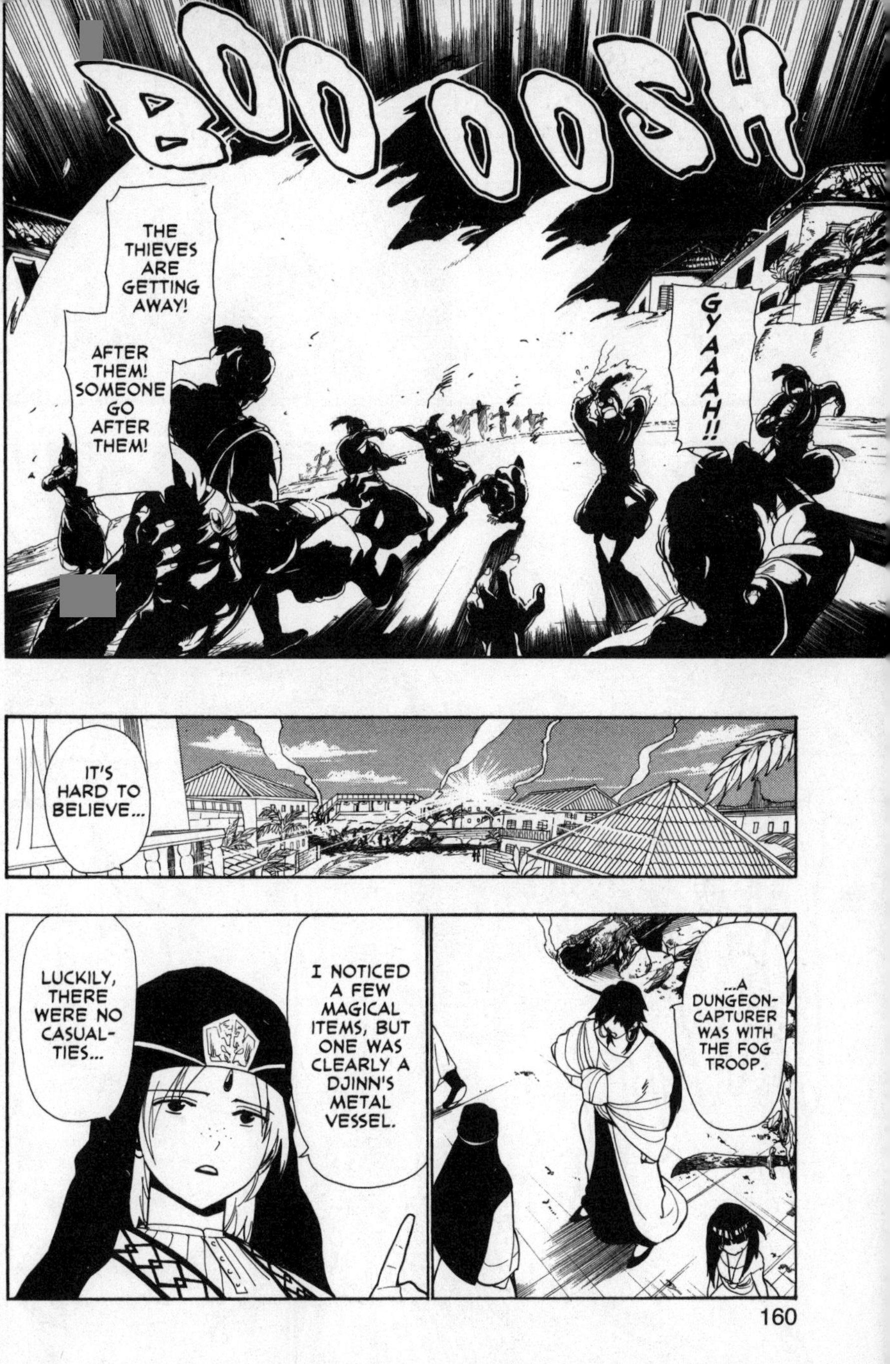
BOOOOSH
GYAAAH!!
THE THIEVES ARE GETTING AWAY!
AFTER THEM! SOMEONE GO AFTER THEM!
IT'S HARD TO BELIEVE...
...A DUNGEON-CAPTURER WAS WITH THE FOG TROOP.
I NOTICED A FEW MAGICAL ITEMS, BUT ONE WAS CLEARLY A DJINN'S METAL VESSEL.
LUCKILY, THERE WERE NO CASUAL-TIES...

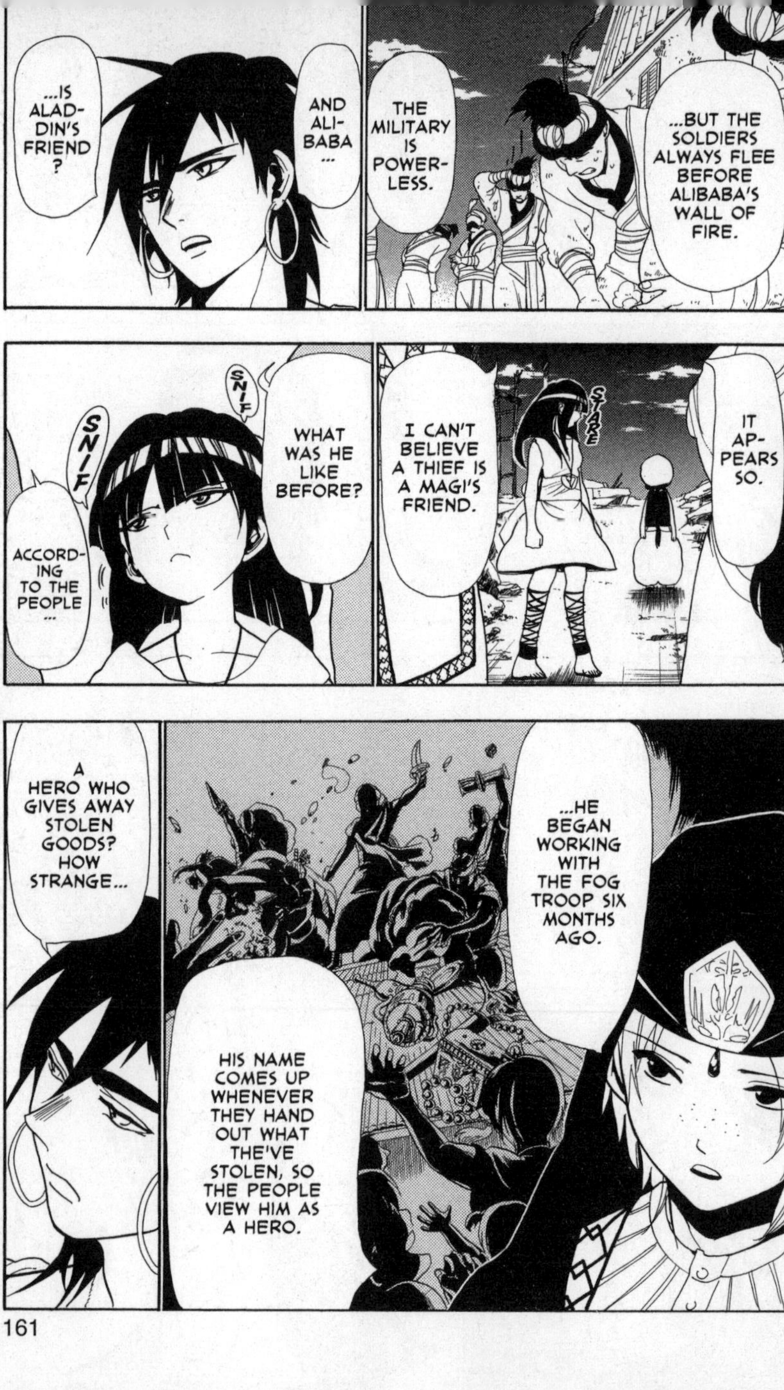
...BUT THE SOLDIERS ALWAYS FLEE BEFORE ALIBABA'S WALL OF FIRE.
THE MILITARY IS POWERLESS.
AND ALI-BABA...
...IS ALAD-DIN'S FRIEND?
IT AP-PEARS SO.
STARE
I CAN'T BELIEVE A THIEF IS A MAGI'S FRIEND.
WHAT WAS HE LIKE BEFORE?
SNIF
SNIF
ACCORD-ING TO THE PEOPLE...
...HE BEGAN WORKING WITH THE FOG TROOP SIX MONTHS AGO.
HIS NAME COMES UP WHENEVER THEY HAND OUT WHAT THE'VE STOLEN, SO THE PEOPLE VIEW HIM AS A HERO.
A HERO WHO GIVES AWAY STOLEN GOODS? HOW STRANGE...

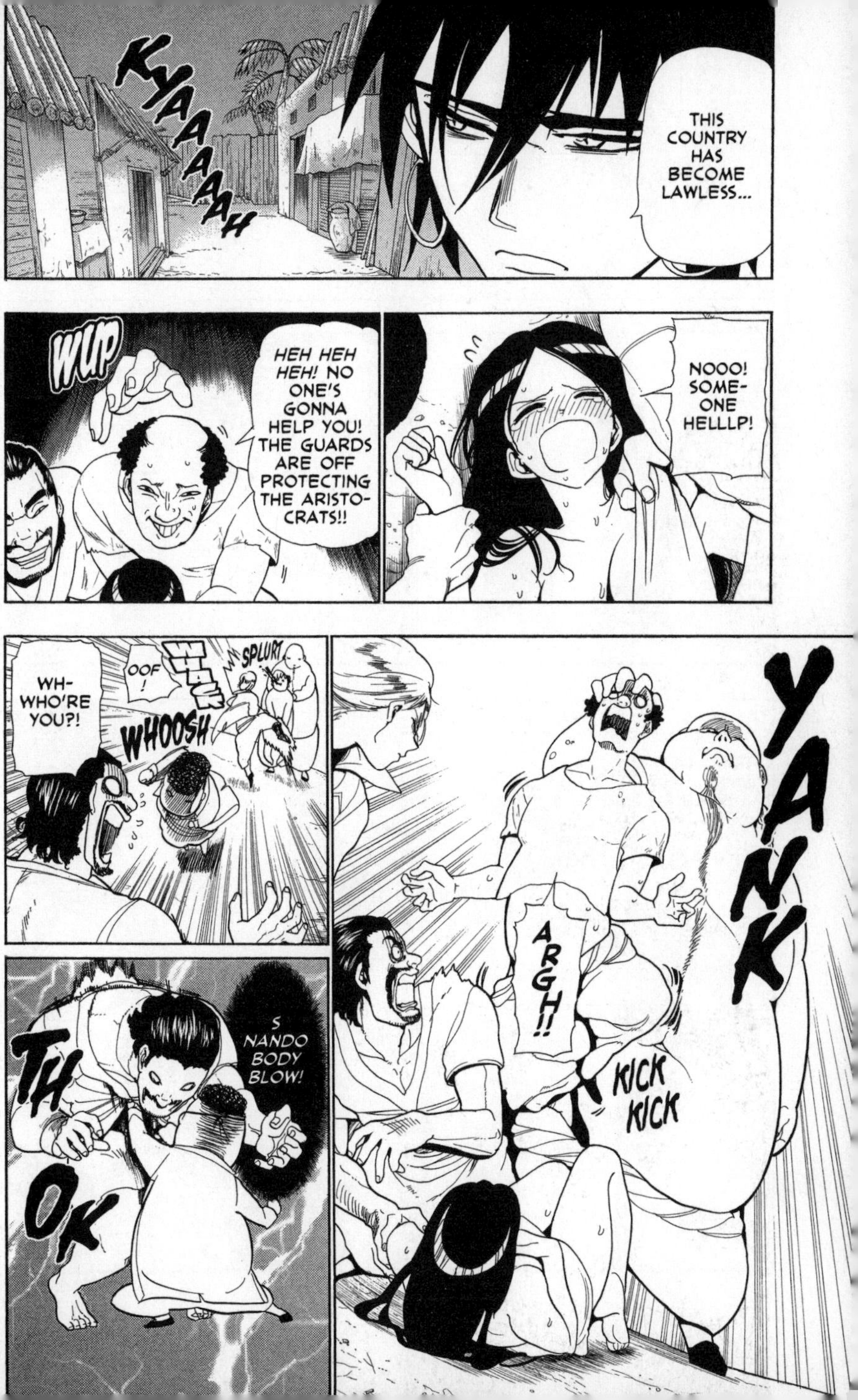
THIS COUNTRY HAS BECOME LAWLESS...
KYAAAAAH
NOOO! SOME-ONE HELLLP!
HEH HEH HEH! NO ONE'S GONNA HELP YOU! THE GUARDS ARE OFF PROTECTING THE ARISTO-CRATS!!
WUP
YANK
ARGH!!
KICK KICK
SPLURT
WHACK
OOF!
WH-WHO'RE YOU?!
WHOOSH
S NANDO BODY BLOW!
THOOK

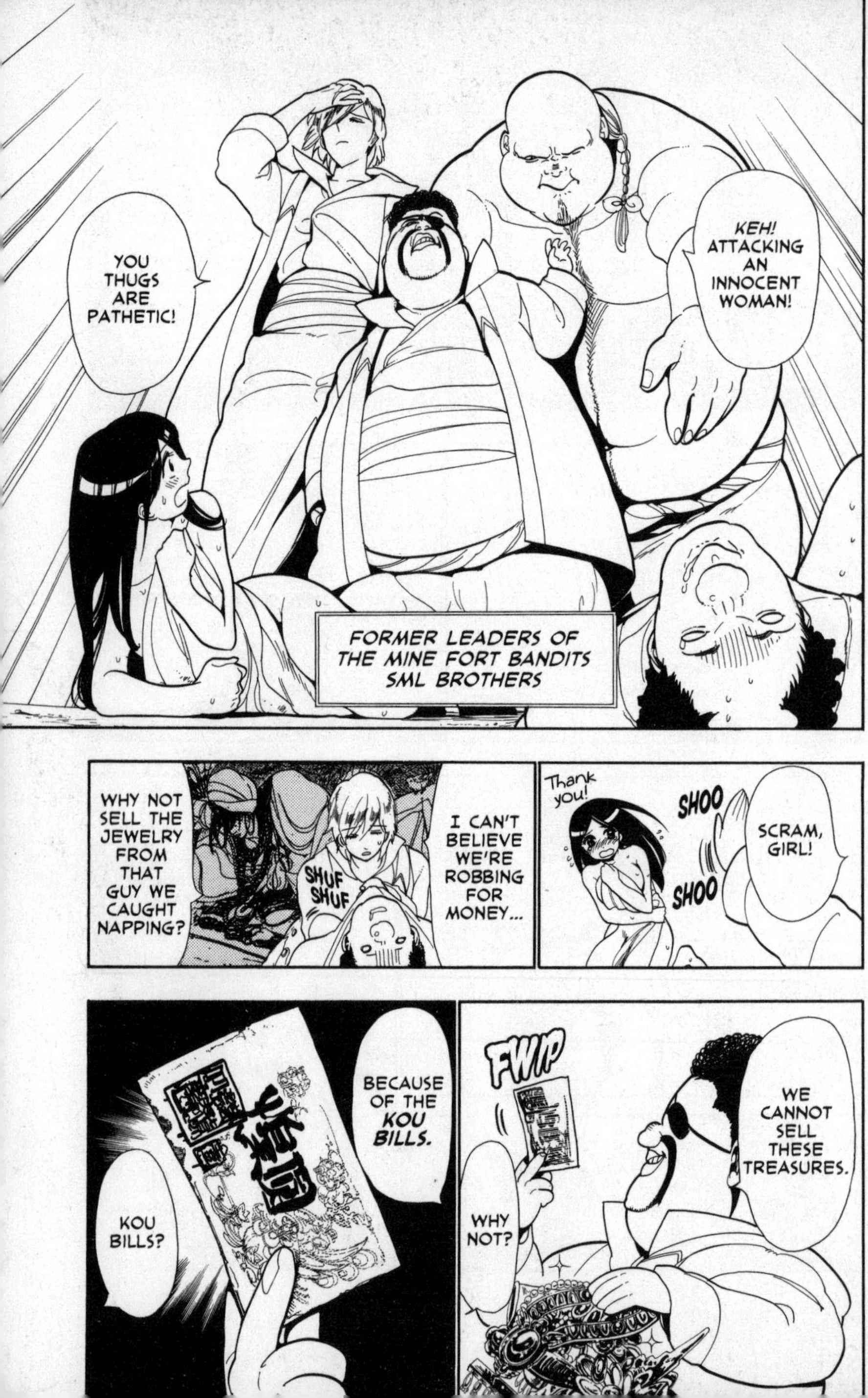
KEH! ATTACKING AN INNOCENT WOMAN!
YOU THUGS ARE PATHETIC!
FORMER LEADERS OF THE MINE FORT BANDITS SML BROTHERS
SCRAM, GIRL!
SHOO
SHOO
Thank you!
I CAN'T BELIEVE WE'RE ROBBING FOR MONEY...
SHUF SHUF
WHY NOT SELL THE JEWELRY FROM THAT GUY WE CAUGHT NAPPING?
WE CANNOT SELL THESE TREASURES.
FWIP
WHY NOT?
BECAUSE OF THE KOU BILLS.
KOU BILLS?

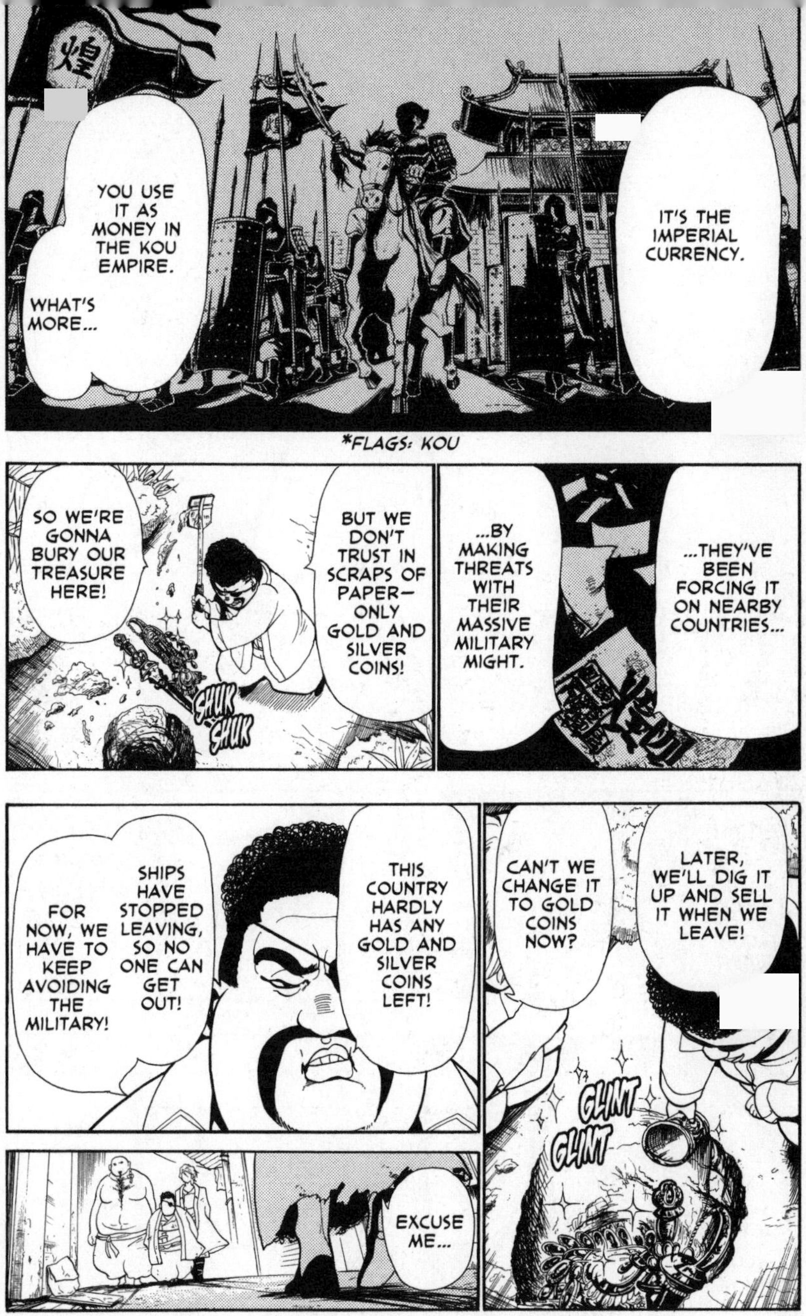
IT'S THE IMPERIAL CURRENCY.
YOU USE IT AS MONEY IN THE KOU EMPIRE.
WHAT'S MORE...
*FLAGS: KOU
...THEY'VE BEEN FORCING IT ON NEARBY COUNTRIES...
...BY MAKING THREATS WITH THEIR MASSIVE MILITARY MIGHT.
BUT WE DON'T TRUST IN SCRAPS OF PAPER—ONLY GOLD AND SILVER COINS!
SO WE'RE GONNA BURY OUR TREASURE HERE!
SHUK SHUK
LATER, WE'LL DIG IT UP AND SELL IT WHEN WE LEAVE!
CAN'T WE CHANGE IT TO GOLD COINS NOW?
GLINT GLINT
THIS COUNTRY HARDLY HAS ANY GOLD AND SILVER COINS LEFT!
SHIPS HAVE STOPPED LEAVING, SO NO ONE CAN GET OUT!
FOR NOW, WE HAVE TO KEEP AVOIDING THE MILITARY!
EXCUSE ME...

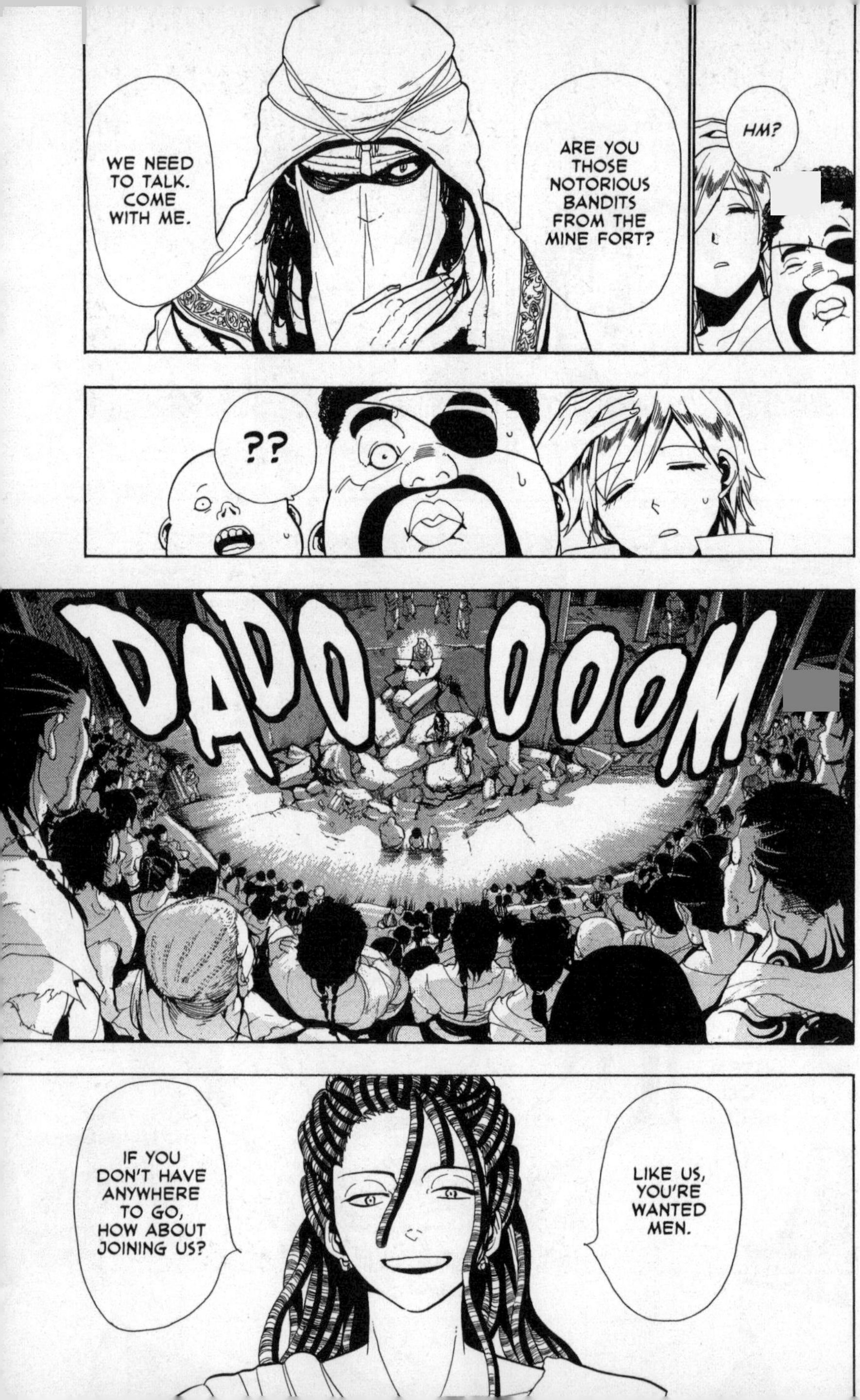
HM?
ARE YOU THOSE NOTORIOUS BANDITS FROM THE MINE FORT?
WE NEED TO TALK. COME WITH ME.
??
DADOOOOM
LIKE US, YOU'RE WANTED MEN.
IF YOU DON'T HAVE ANYWHERE TO GO, HOW ABOUT JOINING US?

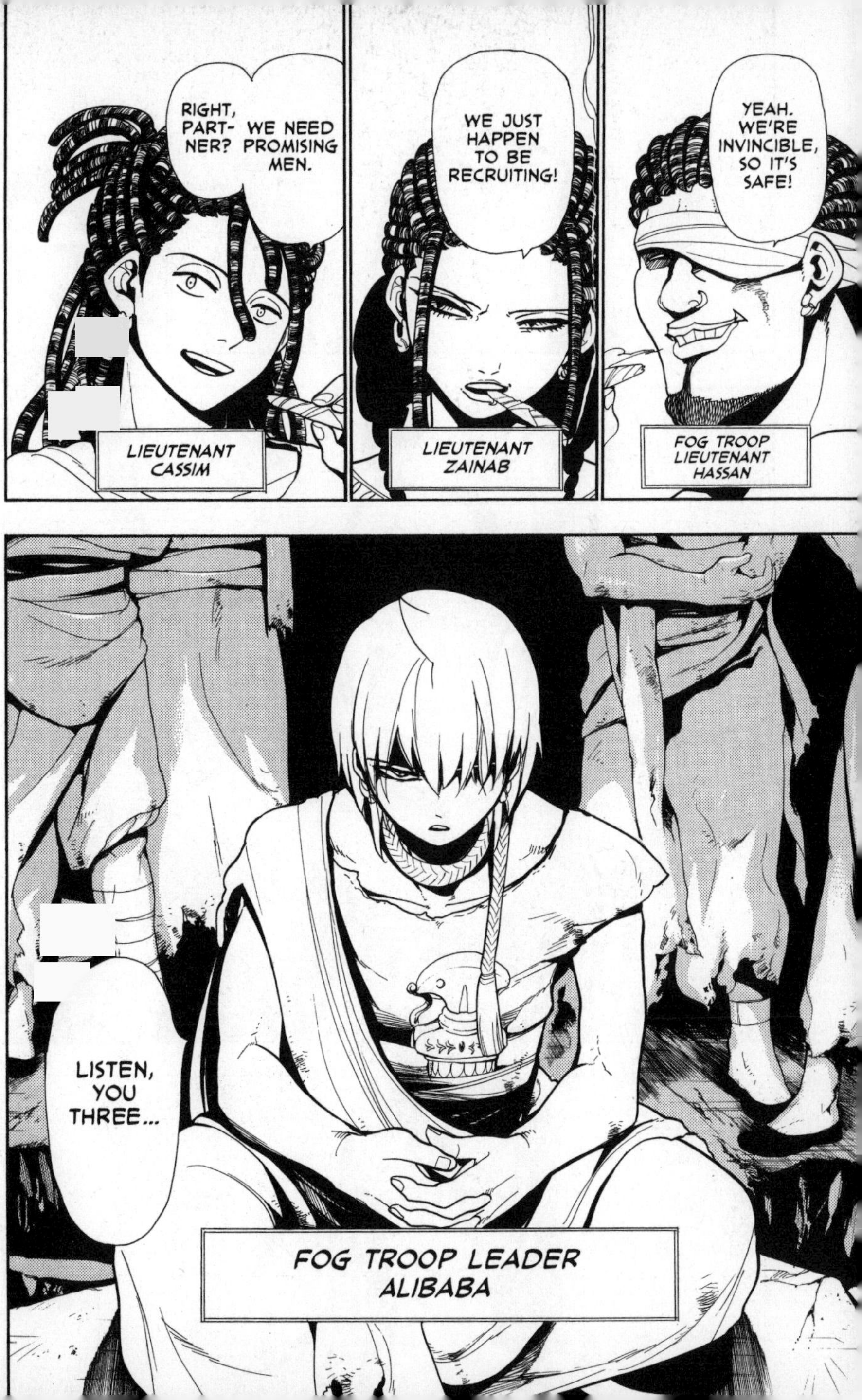
YEAH. WE'RE INVINCIBLE, SO IT'S SAFE!
FOG TROOP LIEUTENANT HASSAN
WE JUST HAPPEN TO BE RECRUITING!
LIEUTENANT ZAINAB
WE NEED PROMISING MEN.
RIGHT, PART-NER?
LIEUTENANT CASSIM
LISTEN, YOU THREE...
FOG TROOP LEADER ALIBABA

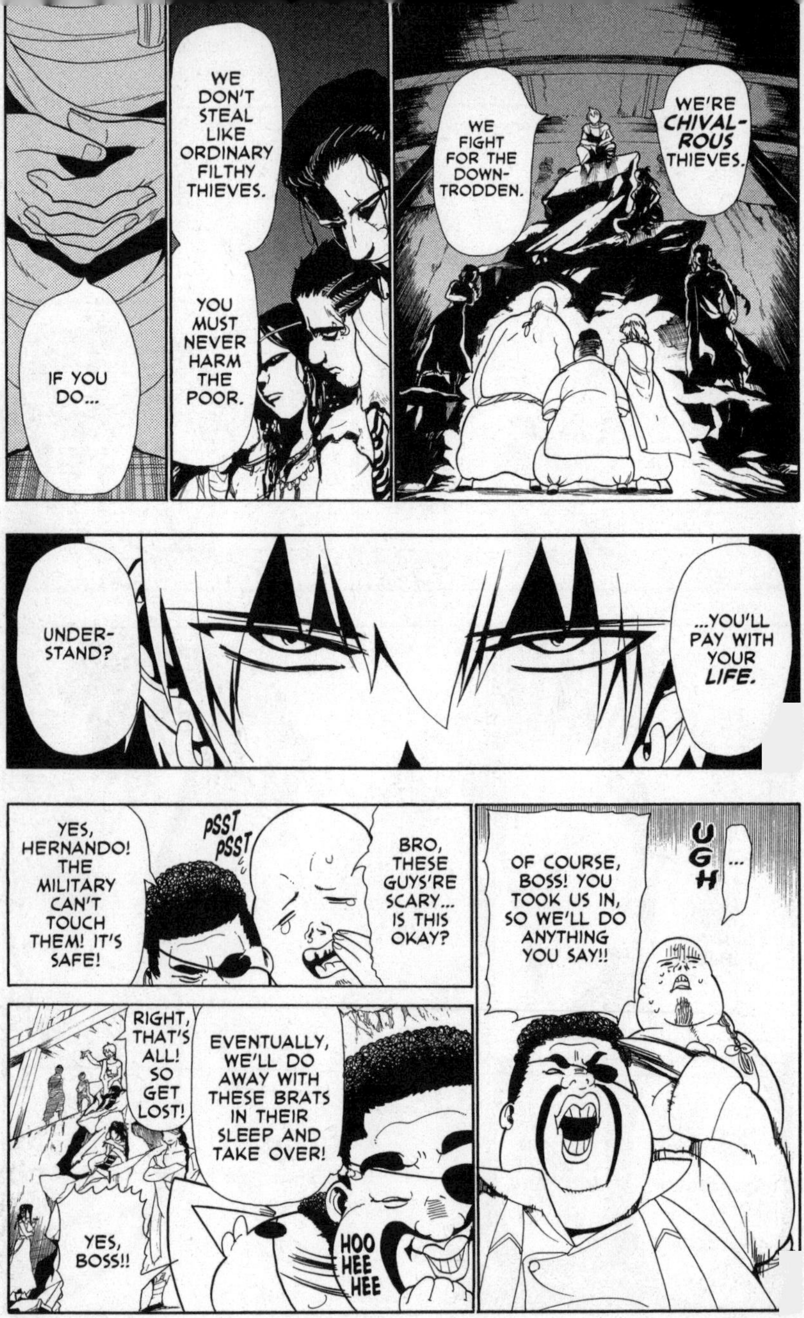
WE'RE CHIVAL-ROUS THIEVES.
WE FIGHT FOR THE DOWN-TRODDEN.
WE DON'T STEAL LIKE ORDINARY FILTHY THIEVES.
YOU MUST NEVER HARM THE POOR.
IF YOU DO...
...YOU'LL PAY WITH YOUR LIFE.
UNDER-STAND?
UGH...
OF COURSE, BOSS! YOU TOOK US IN, SO WE'LL DO ANYTHING YOU SAY!!
BRO, THESE GUYS'RE SCARY... IS THIS OKAY?
PSST PSST
YES, HERNANDO! THE MILITARY CAN'T TOUCH THEM! IT'S SAFE!
EVENTUALLY, WE'LL DO AWAY WITH THESE BRATS IN THEIR SLEEP AND TAKE OVER!
HOO HEE HEE
RIGHT, THAT'S ALL! SO GET LOST!
YES, BOSS!!

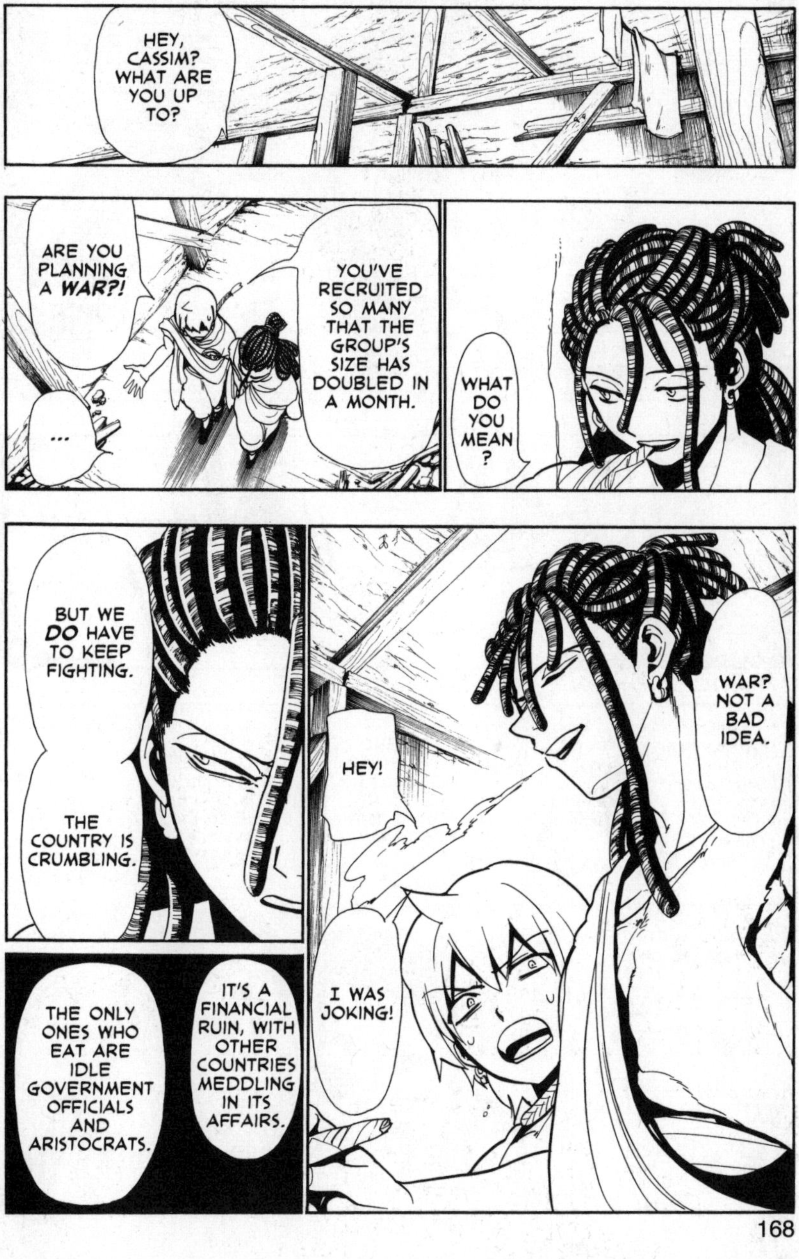
HEY, CASSIM? WHAT ARE YOU UP TO?
WHAT DO YOU MEAN?
YOU'VE RECRUITED SO MANY THAT THE GROUP'S SIZE HAS DOUBLED IN A MONTH.
ARE YOU PLANNING A *WAR?!*
...
WAR? NOT A BAD IDEA.
HEY!
I WAS JOKING!
BUT WE *DO* HAVE TO KEEP FIGHTING.
THE COUNTRY IS CRUMBLING.
IT'S A FINANCIAL RUIN, WITH OTHER COUNTRIES MEDDLING IN ITS AFFAIRS.
THE ONLY ONES WHO EAT ARE IDLE GOVERNMENT OFFICIALS AND ARISTOCRATS.

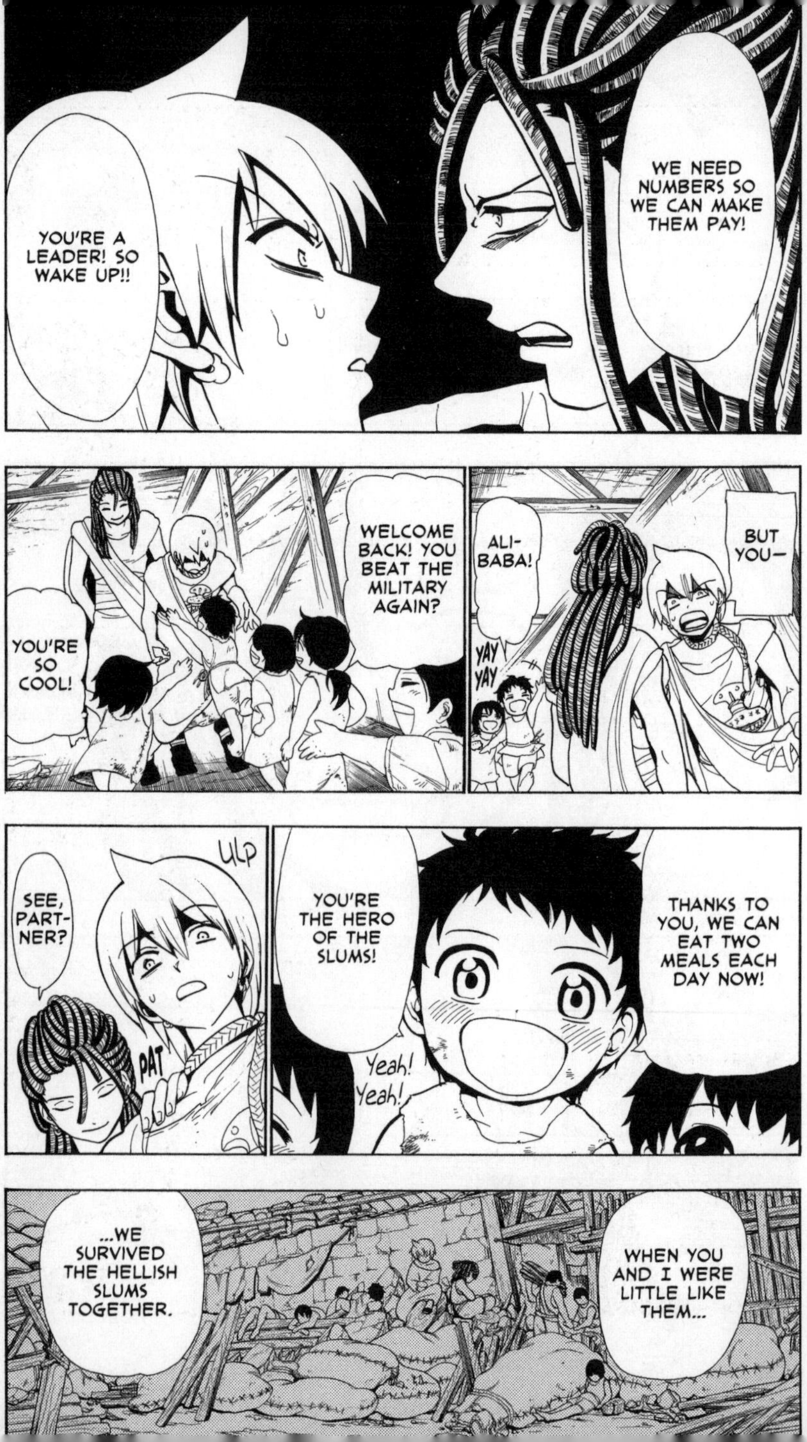
WE NEED NUMBERS SO WE CAN MAKE THEM PAY!
YOU'RE A LEADER! SO WAKE UP!!
BUT YOU—
ALI-BABA!
YAY YAY
WELCOME BACK! YOU BEAT THE MILITARY AGAIN?
YOU'RE SO COOL!
THANKS TO YOU, WE CAN EAT TWO MEALS EACH DAY NOW!
YOU'RE THE HERO OF THE SLUMS!
Yeah! Yeah!
ULP
SEE, PARTNER?
PAT
WHEN YOU AND I WERE LITTLE LIKE THEM...
...WE SURVIVED THE HELLISH SLUMS TOGETHER.

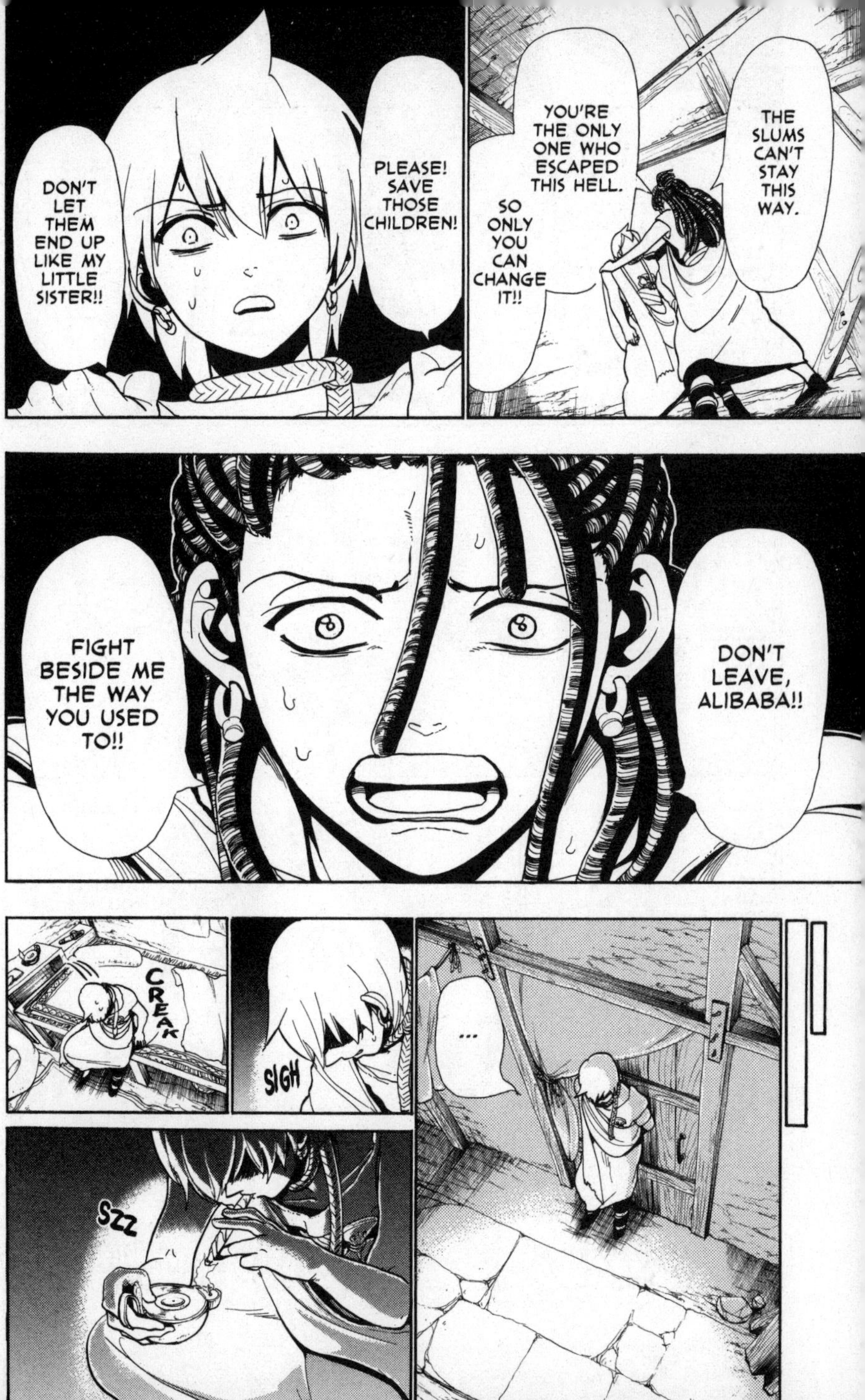
THE SLUMS CAN'T STAY THIS WAY.
YOU'RE THE ONLY ONE WHO ESCAPED THIS HELL.
SO ONLY YOU CAN CHANGE IT!!
PLEASE! SAVE THOSE CHILDREN!
DON'T LET THEM END UP LIKE MY LITTLE SISTER!!
DON'T LEAVE, ALIBABA!!
FIGHT BESIDE ME THE WAY YOU USED TO!!
...
SIGH
CREAK
SZZ

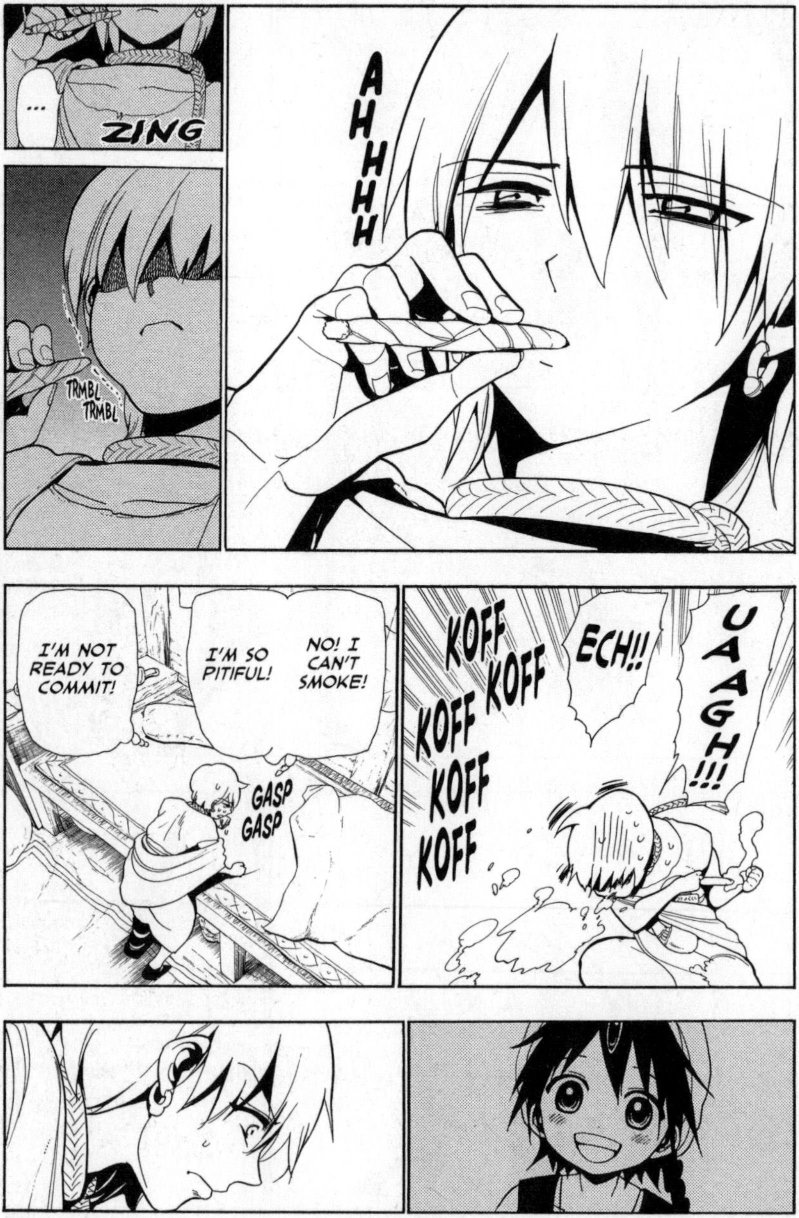
AHHHH
...
ZING
TRMBL TRMBL
UAAGH!!!
ECH!!
KOFF KOFF KOFF KOFF KOFF KOFF
NO! I CAN'T SMOKE!
I'M SO PITIFUL!
I'M NOT READY TO COMMIT!
GASP GASP

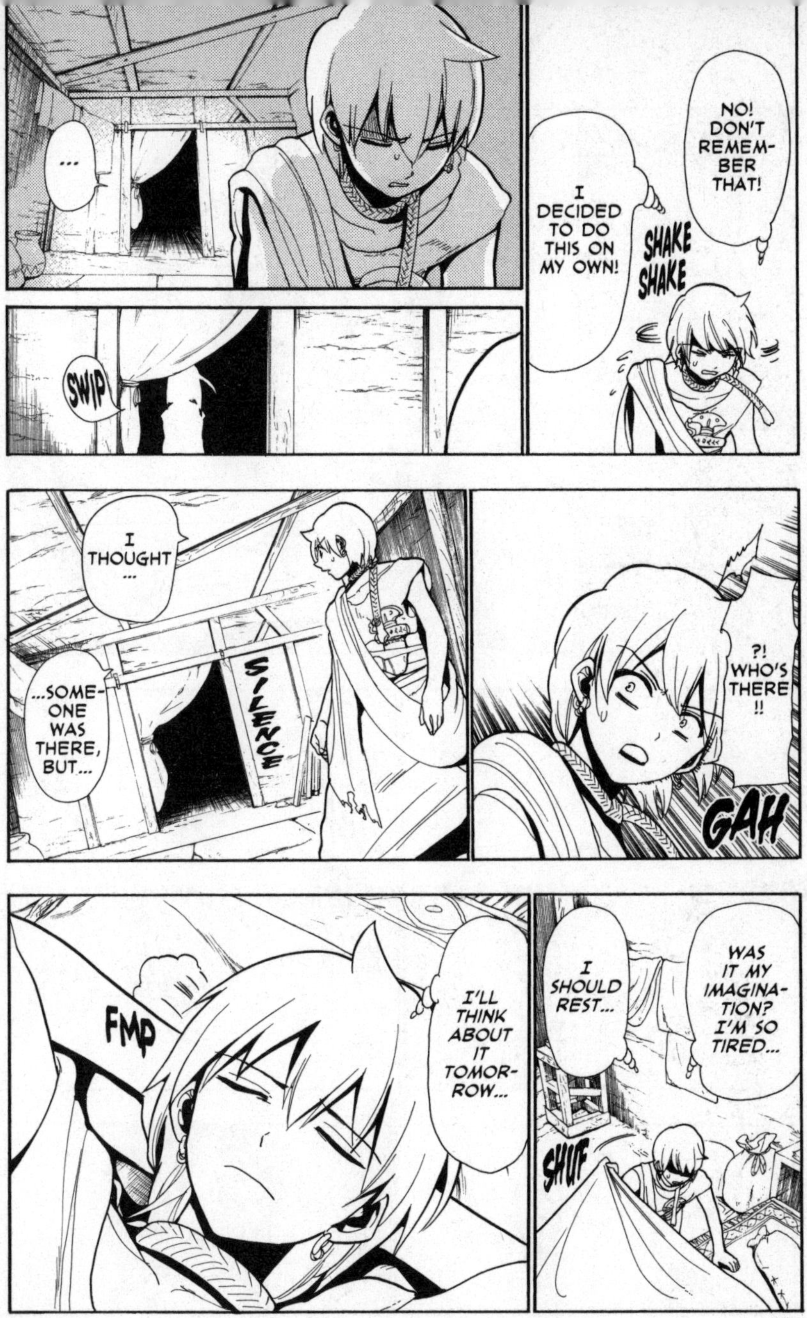
NO! DON'T REMEMBER THAT!
I DECIDED TO DO THIS ON MY OWN!
SHAKE SHAKE
...
SWIP
?! WHO'S THERE !!
GAH
I THOUGHT...
...SOMEONE WAS THERE, BUT...
SILENCE
WAS IT MY IMAGINATION? I'M SO TIRED...
I SHOULD REST...
SHUF
I'LL THINK ABOUT IT TOMORROW...
FMP

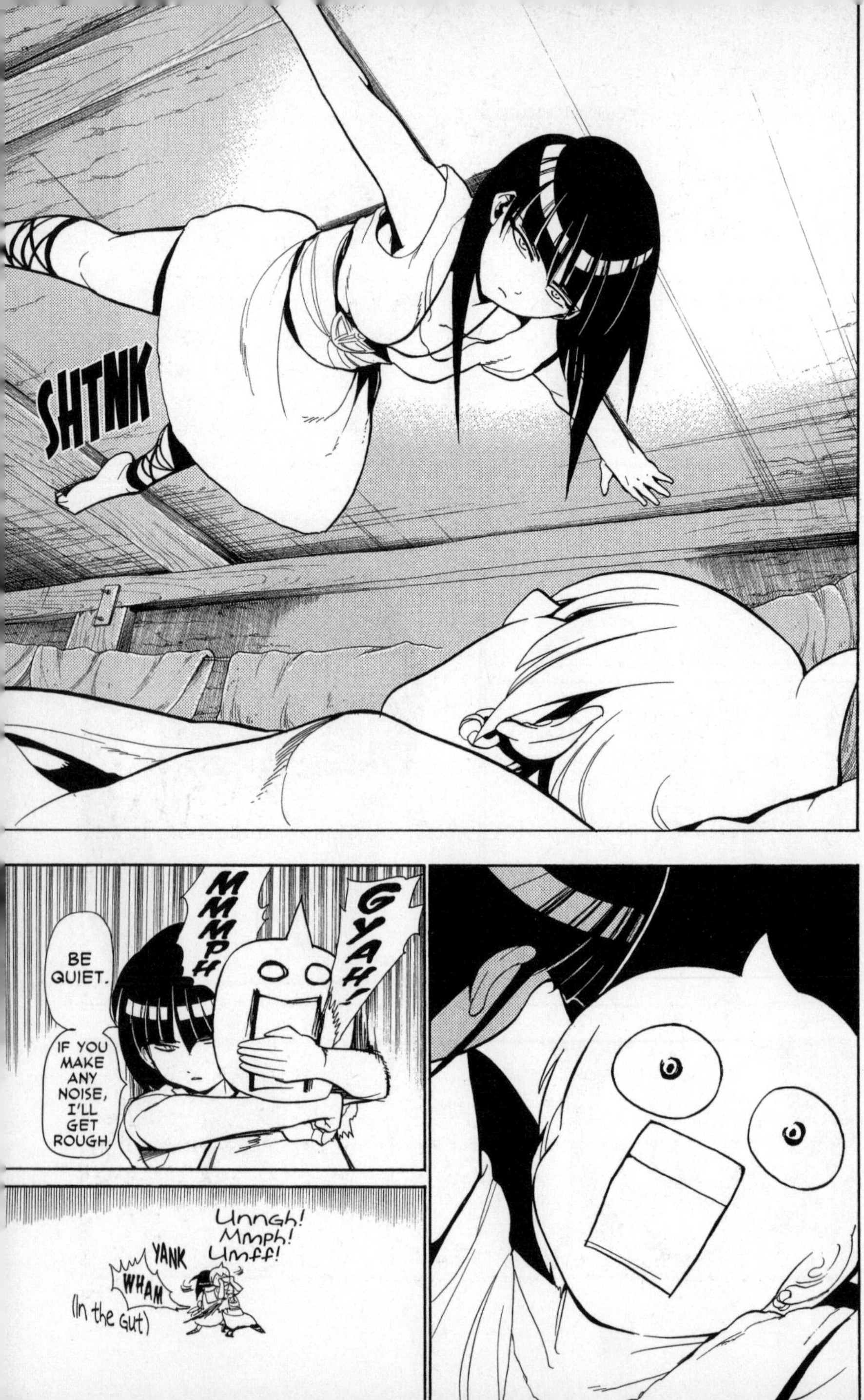
SHTNK
GYAH!
MMMPH
BE QUIET.
IF YOU MAKE ANY NOISE, I'LL GET ROUGH.
Unngh! Mmph! Umff!
YANK
WHAM
(In the Gut)

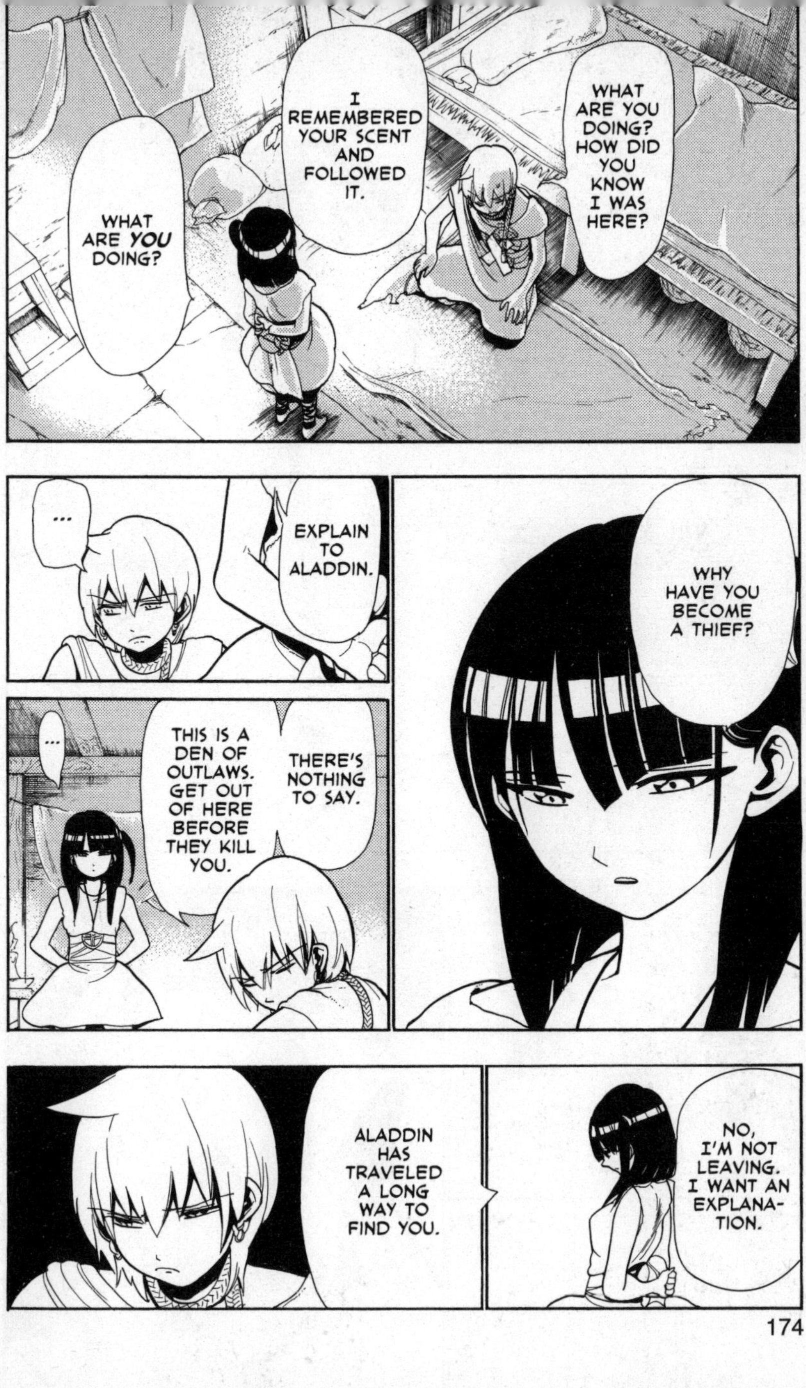
WHAT ARE YOU DOING? HOW DID YOU KNOW I WAS HERE?
I REMEMBERED YOUR SCENT AND FOLLOWED IT.
WHAT ARE *YOU* DOING?
WHY HAVE YOU BECOME A THIEF?
EXPLAIN TO ALADDIN.
...
THERE'S NOTHING TO SAY.
THIS IS A DEN OF OUTLAWS. GET OUT OF HERE BEFORE THEY KILL YOU.
...
NO, I'M NOT LEAVING. I WANT AN EXPLANA-TION.
ALADDIN HAS TRAVELED A LONG WAY TO FIND YOU.

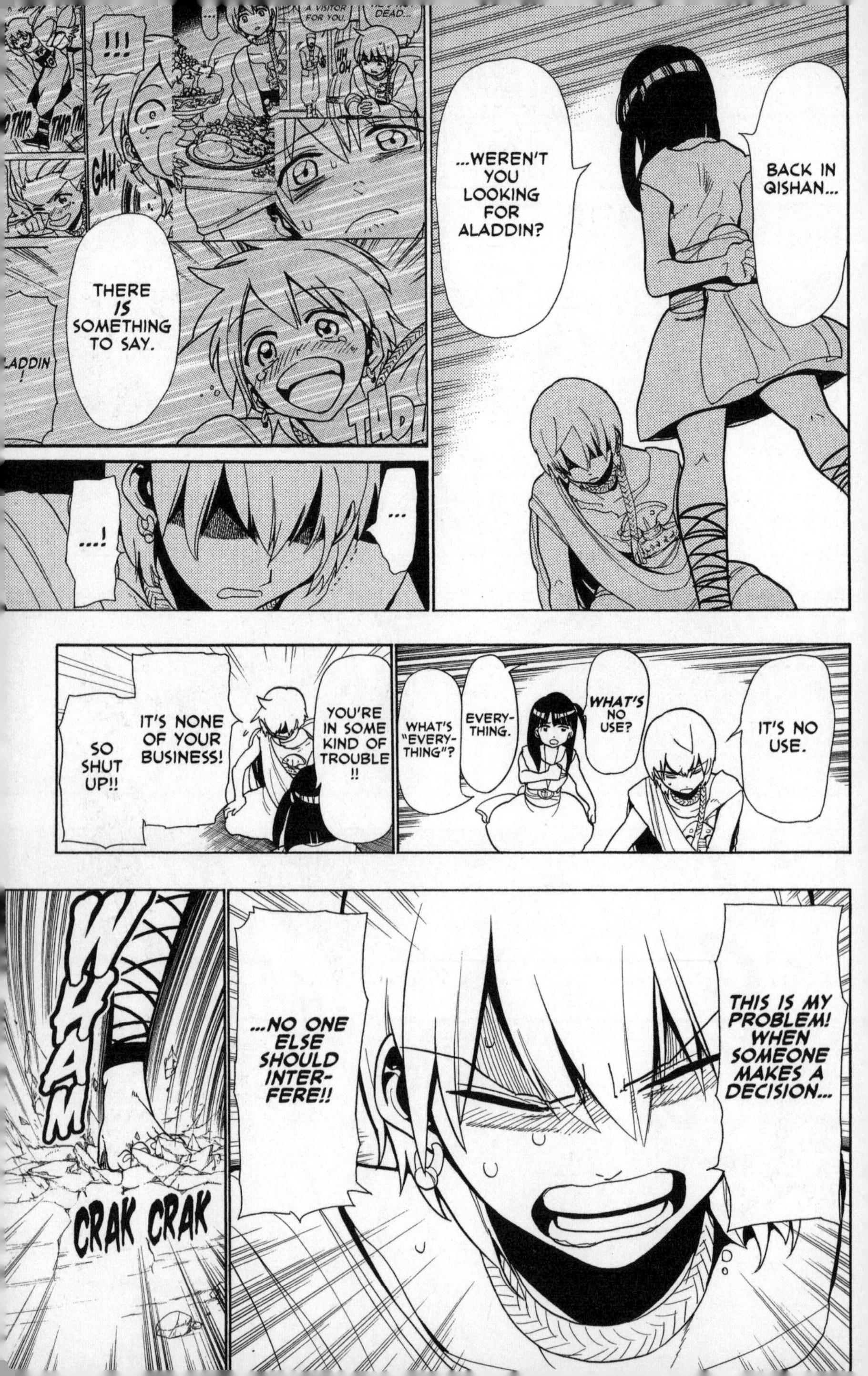
BACK IN QISHAN...
...WEREN'T YOU LOOKING FOR ALADDIN?
DEAD...
A VISITOR FOR YOU
UH OH
...
!!!
GAH
THMP THMP
THERE *IS* SOMETHING TO SAY.
THD
...
...!
IT'S NO USE.
WHAT'S NO USE?
EVERY-THING.
WHAT'S "EVERY-THING"?
YOU'RE IN SOME KIND OF TROUBLE!!
IT'S NONE OF YOUR BUSINESS!
SO SHUT UP!!
THIS IS MY PROBLEM! WHEN SOMEONE MAKES A DECISION...
...NO ONE ELSE SHOULD INTER-FERE!!
WHAM
CRAK CRAK

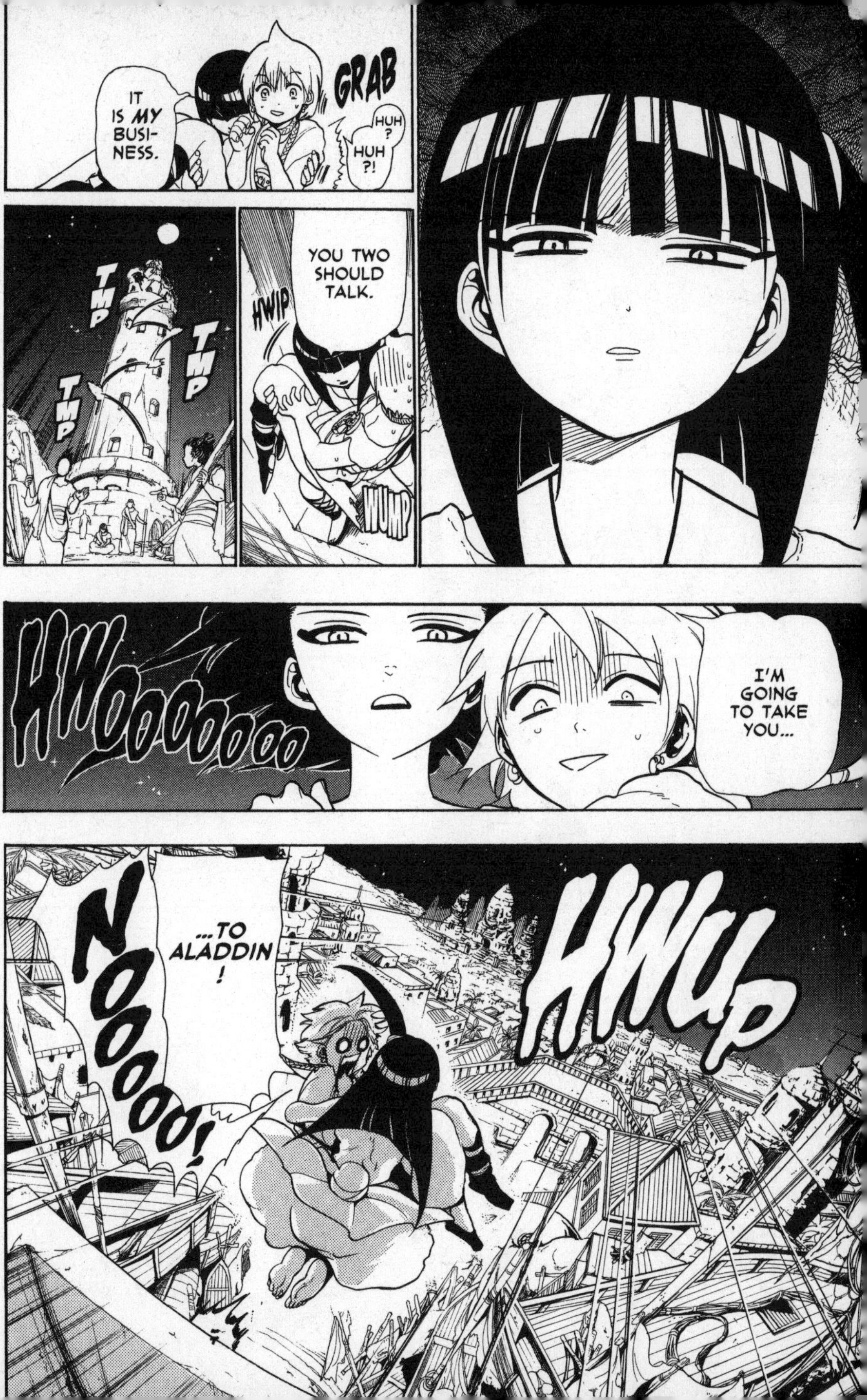
GRAB
HUH?
HUH?!
IT IS MY BUSINESS.
HWIP
YOU TWO SHOULD TALK.
WUMP
TMP
TMP
TMP
I'M GOING TO TAKE YOU...
HWOOOOOOOO
HWUP
...TO ALADDIN!
NOOOOOO!

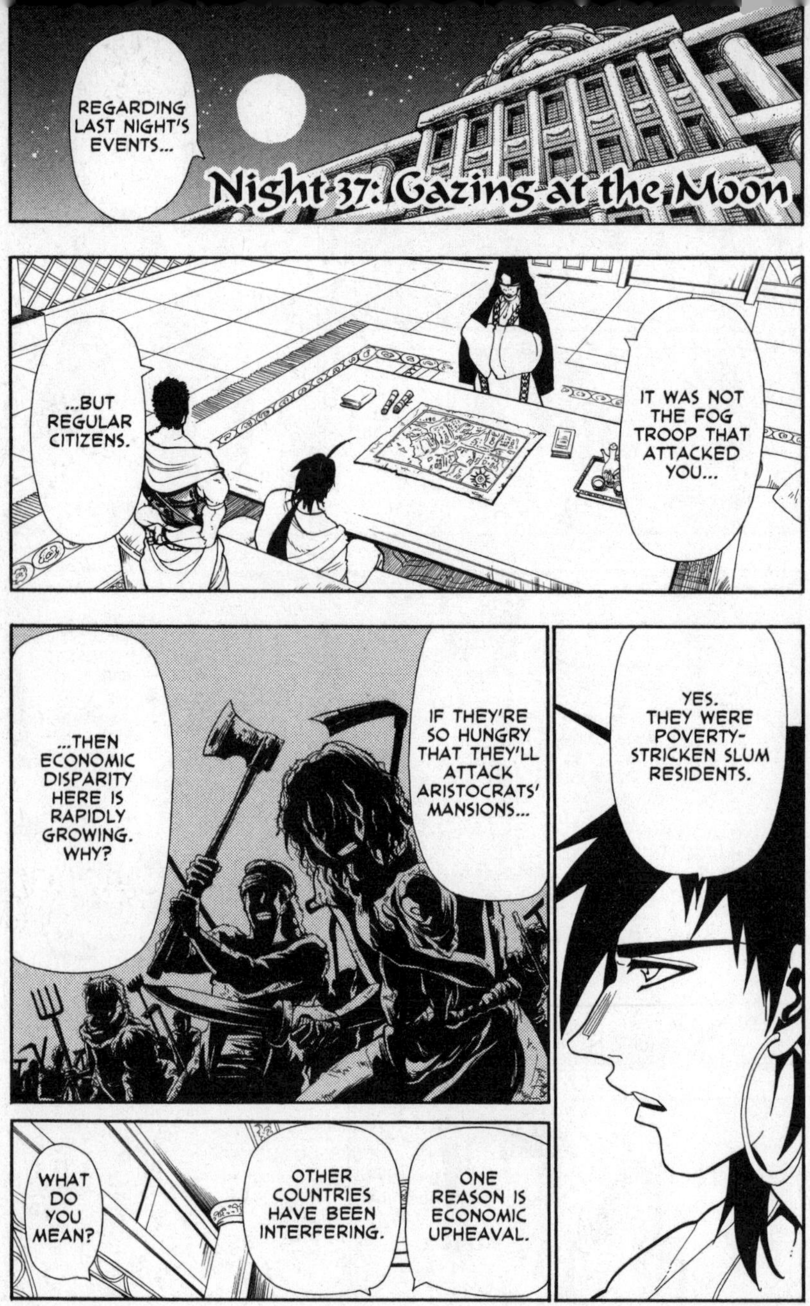
REGARDING LAST NIGHT'S EVENTS...
Night 37: Gazing at the Moon
IT WAS NOT THE FOG TROOP THAT ATTACKED YOU...
...BUT REGULAR CITIZENS.
YES. THEY WERE POVERTY-STRICKEN SLUM RESIDENTS.
IF THEY'RE SO HUNGRY THAT THEY'LL ATTACK ARISTOCRATS' MANSIONS...
...THEN ECONOMIC DISPARITY HERE IS RAPIDLY GROWING. WHY?
ONE REASON IS ECONOMIC UPHEAVAL.
OTHER COUNTRIES HAVE BEEN INTERFERING.
WHAT DO YOU MEAN?

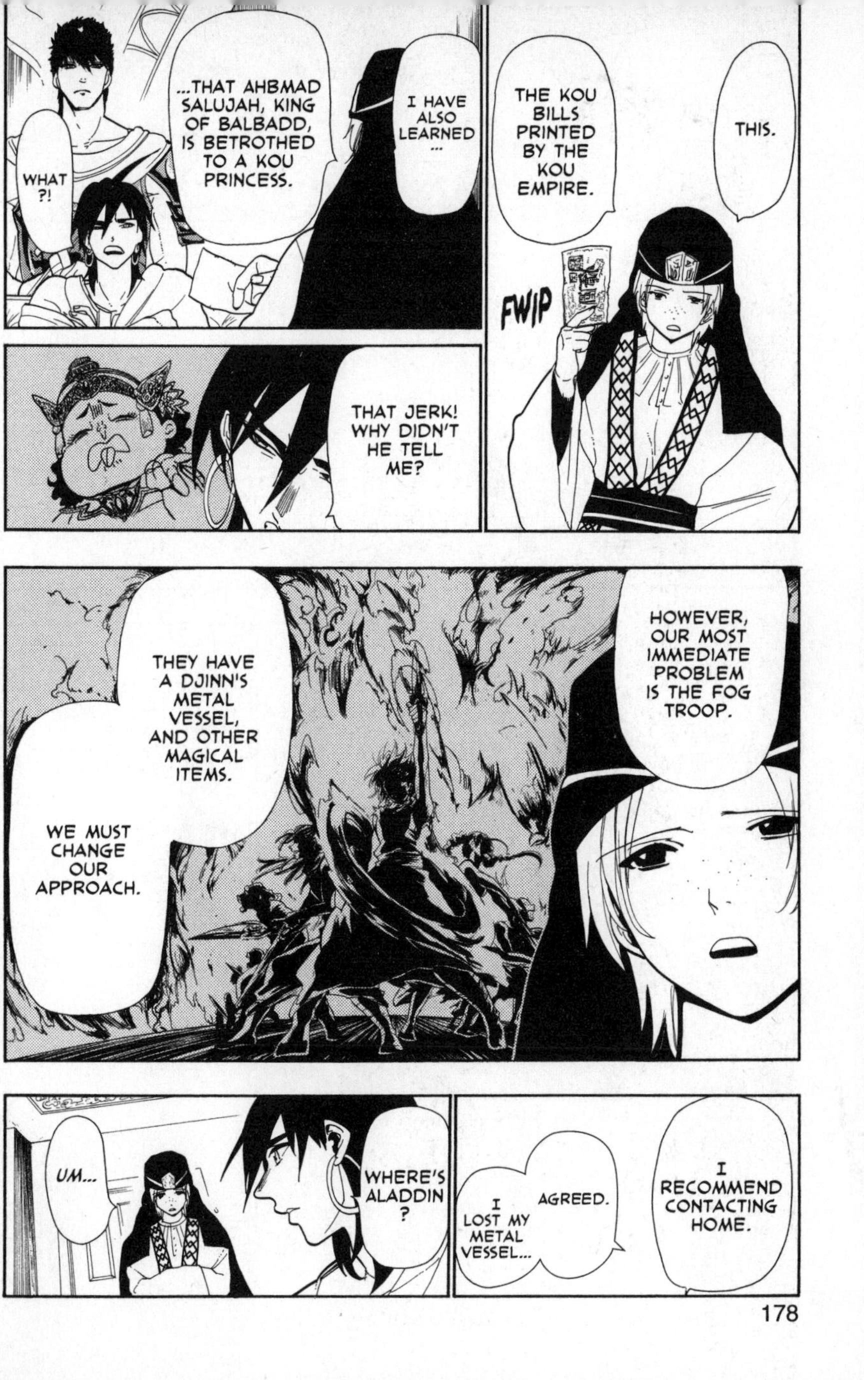
THIS.
THE KOU BILLS PRINTED BY THE KOU EMPIRE.
FWIP
I HAVE ALSO LEARNED ...
...THAT AHBMAD SALUJAH, KING OF BALBADD, IS BETROTHED TO A KOU PRINCESS.
WHAT ?!
THAT JERK! WHY DIDN'T HE TELL ME?
HOWEVER, OUR MOST IMMEDIATE PROBLEM IS THE FOG TROOP.
THEY HAVE A DJINN'S METAL VESSEL, AND OTHER MAGICAL ITEMS.
WE MUST CHANGE OUR APPROACH.
I RECOMMEND CONTACTING HOME.
AGREED.
I LOST MY METAL VESSEL...
WHERE'S ALADDIN ?
UM...

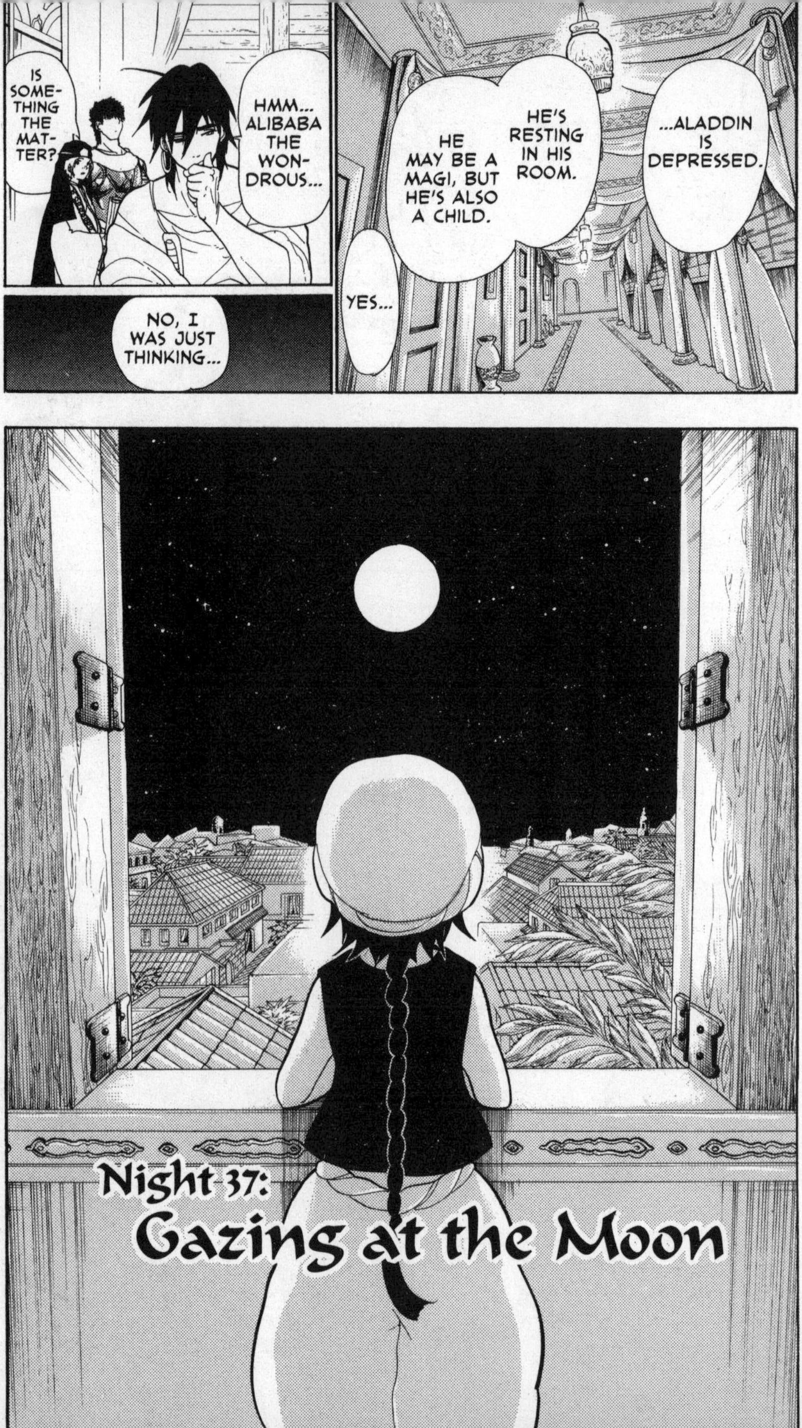
...ALADDIN IS DEPRESSED.
HE'S RESTING IN HIS ROOM.
HE MAY BE A MAGI, BUT HE'S ALSO A CHILD.
YES...
HMM... ALIBABA THE WONDROUS...
IS SOMETHING THE MATTER?
NO, I WAS JUST THINKING...
Night 37:
Gazing at the Moon

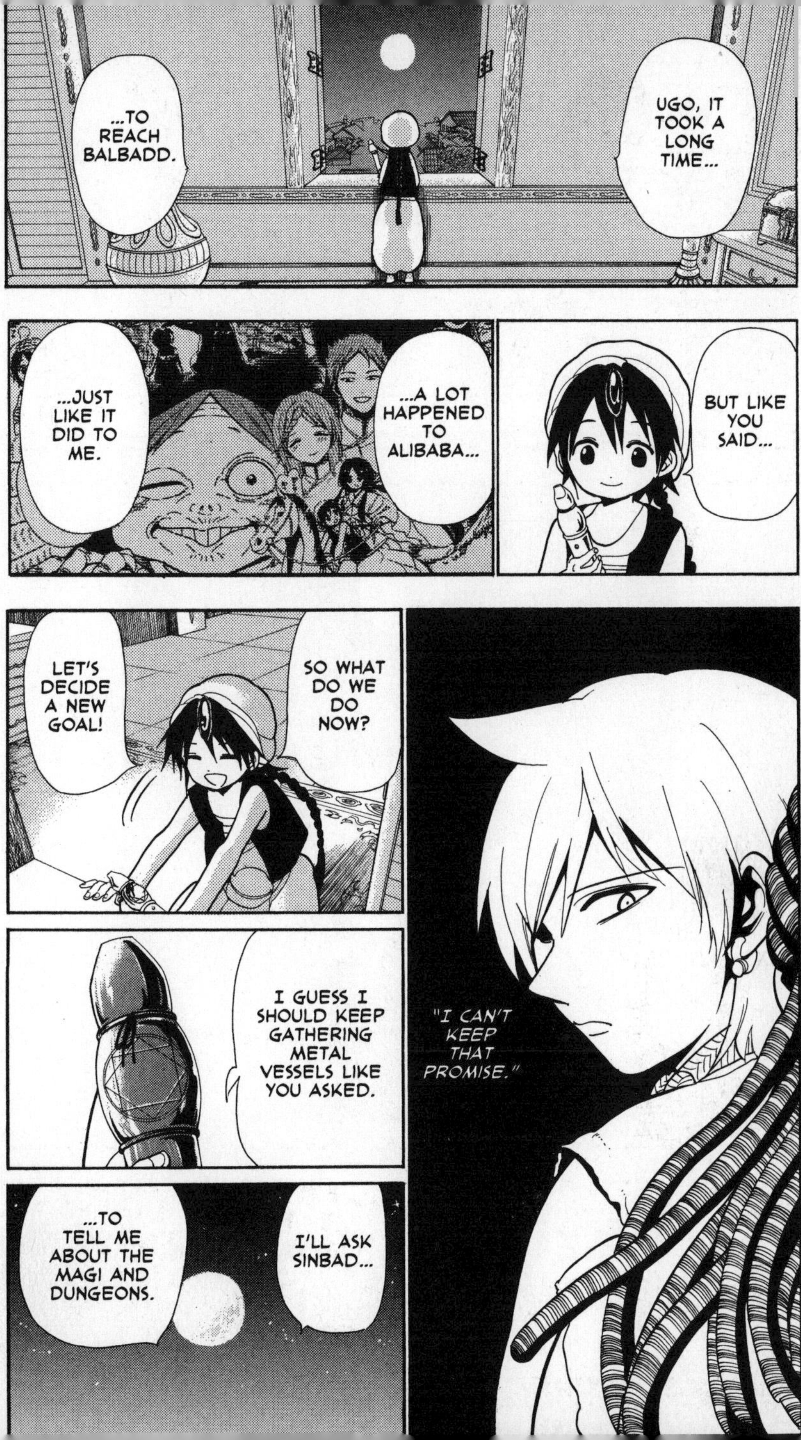
UGO, IT TOOK A LONG TIME...
...TO REACH BALBADD.
BUT LIKE YOU SAID...
...A LOT HAPPENED TO ALIBABA...
...JUST LIKE IT DID TO ME.
"I CAN'T KEEP THAT PROMISE."
SO WHAT DO WE DO NOW?
LET'S DECIDE A NEW GOAL!
I GUESS I SHOULD KEEP GATHERING METAL VESSELS LIKE YOU ASKED.
I'LL ASK SINBAD...
...TO TELL ME ABOUT THE MAGI AND DUNGEONS.

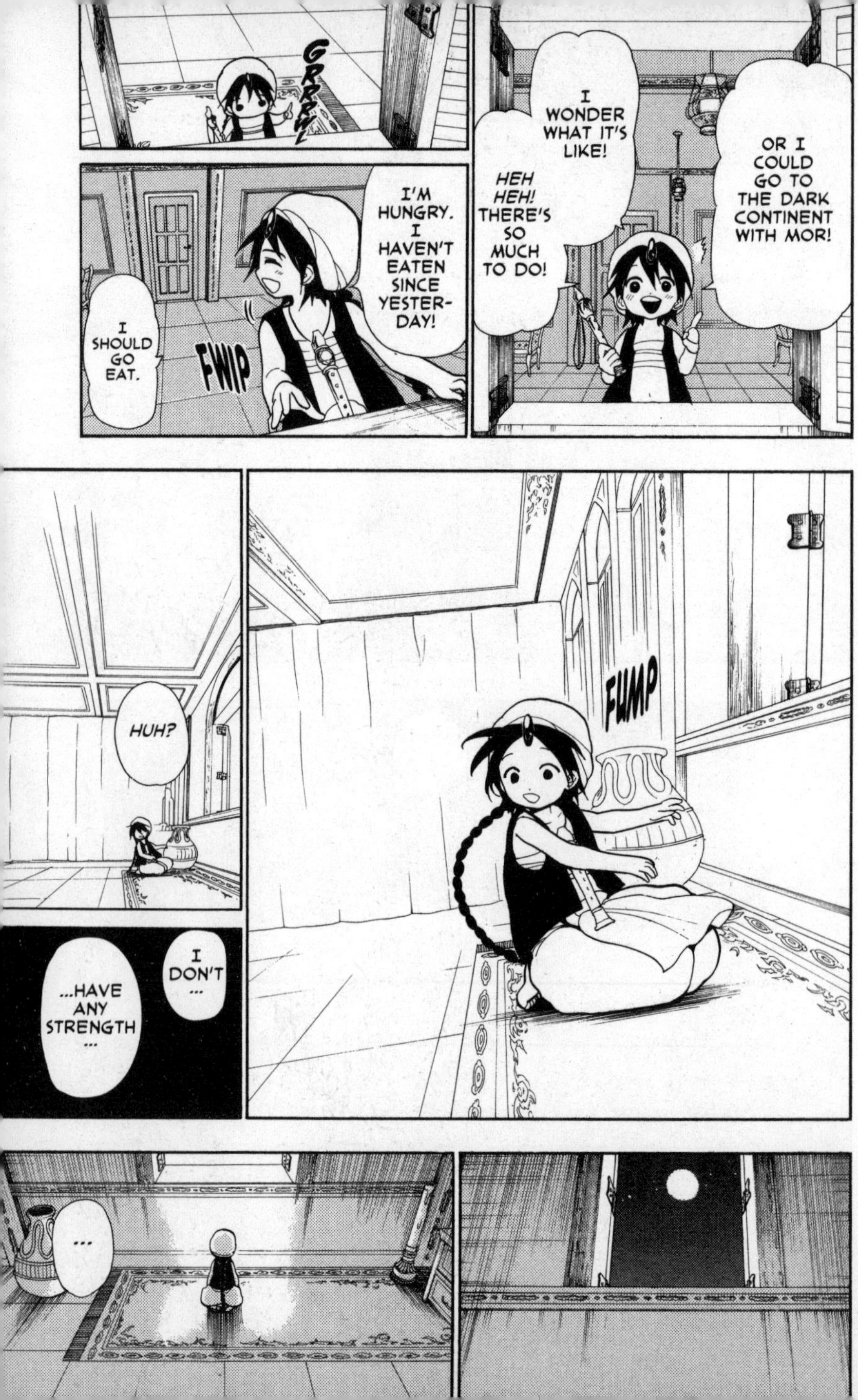
OR I COULD GO TO THE DARK CONTINENT WITH MOR!
I WONDER WHAT IT'S LIKE!
HEH HEH! THERE'S SO MUCH TO DO!
GRRRWL
I'M HUNGRY. I HAVEN'T EATEN SINCE YESTER-DAY!
FWIP
I SHOULD GO EAT.
FUMP
HUH?
I DON'T...
...HAVE ANY STRENGTH...
...

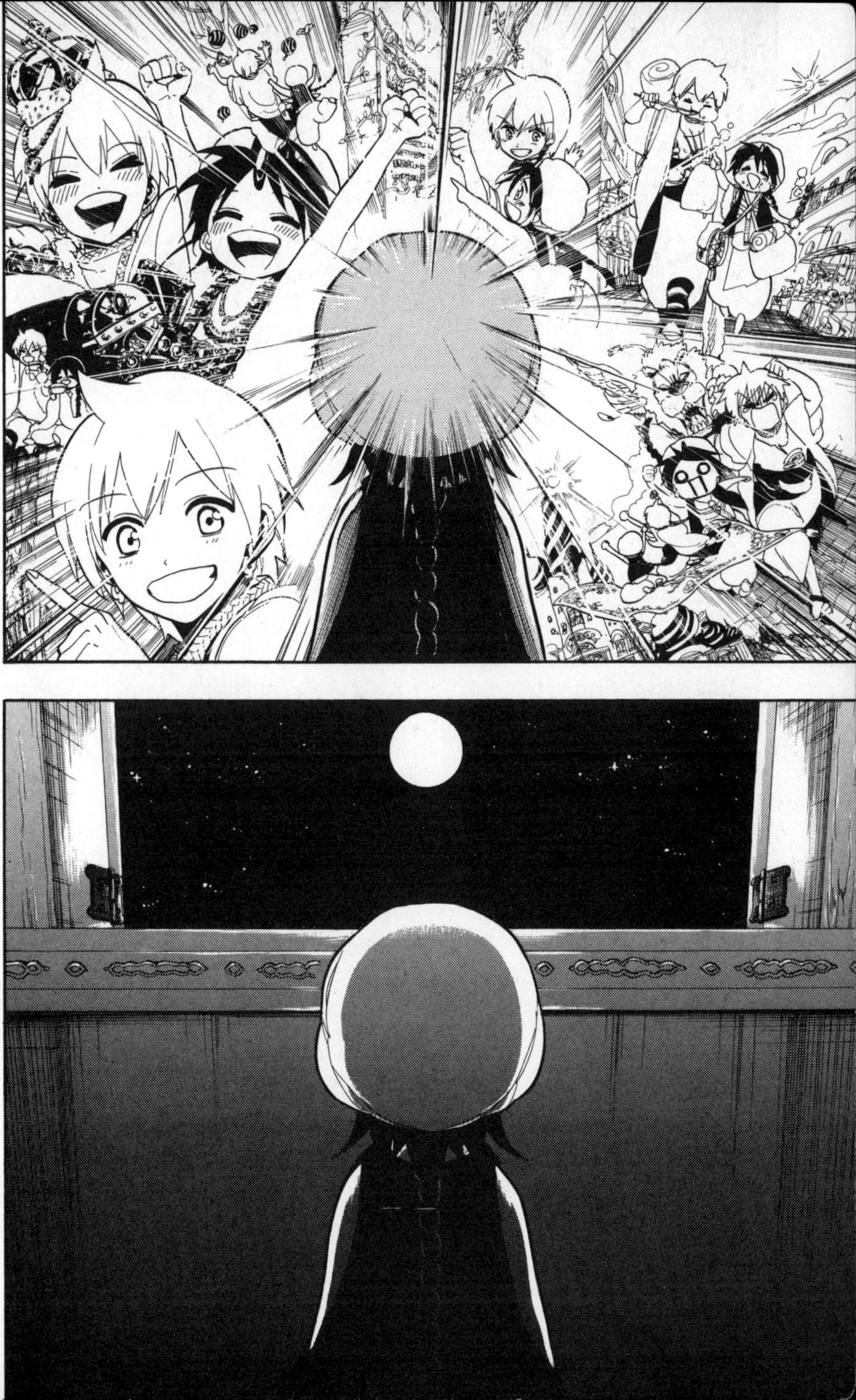

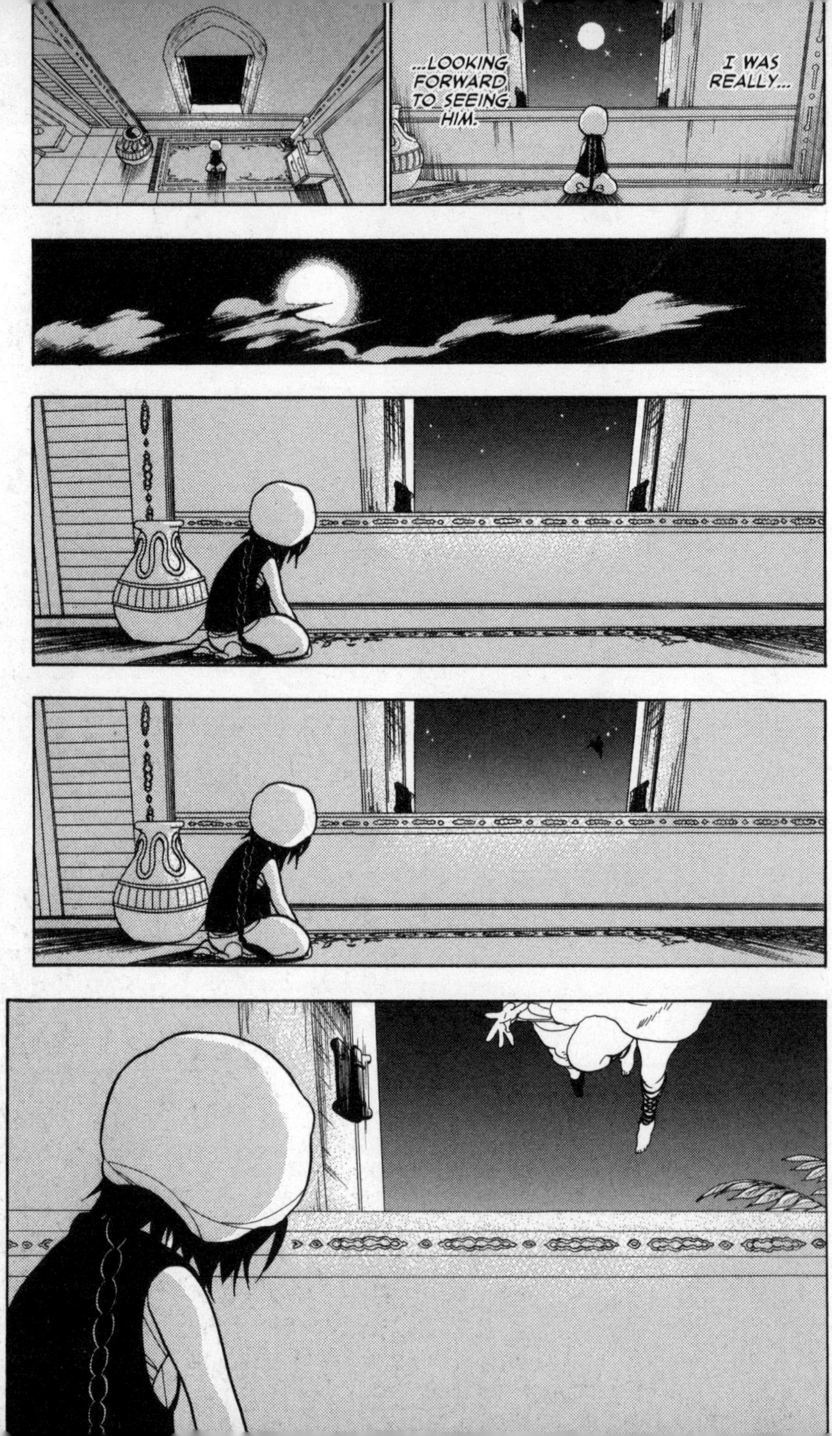
I WAS REALLY...
...LOOKING FORWARD TO SEEING HIM.

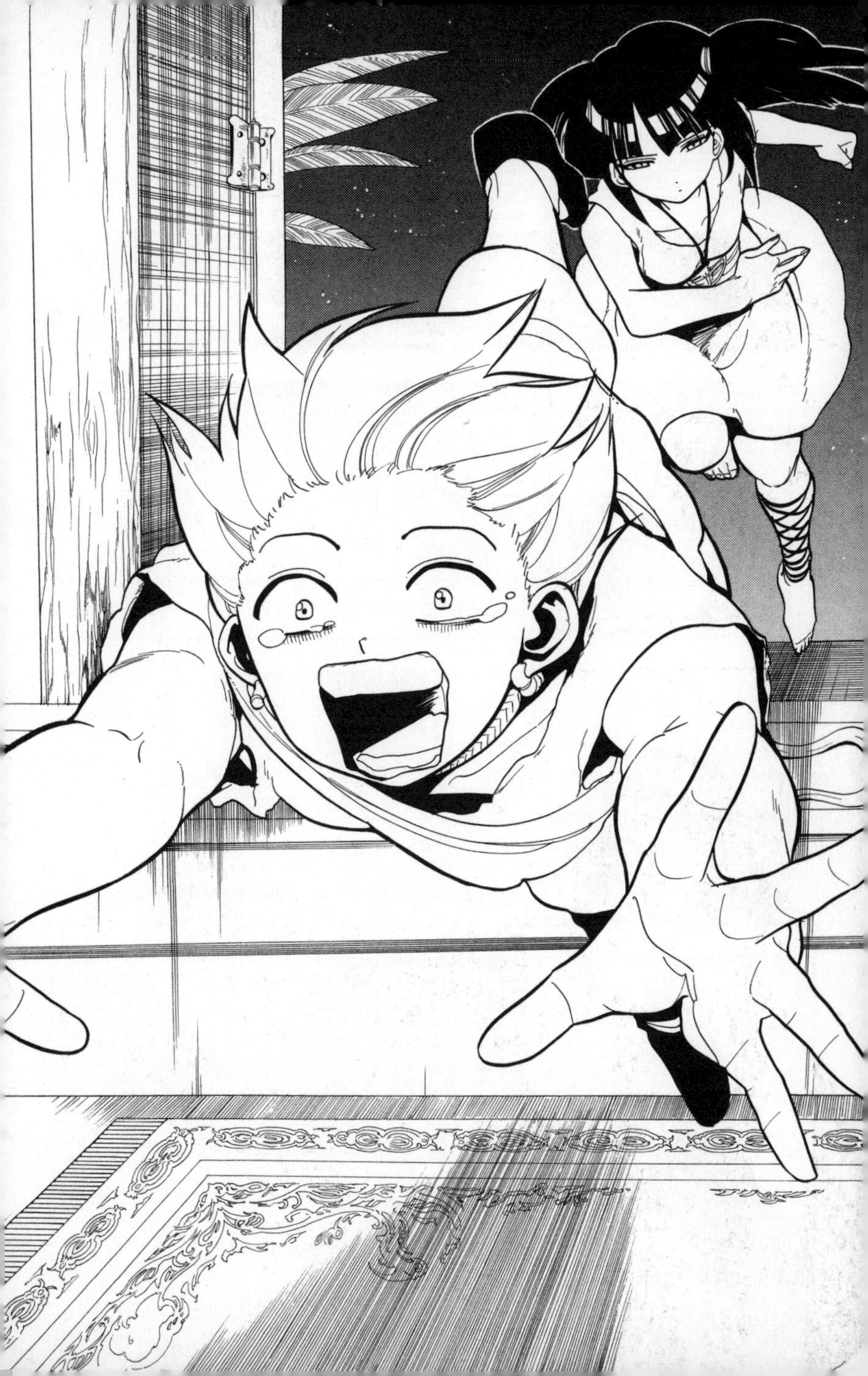

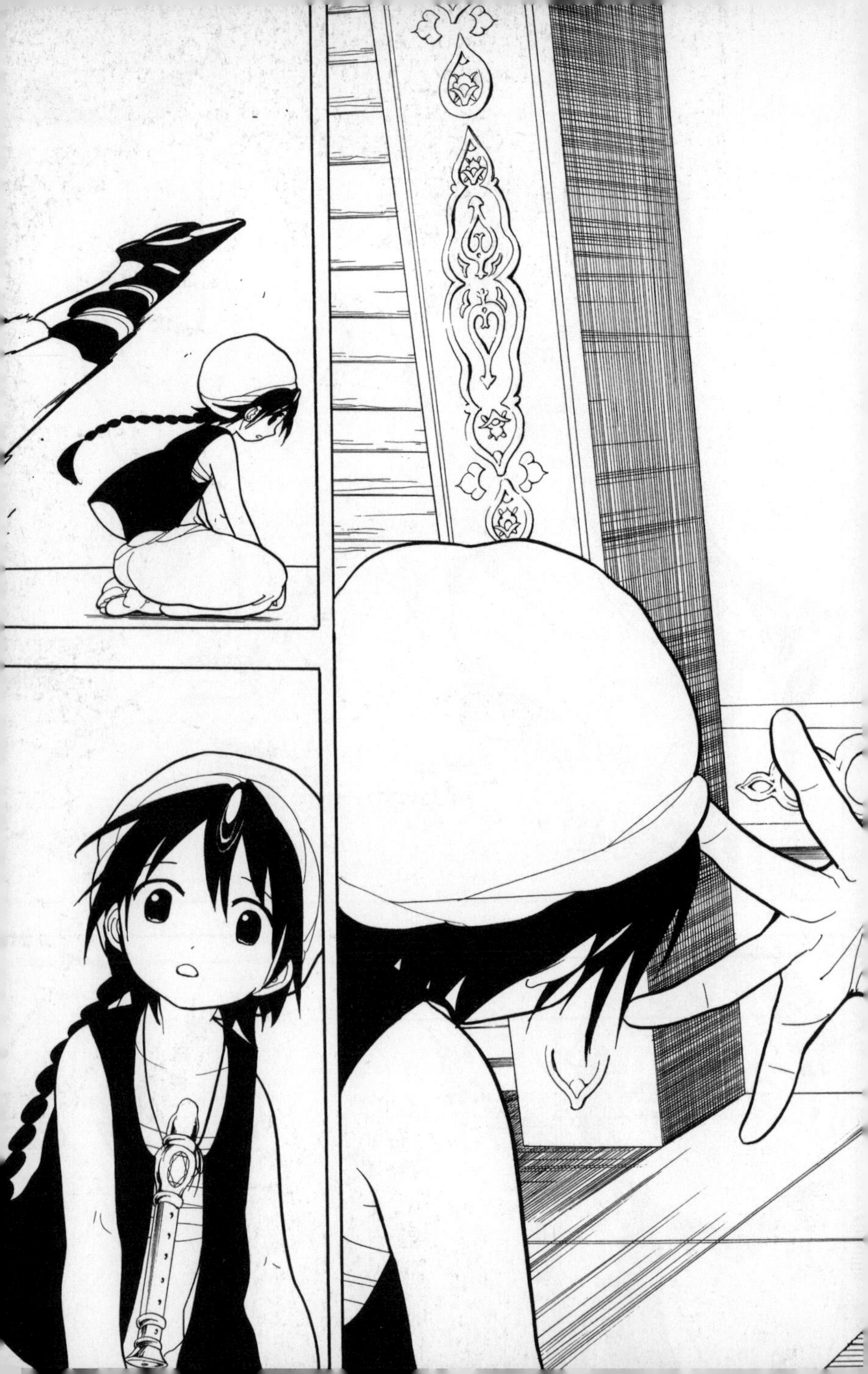

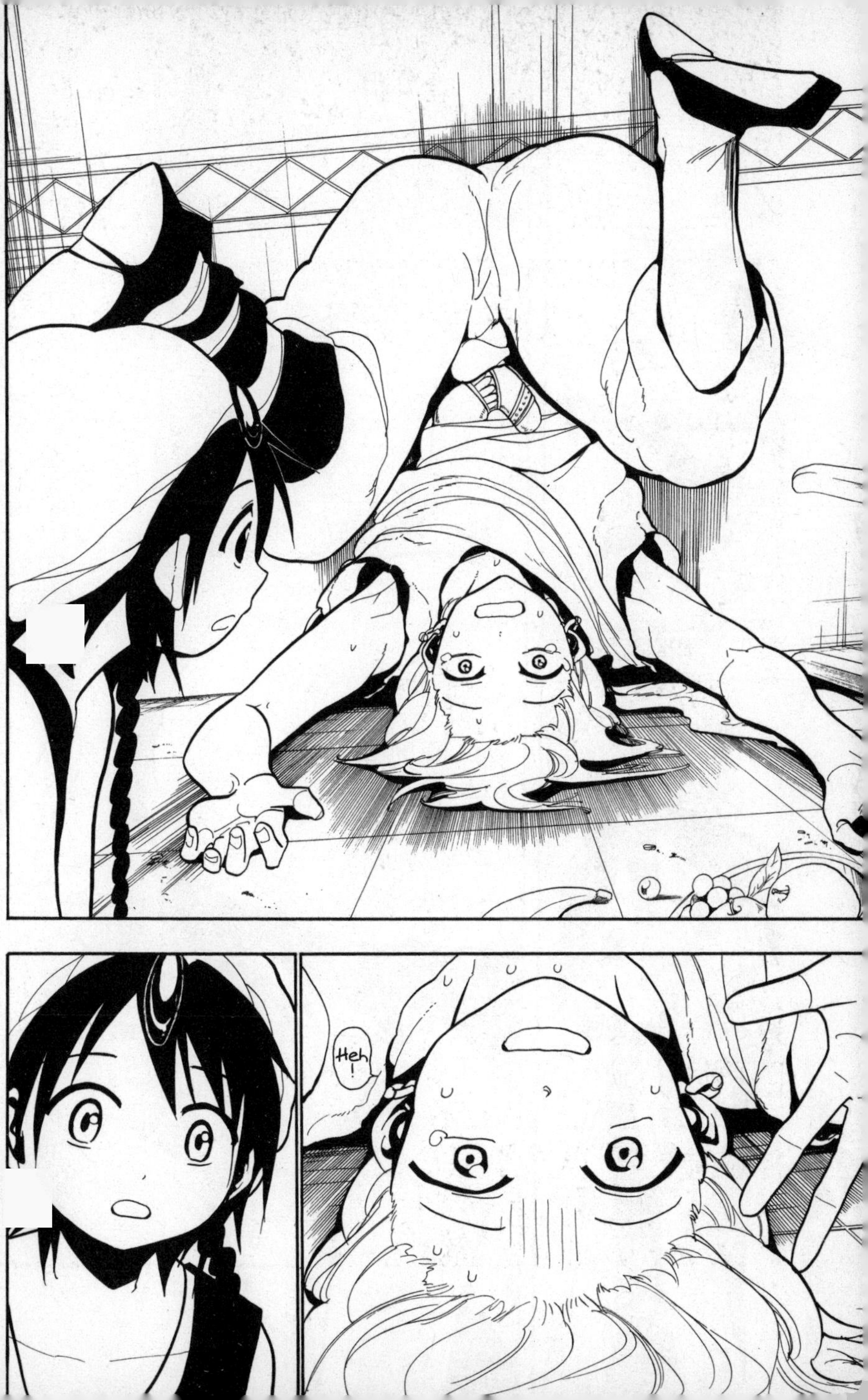
Heh!

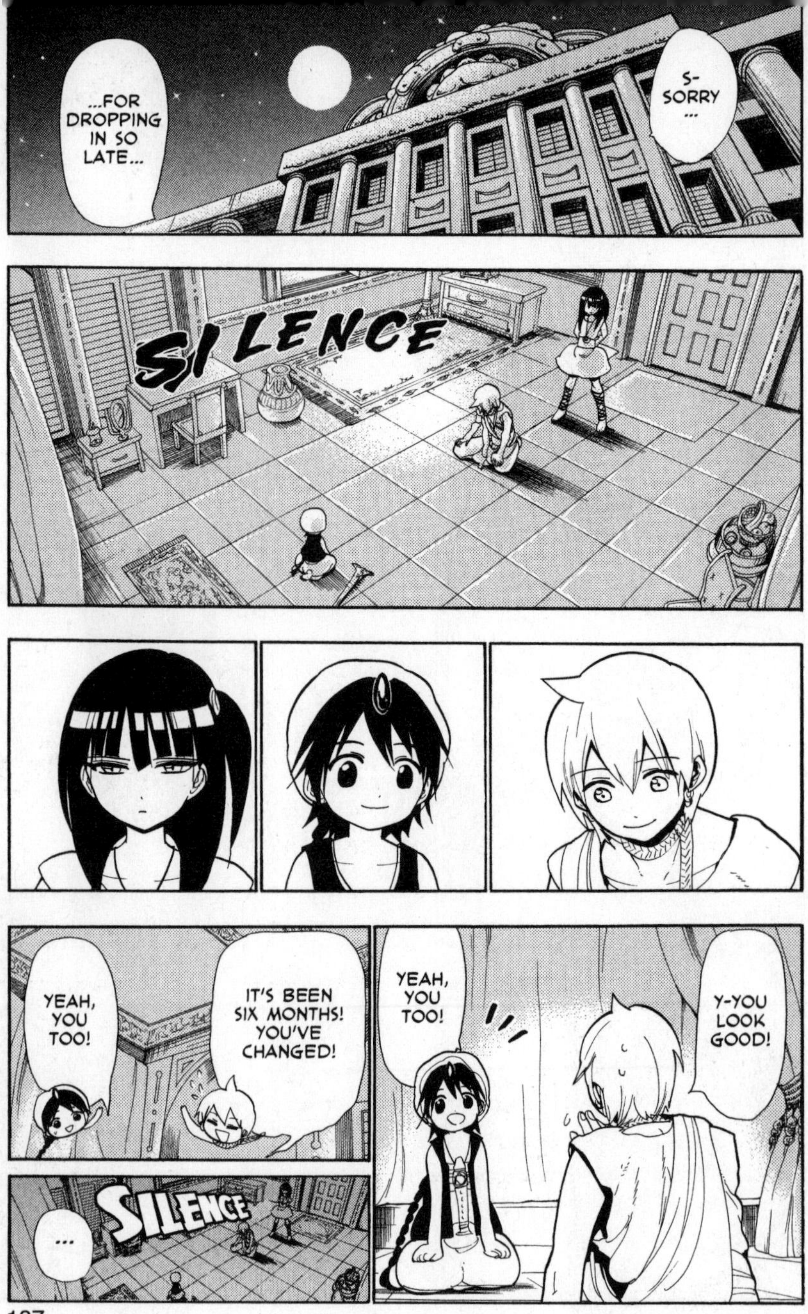
S-SORRY...
...FOR DROPPING IN SO LATE...
SILENCE
Y-YOU LOOK GOOD!
YEAH, YOU TOO!
IT'S BEEN SIX MONTHS! YOU'VE CHANGED!
YEAH, YOU TOO!
SILENCE
...

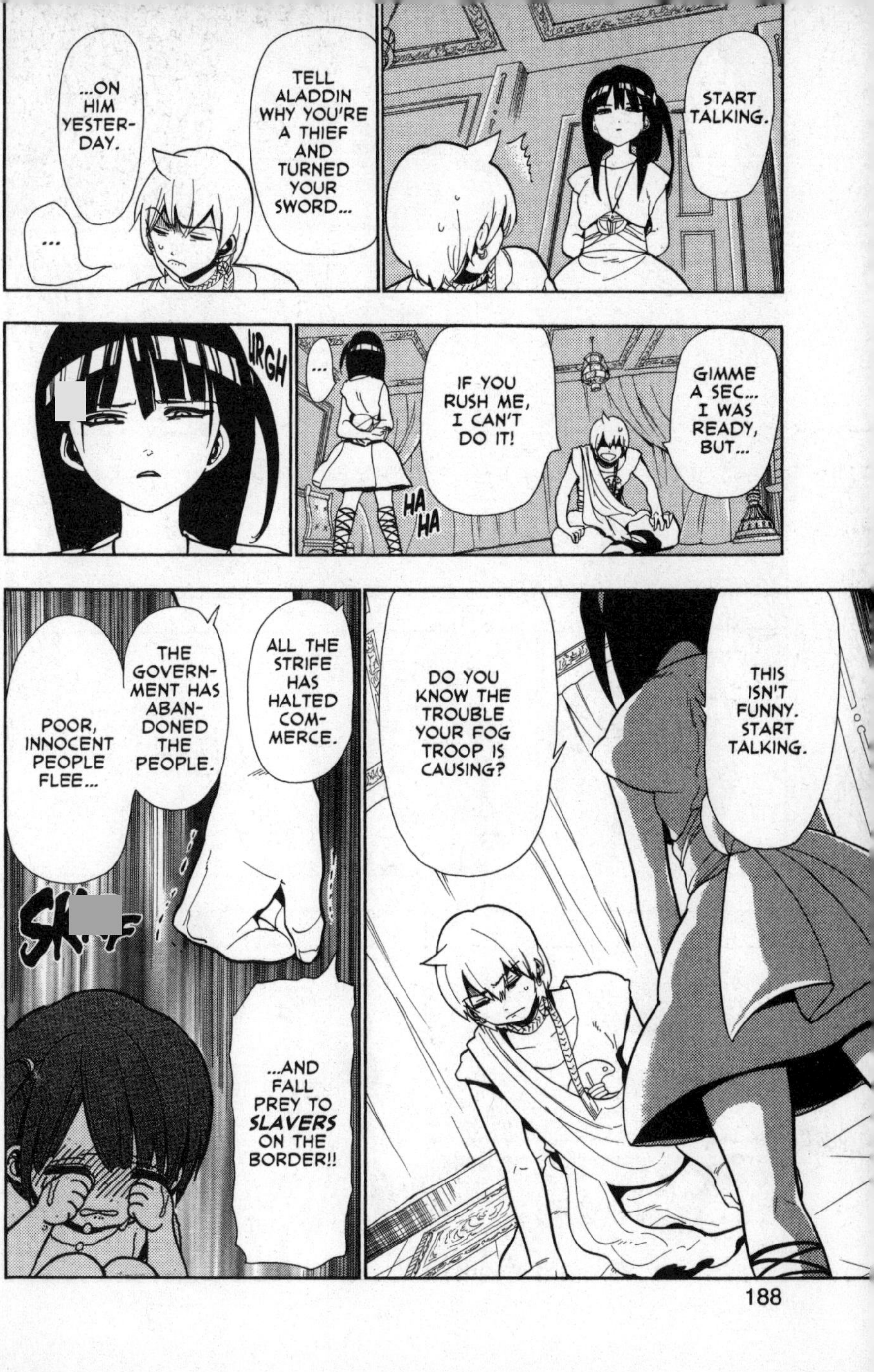
START TALKING.
TELL ALADDIN WHY YOU'RE A THIEF AND TURNED YOUR SWORD...
...ON HIM YESTER-DAY.
...
GIMME A SEC... I WAS READY, BUT...
IF YOU RUSH ME, I CAN'T DO IT!
HA HA
...
URGH
THIS ISN'T FUNNY. START TALKING.
DO YOU KNOW THE TROUBLE YOUR FOG TROOP IS CAUSING?
ALL THE STRIFE HAS HALTED COM-MERCE.
THE GOVERN-MENT HAS ABAN-DONED THE PEOPLE.
POOR, INNOCENT PEOPLE FLEE...
...AND FALL PREY TO *SLAVERS* ON THE BORDER!!

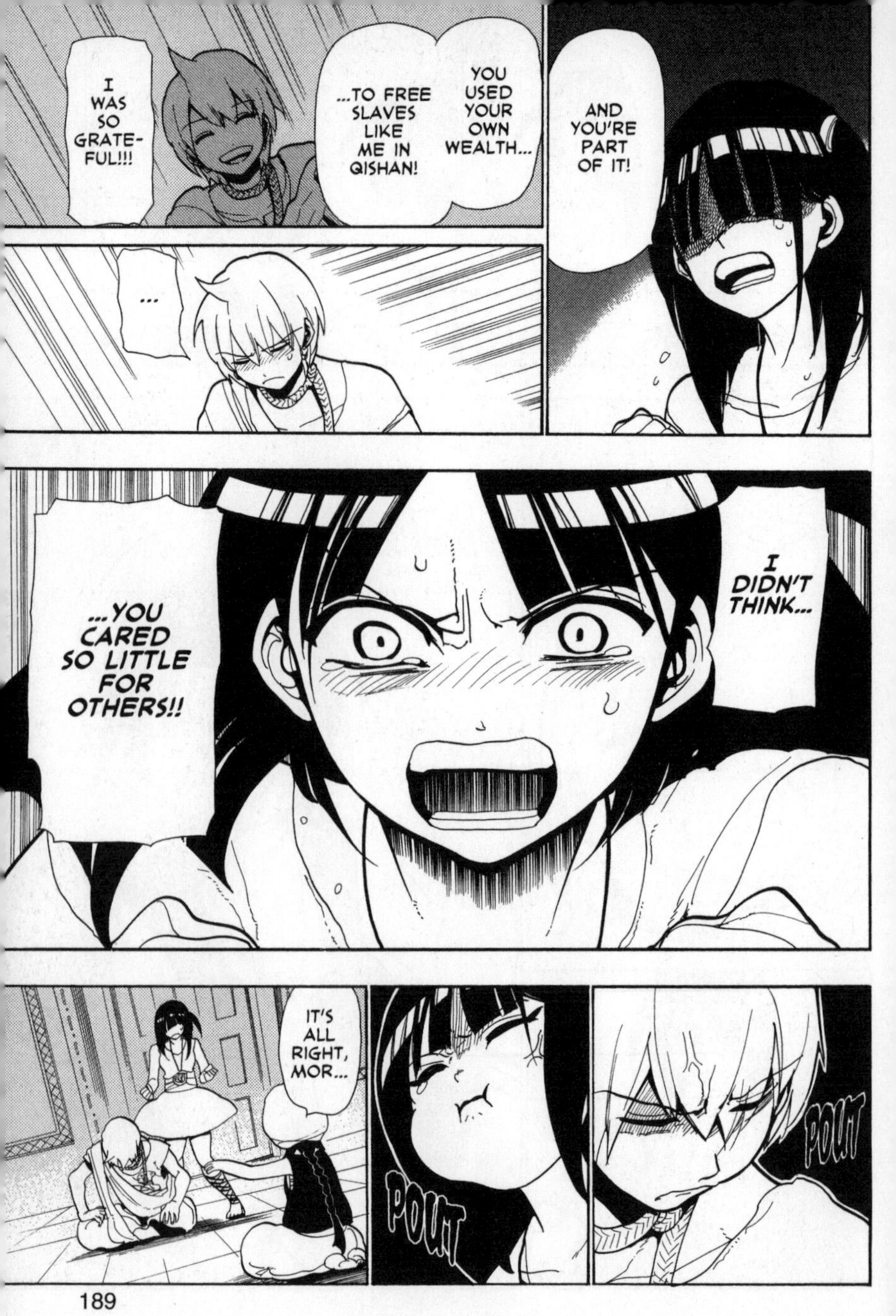
AND YOU'RE PART OF IT!
YOU USED YOUR OWN WEALTH...
...TO FREE SLAVES LIKE ME IN QISHAN!
I WAS SO GRATE-FUL!!!
...
I DIDN'T THINK...
...YOU CARED SO LITTLE FOR OTHERS!!
POUT
POUT
IT'S ALL RIGHT, MOR...

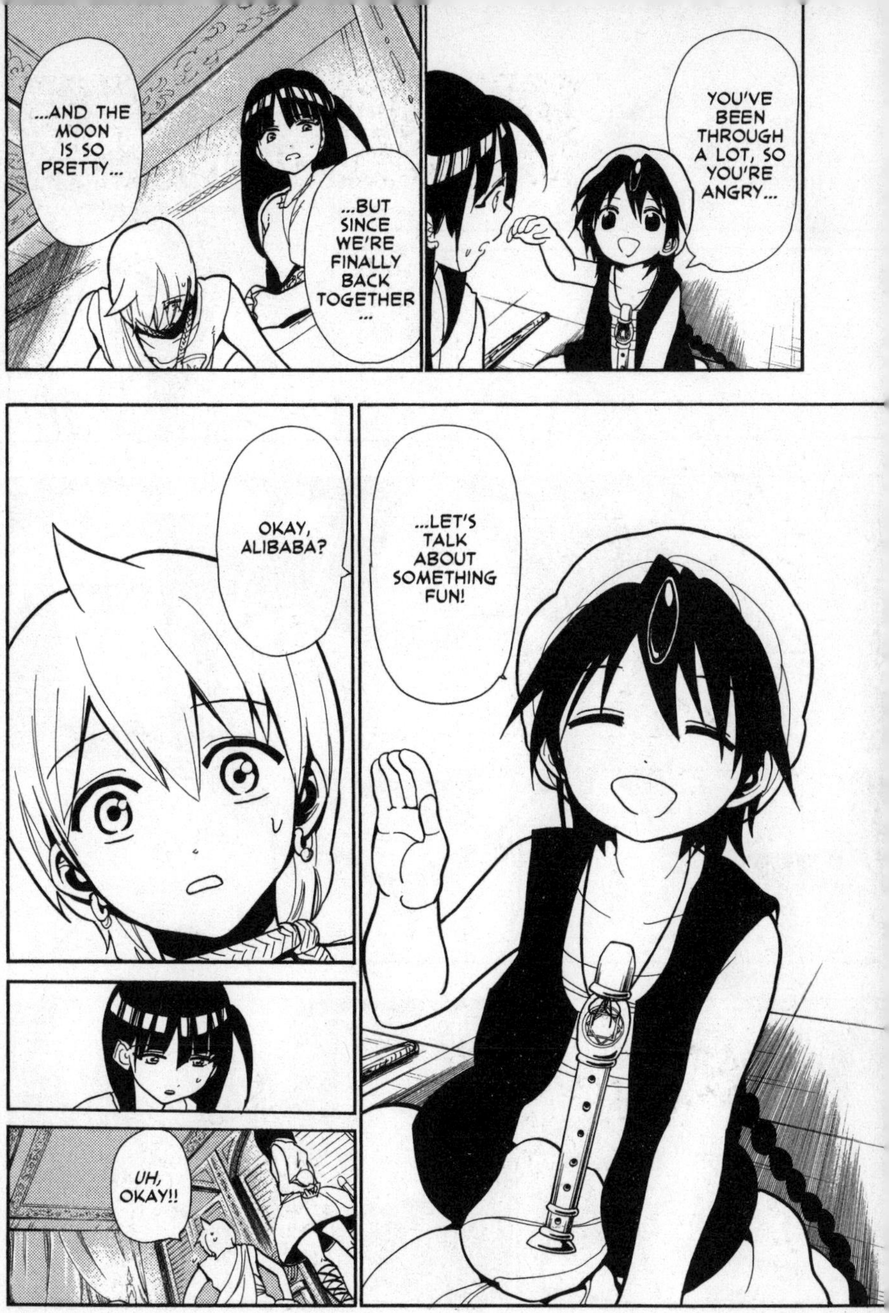
YOU'VE BEEN THROUGH A LOT, SO YOU'RE ANGRY...
...AND THE MOON IS SO PRETTY...
...BUT SINCE WE'RE FINALLY BACK TOGETHER ...
...LET'S TALK ABOUT SOMETHING FUN!
OKAY, ALIBABA?
UH, OKAY!!

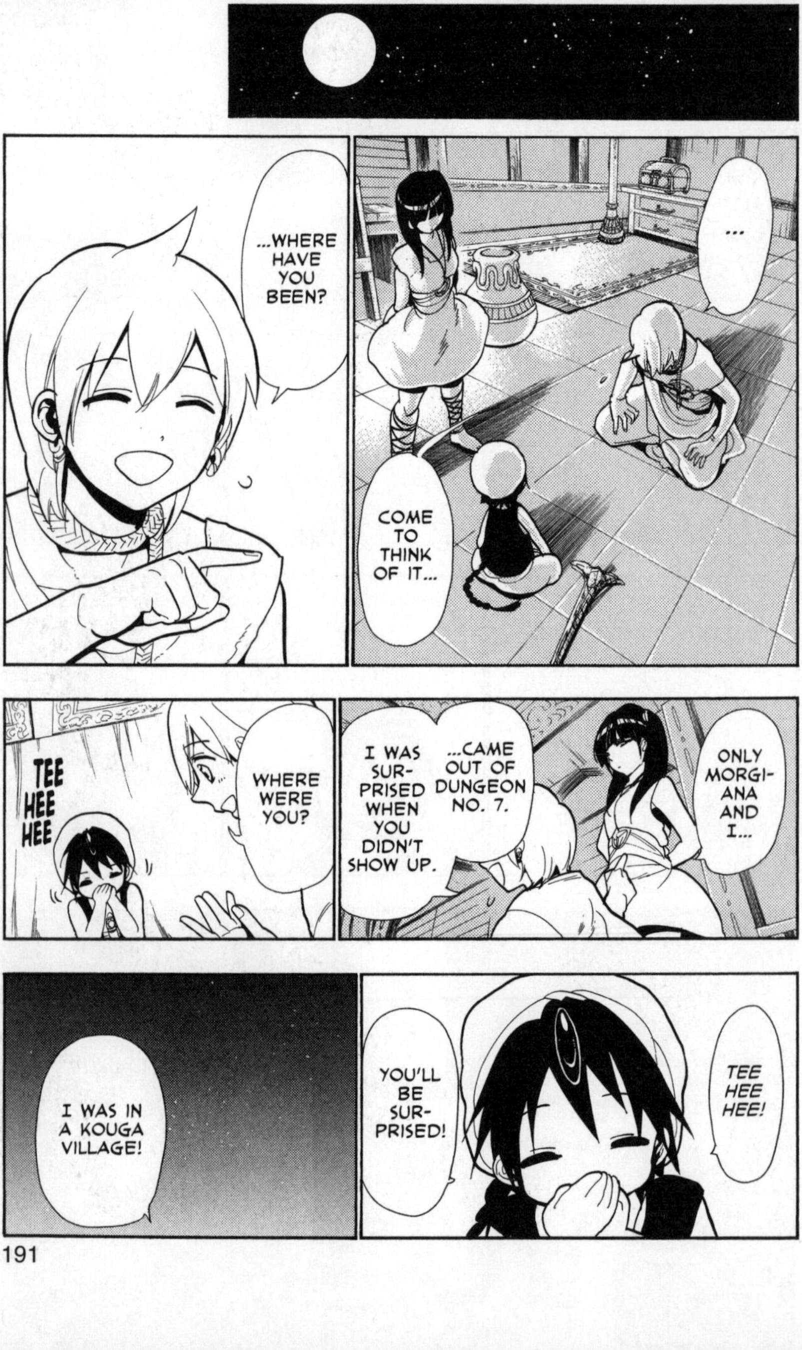
...
COME TO THINK OF IT...
...WHERE HAVE YOU BEEN?
ONLY MORGIANA AND I...
...CAME OUT OF DUNGEON NO. 7.
I WAS SURPRISED WHEN YOU DIDN'T SHOW UP.
WHERE WERE YOU?
TEE HEE HEE
TEE HEE HEE!
YOU'LL BE SURPRISED!
I WAS IN A KOUGA VILLAGE!

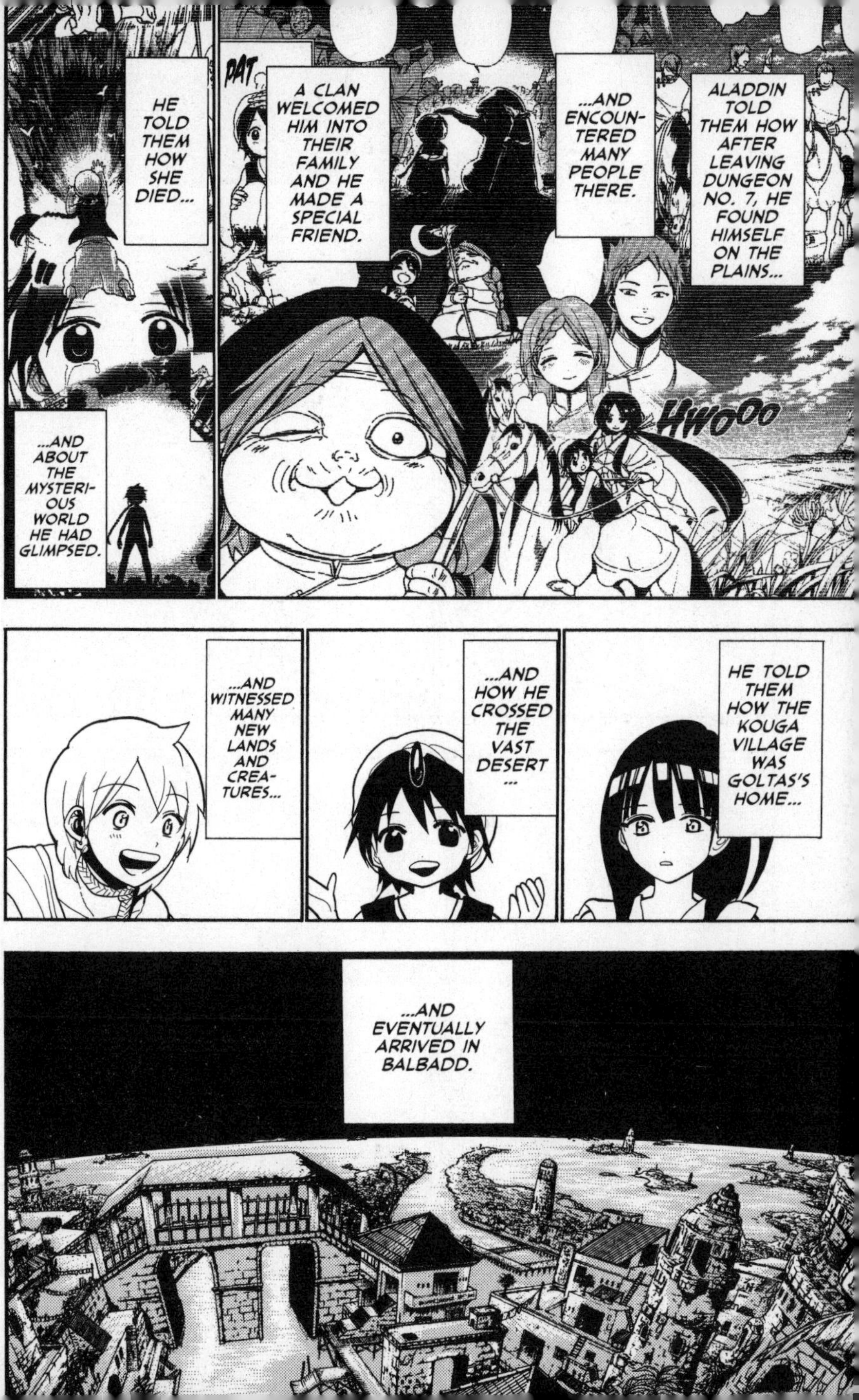
ALADDIN TOLD THEM HOW AFTER LEAVING DUNGEON NO. 7, HE FOUND HIMSELF ON THE PLAINS...
...AND ENCOUNTERED MANY PEOPLE THERE.
HWOOO
A CLAN WELCOMED HIM INTO THEIR FAMILY AND HE MADE A SPECIAL FRIEND.
PAT
HE TOLD THEM HOW SHE DIED...
...AND ABOUT THE MYSTERIOUS WORLD HE HAD GLIMPSED.
HE TOLD THEM HOW THE KOUGA VILLAGE WAS GOLTAS'S HOME...
...AND HOW HE CROSSED THE VAST DESERT ...
...AND WITNESSED MANY NEW LANDS AND CREATURES...
...AND EVENTUALLY ARRIVED IN BALBADD.

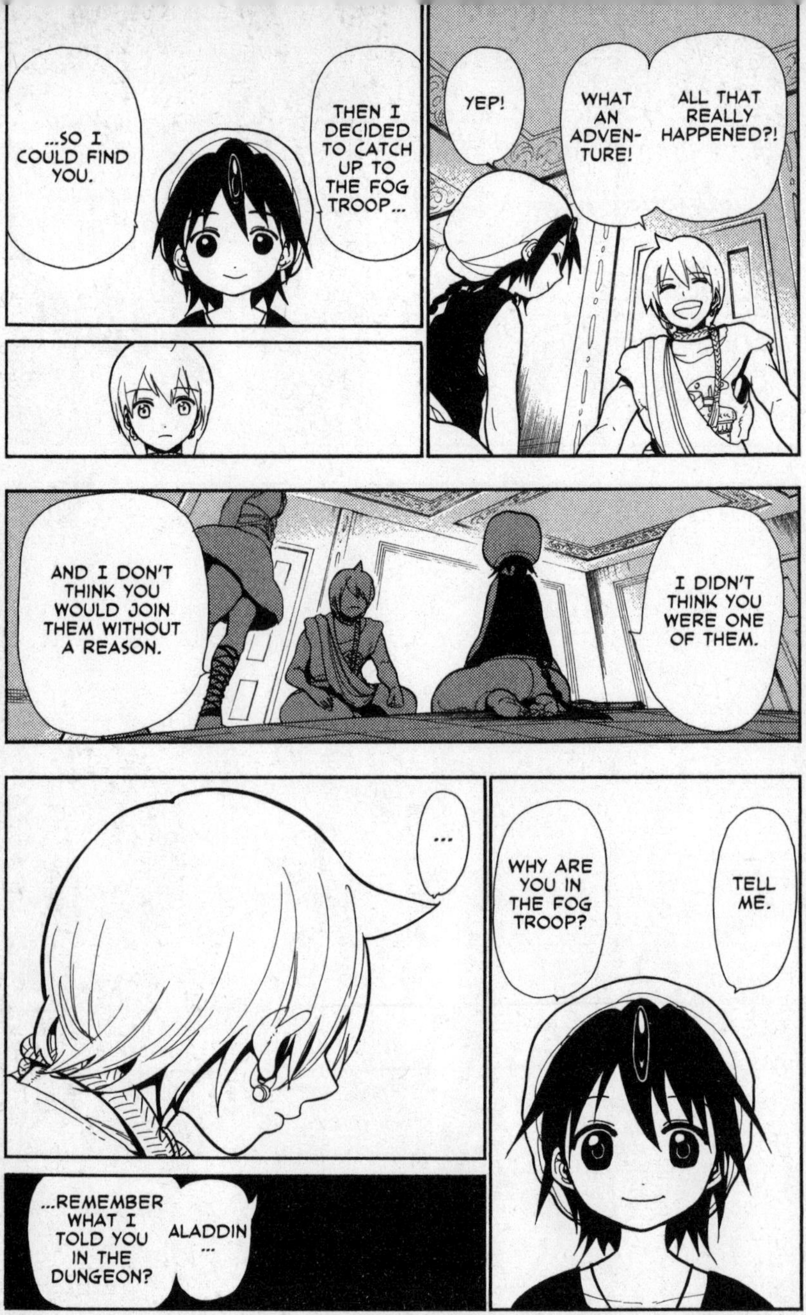
ALL THAT REALLY HAPPENED?!
WHAT AN ADVENTURE!
YEP!
THEN I DECIDED TO CATCH UP TO THE FOG TROOP...
...SO I COULD FIND YOU.
I DIDN'T THINK YOU WERE ONE OF THEM.
AND I DON'T THINK YOU WOULD JOIN THEM WITHOUT A REASON.
TELL ME.
WHY ARE YOU IN THE FOG TROOP?
...
ALADDIN...
...REMEMBER WHAT I TOLD YOU IN THE DUNGEON?

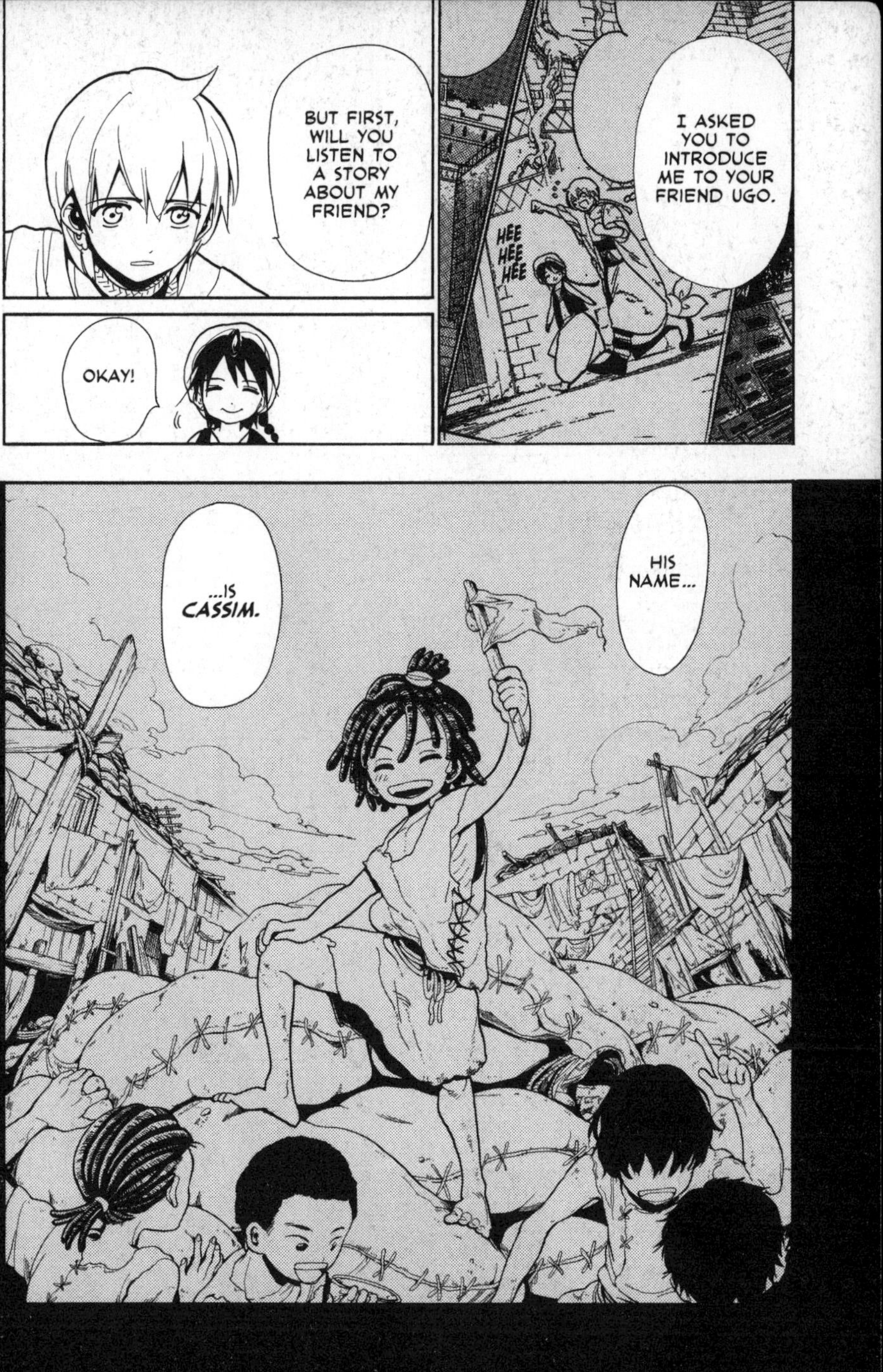
I ASKED YOU TO INTRODUCE ME TO YOUR FRIEND UGO.
HEE HEE HEE
BUT FIRST, WILL YOU LISTEN TO A STORY ABOUT MY FRIEND?
OKAY!
HIS NAME...
...IS CASSIM.

MAGI

The labyrinth of magic

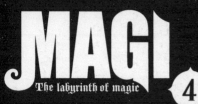

4

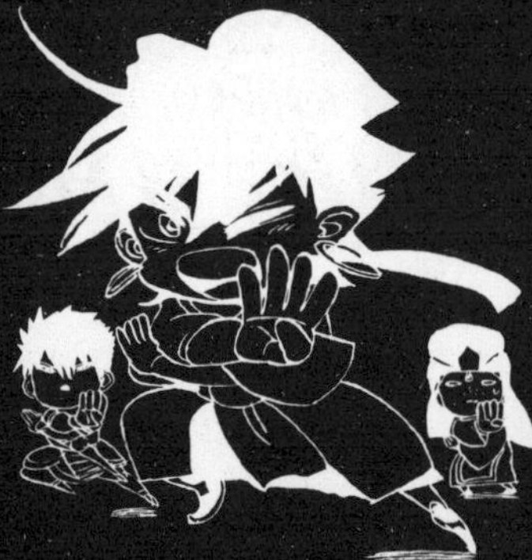

Staff

■ **Story & Art**

Shinobu Ohtaka

Shinobu Ohtaka

■ **Regular Assistants**

Matsubara

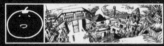

Miho Isshiki

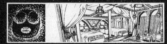

Akira Sugito

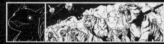

Tanimoto

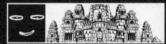

Maru

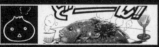

■ **Editor**
Kazuaki Ishibashi

■ **Sales & Promotion**
Akira Ozeki
Shinichirou Todaka

■ **Designers**
Yasuo Shimura + Bay Bridge Studio

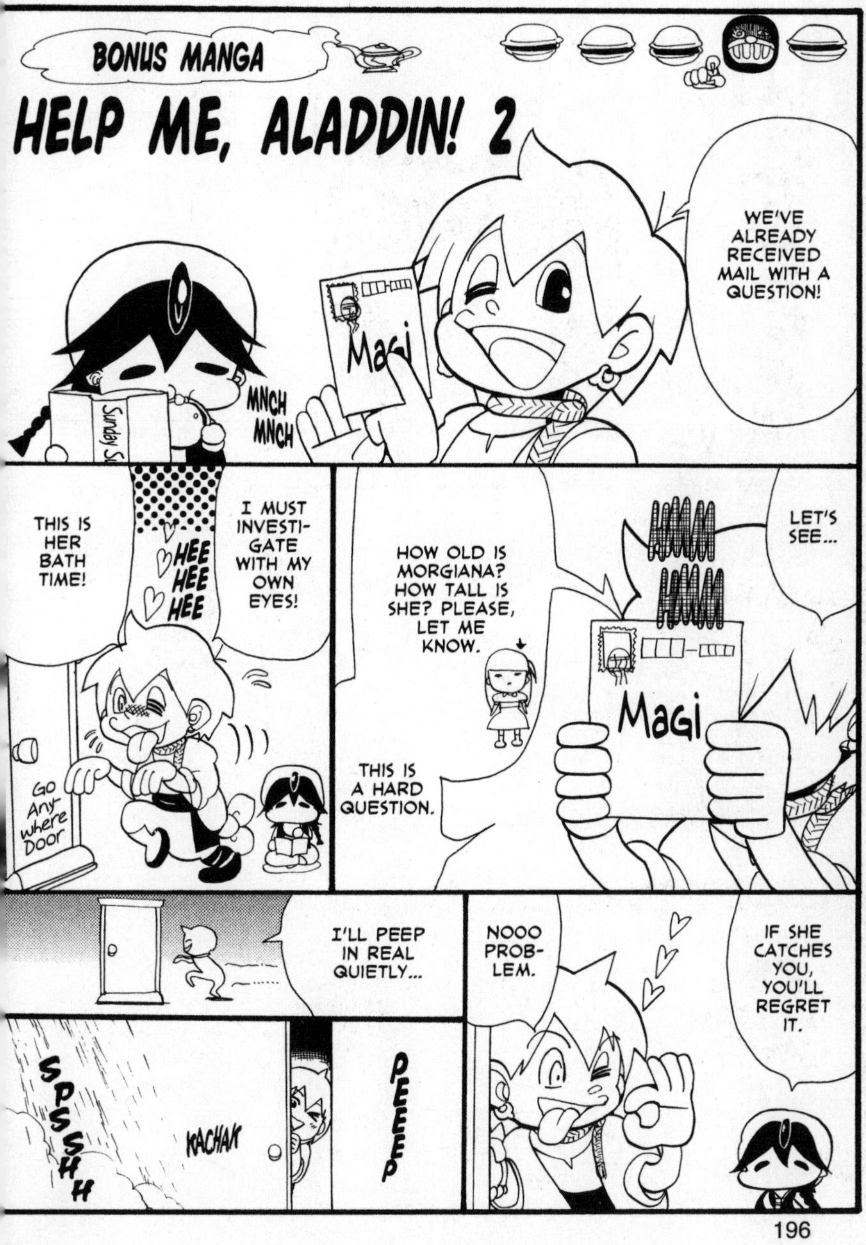
BONUS MANGA
HELP ME, ALADDIN! 2
WE'VE ALREADY RECEIVED MAIL WITH A QUESTION!
Magi
MNCH MNCH
Sunday S
LET'S SEE...
Magi
HOW OLD IS MORGIANA? HOW TALL IS SHE? PLEASE, LET ME KNOW.
THIS IS A HARD QUESTION.
I MUST INVESTIGATE WITH MY OWN EYES!
HEE HEE HEE
THIS IS HER BATH TIME!
Go Anywhere Door
IF SHE CATCHES YOU, YOU'LL REGRET IT.
NOOO PROBLEM.
I'LL PEEP IN REAL QUIETLY...
PEEEP
KACHAK
SPSSHH

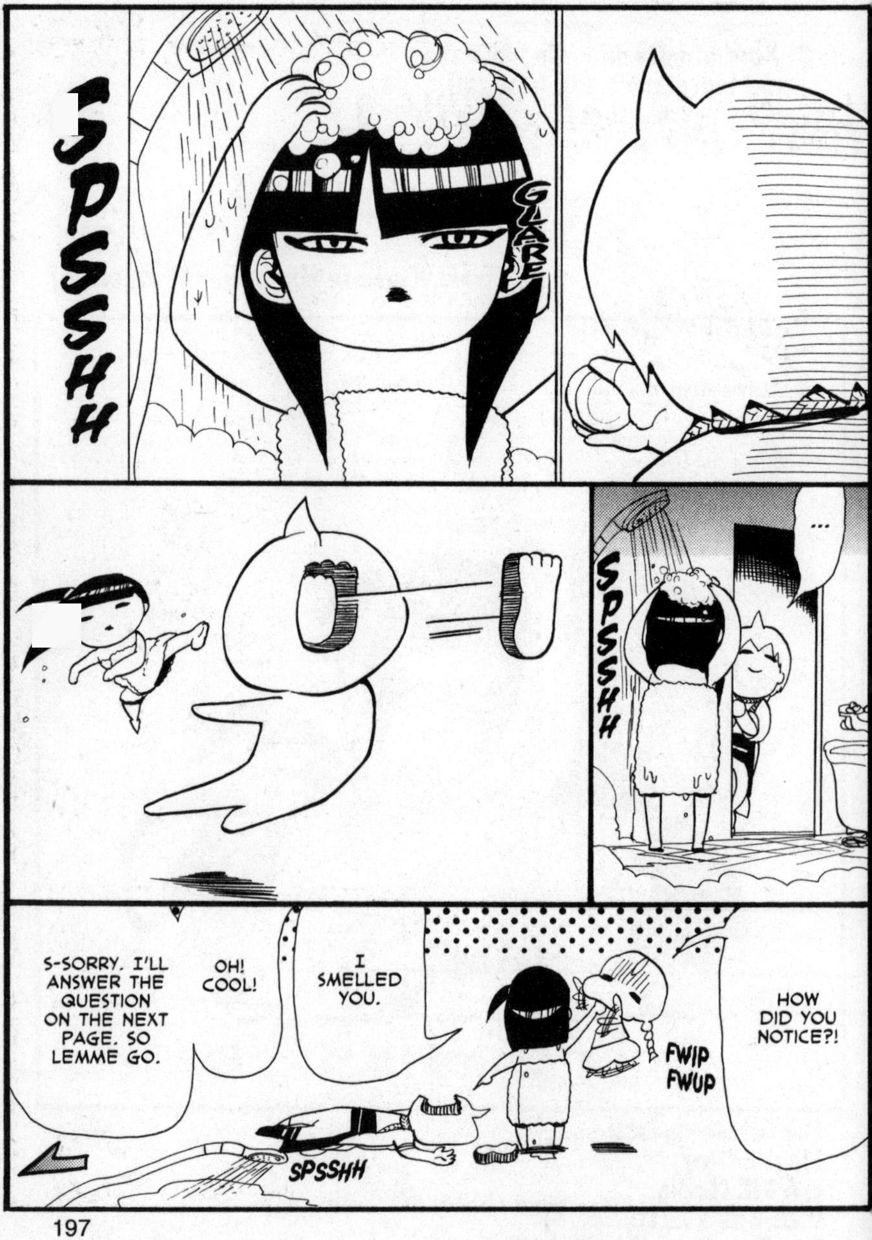
GLARE
SPSSHH
...
SPSSHH
HOW DID YOU NOTICE?!
FWIP FWUP
I SMELLED YOU.
OH! COOL!
S-SORRY. I'LL ANSWER THE QUESTION ON THE NEXT PAGE. SO LEMME GO.
SPSSHH

Q: How old are Aladdin, Alibaba and Morgiana? And how tall are they?

(from X-san in Hiroshima Prefecture)

A: Here you go.

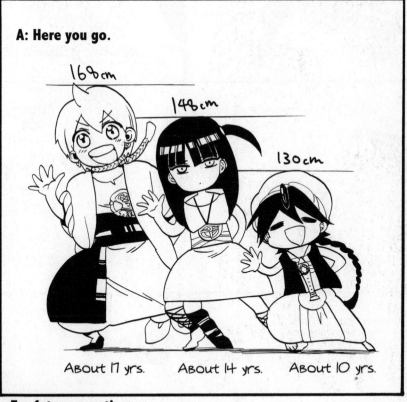

168cm

148cm

130cm

ABOUT 17 yrs. ABOUT 14 yrs. ABOUT 10 yrs.

For future questions...
Magi Editor
c/o VIZ Media
P.O. Box 77010
San Francisco, CA, 94107

MAGI ENEMY PROFILE

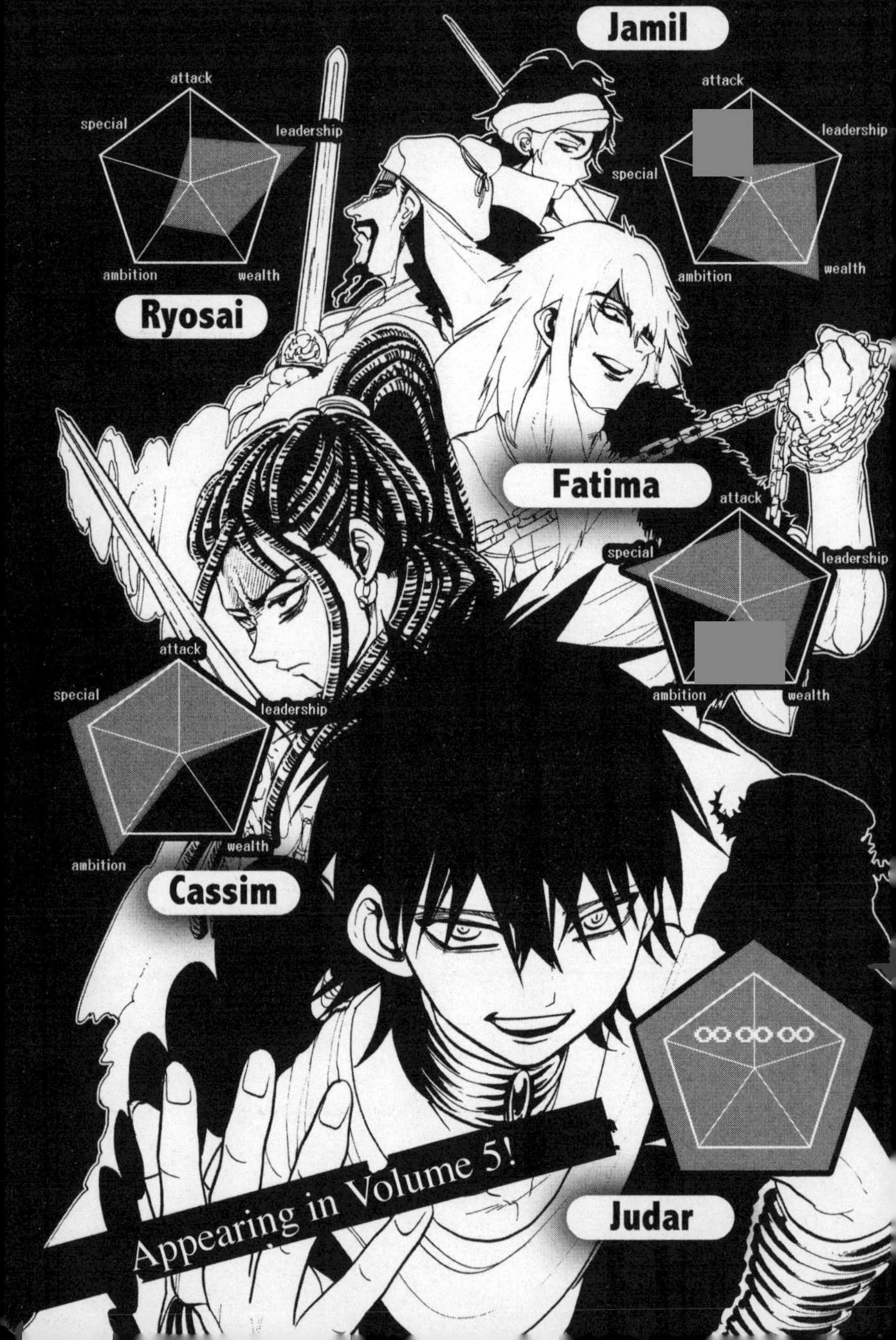

Jamil
attack
leadership
special
ambition
wealth
attack
special
leadership
ambition
wealth
Ryosai
Fatima
attack
special
leadership
ambition
wealth
attack
special
leadership
wealth
ambition
Cassim
Judar
Appearing in Volume 5!

SHINOBU OHTAKA
OHTAKA

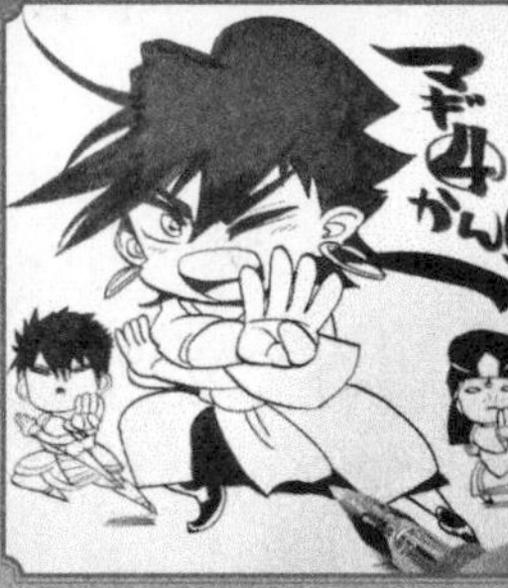
マギ4かん!!

* *Magi* volume 4

Gonna go for it!

MAGI

Volume 4
Shonen Sunday Edition

Story and Art by
SHINOBU OHTAKA

MAGI Vol.4
by Shinobu OHTAKA
© 2009 Shinobu OHTAKA
All rights reserved.
Original Japanese edition published by SHOGAKUKAN.
English translation rights in the United States of America, Canada,
the United Kingdom and Ireland arranged with SHOGAKUKAN.

Translation & English Adaptation 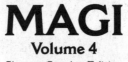 John Werry

Touch-up Art & Lettering ◇ Stephen Dutro

Editor ◇ Mike Montesa

Printed in the U.S.A.

Published by VIZ Media, LLC
P.O. Box 77010
San Francisco, CA 94107

10 9 8 7 6 5 4 3 2 1
First printing, February 2014

WWW.SHONENSUNDAY.COM

PARENTAL ADVISORY
MAGI is rated T for Teen.
This volume contains
suggestive themes.
ratings.viz.com

VIZ
MEDIA
www.viz.com

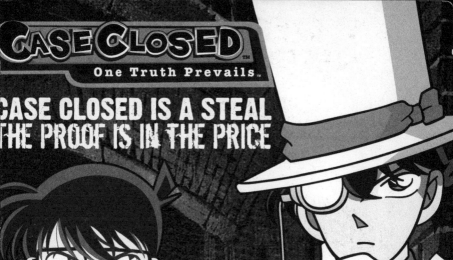
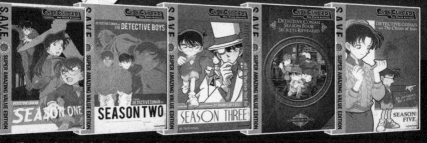

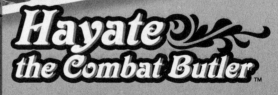
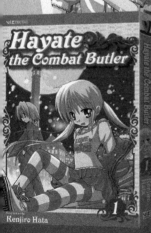

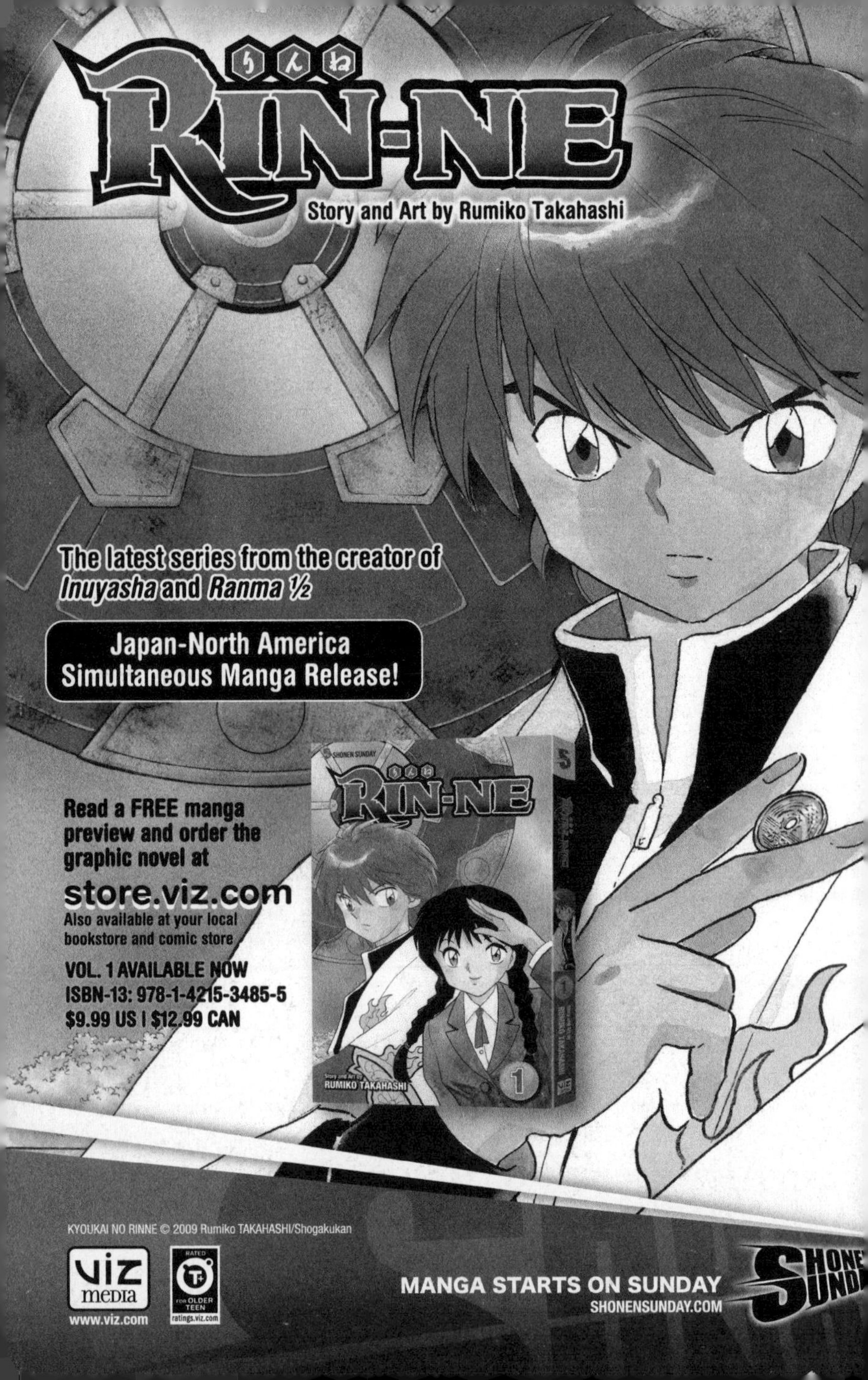
りんね
RIN-NE
Story and Art by Rumiko Takahashi
The latest series from the creator of
Inuyasha and Ranma ½
Japan-North America
Simultaneous Manga Release!
SHONEN SUNDAY
RIN-NE
Story and Art by
RUMIKO TAKAHASHI
1
Read a FREE manga
preview and order the
graphic novel at
store.viz.com
Also available at your local
bookstore and comic store
VOL. 1 AVAILABLE NOW
ISBN-13: 978-1-4215-3485-5
$9.99 US | $12.99 CAN
KYOUKAI NO RINNE © 2009 Rumiko TAKAHASHI/Shogakukan
viz media
www.viz.com
RATED T+ FOR OLDER TEEN
ratings.viz.com
MANGA STARTS ON SUNDAY
SHONENSUNDAY.COM

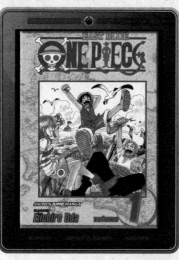
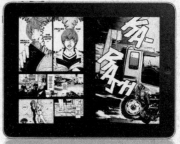
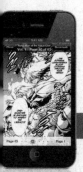

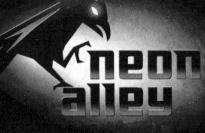
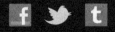

You're reading the
WRONG WAY

MAGI reads from right to left, starting in the upper-right corner. Japanese is read from **right** to **left**, meaning that action, sound effects, and word-balloon order are completely reversed from English order.

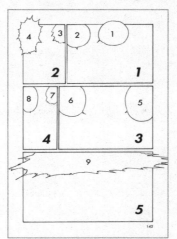